This volume brings a comprehensive perspective to the relationship between anthropology as practiced in museums and other sites of engaged anthropology.

Alaka Wali, Ph.D.; Curator of North American Anthropology;
Field Museum, Chicago; Fellow, The Neubauer Collegium at University of Chicago

In this essential volume, Kreps takes her on-the-ground experiences across the globe and crafts them into sophisticated yet straightforward theoretical arguments about the past and future of museums.

Chip Colwell, Ph.D.; Senior Curator of Anthropology,
Denver Museum of Nature & Science

MUSEUMS AND ANTHROPOLOGY IN THE AGE OF ENGAGEMENT

Museums and Anthropology in the Age of Engagement considers changes that have been taking place in museum anthropology as it has been responding to pressures to be more socially relevant, useful, and accountable to diverse communities.

Based on the author's own research and applied work over the past 30 years, the book gives examples of the wide-ranging work being carried out today in museum anthropology as both an academic, scholarly field and variety of applied, public anthropology. While it examines major trends that characterize our current "age of engagement," the book also critically examines the public role of museums and anthropology in colonial and postcolonial contexts, namely in the US, the Netherlands, and Indonesia. Throughout the book, Kreps questions what purposes and interests museums and anthropology serve in these different times and places.

Museums and Anthropology in the Age of Engagement is a valuable resource for readers interested in an historical and comparative study of museums and anthropology, and the forms engagement has taken. It should be especially useful to students and instructors looking for a text that provides in one volume a history of museum anthropology and methods for doing critical, reflexive museum ethnography and collaborative work.

Christina F. Kreps is a cultural anthropologist specializing in the cross-cultural and comparative study of museums and museological practices. She has carried out ethnographic research on museums and participated in museum development and training programs in the Netherlands, Indonesia, Thailand, and Vietnam. At the University of Denver she is Professor of Anthropology, Director of the Museum of Anthropology and Museum and Heritage Studies Program.

MUSEUMS AND ANTHROPOLOGY IN THE AGE OF ENGAGEMENT

Christina F. Kreps

Routledge
Taylor & Francis Group

NEW YORK AND LONDON

First published 2020
by Routledge
52 Vanderbilt Avenue, New York, NY 10017

and by Routledge
2 Park Square, Milton Park, Abingdon, Oxon OX14 4RN

Routledge is an imprint of the Taylor & Francis Group, an informa business

© 2020 Taylor & Francis

Library of Congress Cataloging-in-Publication Data
Names: Kreps, Christina F. (Christina Faye), 1956- author.
Title: Museums and anthropology in the age of engagement / Christina F. Kreps.
Description: New York, NY : Routledge, 2020. | Includes bibliographical references and index.
Identifiers: LCCN 2019024523 (print) | LCCN 2019024524 (ebook) | ISBN 9781611329155 (hardback) | ISBN 9781611329162 (paperback) | ISBN 9781351332798 (adobe pdf) | ISBN 9781351332774 (mobi) | ISBN 9781351332781 (epub) | ISBN 9780203702208 (ebook)
Subjects: LCSH: Anthropological museums and collections–United States. | Anthropological museums and collections–Netherlands. | Anthropological museums and collections–Indonesia. | Postcolonialism–United States. | Postcolonialism–Netherlands. | Postcolonialism–Indonesia. | Museums–Social aspects–United States. | Museums–Social aspects–Netherlands. | Museums–Social aspects–Indonesia.
Classification: LCC GN35 .K74 2020 (print) | LCC GN35 (ebook) | DDC 301/.074–dc23
LC record available at https://lccn.loc.gov/2019024523
LC ebook record available at https://lccn.loc.gov/2019024524

ISBN: 978-1-61132-915-5 (hbk)
ISBN: 978-1-61132-916-2 (pbk)
ISBN: 978-0-203-70220-8 (ebk)

Typeset in Bembo
by Taylor & Francis Books

This book is dedicated to the legacy of
Michael M. Ames

CONTENTS

FIGURES

ACKNOWLEDGEMENTS

Because this book has been several decades in the making, it is impossible to thank everyone who has contributed to its realization. I will start by thanking the University of Denver for the many research and travel grants and sabbatical leaves I have received over the years. This book project would not have been possible without this generous support. I am especially grateful to my colleagues in the Department of Anthropology and the Denver University Museum of Anthropology for creating a collegial environment in which to work and opportunities to share ideas and projects. I am especially grateful to Anne Amati, Bonnie Clark, Sarah Nelson, Brooke Rohde, and Dean Saitta for their help and guidance.

My sincere appreciation goes to Chip Colwell, Jennifer Shannon, and Alaka Wali for their willingness to read chapters of the book and provide comments at various stages of preparation. I want to thank Joyce Herold, Curator Emeritus of the Denver Museum of Nature and Science, for sharing materials from her archives and for many hours of fascinating conversation about her career as a museum anthropologist.

A special note of gratitude is extended to my colleagues at the School of Museum Studies at Leicester University for hosting me from May to July 2013 while conducting research on museums and public engagement. I want to thank Viv Golding, Janet Marstine, and Richard Sandell for their inspiring work, and for their on-going friendship. I owe Richard Sandell particular recognition for inviting me to join him as co-editor of the Routledge series *Museum Meanings*. During my time in England and thereafter, I benefited from conversations and collaborations with Paul Basu, Beverley Butler, Peter Davis, Sandra Dudley, Rodney Harrison, Serena Iervolino, Bernadette Lynch, Michael Rowlands, and Johanna Zetterstom-Sharp.

Over the course of my many years of association with museums in the Netherlands, I have had the privilege of being mentored by and working with a number of remarkable colleagues in various capacities, many of whom have now retired. This book is, in several respects, a tribute to their visionary thinking and commitment to transforming museums. Heartfelt thanks go to Itie van Hout, Wilhelmina Kal, Susan Legêne, Harrie Leyten, Wayne Modest, and Pim Westerkamp. I also want to say thank you to Peter van Mensch of the Reinwardt Academy for teaching me, early on, how to think critically and deeply about museums.

I am equally indebted to mentors, colleagues, and friends in Indonesia who have taught me to see the world of museums, culture, and heritage through new eyes. Although it has been decades since I did my initial fieldwork at the Provincial Museum of Central Kalimantan, Museum Balanga, memories of the good friends I made there and all that I learned resurfaced while writing this book. Since 2002, I have had the privilege of collaborating with Nata'alui Duha and Father Johannes Hämmerle of the Museum Pusaka Nias and Father Jacques Maessen and Novia Sagita formerly affiliated with the Dayak Ikat Weaving Project. I have been truly astonished by all that they have achieved, and hope I have done their work justice in this book. I must also thank Philip Yampolsky, former Cultural Program Officer of the Ford Foundation in Jakarta, for sending me to Sintang and Nias in the first place, and for securing funding from Ford for the University of Denver/Indonesia Exchange Program in Museum Training. I also want to thank the Asian Cultural Council for helping make the Exchange Program possible.

I had the opportunity to think through many questions raised on the role of museums in heritage preservation in Indonesia and elsewhere when I was awarded a Rockefeller Foundation Humanities Fellowship through the Smithsonian Center for Folklife and Cultural Studies in 2005. I am grateful to Richard Kurin, the exceptional staff at the Center, and to other fellows for giving me the opportunity to spend a highly stimulating summer with them. Over the years, I have gained much from my work with other colleagues at the Smithsonian, including Nancy Fuller, Frank Proschan, and Paul Michael Taylor.

My research and museum practice took on distinctly new directions after 2008 when I became involved in the European Union-sponsored Museums as Places for Intercultural Dialogue (MAPforID) and The Learning Museum (LEM) Projects coordinated by the Instituto Beni Culturali, Emilia Romagna (IBC) in Bologna, Italy. Much gratitude is extended to Antonella Salvi and to Margherita Sani for inviting me to participate in these important and inspiring initiatives. It was through these projects that I also met my dear friend and creative partner Daniele Pario Perra. My understandings of the potential of museums, art, and culture for progressive social change have been considerably expanded through my partnerships with them. I am especially thankful to my colleague at the University of Denver, Roberta Waldbaum, for inviting me to take part in activities organized through the International Center for Civic Engagement in Bologna, jointly sponsored by the University of Denver and University of Bologna. This invitation led to collaborations with my colleagues from the IBC, and to teaching engagements in the University of Bologna Program in the Management and Development of Arts and Cultural Organizations directed by Luca Zan. Special thanks to Luca for our many professional exchanges and good times since 2005.

Over the years, numerous individuals have contributed to this book in some form by inviting me to participate in conferences, contribute to their book projects, to give workshops, or by introducing me to their work. Many also have been kindred spirits and fellow travelers along the way. For these opportunities and blessings, I want to thank: Kathleen Adams, Marilena Alivizatou, Peter Davis, Alexandra Denes, Larissa Förster, Candace Greene, Gwyn Isaac, Laurel Kendall, Paritta Chalermpow Koanantakool, Jennifer Kramer, Corinne Kratz, Cara Krmpotich, Nicola Levell, Sharon Macdonald, Kim Manajek, Nancy Mithlo, Heather Nielsen, Jeanne Rubin, Bernard Sellato, Laurajane Smith, Nick Stanley, Michelle Stefano, Merv Tano, Robert Welsch, Claire Wintle, and Bill Wood. And of course, I am grateful to my students who continue to surprise and invigorate me.

I offer deep gratitude and appreciation to my partner Rupert Jenkins who spent many hours reading and editing seemingly endless versions of chapters, and giving me sound advice. This book would have never been completed without his expertise and unfailing support.

Finally, I thank Routledge editorial staff, especially Heidi Lowther, for their patience and assistance in bringing the project to completion.

1

INTRODUCTION

Museums and Anthropology in the Age of Engagement

Back in the 1990s, two prominent museum anthropologists, Michael Ames and Richard Kurin, criticized museums and the field of anthropology for their lack of useful application and public engagement. Ames, in his influential book *Cannibal Tours and Glass Boxes: The Anthropology of Museums*, declared that "Both museums and the profession of anthropology … are in jeopardy and need to be reformed if they are to play any useful roles in contemporary democratic society; indeed, anthropology at least, likely will have to change if it is even to survive" (Ames 1992, xiii).[1] Five years later, Richard Kurin in a chapter titled "What's with Anthropology?" in his book *Reflections of a Culture Broker: A View from the Smithsonian* faulted anthropologists for not addressing issues of broad public concern. In fact, Kurin asserted that "the field as a whole seems to discourage public engagement," which "portends poorly for the future" (1997, 89). Kurin pointed out that museums had probably done more than academic anthropology departments to bring anthropology's specialized knowledge to the public. Yet, he added that this role had generally been seen by academic anthropologists as "low-priority service rather than a major responsibility" (Kurin 1997, 89).[2]

This book, in large part, was inspired by those of Ames and Kurin and their above-stated concerns. It considers changes that have brought the world of museums and anthropology[3] to a current "age of engagement," or, a time in which both museums and the discipline of anthropology have been responding to pressures to be more socially relevant, publicly engaged, and accountable to diverse communities.

The book focuses on museum anthropology as both a scholarly, academic field and variety of applied anthropology, or in other words, anthropology "put to use" (Van Willigen 2002). I offer examples of the wide-ranging work being carried out in museum anthropology today under the canopy of engagement. In this sense, the book is concerned with the social and public roles of museum anthropology and the forms engagement has taken as a theoretical concept, approach to practice, and ethical stance.

In addition to mapping contemporary trends in museum anthropology, my intention is to provide an historical perspective on engagement and the public role of anthropology practiced in and through museums. I illuminate how at different times and in different places publicly oriented work has been "dominant, residual, and emergent," owing to certain "movements and tendencies" (Williams 1977, 121) in museums and anthropology as well as in their wider social contexts. An historical perspective, or "genealogical history," is important because, in James Clifford's words, "genealogical histories confirm and explain a present; how we got here from somewhere else different; what from the past defines us now" (2013, 34). Genealogical histories can also destabilize orthodoxies in a field and disrupt conventional narratives by surfacing forgotten or ignored ones. Accordingly, one of my tasks is to give a more nuanced reading of what have become conventional narratives of the history of museum anthropology.

As the story goes, anthropology was closely aligned with museums in its early days in the late nineteenth and early twentieth centuries when theory building hinged on the analysis of artifacts (Adams 2015, 88). Museums, in many instances, were the "institutional homes" of the new science and provided financial support for research (Ames 1992, 39, Lurie 1981).[4] In addition to being centers of research, museums were arenas for disseminating anthropological knowledge to the public. Readers familiar with the history of American anthropology know that some of its most notable figures such as Franz Boas and Margaret Mead began or spent their careers working in museums. Boas and Mead were also known for using their positions to participate in public debates on crucial issues of their time, such as racism and war, and for popularizing anthropological insights (Boas 1907, Mead 1970, Sabloff 2011, Liss 2015).

But by the early decades of the twentieth century anthropology had moved from the museum to the university, and a rift had begun to develop between the museum-based study of material culture and the university-based study of ideas and human behavior (Adams 2015, 89). Fieldwork, or the study of culture and society first-hand rather than through artifacts, became the preferred method of research for cultural anthropologists (ethnologists). Increasingly, academic, university-based anthropology came to be seen as more theoretically advanced than museum anthropology. Museums, for many academic anthropologists, were merely repositories for "collecting and housing objects that served little purpose other than as gatherers of dust" (Kahn 2000, 57). The museum anthropologist's role in educating the public also diminished in value in comparison to the research and teaching of academic anthropologists. By the 1950s, museum anthropology had largely receded to the margins of the discipline (Collier and Tschopik 1954, Shelton 2006). Museums and their collections were "rediscovered," however, in the 1980s when they became the subject of critical analysis on the part of academic anthropologists and other scholars influenced by postcolonial and postmodern theory. Especially in the United States and Canada, Native American and First Nation activism and criticism led to a number of watershed events that had a revolutionary impact on the field. Taken together, these movements and tendencies gave rise to the "ree-mergence" and "reinvention" of museum anthropology (Clifford 1988, 1997, Bouquet 2001, 2012, Lonetree 2012, Phillips 2011, Shelton 2006).

This common narrative, however, has tended to overlook critical debates and developments taking place in museum anthropology prior to the 1980s. Alter-natively, I argue that such debates and criticism, both internal and external to the field, laid a foundation and created a climate for the surfacing of a "new" museum anthropology marked by the rise of the anthropology of museums and critical, reflexive museology; more equitable and collaborative practice; and the on-going diversification and decolonization of museums. In the book, I show how the ree-mergence of museum anthropology has not only been due to the critical analysis and "theorizing" of museums (Macdonald and Fyfe 1996) since the 1980s, but also because the field has been grappling with its colonial legacy, paradoxes, Native resistance, and issues of social relevance nearly since its inception (albeit unevenly). I posit an historical narrative of continuity *in* change rather than one characterized by stasis and rupture. In doing so, I attempt to counter what Hannerz sees as a tendency in contemporary anthropology, and that is, for anthropologists to not "engage too seriously with what went before them in their scholarly field" (2010, 136). Given this tendency, Hannerz recommends that "we explore other parts, other nooks and crannies, of twentieth century anthropology ... and see what one finds that might be of current interest. After 'rethinking,' 'reinventing,' and 'recapturing' perhaps there is room for a bit of remembering, retrieving, and even recycling?" (2010, 138–139).

While an historical perspective is crucial for understanding change and "what from the past defines us now" (Clifford 2013, 34), it is equally enlightening to look elsewhere to see what was happening in the world of anthropology and museums in other places and times. For comparative purposes, the book focuses primarily on the historical relationships between museums and anthropology in the United States, the Netherlands, and the Republic of Indonesia—sites of my own research and professional practice over the past 30 years. I am interested in comparing dif-ferences, similarities, connections, and affinities in the social, political, and cultural roles of museums and anthropology in settler-colonial nations like the United States, and former colonial and colonized nations such as the Netherlands and Indonesia, respectively. Through comparison, my intention is to provide insight into variations in the decolonization of museums—a process of on-going concern in museum anthropology that stretches back to the 1950s and 1960s in Indonesia and the Netherlands (Aldrich 2009, Bouquet 2012, 2015, Kreps 1988, 2011, Mohr 2014, Wintle 2016). The story of the Tropenmuseum (Tropical Museum) in Amsterdam, one of the museums featured as a case study, is particularly compelling because it has experienced a number of radical transformations since its founding in 1864. The Tropenmuseum exemplifies how anthropological museums can be transformed from products and tools of colonialism into progressive spaces for intercultural dialogue, exchange, and collaboration in a globalizing and interconnected world.

In the Preface to *Museums, the Public and Anthropology*, the first edition of *Cannibal Tours*, Ames wrote: "Anthropology museums provide windows on other cultures of the world, but when they are examined more closely they can also be seen to mirror the profession of anthropology itself, both its achievements and its foibles" (1986a, xiii). Similar to Ames, I follow a path of critical inquiry that looks at what museum anthropology has been "good for" (Thomas 2016), as well as its dark sides and "difficult heritage" (Macdonald 2009). Overall, my goal is to highlight, in Paolo Freire's words, how "thinking critically about practice, of today and yesterday, makes possible the improvement of tomorrow's practice" (1998, 44).

In the remainder of this introductory chapter, I elaborate on these and other movements, tendencies, and "energies" (Clifford 2013) that have inspired more engaged research, scholarship, and practice in museum anthropology. I also introduce overarching themes that run throughout the book plus theoretical and methodological approaches that have guided my research over the years. Finally, I give a summary of the book's chapters.

An Emerging Age of Convergence

Museum Anthropology as Applied/Public Anthropology

Museum and applied anthropology have historically been considered separate subfields within American anthropology. However, in recent years, they have been increasingly converging with overlapping interests and approaches to practice (Bouquet 2012, Carattini 2015, Lamphere 2004, Silverman 2015).

In an introductory essay to a special issue of *Practicing Anthropology* (a journal of the Society for Applied Anthropology) devoted to current work in museum anthropology, guest editor, Amy Carattini, presents an overview of "what's new and what's going on" in the field. She describes the diverse settings in which museum anthropologists are working, plus their varied roles as applied, practicing anthropologists. These settings include government and non-profit sectors, nongovernmental organizations, cultural centers and historical and heritage sites; education, public folklore, and the arts. One of the aims of the issue is to broaden our collective understanding of the many ways professionals are thinking about the usefulness of anthropology as it is applied "in, out, and around museums." Carattini states that the issue was compiled in an effort to break through the "artificial divisions between practicing, applied, academic and disciplinary professionals" (2015, 4). In so doing, she suggests that we might find ourselves "increasingly united as we learn from one another through shared goals and aspirations, interests and experiences, and desired results" (Carattini 2015, 4).

As will be discussed in Chapter 3, "Museum and Applied Anthropology: Shared Histories and Trajectories," museum and applied anthropology were central to the founding and development of American anthropology (as in other countries such as the Netherlands). But over time and for a variety of reasons, they became peripheral to academic, university-based anthropology. A goal of the book is to show

how museum and applied anthropology have been moving back to the center of the discipline by making theoretical and methodological advancements important to anthropology as a whole, particularly pertaining to matters of engagement.

Defining Museum Anthropology

Museum anthropology is open to multiple interpretations because of the range and variety of work done in the field. But today, museum anthropology may be defined as anthropology practiced *in* museums and the anthropology *of* museums (Kaplan 1996, 813). Flora Kaplan, an anthropologist and former director of the Museum Studies Program at New York University, draws attention to the often overlooked distinction between the two when she writes that "each cuts across the other but is the product of a different history. Current confusion in the field is the result of merging the two without a clear idea of their histories and of the distinction that should be made between practice and theory" (1996, 813).

Anthropology practiced in museums can be described as the application of anthropological research methods, theories, and insights to the collection, documentation, study, care, representation, and safeguarding of people's tangible and intangible culture. Museum anthropology practiced in museums historically has focused on the study and curation of material culture, art, artifacts, and specimens for understanding human cultural and biological diversity across space and through time. American anthropologists working in museums have represented the four main subfields of anthropology, i.e., ethnology or cultural anthropology, archaeology, physical anthropology, and linguistics (Sturtevant 1969). Although for much of its history, museum anthropology has been devoted to the study of material, tangible culture, nowadays, intangible culture—for example in the form of language, knowledge, skills, dance, music, rituals, and the multisensory dimensions of objects—is given much more attention. Furthermore, anthropology in museums has been carried out in museums housing archaeological, ethnographic, and art collections historically originating from non-Western peoples, although this focus too is changing as noted below.

Similar to museum anthropology, the task of defining what constitutes an "anthropology museum" can also be challenging because of the many different types of museums in which anthropological collections can be found (Frese 1960). For instance, many art museums have long housed ethnographic collections albeit classified as art (Clifford 1988, Errington 1998, Price 1989). In the United States, anthropological collections have commonly resided in natural history museums owing to the early history of anthropology in the country and its association with the evolutionary and natural history paradigm. This is despite the fact that such an arrangement has been the source of on-going debate and criticism since the early twentieth century (Boas 1907, Sturtevant 1969, Stocking 1985, Nash, Colwell-Chanthaphonh, and Holen 2011). "Stand alone" anthropology museums in the United States are more typically affiliated with universities, whereas in Europe there is a long tradition of support (on municipal and national levels as well as in universities) for museums classified specifically as ethnographic or ethnology. In recent years, many of these museums have rebranded themselves as "world cultures" museums, such as the Swedish National Museum of World Cultures in Gothenburg, the Rautenstrauch-Joest-Museum of World Culture in Cologne, Germany, and the World Museum in Vienna, Austria. The use of the adjectival "world" projects to the public that ethnographic museums are no longer confined to the study and representation of distant "Others," but are now intended to be for and about everyone in contemporary, multicultural societies. This move can also be interpreted as an attempt to cleanse ethnographic museums of the stain of colonialism. As Shelton has observed, name changes are affected both by external contingencies and the redefinition of institutional objectives (2006, 65).

The anthropology of museums has a more recent history, emerging roughly in the 1980s in tandem with the postmodern, postcolonial, and Native/Aboriginal/ Indigenous critiques of anthropology and museums. Ames was one of the early proponents and practitioners of the anthropology of museums. In *Cannibal Tours* he urged us to examine the social organization, structure, and roles of museums, to view the museum as a cultural artifact, and to "study ourselves, our own exotic customs and traditions, like we study others; view ourselves as 'the Natives'" (1992, 10). Ames also called for a "critical, reflexive museology" and a "critical theory of museums and anthropology," which he saw as a prerequisite for making both more socially relevant and publicly engaged.

When I set out to conduct an anthropological study of Dutch ethnographic museums in 1987, as described in Chapter 4, there was scant literature to draw on for theoretical and methodological guidance. By the time I went to Indonesia in 1991 to begin 18 months of ethnographic fieldwork at the Provincial Museum of Central Kalimantan, Museum Balanga (Chapter 5), the situation had not changed much and the anthropology of museums was still in its infancy. Since that time, the anthropology of museums has matured substantially and become an established genre within museum anthropology.

The anthropology of museums uses the methods of cultural anthropology, namely ethnography, to investigate and understand the role of museums in society (in general and in particular settings), institutional histories, as well as the practices and processes of cultural production, consumption, and action. Anthropologists of museums have shown how museums can be fertile field sites for exploring processes behind the making of collections, exhibitions, and museum-community relations in addition to phenomena such as the politics of cultural representation and identity construction. They have also been producing museum ethnographies, or fine-grained accounts and critical analyses of the development and workings of museums as institutions of public culture in differing social, cultural, and national contexts, generating a body of knowledge for a more inclusive comparative museology (Ames 1992, Bouquet 2012, Clifford 1997, Erikson 2002, Isaac 2007, Kreps 2003a, Lonetree 2012, Macdonald 2002, Shannon 2014). In the next chapter, "Mapping Contemporary Museum Anthropology," I describe the methods of museum ethnography in greater detail, and in subsequent chapters, provide examples drawn from my own research and practice.

As Erikson maintains, "the anthropology of museums has developed a number of analytical tools for understanding that museums can be both powerful authors and a space or terrain where social relations and contestations are played out" (2002, 27). On the whole, the anthropology of museums has been pushing the old museum anthropology in new directions, reinvigorating it, and helping it gain a new status within academic anthropology.

This book is concerned with both the anthropology *of* museums and anthropology *in* museums. Although the anthropology of museums is often associated with the theoretical and critical analysis of museums as compared to the practice of anthropology in museums, I do not draw a sharp distinction between the two since practice and theory are inextricably linked. There can be, in the words of the celebrated sociologist C. Wright Mills, no distinction between the theory of a discipline and its method; rather, both are "part of the practice of a craft" (Mills 1959, 216, quoted in Ingold 2013, 4). Certainly, one of the aims of the book is to demonstrate how theory and practice merge in the idea of praxis. Many museum anthropologists and ethnographers are museum professionals, that is, the people developing exhibitions and educational programming, conducting research on collections and carrying out visitor studies; collaborating with community partners, and administering museums. Many also hold academic positions in universities and teach courses at universities while employed in museums just as anthropologists did during the formative years of the discipline. Bouquet notes that museum anthropologists generally "operate somewhere in between the museum and university and thus breach the boundary between academic and applied anthropology" (Bouquet 2001, 4).

The "Coming of Age" of Museum Studies

As museum anthropologists have become ever more concerned with the "theorizing of museums" (Macdonald and Fyfe 1996), they have been contributing to the development of "new museum theory" (Marstine 2006) and critical museology within the broader field of museum studies. Critical museology illuminates the historical imbalances of power and authority embedded in museum collections and practices, and involves the creation of more democratic, inclusive, and reflexive strategies and interventions (Ames 1992, McCarthy 2015, Phillips 2011, Shelton 2006, Silverman 2015).

Like museum anthropology, museum studies has been undergoing sweeping changes over the past several decades, and assuming more prominence within the academy. While previously relegated to the periphery of academic circles primarily due to its perceived focus on the "how to" of museum work, museum studies has, in Macdonald's words, "come of age" (2006, 1). In addition to museum professionals, contributors to museum studies include anthropologists, art historians, historians, sociologists, and cultural studies scholars. Macdonald suggests that this currently makes museum studies one of the most truly interdisciplinary fields in the academy, merging insights from academic studies with the practical work of museums. In the introduction to the edited volume *Companion to Museum Studies*, Macdonald writes:

> Over the past decade in particular, the number of books, journals, courses, and events dedicated to museum studies has grown enormously. It has moved from being an unusual and minority subject into the mainstream. Disciplines which previously paid little attention to museums have come to see the museum as a site at which some of the most interesting and significant of their debates and questions can be explored in novel, and often excitingly applicable, ways. They have come to recognize that understanding the museum requires moving beyond intra-disciplinary concerns to greater dialogue with others, and to adopting and adapting questions, techniques, and approaches derived from other areas of disciplinary expertise. All of this has contributed to museum studies becoming one of the most genuinely multi- and increasingly inter-disciplinary areas of the academy today.
>
> *(2006, 1)*

Kaplan recognized early on that "museum studies stands at new professional frontiers situated somewhere between universities and museums, signaling that a museum is more than the sum of its parts" (1992, 49). She recommends that instead of seeing museums as a collection of separate disciplines "housed under one roof," it is more productive to focus on common ideas and values that connect those working in museums, and to conceive of museum studies as a social science or as part of an existing discipline like anthropology or sociology. Bouquet suggests too that "museum studies should afford a rich contact zone between the practical and theoretical—a place for learning as well as doing, through interchange instead of segregation" (2001, 15).

Indeed, in recent years, there has been a push to resolve longstanding tensions between theory and practice and integrate academic museum studies and the critical analysis of museums with museum practice, or in other words, with what museum practitioners actually do. McCarthy refers to museum practice as "the broad range of professional work in museums, from the functions of management, collections, exhibitions, and programs to the varied activities that take place within these diverse and complex organizations, as well as indicating a recognizable sphere of work" (2015, xxxv). The division between theory and practice is progressively being seen as a false dichotomy, giving way to the view of theory-as-practice and vice versa. As Shelton argues, the problem is not too much theory but the need to work through the implications of theory and criticism for the redefinition of museum operations, or what he calls "operational museology" (2013).

In his "manifesto for critical museology," Anthony Shelton (Director of the University of British Columbia Museum of Anthropology since 2004) calls for a focus on the study and exploration of "operational museology," which he defines as:

that body of knowledge, rules of application, procedural and ethical protocols, organizational structures and regulatory interdictions, and their products (exhibitions and programs) that constitute the field of 'practical museology.' In addition, it comprises the related professional organizations; accredited courses; systems of internship; mentorship and peer review; conference cycles; and seminars and publications by which it regulates and reproduces its institutionalized narratives and discourses.

(2013, 8)

The anthropology of museums and critical museology take operational museology as one of their main objects of study to denaturalize what have become taken for granted categories of museum work such as "best practices," or ways of doing things that are officially sanctioned and formally described through professional museum organizations. Such designations can not only reproduce the status quo, but also lead to standardization, stifle creativity and limit diversity of methods in the name of "professionalism" (McCarthy 2015, xiv). The task is, Shelton suggests, to establish a theory of practice from which a practice of theory can emerge (2013, 14). To this end, it is also constructive to think of museum practice as social practice, embedded in sets of social relationships and larger social milieus (Kreps 2003b).

My conceptualization of critical museology as presented in this book aligns with that of both Shelton and Ames since much of my work has involved the critique of "operational" or "conventional" museological practice. I use the terms "museum studies" and "museology" throughout the book to refer to the study, theorizing, and critical analysis of all matters related to museums, in the past and present, as well as the methods of museum practice and the museum profession.

The convergence of museum and applied anthropology and museum studies is, I suggest, one of the "energies" (Clifford 2013) that have contributed to the ongoing transformation of museum anthropology. In fact, I view our present age of engagement also as an age of convergence in which the real and perceived boundaries among academic, applied, and professional work have been collapsing around the common cause of engagement. Each of these fields has had its own respective strengths, histories, epistemological and theoretical foundations; professional associations and corresponding conferences, publications, and codes of ethics. Yet they also share many commonalities and nodes of intersection among which are their shared commitment to integrating theory and practice and engaging with audiences beyond the academy.

One of the intentions of the book is to bring these historically separate but complementary fields into even greater dialogue and interaction. Just like museum and applied anthropology, contemporary museum studies emphasizes the public role of museums as part of public culture, or, as Kaplan puts it: "Museum studies or museology views museums as dynamic social institutions engaged in a political process acted out in the public arena" (1992, 49).

Articulations of Engagement

In recent years, "engagement" has become a keyword in anthropological and museological discourse and practice. In his classic text, *Keywords: A Vocabulary of Culture and Society*, British sociologist Raymond Williams described keywords as "ways not only of discussing, but at another level of seeing many of our central experiences ... They are significant binding words in certain activities, and their interpretations; they are significant, indicative words in certain forms of thought" (1983, 15). In *Keywords* Williams was interested in exploring not just the changing meanings of words, but also the ways people cluster or bind words together in a vocabulary, "making explicit or often implicit connections that help to initiate new ways of seeing their world" (Bennett, Grossberg, and Morris 2005, xix).

Williams saw words as generative, noting that "important social and historical processes can occur *within* language in ways that indicate how integral the problems of meanings and of relationships really are" (1983, 22, emphasis in original). He stressed the need to be aware of how issues, problems, and ideologies can be embedded inside vocabularies; and how new kinds of relationships and new ways of seeing existing relationships appear in language.

Following Williams, I am interested in the meanings and relationships the word engagement engenders, and how a new vocabulary and cluster of words has been created around it. This is not to say, however, that the idea of engagement is a new phenomenon in anthropology and the museum world. Again, my aim is to explicate the various modalities engagement has taken and how it has been expressed at various times and places. As will be shown in the following chapters, the notion that anthropology and museums should be publicly oriented and play some useful role in society has been integral to their functions and purposes since their beginnings.

To some anthropologists today, engagement is interpreted as action, and as a means of transgressing the scientific posture of the detached, uninvolved observer or researcher. For applied anthropologists Sam Beck and Carl Maida, engagement is about creating greater access to knowledge gained through anthropological research, and the use of this knowledge to empower individuals and communities to bring about change. "An engaged stance moves the application of anthropological theory, methods and practice further towards action and activism ... and towards a participatory role by becoming increasingly part of those communities or social groupings that we normally study" (Beck and Maida 2013, 1).

Archaeologists Barbara Little and Paul Shackel see their heritage work as a form of civic engagement. This entails, among other things, becoming aware of the political and social contexts of heritage work and how it can be informed by social issues. Civic engagement to Little and Shackel involves participating actively in public life and problem solving, enacting a sense of social responsibility, and promoting social justice locally and globally. The goal of civic engagement "is to become an active player in change, to not only work in communities but with communities, and to work toward creating a better quality of life" (Little and Shackel 2014, 47).

In museum anthropology, engagement has largely taken the form of collaboration, especially with "source" (Peers and Brown 2003) or "originating" peoples—the original producers of the objects found in museum collections (Ames 1990, 161). Nowadays, collaboration is considered by many to be the cornerstone of museum anthropology (Isaac 2015). Not surprisingly, Ames was among the first museum professionals and anthropologists to call for community engaged collaboration (Ames 1990). In recent years, a significant body of literature has developed around the subject (Clifford 1997, 2013, Colwell-Chanthaphonh and Ferguson 2008, Golding and Modest 2013, Kahn 2000, Peers and Brown 2003, Phillips 2011, Shannon 2014, Silverman 2015). Much of the writing on collaboration has consisted of case studies that critically examine the virtues of collaborative, more inclusive partnerships as well as problems encountered and ethical issues raised in the course of collaborative work.

Silverman, in the introduction to the edited volume *Museums as Process: Translating Local and Global Knowledges* (2015), states that much of the important theory that has come out of these studies may be ascribed to the field of sociocultural anthropology. He points out that most of the contributors to the volume are anthropologists whose work has been informed by and shaped discussions in the allied fields of collaborative ethnography, public anthropology, engaged anthropology, and collaborative museology. Moreover, he notes that "unlike the detached analysis of culture and society that has dominated scholarship in the humanities and humanistic social sciences collaborative museology presents an explicitly self-aware engagement with and in communities" (Silverman 2015, 10). Indeed, Silverman stresses that contributors to the volume are not "passive observers," but are writing from the perspective of participants deeply invested in the projects on which they critically reflect. A key theme of *Museums as Process* is that collaborative work is fundamentally processual in nature, and that "museums are spaces in which diverse intellectual, professional, and cultural communities meet and engage in work that yields new ways of thinking, new ways of living" (Silverman 2015, 2).

Collaboration as a contemporary expression of engagement will be elaborated on in more detail in the next chapter, as well as in Chapter 6 in which I assess the vicissitudes of collaboration and "frictions" of encounter (Tsing 2005) while working on museum development and training projects in Indonesia. I address the complex and layered nature of collaborative relationships that can be both compromising and reciprocally rewarding.

The Social Role of Museums

The idea that museums should be public, democratic institutions and play a prominent role in civic life dates back to the nineteenth century (Ames 1992, Watson 2007). But an emphasis on greater public engagement and the social role of museums began to take hold on a large scale in the 1960s and 1970s with the emergence of the "new museology" movement. The birth of the movement is often traced back to the social, political, and civil rights movements and the emergence of neighborhood, community, and eco-museums in the 1960s (Davis 2011, Fuller 1992, Shelton 2013, Watson 2007). Grounded in alternative ways of thinking about the purposes and functions of museums, one of its central tenets was that museums should be primarily concerned with community needs and development, and be integrated into the society around them. The idea that museums existed first and foremost to serve society was formally proclaimed in 1972 at the International Council of Museums (ICOM) roundtable conference in Santiago, Chile. In 1974, the ICOM definition of a museum was revised in line with this new spirit (Fuller 1992, 329). Far from being just a building containing collections and receiving visitors, the definition accentuated how the museum should be seen as a "permanent non-profit institution in service of society and its development" (Boylan 2006, 417). The new museology and ICOM's revision of its museum definition represented a shift from a focus on objects to a focus on people and visitors, and the interests and purposes museums serve (Kreps 2003b, 312).

The new museology is often credited with setting into motion what has become the on-going critique and radical reassessment of museums as social institutions. As Peter Vergo explained in the often cited volume *The New Museology*, the old museology was "too much concerned about museum methods, and too little about the purposes of museums" (1989, 3). The old museology was said to revolve around the practical matters of museums, such as administration, education, conservation, and exhibit making (or "operational museology"), whereas the new museology was more theoretical, critical, and humanistic, emphasizing the museum's relationships to the communities and the contingent meanings and values of objects (Macdonald 2006, Marstine 2006). Essentially, it has emphasized the democratization of museums, in principle and practice, and challenged them to be more socially relevant, responsible, and engaged. At the center of the movement was the argument that museums needed to diversify their audiences, and develop strategies to be more inclusive and accessible to their various publics, particularly historically socioeconomically disadvantaged and marginalized groups. To many, today's critical museology has its roots in new museology (Macdonald 2006, Boylan 2006, Marstine 2006).

The proposition that museums exist to serve society and that service should be a core function of museums is now more or less taken for granted, even if the social role of museums is variably interpreted and deployed for a range of purposes in differing contexts. And while "service to society" remains integral to museological discourse and practice, this function is now more frequently labeled community engagement (Crooke 2006, 170). Nowadays, engagement can be seen as a label for the multiple ways in which museums are in dialogue with and connected to communities, and communities participate in museums. As a sign of the times, the Denver Art Museum in 2015 changed the name of its Education Department to the Department of Learning and Engagement, overseen by a Chief Learning and Engagement Officer and a Director of Learning and Community Engagement.[5]

Museums and Communities

Since the publication of the seminal text *Museums and Communities: The Politics of Public Culture* (Karp, Mullen-Kreamer, and Lavine 1992), numerous volumes have appeared devoted to the relationships between museums and their communities (Crooke 2007, Golding and Modest 2013, Peers and Brown 2003). In addition to presenting reports on specific projects, many authors have been complicating the concept of community. It is now well understood that by using "community" as a general descriptor for a given group we run the risk of masking or erasing political differences and historical experiences that exist within a group (Anderson and Geismar 2017). Like cultures, communities are not static, bounded entities with consistently shared values, beliefs, and interests. Indeed, tensions and disharmony can characterize communities as much as accord. As Onciul notes: "Community is a problematic term as it describes a myriad of complex relations and groupings of individuals ... Thus, community is used as a poor substitute, or shorthand, for a complex, rich, and ever-changing interaction" (2013, 81).

Much of the critical discourse on museums and communities has focused on the issue of identity, and how museums as sites of public culture can be entangled in the "politics of recognition" (Taylor 1992). As the anthropologist Ivan Karp suggests in the introduction to *Museums and Communities*, because museums carry "the power to represent" and "to reproduce structures of belief and experience" (1992, 1–2), museums can be perceived as "places for defining who people are and how they should act and as places for challenging those definitions" (1992, 4). Karp also discusses the multiple roles museums can play as institutions and agents of civil society, or, "the complex of social entities in which we act out our lives and through which we fashion our identity" (1992, 4–5). Museums, along with other institutions of civil society such as voluntary associations, educational organizations, and professional societies, in Karp's words, are the "social apparatuses responsible for providing the arenas and contexts in which people define, debate, and contest their identities, and pro-duce and reproduce their living circumstances, their beliefs and values, and ultimately their social order" (1992, 4–5).

While museums have been historically expected to play active roles in civil society, today these roles are expanding as museums are increasingly being called upon to be engines of community regeneration and a means of building social and cultural capital.[6] Museums may also be expected to provide social services, such as working with "at risk" youth or other "underserved" populations (Gurian 2006, Lynch 2013, 2017). In many instances, they are not just seen as institutions that can address social issues and problems, but also as institutions that can help solve them (Janes 2009). Crooke contends that such developments are linked to the rise of the new political right, and the subsequent shrinkage of the role of government in community life that began to take hold in the 1980s, particularly in the United Kingdom and the United States. The museum's expanded role in civil society, in this regard, is congruent with government policies designed to shift responsibility for society's welfare from the state to civic institutions, such as voluntary organizations and individuals (Crooke 2006, 180–181).

Much of the current interest in engagement across fields, besides being a means of building social capital, is driven by an emphasis on "accountability" (Lynch 2011, Shelton 2006), and by the economic and political realities of the museum and cultural sectors at a time when public funding continues to be cut, and museums must prove their ability to generate their own revenue streams (Janes 2009). Universities have been subjected to similar pressures, and the move toward greater public engagement and community work can be partially credited to these energies.

In the book *Toward Engaged Anthropology*, editors Sam Beck and Carl Maida state that engagement is a concept now used by universities to address decades-long criticism for being unresponsive to the needs of society, government, and the private sector. As a result,

> universities have been challenged to become more actively engaged in society as a whole, rather than reproducing the semi-isolation of the academic enterprise. This has happened as public funding is being withdrawn from higher education, concomitant with universities' expanded contractual arrangements with government and private sectors for product development. These trends are reshaping university operations but also the rationale for higher education itself.
>
> *(2013, 2)*

Critics might say that engagement, in this light, is just another marketing strategy for museums to increase their visitor numbers and revenue, and for museums and universities to justify their existence within the competitive context of neoliberal economics. Certainly, marketing agendas and corporatist thinking are often underlying motivations behind engagement efforts. Yet this perspective belittles the important work that has been and is being done by many to create and promote more useful and relevant practice. The emphasis on engagement, furthermore, can act as a countervailing force against neoliberal individualism, the loss of a sense of community and connection, and the ever expanding commodification of cultural and social life. Accordingly, I use engagement as a unifying concept while remaining mindful of its problematic dimensions.

Although I promote the value of engagement in the book, I am not suggesting that all research, scholarship, and practice in museums and anthropology should be explicitly engaged. On the contrary, there is still much value in the core functions of museums, i.e., collecting, conservation, and research. Certainly, as Kurin asserts, cultural work should be based on sound research, and research-based understandings of culture is one of the most important contributions scholarly disciplines, museums, and cultural institutions can make to the "practice of cultural civics" (1997, 266).

Handler argues along similar lines when he writes that anthropologists have a distinct take on cultural criticism compared to critics from other fields. As he sees it, anthropological cultural critics are anthropologists who expend at least some of their professional effort in dissecting the commonsense presuppositions of their own world and in disseminating the results of that work to as wide an audience of citizens they can reach. As anthropologists they have a distinctive style, or method, of generating critical insight, one born of the historically given tasks of the discipline, its commitment to the comparative study of the variety and particularity of cultural experiences around the globe, and of the fieldwork methods developed to accomplish the task. In my opinion, anthropological training and work make anthropologists particularly insightful cultural critics.

(2005, 4–5)

Handler notes, nevertheless, that while anthropologists may well be insightful they have not been necessarily politically and socially effective or influential, and although there are exceptions, American anthropologists "seem to be almost completely absent from the popular media" (2005, 5).[7]

Museum Anthropology as Cultural Work

The "practice of cultural civics" and "cultural criticism" is among the categories of cultural work in my vision of engaged museum anthropology. I use the term cultural work throughout the book as another unifying concept and as a label for the various kinds of work museum anthropologists do, for example, fieldwork, writing, curating, public programming, teaching and training, and community development, but also as a particular approach to practice—an approach grounded in the idea of *praxis*. Freire defines praxis as "reflection and action upon the world in order to transform it" (1998, 33). The idea of praxis inherently involves critical thinking and reflection on what we do, why we do it, and whose interests are being served by our work. As a particular approach to practice, praxis also requires critical awareness of the structures of power and authority that limit or create obstacles to change. Furthermore, in praxis, theory and practice cannot be separated, but rather, praxis requires theory to illuminate it (Freire 1998, 106). I see cultural work as an appropriate tag for much of museum and anthropological work in the age of engagement, or to borrow from Freire again, an "epoch characterized by a complex of ideas, concepts, hopes, doubts, values and challenges in dialectical interaction with their opposites" (1998, 82).

Today, cultural work is now often associated with the "creative cultural industry" and used to describe "the act of labour within the industrialized process of cultural production" (Banks 2007, 3). However, the terms cultural work and culture worker have long been used by community artists and activists; cultural organizations; educators, folklorists, and public intellectuals to signify work that is for the common good and derived from collective action. The terms also underscore that the work of educators, researchers, curators, artists, and so forth is indeed *work*, is embedded in society's political economy, and contributes to its functioning alongside other professions (Dubin 1987, Maxwell 2001).

One can say that anthropologists have always been doing cultural work, or working the idea of culture, since culture has been the discipline's core concept. Geertz described culture as the concept "around which the whole discipline of anthropology arose" (1973, 4). Yet despite its centrality, the concept of culture has in fact come to be increasingly contested rather than agreed upon. As anthropologist Nestor Garcia Canclini alleges, "anthropologists are unsure whether their object of study should be called 'culture'" anymore (2014, 12). In *Keywords*, Williams famously described culture as "one of the two or three most complicated words in the English language" (1983, 87). The consensus of opinion probably lies with James Clifford, however, who says that even though culture is a "deeply compromised idea," it is one he "cannot yet do without" (1988, 10).

In *New Keywords. A Revised Vocabulary of Culture and Society* (2005), Bennett writes that the diversity of meanings and contexts in which the vocabulary of culture now figures has multiplied extraordinarily in recent years, especially in the use of the "adjectival cultural." This expansion reflects what Williams saw as the versatility of the word as a "map" of social, economic, and political changes (Bennett, Grossberg, and Morris 2005, 64).

Similarly, Breidenbach and Nyiri in their suitably titled book *Seeing Culture Everywhere from Genocide to Consumer Habits*, examine how "today's world is a world shaped by a consciousness of culture that penetrates everyday life as well as matters of the state in an unprecedented way" (2009, 9). Culture is often the central motif of official government policies, the workings of social institutions, in advertising and consumer studies, and a reference point in political struggles and ideologies. The "cultural turn" is not only visible in public debates, but has also steadily infiltrated academic disciplines from the social sciences and humanities to medicine and business (2009, 19). Indeed, "Culture—or rather cultural difference—is now held to be the main explanation for the way the human world functions" (2009, 9).

Certainly, the anthropologist Marshall Sahlins identified, in the early 1990s, how the development of "cultural self-consciousness," especially among "imperialism's erstwhile victims," was one of the more remarkable phenomena of world history in the late twentieth century (Shalins 1993, 3). The deliberate use of culture, its discovery, invention, and reinforcement, or what he termed "culturalism" (1993, 4), had by then already become normative as a means of gaining recognition of a distinctive way of life and relative difference.

Breidenbach and Nyiri suggest, however, that despite the frequency with which the term "culture" is now invoked and the prevalence of "culture consciousness" and "culturalism," the word remains highly ambiguous if not misunderstood and misused. "Many people talk about culture, yet most are not able to describe and define it, let alone point to its actual impact and importance in their institutions and areas of work" (2009, 23). Diverse understanding and uses of culture make it difficult to communicate across disciplines and much less in ways that make sense to the general public.[8] It is the task of anthropologists, as Breidenbach and Nyiri and many others have contended, to make the complexities of culture intelligible to the general public (Handler 2005, Hannerz 2010, Eriksen 2006, Kurin 1997). It is one thing to study and critique culture, but quite another to be able to communicate anthropological understandings of culture to broad audiences.

Kurin offers a set of interpretations of culture that is helpful for comprehending and communicating the diverse meanings and uses of the word culture today. He states that nowadays, culture resides in three general, though overlapping worlds—the worlds of entertainment, scholarship, and politics. As entertainment, culture can be thought of as anything from "high art"—ballet, opera, symphonic music—to popular culture as in television, music, films, and mass commodities. In scholarship,

> culture is treated in the main as ideas, socially embedded praxes, philosophies, historically situated complexes of values, ways of life, and orientations. Culture is an abstraction that sheds light on individuals, groups, nations, historical periods, and even species. You don't buy this kind of culture—you study it, using methodologies of different disciplines from anthropology to art history, from philosophy to ethnomusicology.
>
> *(Kurin 1997, 16)*

In the world of social politics, Kurin states that culture is associated with identities of people, nations, factions, institutions, professions, and members of the electorate. For Kurin culture is: "The symbolic means through which people express their views, values, and interests—and impose them on others. Culture expressed as language, dress, behavioral code, music and specific beliefs, defines who 'we' are" (1997, 17).

The idea of cultural work bridges scholarly understandings of culture with those of "popular thought." It also helps bridge disciplinary and professional divides, for instance between the arts, humanities, anthropology, and museum and heritage studies. On this note, throughout the book I sometimes use "heritage" and "heritage work" interchangeably with culture and cultural work to encapsulate a range of subject areas and spheres of practice that share a close kinship. The word, "heritage," like culture, connotes different things to different people, i.e., scholars, heritage workers, and the "people who use it, shape it, remember it, and forget it" (Little and Shackel 2014, 39). The scholarly literature on heritage, which has grown immensely over the past decade or more, addresses its multiple meanings in diverse contexts as well as its uses and abuses (Harrison 2013, Hoelscher 2006, Kirshenblatt-Gimblett 1998, 2006, Smith 2006, 2009). But it can be loosely understood as "whatever matters [in tangible and intangible forms] to people today that provides some connection between the past and present" (Little and Shackel 2014, 39).

Bridging Disciplinary Divides

The ambiguity of vocabulary and the stubbornness of disciplinary boundaries have hindered the cultural work of museum anthropology and so have the divisions within anthropology. Over its lifetime, American anthropology in particular has fragmented into a number of "subfields" beyond its long-established "Four Fields" of archaeology, sociocultural, linguistic, and physical or biological anthropology. On the one hand this fragmentation reflects the breadth and diversity of a discipline devoted to practically every dimension of human existence. But on the other hand, this tendency has raised questions about anthropology's core identity as a discipline and profession, while contributing to its stratification. However, for decades now, many anthropologists have been admonishing these divides and shedding light on their implications. Nowadays, as described above, there is greater talk of unity as the subfields are coalescing around the shared interests and principles of public and engaged anthropology (Lamphere 2004, Low and Merry 2010).

I write from the perspective and experience of a museum anthropologist trained in the American anthropological tradition while recognizing, as Shelton points out, that "different national traditions cannot be reduced to a single or general developmental model" (2006, 64). Indeed, the distinction between applied and academic work, for example in American anthropology, has been viewed as anachronistic by many anthropologists working in other parts of the world (Eriksen 2006, Hannerz 2010).

Mason notes that the divides that have existed between academic and applied work have also existed in museum studies, that is, divisions between museums and universities, and practitioners and museum critics. According to Mason, such schisms largely come down to practical matters regarding how and under what circumstances research is conducted.

> Academics are rarely able to be immersed within museums, and as such, often find it difficult to access the kind of behind-the-scenes information necessary to reflect on the processes of production and regulation. Conversely, practitioners are often enmeshed in the day-to-day practical issues and may not be inclined to take the longer, historical view preferred by academics.
>
> *(2006, 29)*

Similar to many other authors, Mason argues that we need a "theoretical museology" in which research is located "at the intersection of theory and practice, as opposed to a mode of critique which stands outside looking inward" (2006, 29). She adds: "Recognition of the importance of research to practice and vice versa will only enrich both academics and practitioners" (2006, 30).

Ruth Phillips, an art historian, curator, and former director of the University of British Columbia Museum of Anthropology, astutely circumvents these divisions by labeling herself a "hybrid academic museum professional" (2011, 16). Phillips has also made significant contributions to anthropology and museum studies as a scholar and practitioner. Her description fits the identities of many museum anthropologists whose work cuts across academia and professional museum worlds. I too, like Phillips, have attempted to bridge these worlds, and have assumed multiple identities over the course of my career—professor in a department of anthropology, director of a museum and heritage studies program and university-based museum of anthropology. And as a museum ethnographer, I have critically examined these worlds from both an insider and outsider perspective. I have also worked on several museum development and training programs as an applied museum anthropologist. These multiple positions and identities have given me a number of vantage points from which to critique and reflect on the changes that have been taking place in anthropology, museums, and museum studies over the years. I agree with Ames that "useful criticism needs to combine assessment with the empirical examination of real situations" (Ames 1992, 4).

The book is partly autobiographical in that it chronicles my own trajectory toward engaged research, scholarship and practice in parallel with the field of anthropology as a whole. I write myself into this story through an assembly of personal experience, documentation, and reflexive analysis. What Phillips observes about her own narrative pertains to mine: "Contingencies of biography enter, of course, into every scholarly and critical project, and personal experience always determines the angles of reflection that both open up and limit the resulting narratives" (2011, 4).

Doing Museum Anthropology in a Globalizing and Interconnected World

Back in the late 1970s when Ames began his "anthropology of anthropology and museums" he suggested that we do "applied anthropology in our backyards" (1979), in other words, study ourselves as "museum natives," and our museums as a "culture area" and "exotic new field" (Ames 1986, 61). Ames saw the value of turning the anthropological gaze back on himself, and critically examining his own profession from the "native" or "insider" point of view. For Ames, this reflexive approach was a strategy for reforming both museums and anthropology. When I began studying museums and anthropology in the mid-1980s, I approached my research with a reformer's perspective not unlike that of Ames. However, in addition to studying "museum natives" in my own backyard, I also have been studying them in other national and cultural settings.

This book is the product of nearly 30 years of studying museums and related phenomena mainly in the Netherlands, Indonesia, and the United States. I have been interested in the history of anthropology museums as products and tools of colonialism and their processes of decolonization; the forms museums take, the purposes and interests they serve; and how the museum idea, as a "transnational cultural form" (Appadurai and Breckenridge 1988) and "traveling institution" (Karp and Buntix 2006), is (re)interpreted in diverse settings. In this and many other respects, the book as a whole can be seen as a study in comparative museology (Clifford 1991, Kreps 2003a, 2014). While I have been concerned with the histories and subjectivities of individual institutions and museological traditions and interpretations in different settings and times, I have also paid attention to how these institutions and museologies articulate with larger national and global processes and networks in the past and into the present (Kreps 2003a, 2006).

Kratz and Karp point out in the introduction to *Museum Frictions: Public Cultures/Global Transformations* that "increasing international connections and global orientations is one of the major trends in museum and heritage practice in recent decades, yet, the workings and implications of these trends have gone relatively unexamined" (2006, 4). They go on to say that neither has much consideration been given to "how museums have managed the pushes and pulls that derived from globalizing processes" (2006, 5). Subsequently, the book is intended to help fill gaps in the literature on museums and globalizing processes by providing a comparative case study of how globalizing processes, especially colonialism and decolonization, have shaped museums in the United States, the Netherlands, and Indonesia. Even though I have been concerned with identifying and documenting differences across national boundaries and social and cultural milieus, I have been equally attentive to commonalities and connections. Doing the kind of international and globally oriented museum ethnography I describe in the book has required a mixed methodological toolkit that includes both long-term, immersive and multi-sited ethnography as well as short-term that ranges across a number of different institutions, projects, and countries. It has also necessitated an historical and comparative perspective.

Hannerz suggests that "multi-site" ethnography diverges from the "classical" period of social and cultural anthropology in which field research entailed studying the "entire culture and way of life" of a people in one locale for an extended period of time—at least a year. This style of field work, which he calls the "immersion mode," required a certain degree of fluency in the local language, and the cultivation of close ties and long-term relationships with the people with whom the ethnographer worked. In contrast to the classic ideal of "anthropology by immersion" that relied on extended periods of participant observation for gathering data, multi-site ethnography tends to rely more on interviewing and is more typically "anthropology by appointment" (Hannerz 2010, 76). Notwithstanding these limitations, Hannerz affirms the value of multi-site studies, and the need for "different kinds of fields and different kinds of field work" in anthropology's world today (2010, 77).

Marcus explains that multi-sited ethnography is "an exercise in mapping terrain" that requires "considerable more nuancing and shading" than conventional ethnography (1995, 99–100). He states that it is "mobile ethnography" that is "designed around chains, paths, threads, conjunctions, or juxtapositions of locations" in which the ethnographer establishes some form of logical connection or association among sites (1995, 105). As a research strategy and conceptual framework, multi-sited ethnography characterizes much of contemporary anthropology, and increasingly museum anthropology and museum studies (Alivizatou 2012, Clifford 2013, Levitt 2015). Ever more attuned to how museums are "transnational cultural forms" and part of "transnational cultural flows" (Appadurai and Breckenridge 1988), the tools of multi-sited ethnography allow researchers to "follow ideas, things, or groups across different sites, and the connection between them" (Levitt 2015, 12). And as applied social scientists, we also track problems, needs, and in some cases crises and emergencies for which we might be able to offer some measure of assistance.

Eschewed in anthropology for decades, the comparative method has been re-surfacing not only as a dimension of multi-sited ethnography (Marcus 1995, 102), but also as a particularly useful tool for studying, portraying, discussing, explaining, and experiencing diversity (Hannerz 2010, 56, Van der Veer 2016). Many have come to see how comparison is crucial to understanding processes of differentiation and "the effects of encounter across difference" (Tsing 2005, 4), as much as it is important for grasping claims about universals.

The "New" Museum Ethics

The practice of museum anthropology today is informed by the anthropological code of ethics of "do no harm," and to "do some good" (Nash et al. 2011, 138). As used here, "do some good" is based on the assumption that the pursuits of museum anthropologists should benefit the individuals and communities with whom they work. Indeed, much contemporary museum work is grounded in the rule of "reciprocity," which "requires that each party recognizes, respects, and draws from the expertise of the other" (Lynch in Marstine 2011, 12).

What's more, "do some good" implies action. In fact, Ames saw a commitment to action as an ethical imperative and "part of an individual's and a museum's responsibility to society" (Phillips 2011, 20). Action can mean modifying or even eliminating some practices, such as displaying sacred objects and allowing research on ancestral remains and culturally sensitive collections. Today, for example, many museums are working with Native American and First Nations communities to indigenize curatorial practices through the integration of Indigenous cultural protocols and "traditional care" methods (Kreps 2003a, 2009, 2011, McCarthy 2019, Phillips 2011, Shannon 2017). Action, of course, can also include cultural restitution and the repatriation of collections.

For Nash, Colwell-Chanthaphonh, and Holen, curators in the Department of Anthropology at the Denver Museum of Nature and Science, the idea of "beneficence" embodied in "do some good" comes down to being committed to "stewardship instead of ownership" (2011, 139). They have been acting on this philosophy by instituting a set of guiding principles for the curation of the ethnology collections at their museum. These principles are: respect, reciprocity, justice, and dialogue. They pledge:

> The scientific use and long-term preservation of the American Ethnology Collection will be pursued while embracing the respectful treatment of Native Americans, the mutual benefit of myriad stakeholders, and the evenhanded treatment of all people through open and sincere dialogue.
>
> *(2011, 139)*

Shifts in the ethical principles of museum anthropology echo the changes that have been taking place in the museum world. Marstine contends that these changes signal the need for a "new" museum ethics—an ethics that is not defined merely by professional codes, but also by a "museum ethics of change" that allows museums to change as the needs of society change (2011, 7).

Marstine asserts that progressive institutions embrace rather than shy away from the key ethical issues of the day, and actively enter debates as participants in civic discourse. Museums that are driven by a dynamic ethics discourse have a clear sense of their values, which are continually being assessed in alignment with the communities they serve. "Institutions invested in the new museum ethics discourse effectively communicate the public value of museums. The process empowers museums to change because [the museum] builds public trust through democracy, transparency, and relevance" (2011, 5).

Central to the "new" museum ethics is the assertion that ethics are contingent and relative in nature. Marstine points out that ethics codes, in the Western context, have been based on Enlightenment ideals of virtue and individualism. She maintains though that ethics are culturally defined, and as such, museum ethics should not be seen as a universal set of values that can be applied indiscriminately. Rather, "it is important to differentiate between ethical principles—those ideals and values a society holds dear—and applied ethics—the practice of employing those principles to specific arenas of activity" (2011, 6). Certainly, values change. Many practices that were considered normative and standard in the past are no longer acceptable. Moreover, it is also now apparent that what is considered "best," ethical, or appropriate practice in one cultural context and era may not be in another (Kreps 2008, 2011). The contingent nature of museum ethics, then, infers respect for diversity.

Today, museums are not just concerned with the need to diversify their audiences and represent multiple voices and perspectives, but also with the need to diversify their practices. Through collaboration with Indigenous communities, for example, museum anthropologists have gained a deeper understanding and respect for the diverse ways people know, experience, and make sense of things inside and outside of museums. It is now widely understood that museums must go beyond merely consulting with Indigenous communities (Clifford 1997). Rather, they are expected to actively interrogate previously held conceptions of how collections are classified, stored, interpreted, and exhibited—reconfiguring museums as reflexive stewards of Indigenous peoples' cultural heritage. Harrison, Byrne, and Clarke describe this intervention as "reassembling" collections in ways that "generate new conceptions of care and curation as genuine forms of respect and concern in the contemporary museum and beyond" (2013, 6). Much of contemporary museum anthropology, accordingly, involves "translating knowledges"—multiple epistemologies, multiple ways of knowing—"that often meet and coalesce in the objects upon which various meanings have been inscribed" (Silverman 2015, 3).

To Marstine, contemporary museum ethics, in contrast to the "old," is not a canon of ideas based on consensus and a desire for conformity. Instead, it is marked by strong differences of opinion, contestation, and debate. She asserts that in twenty-first-century societies that purportedly respect difference, consensus and conformity have come to signal exclusivity, like-mindedness, and a fixity of thought that inhibits change, risk taking, and moreover, the moral agency of museums (2011, 6–7).

The conviction that museums have "moral agency" has come to be seen as another key tenet of the "new" museum ethics, and is concomitant with the idea of the socially responsible museum. The moral agency of the museum rests on the premise that museums should contribute to the well-being of society, and actively participate in creating more just and equitable social structures and relationships. Museums that act from a position of moral agency link their work, unapologetically, to issues of social justice, equality, and human rights (Sandell and Nightingale 2012). Besterman sums up the ethos of the new museum ethics when he writes "ethics define relationships of the museum with people, not with things" (2006, 432).

Chapter Summaries

The main of the book draws from my own research, scholarship, and practice carried out over the past several decades. Given its time span, the book is, in part, an assemblage and extension of ideas, lines of inquiry, and case studies that have appeared in previous publications. Material from previous publications serves as background for a deeper understanding of more recent work, and is reinterpreted in light of current theoretical positions in museum anthropology and museum studies. While a large portion of the book is based on "new" material, meaning unpublished, some of it is not new in the sense that I return to material gathered while conducting research as a graduate student in international studies and anthropology in the late 1980s and early 1990s. In this regard, segments of my story recount "beginnings" and "returns" (Clifford 2013).

Chapter 2, "Mapping Contemporary Museum Anthropology" elaborates on many of the themes addressed in this introduction and presents an overview of the main movements and tendencies in museum anthropology over the past few decades that have contributed to more engaged research and practice. While the chapter covers aspects of anthropology practiced in museums, I mainly focus on the rise of the anthropology of museums and critical and reflexive museology. I discuss in detail what has become one of the primary methods for doing the anthropology of museums, i.e., museum ethnography.

Museum anthropology and ethnography are informed by a number of other subfields in anthropology and museums studies, but particularly important is the renewed interest in material culture studies, objects, and materiality. In the section "The Return of the Object," I discuss recent approaches to the study of objects and collections, and how our understanding of the diverse ways people know, experience, relate to, and have cared for the things they value (material and immaterial) has been enriched and expanded through collaboration with originating communities. I consider how collaborative work, along with postcolonial and Indigenous critiques and activism, has radically altered museum practices and powered their indigenization and decolonization. Equally important is the recognition and development of Indigenous and other non-Western museologies. Taken together, these movements have been countering the hegemony of Western museology and contributing to its diversification.

The chapter furthermore addresses some of the on-going challenges confronting museum anthropology, especially related to its standing within the discipline of anthropology as a whole. I discuss the dilemmas many museum anthropologists face when attempting to balance their multiple obligations and responsibilities as both scholars and practicing museum professionals (Ames 1992, Swan 2015, Isaac 2015). Finally, I consider the growing intersection of museum anthropology and museum studies, and what each field has to contribute to the other.

Chapter 3, "Museum and Applied Anthropology: Shared Histories and Trajectories" considers how museum and applied anthropology have been increasingly converging in their interests, purposes, and approaches to practice. Although the two fields have historically been viewed as separate subfields in American anthropology, I consider how they share common histories in their origins and development. Especially significant is their marginalized status within academic anthropology largely due to their practical and public orientation. I describe how many of the criticisms leveled against museum anthropology have also been directed toward applied anthropology. In general, I am concerned with how a shared history of criticism, both internal and external to the fields, has pushed them in new directions and in turn contributed to a more socially relevant and engaged anthropology in general.

The first section of the chapter concerns the historical development of American museum anthropology from its early days to the present. I suggest a more nuanced reading of the field's history by filling in some gaps, for instance, with stories of women and Native American contributions to the field and examples of collaborative and socially relevant exhibitions that took place in the 1960s and 1970s. I also highlight how many of the problems and issues with which early museum anthropologists wrestled remain with us to this day. An historical perspective is valuable for gaining a better understanding of movements and tendencies that have brought us to our current moment, and because, as Phillips maintains, "our most effective studies of museums are those that are informed by history *and* theory *and* practice" (2011, 17 emphasis in the original).

Chapter 4, "Museum Anthropology in the Netherlands: Colonial and Postcolonial Narratives" revisits my research in the late 1980s on the historical development of Dutch anthropology museums in colonial and postcolonial eras. This research was not only my first foray into museum ethnography, but also my first formal investigation into the public role of anthropology museums. I describe how I was motivated to study Dutch museums by their approaches to the representation of culture, which appeared, at that time, to be radically different from the American anthropology museums with which I was familiar.

Briefly, I learned that Dutch anthropology museums were largely products and tools of Dutch colonialism. From their earliest days, their mission was to promote colonialism and enlist the public's support for the colonial enterprise. The ways in which non-Western cultures were represented in museums were shaped by particular economic, political, and social relationships between colonizers and the colonized. After the Dutch lost possession of their colonial territories post-World War II, museums were forced to reorient their missions and undergo a process of decolonization. This meant shifting their mandate from justifying domination and exploitation to fostering cross-cultural understanding and international cooperation. The focus of exhibitions and programs was just as much on people's contemporary realities as it was on their past. In the chapter, I reinterpret these initial research findings in light of recent scholarship on Dutch museums (Aldrich 2009, Bouquet 2012, 2015, Hildering et al. 2015, Kreps 1988, 2011, Mohr 2014, Wintle 2016). My purpose is to show how in some national and social contexts museum anthropology's public role has remained consistently dominant, albeit for questionable ends as an instrument of "governmentality" (Bennett 1995).

My research in the Netherlands led me to Indonesia, a former Dutch colony, to conduct research for my doctoral dissertation in anthropology on the role of museums in national development and how the museum idea was interpreted in a postcolonial, non-Western context. In Chapter 5, "'Museum Frictions' in Colonial and Postcolonial Indonesia," I describe my ethnographic study of the Provincial Museum of Central Kalimantan, Museum Balanga, located in the interior of Indonesian Borneo where, according to the Directorate of Museums of the Ministry of Education and Culture, both museum staff and community members had no idea of what a museum is or should be. In fact, it was said that Indonesians in general were "not yet museum-minded." I discovered, counter to this claim, that many people were museum-minded but in their own ways. Museum staff and community members had their own methods of indigenizing and localizing the museum. I show how Museum Balanga was a site of cultural hybridization wherein Indigenous approaches to representing, taking care of, and preserving what people valued were being mixed with those of international, professional museum culture (Kreps 2003a). While today such practices are seen as progressive in American museums, for instance, at the time of my research they were being discouraged in Museum Balanga in favor of promoting more modern, professional methods. I suggest that the perceived shortcomings of Museum Balanga and other state-sponsored museums had more to do with the bureaucracy of the national museum system and its top-down, authoritarian approach to museum management and development than with people's lack of museum-mindedness. Overall, the chapter provides insights into what the public role of museums and community engagement looks like when executed within the framework of state-controlled cultural policies (Jones 2013).

In the chapter, I also provide an account of the historical development of Indonesian museums from the time of their founding by the Dutch and other Europeans in the late 1700s to the time of my fieldwork in 1991 and 1992. I show how museums during the colonial period existed primarily to serve colonial interests. In the newly independent Republic of Indonesia, museums were to "serve the people and their development." I describe how the government envisioned a role for museums in processes of nation-building, which included the construction of a national culture and identity as well as socioeconomic development and modernization. In this case, the public role of the museum as an instrument of "governmentality" is brought into even sharper focus.

But while the government imagined a new role for museums in postcolonial Indonesia, I highlight how those responsible for museum development did not sever ties with the Dutch or other members of the international museum community. Instead, "international connections and global orientations" (Kratz and Karp 2006) remained critical to the further development of Indonesian museums, as they do today. Museum Balanga serves as a case study in how processes of decolonization and nation-building play out "on the ground," and how local institutions are shaped by and articulate with the wider political, economic, and cultural forces. The chapter also includes a detailed description of my research methods as an example of multi-sited museum ethnography (Levitt 2015).

Chapter 5 serves as background to Chapter 6, "International Collaboration and the Value of Culture and Heritage," in which I discuss my collaboration with the Dayak Ikat Weaving Project in Sintang, West Kalimantan and the Museum Pusaka Nias (Nias Heritage Museum) on the island of Nias off the northwest coast of Sumatra. I describe my work with the organizations as part of the University of Denver/Indonesia Exchange Program in Museum Training, sponsored by the Ford Foundation and Asian Cultural Council. The Exchange Program was conceptualized as a means of providing training (both on-site and at the University of Denver) to the organizations' staff, and as an alternative to the top-down, expert-driven approaches to training I observed during my earlier fieldwork in Indonesia. In this respect, the program was envisioned as an experiment in the development of culturally sensitive, context-specific "appropriate museology" (Kreps 2008). I interpret the Exchange Program as an example of "transnational, transcultural reciprocal collaboration" (Schlele and Hidayah 2014). In contrast to training programs that emphasize the transfer (and reproduction) of standard museum practices, I see training programs as sites of knowledge production.

My work with the Dayak Ikat Weaving Project and Museum Pusaka Nias illustrates the importance of international collaboration and connections in museum and cultural work, and the benefits gained from multi-lateral and multi-pronged strategies. The case studies throw into relief questions regarding the intrinsic and extrinsic values of culture and heritage resources, and the diverse purposes and interests they can serve in different registers. Special attention is given to how the Dayak Ikat Weaving Project and the Museum Pusaka Nias exemplify different configurations of museum/community relations and methods of engagement. Additionally, I show how the ethnography of collaborative projects can generate critical analysis necessary for creating more culturally appropriate, context-specific, and decolonizing methodologies.

The final Chapter 7, "Doing Museum Anthropology 'at Home,'" concentrates on contemporary work in university museums, and the reconnection of academic anthropology to museums. While university museums have historically served as sites for research, teaching, and communicating anthropological knowledge and insights, I am particularly interested in how today they are uniquely positioned to make anthropology socially relevant and useful through engaged research, teaching, and practice. One of my aims is to show how the perceived divides between theoretically oriented anthropology and applied, publicly engaged work are dissolving as it becomes ever more clear how theory informs practice and practice informs theory (McCarthy 2015, Thomas 2010). Academic anthropology's return to the museum also means a return to teaching with objects and collections, and using them to complement theory with time-honored "hands-on" pedagogical approaches (Lubar and Stokes-Rees 2012).

Examples of projects carried out in the Haffenrefer Museum of Anthropology at Brown University (Lubar and Stokes-Rees 2012), the Museum of Anthropology at the University of British Columbia (Kramer 2015, Shelton and Houtman 2009), and at my home institution, the University of Denver Museum of Anthropology (DUMA) illustrate these and other points (Kreps 2015). In the latter case, I describe participatory and community-engaged exhibition projects inspired by my work with the European Union-sponsored Museums as Places for Intercultural Dialogue and The Learning Museum projects. The emphasis here is on how such projects are sites of intercultural dialogue, exchange, and curation.

I also discuss DUMA's work with Native American communities within the context of implementing the Native American Graves Protection and Repatriation Act (NAGPRA), and how this work has forced anthropology museums, in general, to uncover and reconstruct their own particular histories of extractive anthropology and collection formation. I tell the story of how the museum and faculty members' experience working with Native communities and in addressing anthropology's colonial legacy proved valuable in helping the university confront its own difficult heritage related to its founder on the occasion of its 150th anniversary. This narrative leads into a discussion of the ways in which working with Native American and other artists opens channels for addressing dark histories as well as contemporary social issues.

In the section, "Working with Artists," I describe my collaboration with the Italian social practice artist, Daniele Pario Perra, on a multi-sited exhibition project devoted to the topic of graffiti. This project exemplifies the ways in which university anthropology museums have been increasingly working with artists to (re)interpret collections in new and creative ways to generate alternative historical and institutional narratives (Lubar 2017, Marstine 2013, 2017). Working with artists additionally has been part of a trend in anthropology to pay more attention to the border zones between contemporary art and anthropological practice (Schneider and Wright 2010).

I close the chapter by exploring the prospects for the practice of cosmopolitan museum anthropology, which encourages global perspectives and ways of being in the world that acknowledge connections and obligations to others beyond self, family, and nation (Appiah 2006, Mason 2013). Cosmopolitan museum anthropology furthermore encourages new approaches to addressing anthropology museums' long struggle with how to engender greater understandings of what unites us as human beings without eliding our differences. Whereas museums of all kinds are now embracing public engagement and responsiveness to communities as a core mission (Thomas 2016), I stress how museums of anthropology as world cultures museums engage with communities near and far, or local and global.

Overall, in the chapter, I circle back to many of the topics and issues raised in Chapters 1 and 2 regarding the transformation of museum anthropology over the past several decades, its present state, and futures. Ultimately, I consider why museums and anthropology matter in our current age of engagement.

The book should be of interest to anyone interested in an historical and comparative study of museums and anthropology, and the forms engagement takes in different institutional, national, and cultural settings at different moments in time. It should be especially useful for students (and their instructors) looking for a text that provides a history of museum anthropology and major trends in the field, past and present, as well as definitions and a "portfolio of methods" (Tsing 2005) for doing critical, reflexive museum ethnography and collaborative work. Students may also find the text helpful for gaining a better understanding of how theory is applied in practice and how practice inspires theorizing. The book should also be valuable to readers concerned with the intersection of museums, anthropology, colonialism, and decolonization, especially in reference to the Netherlands and Indonesia. Thus, the book is intended to speak to both newcomers to the academic fields of museum anthropology and museum studies as well as to specialist readers. In the end, this book was written with the belief "that it matters what stories we use to tell other stories with" (Haraway 2016, 12).

Notes

1 The late Michael Ames was the Director of the Museum of Anthropology at the University of British Columbia from 1974 to 1997 and from 2002 to 2004, and was a long-time advocate for public museum anthropology. In fact, the first edition of *Cannibal Tours* was titled *Museums, the Public, and Anthropology: A Study in the Anthropology of Anthropology Museums*, published in 1986.
2 Richard Kurin is Distinguished Scholar and Ambassador-at-Large; Acting Director, Arthur M. Sackler Gallery and Freer Gallery of Art at the Smithsonian Institution in Washington, DC; Smithsonian Liaison to the US President's Committee for the Arts and the Humanities and the White House Historical Association, and member of the United States Department of State Cultural Heritage Coordinating Committee. In his lengthy career at the Smithsonian he has served as Acting Provost and Under Secretary for Museums and Research; Under Secretary for History, Art, and Culture, and Director of the Smithsonian Center for Folklife and Cultural Heritage. Kurin also served on the US National Commission for UNESCO (United Nations Educational, Scientific and Cultural Organization) and helped draft the 2003 UNESCO Convention on the Safeguarding of Intangible Cultural Heritage. He holds a PhD in anthropology from the University of Chicago (www.si.edu, accessed June 16, 2018).
3 See Bouquet 2012, Coombes and Phillips 2015, Peers and Brown 2003, Phillips 2011, Shelton 2006, Silverman 2015, and Thomas 2016 for other accounts of these changes.
4 Shelton (2006) points out that anthropology, in its early days, grew out of or resided in learned societies and universities in addition to museums.

5 Personal communication with Heather Nielsen, Director of Learning and Community Engagement, Interpretive Specialist, Native Arts and New World Departments, Denver Art Museum, June 6, 2018.
6 See chapter 4 "Social Capital and the Cultural Sector" in Crooke (2007) for a straightforward discussion on how museums and the arts and culture sector have come to be seen as a means for creating community bonds and social capital.
7 Handler states that this lament is particularly heartfelt among North American anthropologists whose disciplinary ancestors, such as Boas, Benedict, and Mead, had considerable media presence during their careers.
8 Here I am thinking of the distinctions often made between "high Culture" with a capital "C" and culture with a lowercase "c" understood in the anthropological sense of a "whole way of life." The former is often associated with the arts and an attitude of "being cultured," dating back to Arnold's 1868 description of culture as "acquainting ourselves with the best that has been thought and said in the world" (Handler 2005, 77).

References

Adams, Kathleen. 2015. "Back to the Future?: Emergent Visions for Object-Based Teaching in and Beyond the Classroom." *Museum Anthropology* 2:88–95.
Aldrich, Robert. 2009. "Colonial Museums in Postcolonial Europe." *African and Black Diaspora: An International Journal* 2(2):137–156.
Alivizatou, Marilena. 2012. *Intangible Heritage and the Museum. New Perspectives in Cultural Preservation*. London: Routledge.
Ames, Michael. 1979. "Applied Anthropology in Our Backyards." *Practicing Anthropology* 2(1):65–79.
Ames, Michael. 1986a. *Museums, the Public, and Anthropology. A Study of the Anthropology of Anthropology*. Vancouver and New Delhi: UBC Press Concept Publishing.
Ames, Michael. 1986b. "Report from the Field: The Democratization of Anthropology and Museums." *Culture* VI(I):61–64.
Ames, Michael. 1990. "Cultural Empowerment and Museums: Opening Up Anthropology through Collaboration." In *Objects of Knowledge*, edited by Susan Pearce, 158–173. London: The Athlone Press.
Ames, Michael. 1992. *Cannibal Tours and Glass Boxes: The Anthropology of Museums*. Vancouver: University of British Columbia.
Ames, Michael. 1994. "The Politics of Difference: Other Voices in a Not Yet Post-Colonial World." *Museum Anthropology* 18(3):9–17.
Anderson, Jane and Haidy Geismar. 2017. "Introduction." In *The Routledge Companion to Cultural Property*, edited by Jane Anderson and Haidy Geismar, 1–32. London and New York: Routledge.
Appadurai, Arjun and Carol Breckenridge. 1988. "Why Public Culture?" *Public Culture Bulletin* 1(1):1–9.
Appiah, Kwame. 2006. *Cosmopolitanism: Ethics in a World of Strangers*. New York: W. W. Norton and Company, Inc.
Banks, Marcus. 2007. *Theorizing Cultural Work: Labour, Continuity and Change in the Cultural and Creative Industries*. New York and London: Routledge.
Beck, Sam and Carl A. Maida. 2013. *Toward Engaged Anthropology*. New York: Berghahn Books.
Bennett, Tony 1995. *The Birth of the Museum*. London and New York: Routledge.
Bennett, Tony, Lawrence Grossberg, and Meaghan Morris. 2005. *New Keywords. A Revised Vocabulary of Culture and Society*. Oxford: Blackwell.

Besterman, Tristam. 2006. "Museum Ethics." In *Companion to Museum Studies*, edited by Sharon Macdonald, 431–441. Oxford: Blackwell.

Boas, Franz. 1907. "Some Principles of Museum Administration." *Science* 25(649):921–933.

Boast, Robin. 2011. "Neocolonial Collaboration: Museum as Contact Zone Revisited." *Museum Anthropology* 34(1):56–70.

Bouquet, Mary. 2001. "Introduction: Anthropology and the Museum. Back to the Future." In *Academic Anthropology and the Museum. Back to the Future*, edited by Mary Bouquet. New York and Oxford: Berghahn.

Bouquet, Mary. 2012. *Museums. A Visual Anthropology*. London: Berg.

Bouquet, Mary. 2015. "Reactivating the Colonial Collection: Exhibit-Making as Creative Process at the Tropenmuseum, Amsterdam." In *Museum Transformations*, edited by Annie E. Coombes and Ruth B. Phillips, 133–156. Oxford: Wiley-Blackwell.

Boylan, Patrick. 2006. "The Museum Profession." In *Companion to Museum Studies*, edited by Sharon Macdonald, 415–430. Oxford: Blackwell.

Breidenbach, Joana and Pal Nyiri. 2009. *Seeing Culture Everywhere from Genocide to Consumer Habits*. Seattle: University of Washington Press.

Canclini, Nestor Garcia. 2014. *Imagined Globalization*. Durham: Duke University Press.

Carattini, Amy. 2015. "Contemporary Perspectives: In, Out and Around Museums." *Practicing Anthropology* 37(3):4–6.

Chilisa, Bagele. 2012. *Indigenous Research Methodologies*. Los Angeles and London: Sage.

Clifford, James. 1988. *The Predicament of Culture. Twentieth-Century Ethnography, Literature, and Art*. Cambridge, Massachusetts: Harvard University Press.

Clifford, James. 1991. "Four Northwest Coast Museums: Travel Reflections." In *Exhibiting Cultures: The Poetics and Politics of Museum Display*, edited by Ivan Karp and Steven D. Lavine, 212–254. Washington, DC: Smithsonian Institution Press.

Clifford, James. 1997. *Routes. Travel and Translation in the Late Twentieth Century*. Cambridge, MA: Harvard University Press.

Clifford, James. 2013. *Returns. Becoming Indigenous in the Twenty-First Century*. Cambridge, MA: Harvard University Press.

Collier, Donald and Harry Tschopik. 1954. "The Role of Museums in American Anthropology." *American Anthropologist* 56:768–779.

Colwell, Chip. 2017. *Plundered Skulls and Stolen Spirits: Inside the Fight to Reclaim Native America's Culture*. Chicago: University of Chicago Press.

Colwell-Chanthaphonh, Chip and T.J. Ferguson. 2008. *Collaboration and Archaeological Practice. Engaging Descendant Communities*. Lanham, MD: Alta Mira Press.

Coombes, Annie E. and Ruth B. Phillips. 2015. "Introduction: Museums in Transformation: Dynamics of Democratization and Decolonization." In *Museum Transformations*, edited by Annie E. Coombes and Ruth B. Phillips, xxxiii–lxiii. Oxford: Wiley-Blackwell.

Cooper, Karen C. 2008. *Spirited Encounters. American Indian Protest Museum Policies and Practices*. Lanham, MD: Altamira Press.

Crooke, Elizabeth. 2006. "Museums and Community." In *Companion to Museum Studies*, edited by Sharon Macdonald, 170–185. Oxford: Blackwell.

Crooke, Elizabeth. 2007. *Museums and Community: Ideas, Issues, and Challenges*. London and New York: Routledge.

Davis, Peter. 2011. *Ecomuseums: A Sense of Place*. London: Bloomsbury.

Dubin, Steven. 1987. *Bureaucratizing the Muse: Public Funds and the Cultural Worker*. Chicago: University of Chicago Press.

Eriksen, Thomas Hylland. 2006. *Engaging Anthropology*. Oxford: Berg.

Erikson, Patricia. 2002. *Voices of a Thousand People. The Makah Cultural and Research Center*. Lincoln and London: University of Nebraska Press.

Errington, Shelly. 1998. *The Death of Authentic Primitive Art and Other Tales of Progress*. Berkeley: University of California Press.

Freire, Paolo. 1998. *Pedagogy of Freedom: Ethics, Democracy, and Civic Courage*. Lanham: Rowan and Littlefield.

Frese, H. H. 1960. *Anthropology and the Public: The Role of Museums*. Leiden, the Netherlands: E.J. Brill.

Fuller, Nancy. 1992. "The Museum as a Vehicle for Community Empowerment: The Ak-chin Indian Community Ecomuseum Project." In *Museums and Communities*, edited by Ivan Karp, Christine Mullen-Kreamer, and Steven Lavine, 327–365. Washington, DC: Smithsonian Institution Press.

Geertz, Clifford. 1973. *The Interpretation of Cultures*. New York: Basic Books.

Golding, Viv and Wayne Modest. 2013. *Museums and Communities: Curators, Collections, and Collaboration*. London: Bloomsbury.

Gosden, Chris and Francis Larson. 2007. *Knowing Things: Exploring the Collections at the Pitt Rivers Museum 1884–1945*. Oxford: Oxford University Press.

Gurian, Elaine. 2006. *Civilizing the Museum*. London and New York: Routledge.

Handler, Richard. 1993. "An Anthropological Definition of the Museum and Its Purposes." *Museum Anthropology* 17(1):33–36.

Handler, Richard. 2005. *Critics Against Culture. Anthropological Observers of Mass Society*. Madison: University of Wisconsin Press.

Hannerz, Ulf. 2010. *Anthropology's World. Life in a Twenty-first Century Discipline*. London: Pluto Press.

Haraway, Donna. 2016. *Staying with the Trouble. Making Kin in the Chthulucene*. Durham and London: Duke University Press.

Harrison, Rodney. 2013. *Heritage. Critical Approaches*. London and New York: Routledge.

Harrison, Rodney, Sarah Byrne, and Anne Clarke. 2013. *Reassembling the Collection. Ethnographic Museums and Indigenous Agency*. Santa Fe, New Mexico: School of Advanced Research.

Hildering, David, Wayne Modest, and Warda Aztouti. 2015. "Visualizing Development: The Tropenmuseum and International Development Aid." In *Museums, Heritage, and International Development*, edited by Paul Basu and Wayne Modest, 310–332. London and New York: Routledge.

Hoelscher, Steven. 2006. "Heritage." In *A Companion to Museum Studies*, edited by Sharon Macdonald, 198–218. Oxford: Blackwell.

Ingold, Tim. 2013. *Making. Anthropology, Archaeology, Art and Architecture*. London and New York: Routledge.

Isaac, Gwyneira. 2007. *Mediating Knowledges*. Tucson: University of Arizona Press.

Isaac, Gwyneira. 2015. "Museums and the Practice of Anthropology: Whose Responsibility Is It?" *Practicing Anthropology* 37(3):19.

Janes, Robert. 2009. *Museums in a Troubled World*. London and New York: Routledge.

Jones, Anna Laura. 1993. "Exploding Canons: The Anthropology of Museums." *Annual Review of Anthropology* 22:201–220.

Jones, Tod. 2013. *Culture, Power, and Authoritarianism in the Indonesian State*. Leiden: Brill.

Kaeppler, Adrienne. 1996. "Paradise Regained: The Role of Pacific Museums in Forging National Identity." In *Museums and the Making of "Ourselves". The Role of Objects in National Identity*, edited by Flora Kaplan, 19–44. London and New York: Leicester University Press.

Kahn, Miriam. 2000. "Not Really Pacific Voices: Politics of Representation in Collaborative Museum Exhibits." *Museum Anthropology* 24(1):57–74.

Kaplan, Flora. 1992. "Growing Pains." *Museum News* 71(1):49–51.

Kaplan, Flora. 1994. "Introduction." In *Museums and the Making of "Ourselves." The Role of Objects in National Identity*, edited by Flora Kaplan, 1–15. London and New York: Leicester University Press.

Kaplan, Flora. 1996. "Museum Anthropology." In *Encyclopedia of Cultural Anthropology*, edited by David Levinson and Melvin Ember. New York: Henry Holt and Company.

Karp, Ivan. 1992. "Introduction." In *Museums and Communities*, edited by Ivan Karp, Christine Mullen-Kreamer, and Steven Lavine, 1–17. Washington, DC: Smithsonian Institution Press.

Karp, Ivan and Gustavo Buntix. 2006. "Tactical Museologies." In *Museum Frictions: Public Cultures/Global Transformations*, edited by Ivan Karp, Corinne A. Kratz, Lynn Szwaja, and Tomas Ybarra-Frausto, 206–218. Durham, North Carolina: Duke University Press.

Karp, Ivan and Steven Lavine. 1991. "Introduction." In *Exhibiting Cultures: The Poetics and Politics of Museum Display*, edited by Ivan Karp and Steven Lavine, 1–9. Washington, DC: Smithsonian Institution Press.

Karp, Ivan, Christine Mullen-Kreamer, and Steven Lavine, eds. 1992. *Museums and Communities: The Politics of Public Culture*. Washington, DC: Smithsonian Institution Press.

Kirshenblatt-Gimblett, Barbara. 1998. *Destination Culture. Tourism, Museums, and Heritage.* Berkeley and Los Angeles: University of California Press.

Kirshenblatt-Gimblett, Barbara. 2006. "World Heritage and Cultural Economics." In *Museum Frictions. Public Culture/Global Transformations*, edited by Ivan Karp and Corinne Kratz, 161–202. Durham, North Carolina: Duke University Press.

Kramer, Jennifer. 2015. "Mobius Museology: Curating and Critiquing the Multiversity Galleries at the Museum of Anthropology at the University of British Columbia." In *Museum Transformations*, edited by Annie E. Coombes and Ruth B. Phillips, 489–510. Oxford: Wiley Blackwell.

Kratz, Corinne and Ivan Karp. 2006. "Introduction: Museum Frictions: Public Culture/Global Transformation." In *Museum Frictions. Public Cultures/Global Transformations*, edited by Ivan Karp, Corinne A. Kratz, Lynn Szwaja, and Tomas Ybarra-Frausto, 1–31. Durham and London: Duke University Press.

Kreps, Christina. 1988. "Decolonizing Anthropology Museums: The Tropenmuseum, Amsterdam." *Museum Studies Journal* 3(2):56–63.

Kreps, Christina. 1998. "Introduction: Indigenous Curation." *Museum Anthropology* 22(1):3–4.

Kreps, Christina. 2003a. *Liberating Culture: Cross-Cultural Perspectives on Museums, Curation, and Heritage Preservation*. London: Routledge.

Kreps, Christina. 2003b. "Curatorship as Social Practice." *Curator: The Museum Journal* 46 (3):311–323.

Kreps, Christina. 2006. "Non-Western Models of Museums and Curation in Cross-Cultural Perspective." In *A Companion to Museum Studies*, edited by Sharon Macdonald, 457–472. Oxford: Blackwell.

Kreps, Christina. 2008. "Appropriate Museology in Theory and Practice." *Museum Management and Curatorship* 23(1):23–42.

Kreps, Christina. 2009. "Indigenous Curation, Museums, and Intangible Cultural Heritage." In *Intangible Heritage*, edited by Laurajane Smith and Natsuko Akagawa, 193–208. London and New York: Routledge.

Kreps, Christina. 2011. "Changing the Rules of the Road: Post-Colonialism and the New Museum Ethics of Museum Anthropology." In *Routledge Companion to Museum Ethics*, edited by Janet Marstine, 70–84. London and New York: Routledge.

Kreps, Christina. 2012. "Intangible Threads: Curating the Living Heritage of Dayak Ikat Weaving." In *Safeguarding Intangible Cultural Heritage*, edited by Michelle L. Stefano, Peter Davis, and Gerard Corsane, 177–192. Woodbridge: Boydell Press.

Kreps, Christina. 2015. "University Museums as Laboratories for Experiential Learning and Engaged Practice." *Museum Anthropology* 38(2):96–111.

Kurin, Richard. 1997. *Reflections of a Culture Broker: A View from the Smithsonian.* Washington, DC: Smithsonian Institution Press.

Lamphere, Louise. 2004. "The Convergence of Applied, Practicing, and Public Anthropology in the 21st Century." *Human Organization* 63(4):431–443.

Levitt, Peggy. 2015. *Artifacts and Allegiances. How Museums Put the Nation and the World on Display.* Berkeley, CA: University of California Press.

Liss, Julia E. 2015. "Franz Boas on War and Empire. The Making of a Public Intellectual." In *The Franz Boas Papers, Volume 1. Franz Boas as Public Intellectual – Theory, Ethnography, Activism,* edited by Regna Darnell, Michelle Hamilton, Robert L.A. Hancock, and Joshua Smith, 293–330. Lincoln and London: University of Nebraska Press.

Little, Barbara and Paul Shackel. 2014. *Archaeology, Heritage, and Civic Engagement.* Walnut Creek: Left Coast Press.

Lonetree, Amy. 2012. *Decolonizing Museums. Representing Native America in National and Tribal Museums.* Chapel Hill: University of North Carolina.

Low, Setha and Sally Engle Merry. 2010. "Engaged Anthropology: Diversity and Dilemmas." *Current Anthropology* 51 (Supplement 2):s203–226.

Lubar, Steven. 2017. *Inside the Lost Museum: Curating, Past and Present.* Cambridge, Massachusetts: Harvard University Press.

Lubar, Steven and Emily Stokes-Rees. 2012. "From Collections to Curriculum." In *A Handbook for Academic Museums. Beyond Exhibitions and Education,* edited by Stefanie S. Jandl and Mark S. Gold. Edinburgh and Boston: MuseumsEtc.

Luri, Nancy O. 1981. "Museumland Revisited." *Human Organization* 40(2):180–187.

Lynch, Bernadette. 2011. "Collaboration, Contestation, and Creative Conflict: On the Efficacy of Museum/Community Partnerships." In *The Routledge Companion to Museum Ethics,* edited by Janet Marstine, 146–163. London and New York: Routledge.

Lynch, Bernadette. 2013. "Custom-Made Reflexive Practice: Can Museums Realise Their Capacities in Helping Others Realise Theirs?" *Museum Management and Curatorship* 26 (5):441–458.

Lynch, Bernadette. 2017. "The Gate in the Wall: Beyond Happiness Making in Museums." In *Engaging Heritage, Engaging Communities,* edited by Bryony Onciul, Michelle Stefano, and Stephanie Hawke, 11–29. Woodbridge: Boydell Press.

Macdonald, Sharon. 2002. *Behind the Scenes at the Science Museum.* Oxford: Berg.

Macdonald, Sharon. 2006. "Expanding Museum Studies: An Introduction." In *Companion to Museum Studies,* edited by Sharon Macdonald, 1–12. Oxford: Wiley-Blackwell.

Macdonald, Sharon. 2009. *Difficult Heritage: Negotiating the Nazi Past in Nuremberg and Beyond.* London and New York: Routledge.

Macdonald, Sharon and Gordon Fyfe. 1996. "Introduction." In *Theorizing Museums.* Oxford: Blackwell.

Macleod, Suzanne. 2001. "Making Museum Meanings: Training, Education, Research and Practice." *Museum Management and Curatorship* 19(1):51–62.

Marcus, George 1995. "Ethnography In/Of the World System: The Emergence of Multi-Sited Ethnography." *Annual Review of Anthropology* 24:95–117.

Marcus, George and Michael Fischer 1986. *Anthropology as Cultural Critique: An Experimental Moment in the Human Sciences.* Chicago: University of Chicago Press.

Marstine, Janet. 2006. "Introduction." In *The New Museum Theory,* edited by Janet Marstine, 1–36. Oxford: Blackwell.

Marstine, Janet. 2011. "The Contingent Nature of the New Museum Ethics." In *Routledge Companion to Museum Ethics*, edited by Janet Marstine, 1–12. London and New York: Routledge.

Marstine, Janet. 2013. "Cultural Collisions in Socially Engaged Artistic Practice." *Museum Worlds: Advances in Research* 1:153–178.

Marstine, Janet. 2017. *Critical Practice: Artists, Museums, Ethics*. London and New York: Routledge.

Mason, Rhiannon. 2006. "Culture Theory and Museum Studies." In *A Companion to Museum Studies*, edited by Sharon Macdonald, 17–32. Oxford: Wiley-Blackwell.

Mason, Rhiannon. 2013. "National Museums, Globalization, and Postnationalism: Imagining a Cosmopolitan Museology." *Museum Worlds* 1:40–64.

Maxwell, Richard. 2001. *Culture Works*. Minneapolis and London: University of Minnesota Press.

Maynard, Pierre. 1985. "The New Museology Proclaimed." *Museum* 37(148):200–201.

McCarthy, Conal. 2015. "Introduction: Grounding Museum Studies." In *Museum Practice*, edited by Conal McCarthy. Oxford: Wiley Blackwell.

McCarthy, Conal. 2019. "Indigenisation." In *The Contemporary Museum. Shaping Museums for the Global Now*, edited by Simon Knell, 37–54. London and New York: Routledge.

Mead, Margaret. 1970. "Museums in a Media-Saturated World." *Museum News* 49(1):23–25.

Mohr, Sonja. 2014. *Displaying the Colonial. The Exhibitions of the Museum Nasional Indonesia and the Tropenmuseum*. Berlin: Regiospectra Verlag Berlin.

Nash, Stephen, Chip Colwell-Chanthaphonh, and Steven Holen. 2011. "Civic Engagement in Museum Anthropology: A Prolegomenon for the Denver Museum of Nature and Science." *Historical Archaeology* 45(1):135–151.

Onciul, Bryony. 2013. "Community Engagement, Curatorial Practice, and Museum Ethos." In *Museums and Communities. Curators, Collections, and Collaboration*, edited by Viv Golding and Wayne Modest, 79–97. London: Bloomsbury.

Paine, Crispin. 2013. *Religious Objects in Museums: Private Lives and Public Duties*. London: Bloomsbury.

Peers, Laura and Alison Brown, ed. 2003. *Museums and Source Communities*. New York and London: Routledge.

Phillips, Ruth B. 2011. *Museum Pieces. Toward the Indigenization of Canadian Museums*. Montreal: McGill-Queen's University Press.

Price, Sally. 1989. *Primitive Art in Civilized Places*. Chicago, IL: University of Chicago Press.

Sabloff, Jeremy. 2011. "Where Have You Gone, Margaret Mead? Anthropology and Public Intellectuals." *American Anthropologist* 113(3):408–416.

Sandell, Richard and Eithne Nightingale. 2012. "Introduction." In *Museums, Equality, and Social Justice*, 1–9. London and New York: Routledge.

Schlehe, Judith and Sita Hidayah. 2014. "Transcultural Ethnography: Reciprocity in Indonesian-German Tandem Research." In *Methodology and Research Practice in Southeast Asian Studies*, edited by Mikko Huotari, Jürgen Rüland, and Judith Schlehe, 253–272. New York: Palgrave Macmillan.

Schneider, Arnd and Christopher Wright. 2010. "Between Art and Anthropology." In *Between Art and Anthropology: Contemporary Ethnographic Practice*, edited by Arnd Schneider and Christopher Wright, 1–21. Oxford and New York: Berg.

Shalins, Marshall. 1993. "Goodbye to Tristes Tropes: Ethnography in the Context of Modern World History." *Journal of Modern World History* 65(1):1–25.

Shannon, Jennifer. 2014. *Our Lives: Collaboration, Native Voice, and the Making of the National Museum of the American Indian*. Santa Fe School for Advanced Research.

Shannon, Jennifer. 2017. "Collections Care Informed by Native American Perspectives." *Collections: A Journal for Museum and Archives Professionals* 13(3/4):205–224.

Shelton, Anthony. 2001. "Unsettling the Meaning. Critical Museology, Art and Anthropological Discourse." In *Academic Anthropology and the Museum. Back to the Future*, edited by Mary Bouquet, 142–161. New York and Oxford: Berghahn Books.

Shelton, Anthony. 2006. "Museums and Anthropologies: Practices and Narratives." In *A Companion to Museum Studies*, edited by Sharon Macdonald, 64–80. Oxford: Wiley-Blackwell.

Shelton, Anthony. 2013. "Critical Museology: A Manifesto." *Museum Worlds* 1:7–23.

Shelton, Anthony and Gustaaf Houtman. 2009. "Negotiating New Visions: An Interview with Anthony Shelton by Gustaaf Houtman." *Anthropology Today* 25(6):7–13.

Silverman, Raymond A., ed. 2015. *Museums as Process: Translating Local and Global Knowledges.* London and New York: Routledge.

Smith, Laurajane. 2006. *Uses of Heritage.* London and New York: Routledge.

Smith, Laurajane and Natsuko Akagawa, ed. 2009. *Intangible Heritage.* London and New York: Routledge.

Smith, Linda Tuhiwai. 2012. *Decolonizing Methodologies. Research and Indigenous Peoples.* Second ed. London and New York: Zed Books.

Stocking, George. 1985. "Essays on Museums and Material Culture." In *Objects and Others: Essays on Museums and Material Culture*, edited by George Stocking, 3–14. Madison: University of Wisconsin Press.

Sturtevant, William. 1969. "Does Anthropology Need Museums?" *Proceedings of the Biological Society of Washington* 82:619–650.

Swan, Daniel. 2015. "A Museum Anthropologist in Academic Practice." *Practicing Anthropology* 37(3):65.

Taylor, Charles. 1992. "The Politics of Recognition." In *Multiculturalism: The Politics of Recognition*, edited by Amy Gutman, 25–74. Princeton, NJ: Princeton University Press.

Thomas, Nicholas. 2010. "The Museum as Method." *Museum Anthropology* 33(1):6–10.

Thomas, Nicholas. 2016. *The Return of Curiosity. What Museums are Good For in the 21st Century.* London: Reaktion Books

Tsing, Anna. 2005. *Frictions. An Ethnography of Global Connections.* Princeton and Oxford: Princeton University Press.

Van der Veer, Peter. 2016. *The Value of Comparison.* Durham and London: Duke University Press.

Van Willigen, John. 2002. *Applied Anthropology. An Introduction.* Third ed. Westport, Connecticut: Bergin and Garvey.

Vergo, Peter. 1989. *The New Museology.* London: Reaktion Books.

Watson, Sheila. 2007. *Museums and Their Communities.* London and New York: Routledge.

Williams, Raymond. 1958. *Culture and Society: 1780–1950.* London: Chatto and Windus.

Williams, Raymond. 1977. *Marxism and Literature.* Oxford: Oxford University Press.

Williams, Raymond. 1983. *Keywords: A Vocabulary of Culture and Society.* Oxford: Oxford University Press.

Wintle, Claire. 2016. "Decolonizing the Smithsonian: Museums as Microcosms of Political Encounter." *American Historical Review* 121(5):1492–1520.

2

MAPPING CONTEMPORARY MUSEUM ANTHROPOLOGY

Museum anthropology has experienced radical change over the past several decades to the extent that some might say there is a "new" museum anthropology. If so, what are the defining features of this "new" museum anthropology, and how does it differ from the "old"? In this chapter I map what I, along with many other authors, see as some of the major theoretical and methodological movements and tendencies that have come to characterize the field today. My aim is to take stock of the current moment, building on themes addressed in the previous introductory chapter revisited throughout the book.

The chapter begins with a discussion of the maturation of the anthropology of museums and critical, reflexive museology since the 1980s. I describe museum ethnography as the primary method for doing the anthropology of museums, and what it has come to entail as both a research method for "theorizing museums" (Macdonald and Fyfe 1996), and a strategy for the critical analysis of "operational museology" (Shelton 2013), i.e., museum practice.

Museum anthropology and ethnography draw on and are informed by a number of other subfields in anthropology, but particularly important is the renewed interest in material cultural studies. In the section "The Return of the Object" I discuss recent approaches to the study of objects and collections in museums, and how they have led to new interpretations and understandings of the agency of things, for example, in social relations and in the construction of identities. Especially salient has been the focus on materiality, which considers both the tangible properties of objects as well as their intangible, multisensory dimensions. While theoretical advancements in material culture studies have been one of the forces behind the reinvigoration of museum anthropology, I pay special attention to how increased collaboration between museums and originating communities has shed light on the diverse ways people know, are connected to, care for, and value things—ways that can stand in sharp contrast to how they are interpreted and treated in museums. As museums have been pressured to relinquish their position as self-appointed guardians of people's cultural heritage they have increasingly been sharing curatorial authority with those whose cultures are represented in museums. Collaboration and the co-curation of collections have revealed how many communities have long had their own methods of "traditional care," or Indigenous museologies. In turn, many museums have been reconceptualizing curatorial practice as they have become spaces of intercultural dialogue and translation (Clifford 2013, 2019, Isaac 2009, Kramer 2015, McCarthy 2019, Shannon 2017). What we have been increasingly witnessing is the indigenization of mainstream, dominant culture museums as a critical component of decolonization.

I see the decolonization of museums as "deep engagement" because it is predicated on "decolonizing the mind" (Memmi 1965), or reconfiguring patterned ways of thinking about museums and their purposes, and "liberating culture" from the hegemony of Eurocentric museology (Kreps 2003a, xiii). At the same time, I consider recent meanings and uses of the term decolonization in comparison to those in the past. The point is to highlight how decolonization, despite its widespread usage today, remains a contested and burdened term (Bhambra, Gebrial, and Nişancioğlu 2018).

These movements not only reflect the expansion of museum anthropology, but also its diversification as we become ever more attuned to the ways in which diverse voices, experiences, and museological approaches have been broadening and enriching the field. Indeed, diversity, in various manifestations, is a prevailing theme running throughout the chapter.

While the new, change, and transformation are overarching themes of the chapter, I also draw attention to remaining challenges in the field and dilemmas that museum anthropologists continue to face. Here I am particularly concerned with the field's evolving status in and relationship to the discipline of anthropology as a whole and how its various publics are being reframed, invoked, and understood (Barrett 2012, 1). In the final section of the chapter, I focus on the increasing convergence of museum anthropology, museum studies, and the museum profession through an emphasis on praxis—the merging of theory, reflection, and action. In sum, I consider what museum studies has to offer anthropology, and what anthropology has to offer museum studies, and finally, what both have to offer their publics in the age of engagement.

The Anthropology of Museums and Critical, Reflexive Museology

Today, museum anthropology is understood as both anthropology practiced *in* museums and the anthropology *of* museums, as outlined in the previous chapter. While this chapter covers elements of both genres, I begin with a discussion of the anthropology of museums and critical, reflexive museology. Taken together, these movements have pushed the field in new directions and back to the forefront of anthropology in general while contributing to more critically informed practice (Shelton 2001, 2006a).

Michael Ames, as noted in the previous chapter, was a pioneer of the anthropology and critical theory of museums. In an article titled "Report from the Field: The Democratization of Anthropology and Museums" (1986), he explains that he came to museum ethnography when he realized that due to his administrative responsibilities at the University of British Columbia Museum of Anthropology he no longer had time for long field trips to South Asia where he had been doing fieldwork. In his words: "I needed a field station closer to home ... Why not, I thought, study anthropology and museums? Given my own dual location, embedded in both a museum and university department of anthropology, what could be homier?" (1986, 61). Ames began his research with what he states was a simple question: What would anthropology and museums look like if we looked at them as if they were Indians? (Ames 1986, 61).

Ames, in this and later work, pressed us to study ourselves as "the natives" and to examine our own exotic customs as we study those of "others." To Ames, there was much to be learned from studying ourselves and the cultures of our own profession as a means of changing them. He stressed that it is not enough to criticize museums and the work of museum professionals. Rather, "Useful criticism needs to combine assessment with the empirical examination of real situations, recognizing the complexity and intermingling of interests involved, as well as the relations between the individual and the social, and the conditions within which they operate" (1992, 4). The objective is to locate critiques within their social, political, and economic contexts. This is "the agenda for a critical anthropology of museums" (1992, 5), which calls for a "critical, reflexive museology" and a critical theory of museums and anthropology. Writing from the standpoint of a scholar, teacher, and museum professional (or "native" museum anthropologist), his approach was to relate experience to critique and then to action. Ames's emphasis on the practical and on action reflected the innovative environment in which he and the staff worked at the University of British Columbia Museum of Anthropology (UBCMOA) during the 1980s, laying a foundation for anthropological and critical museology (Phillips 2011, Shelton 2001, 2006a, 2006b).[1]

Decades before Ames published his groundbreaking *Cannibal Tours and Glass Boxes*, however, the Dutch museologist H. H. Frese conducted an extensive study of anthropology museums in Europe, North America, Australia, and New Zealand from 1957 to 1958. His findings were published in *Anthropology and the Public: The Role of Museums* for which he earned a PhD in anthropology. By Frese's own account, this was the first study of its kind (1960, 3).[2]

But despite the pioneering work of Ames and Frese, the anthropology of museums, defined as such, did not really begin to take hold until the 1990s. As Handler and Gable, two anthropologists who also took an early interest in the ethnographic study of museums and historical sites, observed in the late 1990s, "there has been almost no ethnographic inquiry into museums as arenas of ongoing, organized activities. As a result, most research on museums has proceeded by ignoring much of what happens in them" (1997, 8–9).

This is no longer the case. Nowadays, the museum is an accepted object of study, and museum ethnography is an established method for examining nearly every aspect of museological phenomena in nearly every corner of the world. The anthropology of museums and museum ethnography has expanded our knowledge of the diversity of museum models and museological behavior in different national, cultural, and historical contexts, contributing to a more comprehensive and nuanced comparative museology. As both a research method and analytical framework in the anthropology of museums, comparative museology can reveal how people in varied times and places similarly and differently make sense of the museum idea and the things that end up in museums (Byrne 2014, Clifford 1991, Kaplan 1994, Kreps 1998, 2003, Shelton 2006b). Comparative museology also has implications for practice because, as Karp and Lavine suggest, we begin to discover the artifice of our practices when we look at them in comparison to those in other cultural contexts (1991, 1). Thus, comparative museology can be a strategy for understanding museological diversity and diversifying museum anthropology. And as will be shown in subsequent chapters, the anthropology of museums through the lens of comparative museology makes for a broader and more inclusive historiography of museum anthropology.

For museum ethnographers, the museum and related spaces are multifaceted field sites for exploring internal processes behind the making of collections, exhibitions, and educational programming besides subjects such as the politics of cultural representation, identity construction and nation-building; museum/community relations; and the nature of cultural production and consumption. In addition to ethnographies of particular areas of museum work, ethnographic studies have been carried out on individual museums and their development, for example, Native American museums and cultural centers (Erikson 2002, Harrison, Byrne, and Clarke 2013, Isaac 2007, Lonetree 2012, Message 2014, Onciul 2013, Shannon 2014, Sleeper-Smith 2009), and non-Western museums (Bhatti 2012, Evans and Rowlands 2015, Kaplan 1994, Kreps 2003a, Simpson 1996, Stanley 1998, 2007, Varutti 2012, 2014). Critical analysis and the theorizing of museums has led to a rethinking of museums in terms of the kinds of roles they play in society (or particular communities) and the purposes and interests they serve (Marstine 2006). Erikson, in her ethnography of the Makah Cultural and Research Center in Neah Bay, Washington, writes that in the anthropology of museums literature,

> the museum is considered an arena for social relationships between and among diverse peoples of often unequal status ... Museums—whether ethnic, mainstream, or national—are ideal places for theorizing how representation, identity formation, and power relations work ... [and] ... where the tension between cultural homogenization and cultural heterogenization plays itself out.
>
> *(2002, 6)*

Shelly Ruth Butler's pioneering study of the controversial exhibition *Into the Heart of Africa* shown at the Royal Ontario Museum in Toronto from 1989 to 1990 is an early museum ethnography that addressed both the possibilities and pitfalls of critical, reflexive museology. In her book *Contested Representations:*

Revisiting "Into the Heart of Africa," first published in 1999, she describes the premises of reflexive museology.

> Whereas curators have traditionally focused on the goals of acquiring and preserving objects, and have been preoccupied with presenting artifacts in reconstructions of their 'original settings,' reflexive museology changes the way in which we think about museums and their collections. Focusing on museum practices of collecting, classifying, and displaying material culture, reflexive museology is informed by the premise that exhibits of other cultures are neither neutral nor tropeless, despite claims otherwise. Rather, exhibits are informed by the cultural, historical, institutional, and political contexts of the people who make them.
>
> *(2008, 22)*

In a 2015 publication, Butler writes that whereas early iterations of reflexive museology, exemplified by the "flawed" case of *Into the Heart of Africa*, were shaped by postmodern theoretical projects and critiques of museums' colonial legacies, these days reflexive museology is more typically informed by calls for socially relevant scholarship and practice. The contemporary reflexive museum is associated with self-awareness and self-critique as well as awareness of the need for democratic participation on the part of visitors and various stakeholders. In short, "reflexivity is a crucial first step toward creating collaborative models of representation and creation" (Butler 2015, 167).

Butler's *Contested Representations* is an example of how museum ethnography can be employed in the important work of cultural criticism (Marcus and Fischer 1986). In addition to its theoretical insights, her book serves as an instructional text in the "how to" of museum ethnography and the ways its methods are similar to and differ from conventional ethnography. She presents detailed descriptions of her research methods, for example her collection and critical analysis of museum policy statements, press clippings and media packages; exhibition texts and object labels; and materials produced by community members such as protesters' pamphlets. Butler also made extensive use of personal interviews with a variety of people involved in or touched by the controversy. These included: museum professionals, academics, curators, members of the African–Canadian community, members of the protest group Coalition for the Truth about Africa, and students in the fields of anthropology, museum studies, history, and film. Butler writes that her goal in choosing who to interview was to bring together and juxtapose different perspectives on the controversy and "to examine the intersections of these voices. In this sense, my ethnography is driven by themes, images, and issues as opposed to a more traditional focus on a particular community or geographic area" (2008, 14).

Museum ethnographers see museums as field sites for the investigation and analysis of museum workings on many levels from how knowledge is constructed and conveyed through exhibitions to revealing underlying institutional power structures and organizational hierarchies. In this latter respect, the study of museums often entails what Nader calls "studying up" or looking at processes whereby power and responsibility are exercised within our own societies' institutions and organizations (Nader 1969). Sharon Macdonald, for instance, in her now classic ethnography of the Science Museum in London, was interested in the construction of science, and how it is presented and understood by various publics. Macdonald's research not only required "studying up" but also "defamiliarizing the familiar," a long-standing anthropological trope for rendering the familiar exotic (Eriksen 2006, 10). Macdonald states that this tactic was critical for helping overcome her own cultural presuppositions and to "see, or frame, things in new ways" (2002, 7).

In her book *Museums. A Visual Anthropology* (2012), Bouquet discusses the particular contributions anthropology, and more specifically the use of ethnographic research methods, can make to both anthropology and museum studies. She describes how museum ethnographies can approach institutions as field sites from various starting points and forms of engagement, such as collections, exhibitions, and public programming. Bouquet shows through case studies how ethnographic methods, especially participant observation, can be used to examine "the microdynamics of collection, representation, and public mediation practices in museums" (2012, 92). She sees ethnography as a productive way of contextualizing the details of everyday museum activities and placing them within broader frames of reference, and broader cultural issues and debates "both on and off stage, on and off site" (2012, 99). Ethnography further provides an avenue for "understanding the intersection between worlds of professional expertise and the general public" (2012, 3). Bouquet additionally points out how museum ethnographies can be informed by diverse theoretical perspectives, such as object agency and exchange; brokerage, actor-network and practice theory; semiotics; and narratives that interrogate questions of authorship, cultural production, and consumption (2012, 98). She indicates how museum ethnographies, and more generally, an anthropology of museums, fits into and draws from broader developments in visual anthropology and material culture studies (2012, 4).

The Return of the Object

While much of the anthropology of museums has concentrated on the museum as an object of study in itself, this movement has coincided with a resurgence of scholarly interest in objects and material culture (Buchli 2002, Meyers 2001, Tilley et al. 2006). Renewed interest in material culture studies has been one of the energies behind the reinvigoration of museum anthropology within the academy, shedding new light on the multiple roles things play in people's lives and the diverse ways they relate to them inside and outside of museums. The recent emphasis on the materiality of things, their physical properties as well as multisensory dimensions, enriched by originating communities' teachings on the numinous qualities of belongings have generated fresh and alternative understandings of things.

The return of the object in museum anthropology has come at a time when the intangible dimensions of material or tangible culture have been receiving greater recognition and respect within the international museum community (Stefano and Davis 2017, Kirshenblatt-Gimblett 2006, Kreps 2009, 2012, Stefano, Davis, and Corsane 2012, Smith and Akagawa 2009). Since the adoption of the Convention on the Safeguarding of Intangible Cultural Heritage by UNESCO in 2003, museums have also been paying more attention to intangible culture. As defined in the Convention, intangible cultural heritage is: "the practices, representations, expressions, knowledge, skills—as well as instruments, objects, artefacts and cultural spaces associated therewith—that communities, groups and in some cases individuals recognize as part of their cultural heritage" (UNESCO Convention on the Safeguarding of Intangible Cultural Heritage Article 2.1, Definitions). Article 2.2 of the Convention states: "Intangible cultural heritage is manifested in oral traditions, including language; performing arts (traditional dance, music, and theatre); social practices, rituals, and festive events; knowledge and practices; and traditional craftsmanship."

At first glance, movements to pay greater attention to intangible qualities of objects and ephemeral cultural expressions may seem contradictory and even oppositional to museum anthropology's return to the object. But rather than undermining the value of objects to museums, they have elevated it by stimulating greater dialogue around the importance of museum collections to various constituencies. What's more, they have generated more complex understandings of the multiple meanings and agency of objects (Dudley 2010, 2012, Rowlands 2006, Thomas 1991), and significantly reshaped curatorial practice.

In the words of Crispin Paine: "Since the 1980s, there has been a revolution in academic understandings of objects ... Led by anthropologists and archaeologists this revolution has been fought under the banner of 'material culture studies' ... It has given back to museums and their collections an academic importance that had been lost" (2013, 4). Paine underscores how the so-called "new material culture studies" is no longer so much about how people make things or how things function in a society as it is about the subjectivity and agency of things and how they mediate social relationships. "The new approach to material culture studies ... is crucially concerned with social relationships and the relationships of things with people" (Paine 2013, 4–5).

Recent material culture studies have been concerned with gaining insight into how "persons make things and things make persons" (Tilley et al. 2006, 3), and how subjects and objects are indelibly linked. Material culture studies scholars may take the object, the human subject, the social, or a combination thereof, as their starting point. This approach has been especially important for understanding the place of material culture in the construction and assertion of group identity as an element of the "politics of belonging" and "recognition" (Rowlands 2006, 443).

Sandra Dudley contends that while studies on the social lives of objects and the roles objects play in social relations (Appadurai 1986, Hoskins 1998, Kopytoff 1986) have provided useful historical perspectives and cultural insights, they have tended to emphasize the *cultural* over the *material* aspects of objects rather than the materiality of objects per se (Dudley's emphasis). Consequently, they "are limited in helping us understand how people actually experience and interact with objects on a physical, sensory, or emotional level, whether in a museum or not" (Dudley 2012, 4). Dudley argues for greater sensitivity to the culturally nuanced sensory modalities through which the qualities of things are experienced and valued, particularly in museums.

> It is time to see a materially focused, material culture studies back in the centre of museum practice and museum studies. It has not held such a place since the late nineteenth century and it deserves to return—not in a positivist, static form and role it held in the past, but through a gentle, twenty-first century revolution in which the object is once more at the heart of the museum.
>
> *(2012, 5)*

As visual symbols, objects in museums are not only predominantly for the eyes, but are also primarily understood through the lens of "object-based epistemology," or the view that objects embody and convey knowledge and information (Conn 2010). Thus, museums are not only visual symbol systems but also information systems in which things become part of "object-information packages." As Dudley puts it:

> There is a current, indeed dominant, view within museum studies and practice, that the museum is about information and that the object is just a part—and indeed not always an essential part—of that informational culture … objects have value and import only because of the cultural meanings which immediately overlie them and as a result of the real or imagined stories they can be used to construct. The material object thus becomes part of an object-information package.
>
> *(2010, 3)*

Positioning objects merely as part of information packages, Dudley argues, ignores the multisensory and multidimensional aspects of objects—"the very materiality of the material." In Dudley's view, it is time to see beyond the narrow (but still important) discussion of aesthetics and formal qualities of artworks or technical analyses of artifacts and natural history specimens. We need to enrich an existing preoccupation with the symbolic, representational, and communicative dimension of objects with emotion and physical sensation (Dudley 2010, 6–7).

A focus on the materiality of objects and their sensorial qualities in the work of Dudley and others has illuminated how the ways in which objects are seen, valued, and experienced in museums can stand in stark contrast to how they are perceived and experienced in their originating contexts. As anthropologists Constance Classen and David Howes assert in "The Museum as Sensescape: Western Sensibilities and Indigenous Artifacts":

> In western museum settings, artifacts are preeminently objects for the eyes. Within their cultures of origin, visual appearance is only one part and often

not the most important part of an artifact's sensory significance. The sensory values of an artifact do not reside in the artifact alone, but in its social use and environmental context. The dynamic web of sensuous and social meaning is broken when an object is removed from its cultural setting and inserted into the visual symbol system of the museum.

(2006, 200)

For some time now, scholars and members of originating communities have critically examined how the meanings, values, and functions of objects change when they are removed from their originating context and reframed within the episte-mological paradigms of Western museums (Clavir 2002, Kirshenblatt-Gimblett 1991, Cooper 2008, Clifford 1991, 1988, Erikson 2002, Gurian 2006, Isaac 2007, 2009, Kreps 2003a, 2003b, McCarthy 2011, Mithlo 2004, Shelton 2006b, Simpson 2006). It is now widely recognized that Western museology has rested almost exclusively on one knowledge system, or epistemology, which has dictated why and how non-Western cultural materials have been collected as well as the ways in which they have been treated and represented in museums. Within this knowledge system, objects have been reconfigured to fit into Western constructs of science, culture, art, history, and heritage. In museums, they become art objects, appreciated for their aesthetic qualities, craftsmanship, technological ingenuity, and ethnographic objects or "data" valued for what they can tell us about a people's culture (Kreps 2003a, 30–31). In short, they have been decontextualized and largely de-sensualized, and reduced to visual metaphors.

By looking at how certain objects are understood and experienced in non-Western contexts, for example among Native American and other Indigenous communities, we can see how the emphasis on the visual and objects as informa-tion carriers has diminished the importance of not only the multi-sensory dimen-sions of objects now in museums, but also the multiple meanings and values they can hold as well as their multiple agencies.[3] Objects in their originating commu-nities can be family heirlooms, symbols of rank and status, sacred materials neces-sary for the perpetuation of religious beliefs and practices, documents of a community's history, works of art, and mnemonic devices for evoking memories, biographies, songs, and stories. Objects stand for significant traditions, ideas, cus-toms, social relations, and it is the stories they tell, the performances they are a part of, and the relationships among people and between people and places that are as important as the objects themselves (Clavir 2002, Clifford 1991, Cruikshank 1995, Erikson 2002, McCarthy 2011, 2019, Tapsell 2015).

In addition to standing for or representing some aspect of culture, as they often do in anthropology museums, it also can be true that objects simply are what they are. A figure or image does not *represent* a spirit or ancestor, but *is* that spirit or ancestor. Its sheer materiality, presence, and singularity as an individual are what matters and what gives it meaning and value. To many Native Americans and other peoples, objects are alive, imbued with a life force and spirit. In fact, as Karen Coody Cooper (member of the Cherokee Nation of Oklahoma and former staff of the Smithsonian National Museum of the American Indian) states that the term "object" is "patently offensive to many Native Americans because it refutes the idea of animism, or life within the materials" (2008, 65).

Many scholars have elucidated how Native American views of Native-made things in museums diverge from the views of Western museum curators, collections managers, conservators, educators, and scientists. Kelley Hays-Gilpin and Ramson Lomatewama (Hopi artist, scholar, and curator) describe how Hopi ontology is reshaping curation practices at the Museum of Northern Arizona. These authors also comment on the problematic nature of museum terminology and the different epistemologies and ontologies they reflect. They write:

> we use the term 'artifact' to refer to something made or modified by humans, because this term implies relationships in ways that 'object' does not … What Hopi speakers would do is call it what it is—a rain sash, a *katsina* doll, a water jar—not invent superordinate terms like 'textiles, carvings, pottery, or objects' … So 'artifacts' is still not a perfect term, and there may not yet exist a perfect term in English. In short, we are not talking about passive, inanimate objects whose primary use is to serve as evidence or data for past lifeways, although educating humans in that way is often among their many active roles.
>
> *(2013, 260–261)*

Hays-Gilpin and Lomatewama point out that Hopi generally perceive the museum as privileging rational thought over emotion and secular over spiritual concerns. They assert that while these hierarchical dichotomies were constructed by science for science, Hopi and other Native Americans see this as "how science is, but not how the world is" (2013, 262).

To avoid offensive connotations that can be associated with the terms objects, artifact, material culture, or cultural property, increasingly museum anthropologists are adopting Indigenous names, words, and signifiers. In the Museum of New Zealand Te Papa, for instance, the Māori word *taonga* (treasure) is used, "which in the Māori world are ancestral heirlooms of great spiritual power and sometimes object-beings who are treated like a person" (McCarthy 2019, 37). Kramer relates that the UBCMOA refers to the material the museum holds from originating communities as "belongings" rather than cultural property. This practice is meant to show respect for the on-going relationships some First Nation maintain with objects residing in the museum, such as the Coast Salish Musqueam people on whose land the museum sits. While the Musqueam do not technically "own" their "cultural property" in the museum, Kramer states that they have continuous and unbroken relationships to it and thus refer to it as "belongings." "The use of the term 'belongings' is a tactic to recognize cultural values and the multiplicity of ways of knowing the world, and acknowledges the right of people to self-represent and self-define. Belongings in museums can have Indigenous owners but can also be stewarded outside Indigenous communities" (Kramer 2017, 157–158).

Differences between Western and non-Western worldviews and values (or those between science and spirituality) have been cast as oppositional and indeed irreconcilable to some. But others have challenged this kind of dichotomous thinking. Nancy Mithlo (scholar, curator, and member of the Fort Still Chiricahua Warm Springs Apache Tribe), for one, asserts that: "Indigenous knowledge can exist within a scientific paradigm without sacrificing the contours of unique worldviews" (2004, 745). What's more, Mithlo argues that the "adoption of oppositional credos, while serving to maintain boundaries and differentiate values, ultimately oversimplifies and thus mischaracterizes the aims of both parties, Natives and anthropologists" (2004, 276).

Since the 1990s, Indigenous people have been progressively working with and within museums to exert authority over the care, display, and interpretation of their material heritage. Over the decades, museums have come to increasingly understand that originating communities' relationships to belongings as well as their values and meanings must be respected (Kramer 2017, Peers and Brown 2003, Lonetree 2012, McCarthy 2011, Sleeper-Smith 2009). Through greater interaction and collaboration, Indigenous communities and museums have been creating more culturally sensitive and appropriate curatorial practices. In the process, we have also learned how many communities have their own museological traditions, or what among some Native Americans is referred to methods of "traditional care," especially for the care and treatment of culturally sensitive objects (e.g., sacred and ceremonial objects) now housed in museums (Clavir 2002, Flynn and Hull-Walski 2001, Kreps 2003a, 2009, Rosoff 1998, Simpson 2006, Tapsell 2015). Because communities are diverse, each determines what methods are appropriate in keeping with their own particular cultural protocol and how they define traditional care (Shannon 2017). As Clavir notes: "Having control over the tangible objects in museums plays a role in having control over the intangibles" (2002, 76).

The movement to integrate Indigenous museological traditions into museums and to indigenize them has been challenging the Eurocentric biases and assumptions lodged in science-based museology. The ways in which we store, conserve, handle, display, and interpret belongings have been called into question and critically re-examined, showing us that what is seen as appropriate in one cultural context may not be in another (Clavir 2002, Colwell 2014, Kreps 2009, Peers and Brown 2003, McCarthy 2019, Phillips 2011, Schorch, McCarthy, and Dürr 2019, Sully 2008). In addition to being asked to remove culturally sensitive items from displays or restrict access to them, we are also being instructed in how to appropriately store and care for them based on Indigenous cultural protocol. Nowadays, greater sensitivity is being shown to the numinous qualities of belongings, and how religious, sacred, and ceremonial objects should be treated in museums (Colwell 2014, 2017, Kramer 2015, Paine 2013, Peers and Brown 2003, Sullivan and Edwards 2004).

Changes in curatorial practices and the treatment of Native objects in anthropology museums in the United States are some of the many outcomes of the Native American Graves Protection and Repatriation Act (NAGPRA) enacted in 1990. NAGPRA is federal legislation that applies to Native American and

Hawai'ian human remains, funerary objects, sacred objects, and objects of cultural patrimony—as defined by law—held in institutions that receive federal funding of any kind. Achieved after decades of Native activism, NAGPRA created a process for repatriating ancestors and belongings to culturally affiliated tribes. The law mandated that museums consult with Native communities to determine cultural affiliation and on all NAGPRA-related matters (Colwell 2017, Fine-Dare 2002, Benton 2017, Trope and Echo-Hawk 2000).

NAGPRA is seen by many as important human rights legislation that has given Native American peoples unprecedented voice and power in their search to care for their ancestors and for sacred and ceremonial objects.

> The displacement of people and objects over the centuries since European arrival has been immense, playing out through forced relocation, excavation of graves, the removal of bodies from battlefields for scientific research, and collection of objects. NAGPRA provides important, albeit limited, power for Native American groups to shift control and apply their own value systems to decisions about how graves, human remains, and important cultural items are cared for.
>
> *(Benton 2017, 111)*

The passing of NAGPRA is an example of how a professional body's code of ethics can be inadequate in dealing with particular concerns, and how law, in turn, can stimulate new ethical agendas. In Edson's words, "The law is sometimes the last resort for those confronted by unethical acts" (1997, 27).

NAGPRA is still opposed in some quarters on the grounds that it breaches the boundaries between science and religion in museums (Colwell 2014, Paine 2013), and because policies restricting access to collections (particularly human remains) run counter to the idea of the museum as a modern, secular, public institution open to all (Kreps 2014). But today the presence of religion and spirituality in museums is no longer the taboo subject it once was. In fact, the intersection of religion and museums has become a "hot topic" as museums are being called upon to foster social cohesion and cross-cultural understanding through the promotion of respect for religious diversity. There is now a growing body of literature on this subject that includes numerous case studies on how museums are working with members of religious communities—for example, Buddhist, Hindu, Muslim, Jewish, and Christian—to respectfully conserve and display sacred objects in their care. Nowadays, it is common to read accounts of how religious practitioners are being welcomed into museums to co-curate exhibitions and care for objects on display or in storage (Buggeln 2015, Davis 1997, Gaskell 2003, Kreps 2014, Sullivan and Edwards 2004, Macdonald 2005, O'Neill 2011, Sullivan 2015).[4]

Just as the religious, sensory, and ontological turns in material culture studies and museum practice have been contributing to new understandings of and appreciation for the intangible dimensions of objects, so has the digital turn. Digital technology has not only allowed for greater integration of intangible culture into museum practice, such as Indigenous peoples' epistemologies and ontologies, but it has also, in Morphy's words, enabled "Indigenous communities, the producers of the objects in ethnographic museums, to reconnect with objects in museums and make them part of their contemporary lives" (2015, 91).

Aaron Glass, in "Indigenous Ontologies, Digital Futures," describes a collaborative project between the U'Mista Cultural Centre in Alert Bay, British Columbia and the Ethnology Museum in Berlin. The goal of the project was to supplement the Ethnology Museum of Berlin's existing collections records with current Kwakwaka'wakw Indigenous cultural knowledge, and to develop a digital database information management system that encodes and conveys key aspects of an object's complex cultural and material being (Glass 2015).

Glass outlines the benefits of using digital media to bring Indigenous ontologies (in this case, Kwakwaka'wakw theories of the object and person) into productive proximity with anthropological epistemologies (histories of ethnographic knowledge production) surrounding a nineteenth-century collection (2015, 22). He suggests that such information management systems can become powerful conceptual tools for arranging and constructing knowledge about objects, which in turn can be used by museums, researchers, the public, and originating communities. These information management systems can help situate objects and the knowledge about them more thoroughly within their ethnographic milieu by taking different ontologies seriously, especially as they inform conditions of object production and circulation (2015, 22). Glass states that "[b]y doing so, we simultaneously enrich museum collection information, increase the capacity for quality public education and scholarly research, and make collections more accessible, relevant and useful to Kwakwaka'wakw, for whom the art of their ancestors provides an important foundation for current and future social, material and spiritual practice" (2015, 24).

As Indigenous communities are exerting greater control over how their belongings are treated in museums, museums have become "critical sites for shaping debates and discourses around cultural property" (Anderson and Geismar 2017, 129). Indeed, today, like material culture, cultural property is understood in much wider terms than in previous iterations. Anderson and Geismar define cultural property broadly as, "the recognition of collective rights in both material and intangible culture within international policy, national law, cultural institutions, local contexts, and everyday practices" (2017, 1).

Museum anthropology's return to the object and greater collaboration between museums and originating communities have expanded our understandings of how objects can be perceived, interpreted, valued, and treated in diverse cultural contexts. These developments have contributed to the diversification of curatorial practices in museums, and have been a major force behind the indigenization and decolonization of museums.

Collaboration, Indigenization, and Decolonization of Museums

Collaboration between museums and originating communities is now considered a cornerstone of contemporary museum anthropology (Isaac 2015, Shannon 2014), particularly in settler nations like Australia, Canada, New Zealand, and the United States (Peers and Brown 2003). Collaborative work on collections care, repatriation, exhibitions, research, language revival, and cultural heritage preservation projects has reconfigured power relations and opened possibilities for new kinds of engagement on more equal terms (Clifford 2013, Krmpotich 2014, Kramer 2017, Peers and Brown 2003, Schultz 2011). Collaboration can be seen as a specific approach to engagement directed toward building mutually beneficial and respectful relationships between museums and stakeholder communities (Colwell-Chanthaphonth and Ferguson 2008, Shannon 2014, 2009, Silverman 2015). As Butler asserts, "The negotiation of more equitable, collaborative, and sensitive relations between establishment museums and aboriginal communities has been *the* major development in museum practice in settler societies during the last few decades" (2015, 166). In many respects, collaboration represents a shift in both ideology and practice from a "colonial" to a more "cooperative" and "collaborative" museology (Clifford 1997, 120, Schultz 2011, Basu 2011). In turn, anthropology museums have increasingly come to be conceptualized as "contact" (Clifford 1997) and "engagement zones" (Onciul 2013), or hybrid spaces of intercultural curation and translation (Kramer 2015).

Duggan states that collaboration with Indigenous peoples has been "a hallmark of ethnology since the mid-19th century, and throughout the 20th century numerous anthropologists acknowledged indigenous and local cultural specialists as co-producers of project results and knowledge" (2011, 2). Much has been written, for example, about the partnership between Franz Boas and George Hunt (Kwakwaka'wakw), who worked alongside Boas as a "fieldworker/objects collector/collaborator" (Berlo and Phillips 1992, 38, Archambault 2011, 16). Yet it needs to be recognized that this early collaboration took place within the context of internal-colonialism, brutal assimilationist policies, unequal power relationships, and communities under duress (Lonetree 2012, Mithlo 2004, Shannon 2009). Undeniably, much of collaboration today is devoted to rectifying this troubled history by coming to terms with how it has influenced relationships between museums and Indigenous communities.

Even though the collaborative movement has been, as Lonetree (Ho-Chunk) says, "a welcome shift in power dynamics within museums," she also reminds us that "ongoing issues remain. We must not allow these narratives of collaboration to become too tidy or celebratory, or we could become complacent" (2012, 22). Indeed, we must continually critically assess the terms of collaboration and partnerships by asking who is defining, setting, and controlling them (Clifford 1997). Indeed, Boast argues that in some situations collaboration can take the form of neocolonialism by perpetuating asymmetrical power relations embedded in the institutional, structural inequalities of museums (Boast 2011). Moreover, while collaboration is inherently grounded in the principles of inclusivity and "shared authority," Mithlo points out, policies of inclusion can place an "undue and often unworkable burden upon Native museum professionals to bridge broad conceptual gaps. Museums are self-perpetuating institutions that generally maintain authority, despite efforts to 'give Natives a voice'" (2004, 746).

Bryony Onciul, who has documented interactions between Indigenous Black-foot First Nations communities in Canada and museums and heritage sites, openly discusses the successes and failures of collaboration as it occurs in "engagement zones." Onciul stresses that for community members engagement is not always as positive or empowering as museums assume. Expanding on Clifford's concept of the museum as a "contact zone," Onciul proposes engagement zones to spotlight internal community collaboration and work that occurs in cross-cultural engagement and citizen-controlled grassroots community development projects (2013, 83). Engagement has great potential to benefit museums and communities, to share knowledge, create new relationships, exhibits, programs, policies, and curatorial practices. However, she emphasizes that these are not automatic products of engagement. Rather they "depend upon the process and power sharing within the engagement zone" (2013, 92–93). In Onciul's view, "engagement is limited by the context in which it occurs and the extent to which a museum is willing to take on, adapt, and indigenize its practice, products, and ethos" (2013, 94). Engagement is a step toward indigenizing museums and museology provided that Indigenous approaches are supported and respected as distinct but equally valid, and potentially complementary ways of maintaining cultural knowledge and material (Onciul 2015, 243–244).

Despite these limitations and pitfalls, collaboration and engagement are indispensable ingredients for the indigenization of mainstream museums. Phillips describes the nature of indigenizing processes in Canada that entail the

> incorporation into the mainstream museum world of concepts, protocols, and processes that originate in Aboriginal societies. These include ways of thinking about key issues that are central to museum work, such as the nature of materiality, spirituality, community, and history … The result of indigenization in this sense has been a kind of hybridization, leading us toward more dialogical ways of determining how the public presentation of distinctive cultural traditions should be enacted.
>
> *(2011, 10)*

Indigenization of museums has the power to provoke more relational, culturally sensitive, and appropriate approaches to practice, and the realization that just as museums are diverse in the multiple voices, perspectives, and identities they represent, so too should be curatorial practices (Kreps 2003a, 2008).

Another key element of the indigenization of museums is recognition of Indigenous museologies, or the "multiple practices through which Indigenous people adapt, remake, revise, and Indigenise museological processes" (McCarthy 2019, 38–39). According to Sarah Carr-Locke, Indigenous museology can be defined as "museum work done with, for, and by Indigenous peoples, whereby standard museum practices are altered to suit their needs" (Carr-Locke quoted in McCarthy 2019, 40). It is a way of looking at museology in alternative ways to maintain and sustain living culture.

The indigenization of museums acknowledges that not only Aboriginal/Indigenous peoples in settler-colonial nations but peoples throughout the world have had their own ways of taking care of and safeguarding what they value, their own models of museums, as well as cultural guardians/curators long before the introduction of the Western museum concept. As we now know, in many cases, contemporary, Indigenous and non-Western museums and museological practices build on and are extensions of earlier forms and behaviors (McCarthy 2011, 2019, Onciul 2013, 2015, Kreps 2003a, 2003b, Simpson 1996, 2006). For example, in my own research in Indonesia and other parts of Southeast Asia, I have discovered that Indigenous models of museums and museological behavior (including collecting, conservation, display practices, and conceptual frameworks for cultural heritage transmission and preservation) can be found in vernacular architecture, religious beliefs and practices, social organization and structure (especially kinship systems and ancestor worship); artistic traditions and aesthetics; and Indigenous epistemologies and ontologies (Kreps 2003a, 2003b, 2009, 2014). The identification, documentation, and critical analysis of non-Western models of museums and museological behavior not only makes a valuable contribution to comparative museology, but is also part of the on-going process of decolonizing Western museology and museum studies.

Since the 1980s, decolonization has come to signify a form of "progressive, postcolonial museology" (Wintle 2016) for transforming museums into more just and equitable institutions. For many, the decolonization of museums begins with acknowledging the historical fact of museum anthropology's colonial legacy, the impact of European imperialism and colonialism on colonized peoples (Lonetree 2012), and how museums have functioned within dominant and oppressive power structures informed by racist agendas. Institutions that adopt decolonizing methodologies accept that current practices cannot be divorced from colonial pasts, and that the onus for decolonization and change rests mainly on dominant culture museums, not on historically oppressed communities (Smith 2012). Decolonization, furthermore, acknowledges the existence of alternative stories and parallel ways of understanding, utilizing, and caring for tangible and intangible cultural heritage (Sully 2008, 19).

A discourse on colonialism and museums began to appear in the scholarly literature in the 1980s, influenced by the postcolonial critique and reflexive turn in anthropology more generally, gaining momentum in the 1990s (Ames 1992, Clifford 1988, Cole 1985, Harrison 1993, 1991, Hymes 1969, Jones 1993, Simpson 1996, Stocking 1985). Over the years, postcolonial museum theorists have been exploring questions, such as:

What impact did the imposition of colonial power have on indigenous societies and on cultural production within them? How have objects imported or appropriated from colonies been displayed at the imperial centre? What impact do the power relations of colonialism have on the interpretation of objects? What are the possibilities for the display of 'colonial' objects in the present day and how can contemporary museum practice address the inheritance of colonialism?

(Barringer and Flynn 1998, 1)

Lonetree reminds us, however, that Indigenous communities had been delivering their own critiques of museums for decades prior to the 1980s through scholarship, activism, legal channels, and the establishment of tribal museums and cultural centers (Cooper 2008, Haakanson 2015, Lonetree 2012, Message 2014, Nicks 2003, Onciul 2013, Phillips 2011, Sleeper-Smith 2009). Taken together, on-going criticism and Native activism have been driving the decolonization of museums intended to dislodge existing power structures and relationships that obstruct the reversal or sharing of power and authority.

To Lonetree, decolonizing museum practice for Native Americans is a way of attending to the historical trauma of colonialism and its enduring effects.

Decolonizing museum practices must involve assisting our [Native American] communities in addressing the legacies of historical unresolved grief. Doing this necessarily cuts through the veil of silence around colonialism and its consequences for Native families and communities ... Given that the Native American holocaust, which spanned centuries, remains unaddressed in both Native and non-Native communities, truth telling is the most important aspect of decolonizing museum practice of the twenty-first century, however painful it may be. The process assists in healing and promotes community well-being, empowerment, and nation building.

(2012, 5)

Lonetree's interpretation of decolonization speaks directly to the Native American experience of genocide, and the responsibility of dominant-culture as well as tribal museums to address this history.

In the article "Decolonizing Anthropology Museums: The Tropenmuseum, Amsterdam," based on my early study of Dutch anthropology museums in colonial and postcolonial eras, I described decolonization as a "conscious process of recognizing the inherent ideologies lodged in any collection and exhibition." I saw decolonization as "a means of revealing how historical and sociocultural factors have shaped museum methods, and how these methods can reflect the relations between Westerners and non-Westerners" (Kreps 1988, 56). Years later, in a chapter on decolonizing processes in the Tropenmuseum, Amsterdam and the Smithsonian National Museum of the American Indian, I defined decolonization as a

process of acknowledging the historical, colonial contingencies under which collections were acquired revealing Eurocentric ideologies and biases in the Western museum concept, discourse and practice; acknowledging and including diverse voices and multiple perspectives; and transforming museums through sustained critical analysis and concrete actions.

(2011, 72)

While this latter, modified iteration reflects my evolving understanding of the process, the earlier version was conceptualized to describe decolonizing processes as they unfolded in Dutch museums and the Netherlands as a former colonial empire.

The point is that decolonizing processes, like indigenization, are context-specific in time, place, and institutional setting. And although today, decolonization has become a keyword in museum anthropology, museum studies, and activist movements, it also is important to keep in mind how the term has been used at different historical moments to refer to particular circumstances and for certain purposes. In short, the term decolonization, like all keywords, has a genealogy.

The German scholar Moritz Julius Bonn is said to have coined the term decolonization in his section on "Imperialism" in the *Encyclopedia of the Social Sciences* published in 1932. It came into general use in the 1950s and 1960s as a label for the process by which colonized peoples in Asia and Africa gained their independence from their colonial rulers (Chamberlain 1999, 2). Chamberlain notes that the word decolonization was not favored by Asians and Africans because it implied that initiatives for decolonization were taken by metropolitan powers. Consequently, Asians and Africans have instead sometimes preferred to speak of their "liberation struggles" or "resumption of independence" (Chamberlain 1999, 2). This reading frames decolonization within the context of the "formal acts of withdrawal from the colonies, but also acknowledges the impact of anticolonial struggles and neocolonial models of 'freedom,' pointing as well to the social processes of reimagining and practicing European, American, and colonial lives after empire" (Wintle 2016, 1495).

The particularities of decolonization associated with the end of empire have had a profound impact on museums in former colonial and colonized nations, as will be shown in later chapters where I discuss the historical development of Dutch and Indonesian museums in colonial and postcolonial contexts. In the Indonesian case, the process of decolonizing museums was complicated by the on-going hegemony of Western museology promulgated not only by the Dutch and other international agents, but also by the Indonesian state. What this example recommends is the need to locate the nexus of power in all decolonizing landscapes, and to think carefully about what decolonization means in both theory and praxis in different places and times (Bhambra, Gebrial, and Nişancioğlu 2018, 2).

Remaining mindful of the complexities of the term, decolonization marks a humanistic turn in museum anthropology that places human rights, social justice, and cultural restitution at the center of museological discourse and practice. Moreover, it signals how a history of scientific detachment and aversion to politics has been giving way to advocacy and engagement (Kreps 2011, 71). Decolonization also represents a radical rethinking of museum ethics as compared to the past. As Marstine has pointed out, ethics require continual reassessment in light of current concerns and contexts (2011). The rise of the anthropology of museums and critical, reflexive museology has played a pivotal role in bringing about these changes. But while much progress has been made, much work remains to be done to "liberate culture" (Kreps 2003a) from the hegemony of Western museology, museum studies, and heritage work.

Countering Hegemonic Museology

Although the museum, as James Clifford reminds us, "is an inventive, globally and locally translated form, no longer anchored to its modern origins in Europe" (2019, 109), Western museology and heritage practices still dominate the literature in museum studies (McCarthy 2019, 38). And while a large body of literature now exists on changing relationships between museums and source communities, this literature has tended to focus on the impact of these changes on dominant-culture curatorial and exhibitionary practices. What remain largely under-examined are concrete examples of the forms museums, curatorial practices, and approaches to heritage preservation take in non-Western cultural and national contexts. We need more studies of these subjects to continue to counter the hegemony of Western museology, and further its decolonization (Byrne 2014, Hitchcock, King, and Parnwell 2010).

In my 2003 book *Liberating Culture: Cross-Cultural Perspectives on Museums, Curation, and Heritage Preservation*, I wrote that a goal of the book was to help

> liberate culture, and its collection, curation, interpretation, and preservation in museums from the management regimes of Eurocentric museology. The liberation of culture is not only about giving back or restoring a people's right to and control over the management of their cultural heritage. It is also about liberating our thinking from the Eurocentric view of what constitutes a museum, artifact, and museological practice so that we might better recognize alternative forms. The liberation of culture allows for the emergence of a new museological discourse in which points of reference are no longer solely determined and defined by the West. The aim is to open the field to include multiple voices, which represent a wide range of experiences and perspectives, and to give credence to bodies of knowledge and practice that have been historically overlooked or devalued. This 'new inclusiveness' acknowledges that those who have been marginalized as 'the others' are central to the creation of new museological paradigms.
>
> *(2003a, 145)*

Certainly, profound changes have taken place since 2003, many of which I address in this book. For one, those on the margins have continued to "talk back" in even louder voices and on even larger platforms (e.g., the Internet).

Indicative of this trend, in 2014 I was invited to participate in the conference *Museum of Our Own: In Search of Local Museology in Asia*, held in Yogyakarta,

Indonesia. In her review of the conference, Yunci Cai declared that the conference was a "significant milestone in the development of Southeast Asian museology." It was "one of the first few attempts" to respond to and add Asian voices to critical debates on museums that had been taking place for several decades" (2015, 2–3). The conference brought together some 100 museum professionals to explore museological models unique to Asia, and to discuss key contemporary trends.[5]

In the same year, I was invited to speak at the conference *Museums in Arabia* held in Doha at the Museum of Islamic Art.[6] In light of the investment in high-profile museums in a number of states of the Arabian Peninsula (Matar 2015), the conference was organized to critically assess the implications of this "museum boom" for local forms of heritage performance and preservation.[7] Intended to serve as a platform for museum professionals, researchers, and academics to discuss, debate, and exchange ideas, the conference explored a number of themes and issues, and addressed the challenges museums in the region face in their development; the ways that international museum models and museology are impacting local forms of heritage representation; and the kinds of audiences museums are speaking to, and how local communities engage with museums (Exell and Wakefield 2016, 8–9).

Back in 1983, in his prescient article "Indigenous Models of Museums in Oceania," Sidney Moko Mead, the noted Māori art historian and anthropologist, wrote about the meeting houses of the Māori and other Pacific islanders. In the article he asserted that instead of dismantling these Indigenous museological structures for the "sake of setting up European style museums, we should work within these systems as much as possible" (1983, 101). Indeed, as I have now long argued, Indigenous/non-Western models of museums, curatorial methods, and concepts of heritage preservation are worthy of recognition and protection in their own right as expressions of cultural diversity and living culture (Kreps 1998, 2003a). They are, at once, expressions of cultural diversity and a means of protecting it. But while awareness of and respect for museological diversity has been growing, much of the international museum profession continues to promote "best practices" and the standardization of "operational museology" (McCarthy 2015, Shelton 2013), running the risk of erasing the very diversity museums seek to protect (Kreps 1994).

Furthermore, while interest in non-Western museums has grown steadily and more Indigenous/non-Western scholars and practitioners have been making their mark, their representation in the literature is comparatively limited. As Bhatti emphasizes below, this gap restricts how we think about museums since museological discourse and practice continue to be dominated by Western perspectives. In the book *Translating Museums: A Counterhistory of South Asian Museology*—an ethnography of the Lahore Museum in Pakistan—Bhatti contends that:

> The intellectual reinvestment and interest in the museum by fields such as anthropology is a positive step, however, where they fail is in the ability to disrupt or question the prominence of the so-called ideal Eurocentric museum model that continues to be dominant and propagated from the 'centre'. This

situation has led to in-depth studies of non-western or post-colonial museums still remaining on the periphery in the global discourse on museums and cultural heritage ... It is this lacuna that I want to address in this ethnography of the Lahore Museum and the museum culture of South Asia generally, to break the Eurocentric hegemony and hold on museology and to allow for the possibility of museologies.

(2012, 27)

Bhatti states that the purpose of the book is "to redress this theoretical and conceptual imbalance," and fill in the missing gaps in world museum history (2012, 27–28). Her ethnography reveals how there is not one universal museology but a world full of museologies, and how we have much to learn from those who have existed on the margins of the international academic and professional museum community (Kreps 2003a, xiii, Hooper-Greenhill 2000, 153, Shelton 2013).

Conal McCarthy, in a book chapter titled "Indigenisation: Reconceptualising Museology," describes the on-going conceptualization of Māori museology, which has been on the forefront of the Indigenous museology and decolonization movement for decades. Since the 1970s, and particularly after the influential, international traveling *Te Māori: Māori Art from New Zealand Collections* exhibition of 1984 through 1987, mainstream museums in New Zealand (Aotearoa) have witnessed an increase in Māori staff and the evolution of a Māori style of museum policy and practice that incorporates customary knowledge and values. Consequently, Māori concepts have become embedded in nearly all aspects of museum work (2019, 45–46).

McCarthy writes that according to the Māori scholar and museologist Arapata Hakiwai, "Māori tribes in Aotearoa are now at the stage where they want and need a larger cosmopolitan and comparative framework to underpin the future development of Māori museology within museums *and* tribal heritage settings outside of museums" (2019, 48). This involves reaching out and making connections across communities and nations. The development of "larger cosmopolitan and comparative frameworks" that acknowledge differences between and commonalities among museological traditions on a global scale is a worthwhile aspiration for museum anthropology and museum studies.

Promoting Anthropological Understandings of Diversity

Ulf Hannerz, in *Anthropology's World: Life in a Twenty-first Century Discipline* (2010), argues that it has become both legitimate and necessary to engage with anthropology at home to free the discipline of its legacy of "othering" and exoticism, especially in the eyes of the general public. One of the enduring consequences of the decolonization of anthropology, he asserts, is that it is

no longer intellectually, morally, or politically defensible to have a separate discipline for those parts of humanity which were 'non-western' ... It is from this point on that anthropology has moved towards being more explicit and consistent in identifying itself as a discipline concerned with all of humanity.

(2010, 3)

This more inclusive anthropology supports what Hannerz sees as the field's central mission, and that is "the scholarly and practical understanding of human diversity" (2010, 48). In fact, he argues that this pursuit should be anthropology's "brand." Since its beginnings, anthropology has "sought to map the variety of human life, even if for some time we applied this preoccupation preponderantly to what was geographically distant, exotic—expressing a shared stance toward what is 'out there'" (2010, 49). Hannerz emphasizes how anthropology's focus on diversity makes an important contribution to knowledge, and what is more, "a study of diversity remains the best antidote to unthinking ethnocentrism" (2010, 49). In Hannerz's view, anthropology has had a special relationship to diversity based on the knowledge that other ways of thinking and acting are possible, and that alternatives exist.

Anthropology can assist, in Hannerz's words, in "building intelligibility where both diversity and connection are ever present" (2010, 89), since anthropologists have shared a kind of "double cosmopolitanism." For Hannerz, double cosmopolitism entails, on the one hand, embracing a concern for humanity and its condition, and on the other hand, fostering awareness and appreciation of diversity in particular, meaningful forms. Museums of anthropology are venues for performing a kind of cosmopolitanism that encourages critical thinking about one's own position in the world, and the willingness, curiosity, and courage to openly and respectfully engage with people who are different (Levitt 2015, 136). Mason even suggests a "cosmopolitan museology" that facilitates encounters beyond the known and the self in order to "take oneself out of and to encourage reflexive awareness of one's 'own location'" (2013, 45).

While diversity has become a keyword in contemporary anthropological and museological thinking and practice, Nancy Parezo, a museum anthropologist at the University of Arizona, points out that anthropology museums have been, since their founding, devoted to understanding human diversity, and nudging "the public to see the world in new ways" (2015, 10). Anthropology museums have helped society grapple with fundamental philosophical questions like "Where did we come from?" and "Why is everyone not like us?" by promoting the anthropological values of respect for cultural diversity and disseminating facts and alternative perspectives. Parezo states that museums have helped combat all-too-prevalent misinformation, stereotypes, and prejudices about people of the world. "Museums have thus been key sites where the discipline has tried to inculcate its central messages that practitioners have felt will make the world a better place: cultural diversity should be respected and cultures should be studied and understood" (2015, 12). To Parezo, museums are sites where the public is confronted with the fact that cultural diversity exists, and that society must learn to deal with cultural and social differences if it is to survive. She emphasizes how museum anthropologists have been able to disseminate this message because museums, by definition, are "institutions that serve their communities be they towns, cities, states, nations, universities or businesses" (2015, 12).

Museums by definition should also serve the public good, and serving the public good is not only one of the many responsibilities of museum anthropologists, but an underlying principle motivating their work. Museums of anthropology, in Parezo's view, are particularly appropriate platforms for debating what actually constitutes the public good, and what is beneficial or not to the betterment of society. They are sites of opportunity for community and individual engagement and forums in which to tackle socially relevant problems (2015, 12).

While acknowledging that the nature of engagement and what constitutes the fundamental activities of museums have changed over time and led to important debates about the museum's relevance, Parezo also contends that public engagement and serving the public good are not new in anthropology. Rather, she upholds that anthropology museums have always been arenas for social engagement, and museum-based anthropologists have continually advanced anthropology's idea of the public good "even during a period when the rest of the profession has been insular, worried more about socially and intellectually reproducing itself rather than demonstrating its social relevancy. Such engagement must continue today if anthropology is to matter" (2015, 13).

Indeed, more and more anthropologists, including museum anthropologists, are doing anthropology "at home" by working with diverse communities on an array of issues of public concern, such as access to health care, immigration and migration, climate change and environmental racism, homelessness and gentrification, gender inequality, and many other social justice issues. What this tells us is that museum anthropology today is not only about and for everyone, but can also encompass almost anything that speaks to the human condition. It can help shed light on the ways that various communities perceive and are affected by certain issues and problems on different scales and in different registers.

On-Going Challenges and Dilemmas

Remarkable methodological, theoretical, and ethical advancements have been made in museum anthropology since the 1980s that have reconfigured and even revolutionized practice. And while museum anthropologists have gained considerable ground in moving their field from the margins of academic anthropology, they can still be burdened with confronting entrenched and often misinformed views within the academy regarding the nature and value of museum work. Many museum anthropologists and museums (even those based at universities) continue to be faced with a number of challenges. Not the least of which, is what many have long referred to as the "curator's dilemma" and a kind of "schizophrenia" due to their multiple roles and obligations.[8]

In the chapter "Dilemmas of the Practical Anthropologist" in *Cannibal Tours*, Ames summed up the situation for many museum anthropology curators in the following passage:

The curator trains in the university system where individual research is presented as the primary good, and then works where the collective need to serve the public is given primacy … The museum ethnologist is caught between what often appear to be rapidly diverging standards. This is the 'curator's dilemma,' a conflict of interest between duties towards the collections and personal research, to say nothing of the exhibits and meeting the visiting public, a situation some more dramatically refer to as curatorial schizophrenia.

(1992, 31)

Some might say that Ames's comments are no longer pertinent given that they were published nearly 30 years ago. But the dilemmas to which he refers continue to pull museum anthropologists in different directions, and can have a bearing on for what kind of work they are recognized and rewarded.

In a 2015 essay Daniel Swan discusses "the double jeopardy of practice and academy" (2015, 65), and the strains of meeting his administrative duties as director of a museum while keeping up with his research and publication goals. Fortunately, he states, he was hired with tenure in "an academic appointment in which practice trumped scholarship" (2015, 65). Acknowledging that this is not always the case, he stresses how "We must work with increased diligence as a professional, practicing community to insure that our colleagues in academic settings receive the proper credit for their efforts in the practice of museum anthropology" (2015, 65). Swan describes how over the course of his 35-year career he has been a curator in a range of museum settings; a museum director, university professor, and academic division head. Swan's professional trajectory was from the museum to the academy, a background he believes has given him vantage points from which to see the value of working in both museum and academic arenas:

My message to current and future colleagues in museum anthropology is quite straightforward. I encourage you to embrace movement in and out of practice, regardless of duration or scale. In my experience, the dynamic tension between practice and academy provided me with opportunities to engage additional constituencies and explore new aspects of my community collaboration as a museum anthropologist. The relationship between museum and academy is reciprocal and mutually instructive.

(2015, 65)

A point of contention for many museum anthropologists affiliated with universities is that they are not adequately recognized for their curatorial work on exhibitions, a task that generally requires considerable research and subject expertise. The archaeologist Jeremy Sabloff sums up the amount of work involved in exhibit making below.

An exhibit is typically a complex endeavor that includes grant writing, research, and publication. Moreover, it often requires a significant investment of labor; field or collections research; initial conceptualization and planning; grant submission and fund raising; label, text panel, and catalog writing; exhibit preparation and installation; docent and teacher training; opening lectures; digital outreach on the Internet; and so forth ... Yet such scholarly curatorial work is frequently ignored in tenure and promotion dossiers. Moreover, the catalog, which may well have undergone peer review, is frequently given little or no weight in analyses of publications.

(2011, 412)

Sabloff sees curatorial work on exhibitions as a form of public engagement that should be recognized in academic evaluations because, in addition to being a form of scholarship, exhibits are a "critical component of public communication" (2011, 412).

Silverman points to similar dilemmas faced by museum anthropologists engaged in community-based collaborative research. He writes that "In the Academy there is a longstanding tradition associated with the humanities and humanistic social sciences (e.g., sociocultural anthropology) that eschews collaboration in scholarly endeavors. Single- authored monographs and articles are the standard" (2015, 14). And even though academic culture is changing, he says "change is slow in coming." Because there is now an ethical imperative for pursuing collaborative work, "museums and universities need to open intellectual spaces that encourage rather than discourage community-based scholarship" (2015, 14).

Museum anthropology, in many respects, occupies the border zones between what Roger Sanjek calls the "two contending value systems" that motivate anthropological work. One is the "academic-career complex" and the other is what he calls "mutuality." The values of the academic career complex that motivate anthropologists as professionals are the satisfaction of discovering and deepening an expansive anthropological worldview; advancement along career paths; and the approval and esteem we receive from colleagues. According to Sanjek, "As we are thus 'disciplined' by the discipline, these values and rewards define us as individuals within a professional world, aspects of which we become aware of only after we enter it" (2015, 1).

Yet for many anthropologists, Sanjek claims there are other values that motivate them too. These include the value they place on mutually positive relations with the people they study, work with, write about and for, and communicate with more broadly as anthropologists. These values, he attests, may complement or outweigh professional goals and achievements. At the heart of this value set is the idea of mutuality (2015, 2).

Sanjek stresses that the two value sets can pull an anthropologist in opposite directions—either inwardly, toward the world of professional anthropology, or outwardly, toward their larger social worlds. Sometimes, they can also be "compatible, even 'in sync,'" motivating anthropologists to pursue both professional academic goals while adhering to and advancing the values of the people and communities they study, work with, and live in (2015, 2). Mutuality as a concept, research strategy, and political position is not new, Sanjek explains. Many anthropologists, past and present, have practiced mutuality in their choices regarding "where and what to study, how they conduct fieldwork, and with what audiences and publics and in what forms they share and disseminate their anthropological findings and knowledge (2015, 2). Mutuality can be seen as a kind of collaborative work, but it is collaboration "with an edge" since it can involve taking political risks and accepting a degree of marginality vis-à-vis the academic career complex.

Indeed, as Alaka Wali, an applied museum anthropologist at the Field Museum in Chicago, testifies, "Accepting marginalization makes the decision to pursue mutuality a political act" (2015a, 175). For Wali, mutuality must also be "an act of passion" because as a research strategy it implies that the researcher, first and foremost, is guided by the concerns and questions of importance to research subjects. This means that research projects are grounded in and driven by people's real life experiences, and are intended to add in some way to their quality of life. Wali further emphasizes that "mutuality must also be an act of patience" because deeper collaboration requires an investment in time that may not fit with typical research or funding cycles (2015a, 175–176).

Wali's work, if not career, is exemplary of how applied and museum anthropologists find ways of working around and within different institutional systems and value sets. Wali, like Swan and others, has straddled the worlds of academia and publicly oriented work by learning to speak their respective languages and navigate their respective cultures. She has shown how one interest group or audience need not be exclusive of another. Over the course of her career, Wali has conducted ethnographic research on the impact of hydroelectric dams on Indigenous populations in Panama; on infant mortality among African-Americans in Harlem, New York; and more recently, on creativity, art, and resilience in communities in Chicago. She established the Center for Cultural Understanding and Change at the Field Museum in 1995 as part of the Field's efforts to better engage with Chicago-area communities and organizations on projects related to art, activism, environmental conservation, and restoration (Wali 2006, 2015a, 2015b).

Wali has chosen to conduct research that will reach and influence audiences beyond the academy, such as policy makers and public officials. As a case in point, the results of an ethnographic study she and other Field Museum staff carried out on "informal" artists in Chicago were not published in a peer-reviewed academic journal. Instead they were disseminated in the form of a report that she states had a "strong impact on the arts policy community" (2015a, 184), namely the National Endowment for the Arts and the city of Chicago's Department of Cultural Affairs. The report, Wali recounts, contributed to a shift in resource allocation from the funding of formal, institutionalized venues and arts programs to more support for informal art making and artists in neighborhoods. Although based at a museum and holding the title of curator, Wali writes that she did not start performing more traditional tasks such as collecting objects for the museum's collection and curating exhibits until after she had been at the museum for ten years (2015a, 180).

Doing cultural work that has real impact and matters to individuals and communities has been both personally and professionally gratifying to Wali, leading her to proclaim in 2015 "that this is a great time to be a museum anthropologist. Museums of all kinds are seeking insights into how to better engage their diverse publics, and how to more creatively represent cultural issues" (Wali and Tudor 2015, 24). But while it may be a great time for museum anthropologists working in large institutions like the Field Museum, for those working in smaller arenas such as university museums, the present moment can feel precarious.

According to Isaac, since the early 2000s a number of university museums and ethnographic collections have closed due to the financial and spatial burdens of maintaining collections. With universities looking for ways to cut costs, anthropology museums have become easy targets. Isaac states that this situation should raise concerns since it means that university administrators or anthropology departments do not see museums as vital resources. Closures cut access to collections, and impede teaching and training anthropology students in museum anthropology. She is especially concerned about the fate of ethnology collections, which she states carry a "low status" in comparison to art and even archaeology collections.

> It is worth noting that I do not know of any art historians or artists who argue they would rather run their degree programs without art collections or museums. The low status of ethnology collections is further complicated by the fact that university-based archaeology collections often receive state funding if they serve as a mandated state repository, leaving ethnology collections unfunded and often orphaned within larger state and federal systems.
>
> *(2015, 19)*

Isaac believes that museum anthropology is at a crucial turning point because the closing of museums and collections inhibits the ability of anthropology programs to teach "critical museology in practice" and to foster the kind of cross-cultural and collaborative frameworks and methodologies that have come to characterize contemporary museum work, especially with originating communities. Anthropology collections and museums are not just of value to anthropology, she argues, but also to these communities. Isaac asserts that as the founder of these collections, "anthropology as a discipline has a responsibility towards them—and this does not mean only to take this up by writing about them as an exercise in post-colonial detachment therapy" (2015, 19). In Isaac's words,

> the museum environment enables us to experience cultural diversity and different cultural approaches to knowledge firsthand, and last but not least, the exploration of effective cross-cultural frameworks that enable these shared histories, knowledges, and collaborations to shape how cultural and political landscapes are not just conceived but lived.
>
> *(2015, 19)*

Many still ponder the relevance of ethnographic collections and museums in today's world. As Bouquet submits, despite their persistence into the twenty-first century anthropology museums remain essentially nineteenth-century institutions with collections largely dating back to the colonial era and tainted by the Eurocentric premises on which they were established (2012, 90). Certainly given their entanglement in colonialism, there are some who believe it will never be possible to fully decolonize anthropology museums and museum anthropology (Lonetree 2012, Mithlo 2004, Shannon 2009, 2014). Nevertheless, efforts continue to be made to reconcile this past with the present.

In spite of on-going criticism, new generations of anthropology students are turning to museum anthropology not only because it provides them with another career option, but also because it offers them the opportunity to do applied, publicly engaged work. Indeed, the up and coming generation of museum anthropologists is savvy to the directions their chosen field is taking in what Ruth Phillips calls the "second museum age." She suggests that: "The truly exciting and innovative potential of the second museum age lies in the advanced programs of socially responsible research and representation that they can support and embody" (2005, 85).

The Convergence of Museum Anthropology and Museum Studies

Many of the developments in museum anthropology discussed thus far have concurrently been taking place in museum studies and the museum profession. And many of the issues, concerns, and questions currently being debated in the museum world are similar to those in anthropology. Today, the fields of museum anthropology and museum studies are closely aligned, if not inseparable, since many anthropologists contribute to museum studies as scholars, teachers, and practitioners (Silverman 2015).

Not unlike museum anthropology, until relatively recently museum studies was considered mostly an applied field, concerned foremost with museum methods and practical matters (Vergo 1989, 3, Macdonald 2006). But over the past decade or more, museum studies has become much more than the "how to" of museum work. It is now a domain of scholarship with its own body of literature, an academic discipline as well as a field of practice.

The changing status of museum studies within the academy and its growth in general can be attributed to a number of developments that have been taking place over the past half-century or more. One is the phenomenal growth in the number and kinds of museum worldwide since the mid-twentieth century. The International Council of Museums (ICOM), an organization created in 1946 by UNESCO by and for museum professionals, now has some 35,000 members that represent the global museum community. As of 2014 there were some 35,000 active museums in the United States, according to the Institute of Museum and Library Sciences.[9] Guerzoni estimates that the world total is close to 80,000, and "it is not unrealistic to estimate that 50 percent of this astonishing total was built and/or extended in the last 40 years, with a thousand new museums each year" (2015, 189).

Another development is the need for better-trained museum professionals and the evolution of the museum profession (Kaplan 1996, 818, 2006). Generally speaking, professionalization of the field has involved the establishment of international, national, regional, and local museum associations each with their own conferences, publications, and sub-committees devoted to specific areas of museum practice; the formulation of professional codes of ethics for promulgating standards of conduct; and the expansion of museum studies and training programs in universities, art schools and institutes, and in some cases, museums. According to Kaplan, in 1994 there were a few hundred museum studies programs in the United States (1996, 818). Over the past few decades the number and kinds of programs and specialized courses have swelled to meet the demands of the profession just as universities and colleges seek to partake in the growth of the "culture industry" and "creative economy."[10]

Whether or not a degree or formal training in museum studies is necessary remains open to debate. There are some who believe that disciplinary training, for example in anthropology or art history, or an internship is sufficient preparation for a career in museums (Harrison 1991). Increasingly, however, others find museum studies as a "precondition for its acceptance as a new discipline or sub-disciplinary area and profession in its own right" (Kaplan 1996, 820). Regardless of such debates, Kaplan points out that the burgeoning literature in museum studies

> attests to the validity of the discipline and the process of codifying a body of knowledge dating back to the eighteenth century ... Museum studies, like museums themselves, is interdisciplinary. It may be used as a prism through which traditional academic disciplines are refracted, and it may be seen as a discipline on its own.
>
> *(1996, 820)*

What has contributed most significantly to the growth of museum studies as an academic field and its increasing acceptance within the academy has been the "theorizing of museums," as noted in the last chapter. According to Macdonald, up until the 1990s, the social and cultural theorizing of museums remained relatively under-developed. In their path-breaking volume *Theorizing Museums* (1996), Macdonald and Fyfe brought together a range of theoretically informed studies by European and American scholars. The aim of the volume was to highlight the pertinence and rich theoretical potential of the museum as an analytical locus for anthropological, sociological, and cultural studies; and to show how social and cultural theorizing can illuminate many contemporary museum issues (1996, 3). The book was intended to contribute to the development of an anthropology and sociology of museums, and its authors were primarily concerned with how the nature and context of museums had been changing since the 1980s, and how such changes affected practice.

In her edited volume *A Companion to Museum Studies*, Macdonald maintains that museum studies has gone beyond the "first wave" of new museological work by broadening its scope, expanding methodological approaches, and deepening an empirical base. She suggests, "Perhaps more than anything, museum studies today recognize … the multiplicity and complexity of museums, and call for a correspondingly rich and multi-faceted range of perspectives and approaches to comprehend and provoke museums themselves" (2006, 2).

Altogether, the theorizing of museums has had significant implications for museum policy and practice by providing more nuanced theoretical and methodological tools for more robust empirical research and critical accounts of existing museum practice (McCarthy 2015). For Macdonald, the recent critical study of the museum reconnects with the critical orientation of the new museology movement that began to emerge in the 1960s. This reconnection, she contends, is not only "evident on paper but is also underway in many museums, though to varying extents in different places and in different types of museums" (2006, 9). Reconnecting critical theory with the new museology opens paths for strengthening alliances between those who study museums with those who work in them (2006, 8–9).

Kaplan points out that the critical study of museums as social institutions began to develop in the 1970s in Europe and later spread to North America and other parts of the world (2006, 165). She notes that even though anthropology as a discipline had a long association with museums, it "lagged behind in the study of museums in the United States" (2006, 166). According to both Kaplan and Lurie, the Council for Museum Anthropology (CMA) was created in 1974 partly in reaction to a sense of isolation museum anthropologists felt in dealing with museum-related problems as anthropologists (Kaplan 2006, 166, Lurie 1981, 183–184). The CMA held its first meeting at the American Anthropological Association (AAA) conference in Mexico City that same year. The CMA also began publishing a quarterly newsletter in 1976 that included reports on museum-based research, exhibit announcements and reviews, bibliographies, and job postings. It also included guidelines for training in museum studies programs, and announcements of grants the CMA received for such purposes from the federal government and other agencies.[11] The CMA was initially affiliated with the American Association of Museums (now the American Alliance of Museums—AAM), but in 1990 it departed from the AAM and joined the AAA, "giving notice of the disciplinary acceptance of the study of museums and their roles as a subfield of anthropology" (Kaplan 1992, 51, 2006). The newsletter was transformed into a peer-reviewed journal, *Museum Anthropology*, in 1992, which continues to be a leading journal in both anthropology and museum studies.[12] In an editorial statement "On Becoming a Journal," then editor of the Newsletter Enid Schildkrout wrote:

> *Museum Anthropology* has a very important role to play within the discipline of anthropology and within the museum profession. These two constituencies combine to make up a diverse and demanding audience. From different

vantage points both are concerned with many controversial issues that are also of great public interest ... We hope to publish many cogently argued, diverse viewpoints.

(1991, 5)

Certainly, academically oriented museum anthropologists and museum professionals have a great deal to learn from one another through continual dialogue and exchange. Museum ethnographers have much to offer, for instance, in terms of fine-grained critical analyses of "operational museology" (Shelton 2013, McCarthy 2015), but also as trained fieldworkers in how to establish rapport within a community and build and maintain meaningful collaborative partnerships. As students of cultural diversity, they can add insight and depth to the representation of culture in exhibitions and educational programming. As "cultural brokers" (Kurin 1997) and "translators" (Silverman 2015), museum anthropologists model approaches to intercultural dialogue that can be of crucial importance to the development of more inclusive and equitable policies and programs. Conversely, museum professionals can offer practical advice to anthropologists in general on how to better reach the public through exhibitions, educational programming, and other forms of popular media.

Shelton has argued that museums need anthropology for "charting new courses" in an increasingly globalized and diverse world (2006a, 79). But we can equally say that anthropology needs museums for exploring alternative paths for reaching and speaking to audiences beyond the academy about pressing cultural issues of our times. Over two decades ago, Kurin asked: "Where are we as academic departments, public institutions, professional societies, and practitioners in the contemporary debates about culture? We should be at the forefront of national and international debates on fundamental cultural issues. Yet we are not" (1997, 277). While progress is being made, anthropology in the United States continues to lag behind the discipline as practiced in Europe and Latin America, for example, where anthropologists as public intellectuals regularly participate in public discourse (Beck and Maida 2015, 11).

Anthropologists could furthermore take lessons from museum professionals regarding how to create more equitable and democratic working environments within their own institutions and the anthropological community at large. For example, Ames, in the previously mentioned article "Report from the Field: The Democratization of Anthropology and Museums," describes two museum conferences he attended in Canada in the early 1980s. He observed that at both conferences considerable time was spent discussing the professional needs of attendees as well as the needs of the visiting public. He noted that the focus was on improving institutional as well as individual professional standing, and "individual and collective interests" were more closely linked than one usually finds in a university setting (1986, 63). In *Cannibal Tours*, Ames elaborated on this theme, highlighting the difference between the degree to which academic anthropologists and museums are held accountable to the public.

In contrast to universities, which have maintained a degree of autonomy and insulation from the communities that support them, museums have, for better or worse, become more closely integrated into and involved with the communities in which they are located and thus, in a sense, more democratized than universities. Museum personnel, therefore, have had to become more responsive to a wider public ... Academic anthropologists, by contrast, are still, by and large, responsible only to their professional peers and to foundations that provide personal research funds. They do not have to answer, except in a more generalized way, to the public.

(1992, 41)

Museum studies mirrors anthropology in its breadth of subject matter, areas of concern, and disciplinary coverage. Moreover, museums and the field of anthropology share interlocking histories and have proven to be enduring institutions despite their compromising pasts. Museum studies in dialogue with anthropology can illuminate the contingencies of these histories, and what bearing they might have on current and future practice. Indeed, the dichotomies that have long separated the fields are breaking down as more and more museum anthropologists consider themselves "professional hybrids" (Phillips 2011), and cultural workers.

In the inaugural issue of the journal *Museum Worlds*, editors Sandra Dudley and Kylie Message summarize the meaning of museums today, and the value of museum studies.

Museums engage with and are embedded within the societies and histories of which they are a part, and in doing so they are not only influenced by, but also impact upon, wider social and cultural patterns. Studies of museums, in their increasing range of disciplinary influences and subject focus, reflect this embeddedness and dynamism. Museums and the ever developing field of museum studies, are variously concerned, on different levels and in a diversity of ways with institutions, nations, people, communities, governments, exhibitions, displays, public programs, collections, material culture, audiences, public memory, and concepts and experiences of place, identity, and belonging.

(2013, 1)

Anthropologists have something to say about all of the subjects listed above, but the social "embeddedness" and "dynamism" characteristic of museums remains largely aspirational for the discipline of anthropology. The convergence of museum anthropology and museum studies can help "embed" anthropology more deeply in society so that it has a more dynamic and lasting impact on people's lives and the societies and cultures in which they live. As Kurin observes:

Curation for the museum of the new millennium is processual, not static. It relies on the idea of partnership and trust between community and institution, a proactive effort to serve the public, increase understandability, and use the museum as a vehicle of inter- and intracultural communication. Helpful, skilled, and connected, the museum is enmeshed in the social and economic life of the people around it.

(1997, 284)

In this chapter, I have considered major movements and tendencies in the recent history of museum anthropology, and how they have been adding to the development of more engaged research, scholarship, and practice. In the next chapter, I present an overview of the origins and historical trajectories of museum and applied anthropology to show how these two subfields of anthropology have also been converging over the past couple of decades. I pay special attention to how a history of critique, internal and external, has been a defining characteristic of the fields throughout their lifetimes, and has been necessary for moving them in new directions.

Notes

1 Actually, Schultz points out that meaningful engagement with communities, especially First Nations, has been a priority at UBCMOA since its inception in 1949. According to Schultz, Harry and Audrey Hawthorn, the first director and curator, built the museum on the foundation of "useful anthropology," defined as "a discipline that serves the people being studied as well as the academy" (2011, 2).
2 Frese's work will be discussed in more detail in Chapter 4. It is also worth noting here that Ames might have been influenced by Frese's *Anthropology and the Public* since the first edition *Cannibal Tours and Glass Boxes: The Anthropology of Museums* was titled *Museums, the Public and Anthropology* (1986). Ames also cited Frese's book in this first edition.
3 As will be discussed in the next chapter, it was precisely for these reasons that Boas saw the study of material culture in museums as a limited method for understanding the complexities of a culture. Early on, he recognized that objects held multiple meanings and functions in their originating contexts that became lost as they were "recontextualized" in museums (Boas 1907, Jacknis 1985). Rowlands has pointed out that an emphasis on "decontextualized" material culture at the beginning of the twenty-first century is somewhat ironic given that decontextualization is what led to the demise of material culture as a research and teaching tool at the beginning of the twentieth century (2006, 443).
4 Recognizing the importance of religion in American history and life, the Smithsonian National Museum of American History hired a religion curator in 2016. It had not had such a curator since the 1890s. As reported in the *Washington Post*, the curator's job is to "remind Americans of our nation's religious history, in all its diversity, messiness, import and splendor" (Zauzmer 2016).
5 The conference was organized by the University of Gadjah Mada in Yogyakarta, one of Indonesia's leading universities, and the National Museum of World Cultures in the Netherlands. Organizers invited participants to contribute papers on one of five themes: Writing museum histories in Southeast Asia; The West and the Rest: the development of the theory of museology; Museums and heritage; Conservation; and Museology education in Southeast Asia (Cai 2015, 2–3). I was invited to participate based on my many years of research on museum development in Indonesia, and my work with museum training programs in Thailand and Vietnam.
6 The conference was organized in cooperation with University College London-Qatar and the Museum of Islamic Art, Doha and with support from the Qatar National Research Fund.

7 For example, the Louvre Abu Dhabi (opened in 2016), the Guggenheim Abu Dhabi and the Zayed National Museum, and the King Abdulaziz Center for World Culture in Dhahran, Saudi Arabia (2016), and the National Museum of Qatar (2017).
8 The curator's dilemma is an enduring issue in museum anthropology that I will return to in the next chapter.
9 Institute of Museum and Library Sciences website imls.gov (accessed September 4, 2017).
10 On the development of the museum profession see Ames 1992, Boylan 2006, Kaplan 1992, 1994, Weil 1990.
11 See Council for Museum Anthropology Newsletters 1976 and 1977.
12 I served as editor of the journal from 2000 to 2005.

References

Ames, Michael. 1986. "Report from the Field: The Democratization of Anthropology and Museums." *Culture* VI(I):61–64.

Ames, Michael. 1992. *Cannibal Tours and Glass Boxes: The Anthropology of Museums*. Vancouver: University of British Columbia.

Anderson, Jane and Haidy Geismar. 2017. "Introduction." In *The Routledge Companion to Cultural Property*, edited by Jane Anderson and Haidy Geismar, 1–32. London and New York: Routledge.

Appadurai, Arjun, ed. 1986. *The Social Life of Things*. Cambridge: Cambridge University Press.

Appadurai, Arjun and Carol Breckenridge. 1988. "Why Public Culture?" *Public Culture Bulletin* 1(1):1–9.

Archambault, JoAllyn. 2011. "Native Communities, Museums and Collaboration." *Practicing Anthropology* 33(2):16–20.

Barrett, Jennifer. 2012. *Museums and the Public Sphere*. Oxford: Blackwell.

Barringer, Tim and Tom Flynn. 1998. "Introduction." In *Colonialism and the Object. Empire, Material Culture and the Museum*, edited by Tim Barringer and Tom Flynn, 1–8. London: Routledge.

Basu, Paul. 2011. "Object Diasporas, Resourcing Communities: Sierra Leonean Collections in Global Museumscape." *Museum Anthropology* 34(1):28–42.

Beck, Sam and Carl A. Maida. 2015. "Introduction." In *Public Anthropology in a Borderless World*, edited by Sam Beck and Carl A. Maida, 1–35. New York and Oxford: Berghahn.

Benton, Susan. 2017. "A Paradox of Cultural Property. NAGPRA and (Dis)Possession." In *The Routledge Companion to Cultural Property*, edited by Jane Anderson and Haidy Geismar, 108–127. London and New York: Routledge.

Berlo, Janet Catherine and Ruth B. Phillips. 1992. "Vitalizing the Things of the Past. Museum Representations of Native North American Art in the 1990s." *Museum Anthropology* 16(1):29–43.

Bhambra, Gurminder, Dalia Gebrial, and Karem Nişancioğlu. 2018. "Introduction: Decolonising the University?" In *Decolonising the University*, edited by Gurminder Bhambra, Dalia Gebrial, and Karem Nişancioğlu, 1–15. London: Pluto Press.

Bhatti, Shaila. 2012. *Translating Museums. A Counterhistory of South Asian Museology*. Walnut Creek, California: Left Coast Press.

Boas, Franz. 1907. "Some Principles of Museum Administration." *Science* 25(649):921–933.

Boast, Robin. 2011. "Neocolonial Collaboration: Museum as Contact Zone Revisited." *Museum Anthropology* 34(1):56–70.

Bouquet, Mary. 2001. "Introduction: Anthropology and the Museum. Back to the Future." In *Academic Anthropology and the Museum. Back to the Future*, edited by Mary Bouquet. New York and Oxford: Berghahn.

Bouquet, Mary. 2012. *Museums. A Visual Anthropology*. London: Berg.

Boylan, Patrick. 2006. "The Museum Profession." In *Companion to Museum Studies*, edited by Sharon Macdonald, 415–430. Oxford: Blackwell.

Buchli, Victor, ed. 2002. *The Material Culture Reader*. Oxford and New York: Berg.

Buggeln, Gretchen. 2015. "Museum Space and the Experience of the Sacred." *Material Religion. The Journal of Objects, Art and Belief* 8(1):30–50.

Butler, Shelley. 2008. *Contested Representations: Revisiting "Into the Heart of Africa"*. Peterborough, Ontario: Broadview Press.

Butler, Shelley. 2015. "Reflexive Museology Lost and Found." In *The International Handbook of Museum Studies. Museum Theory*, edited by Andrea Whitcomb and Kyle Message, 159–182. Oxford: Wiley Blackwell.

Byrne, Denis. 2014. *Counterheritage: Critical Perspectives on Heritage Conservation in Asia*. London and New York: Routledge.

Cai, Yunci. 2015. "Review of Museum of Our Own: In Search of Local Museology for Asia." *Papers from the Institute of Archaeology* 25(2):2–7.

Chamberlain, M.E. 1999. *Decolonization*. Oxford: Blackwell Publishers. Original edition, 1985.

Classen, Constance and David Howes. 2006. "The Museum as Sensescape: Western Sensibilities and Material Artifacts." In *Sensible Objects: Colonialism, Museums, and Material Culture*, edited by Elizabeth Edwards, Chris Gosden and Ruth B. Philips, 199–222. Oxford: Berg.

Clavir, Miriam. 2002. *Preserving What is Valued: Museums, Conservation, and First Nations* Vancouver: University of British Columbia Press.

Clifford, James. 1988. *The Predicament of Culture. Twentieth-Century Ethnography, Literature, and Art*. Cambridge, MA: Harvard University Press.

Clifford, James. 1991. "Four Northwest Coast Museums: Travel Reflections." In *Exhibiting Cultures: The Poetics and Politics of Museum Display*, edited by Ivan Karp and Steven D. Lavine, 212–254. Washington, DC: Smithsonian Institution Press.

Clifford, James. 1997. *Routes. Travel and Translation in the Late Twentieth Century*. Cambridge, MA: Harvard University Press.

Clifford, James. 2013. *Returns. Becoming Indigenous in the Twenty-First Century*. Cambridge, MA: Harvard University Press.

Clifford, James. 2019. "The Times of the Curator." In *Curatopia. Museums and the Future of Curatorship*, edited by Philipp Schorch and Conal McCarthy, 109–123. Manchester: Manchester University Press.

Cole, Douglas. 1985. *Captured Heritage. The Scramble for Northwest Coast Artifacts*. Seattle: University of Washington Press.

Colwell, Chip. 2014. "The Sacred and the Museum: Repatriation and the Trajectories of Inalienable Possessions." *Museum Worlds* 2:10–24.

Colwell, Chip. 2017. *Plundered Skulls and Stolen Spirits: Inside the Fight to Reclaim Native America's Culture*. Chicago, IL: University of Chicago Press.

Colwell-Chanthaphonh, Chip and T.J. Ferguson. 2008. *Collaboration and Archaeological Practice. Engaging Descendant Communities*. Lanham, MD: Alta Mira Press.

Conn, Steven. 2010. *Do Museums Still Need Objects?* Philadelphia: University of Pennsylvania Press.

Cooper, Karen C. 2008. *Spirited Encounters. American Indian Protest Museum Policies and Practices*. Lanham, MD: Altamira Press.

Cruikshank, Julie. 1995. "Imperfect Translations: Rethinking Objects in Ethnographic Collections." *Museum Anthropology* 19(1):25–38.

Davis, Richard. 1997. *Lives of Indian Images*. Princeton, NJ: Princeton University Press.

Dudley, Sandra. 2010. "Museum Materialities: Objects, Sense, Feeling." In *Museum Materialities: Objects, Engagements, Interpretations*, edited by Sandra Dudley, 1–17. London and New York: Routledge.

Dudley, Sandra. 2012. "Encountering a Chinese Horse: Engaging with the Thingness of Things." In *Museum Objects: Experiencing the Properties of Things*, edited by Sandra Dudley, 1–16. London and New York: Routledge.

Dudley, Sandra and Kylie Message. 2013. "Editorial." *Museum Worlds* 1:1–6.

Duggan, Betty. 2011. "Introduction: Collaborative Ethnography and the Changing Worlds of Museums." *Practicing Anthropology* 33(2):2–3.

Edson, G. 1997. *Museum Ethics*. London and New York: Routledge.

Eriksen, Thomas Hylland. 2006. *Engaging Anthropology*. Oxford: Berg.

Erikson, Patricia. 2002. *Voices of a Thousand People. The Makah Cultural and Research Center*. Lincoln and London: University of Nebraska Press.

Erskine-Loftus, Pamela, ed. 2014. *Reimagining Museums Practice in the Arabian Peninsula*. Cambridge: Museums ETC.

Evans, Harriet and Michael Rowlands. 2015. "Reconceptualizing Heritage in China. Museums, Development and the Shifting Dynamics of Power." In *Museums, Heritage and International Development*, edited by Paul Basu and Wayne Modest, 272–294. London and New York: Routledge.

Exell, Karen and Sarina Wakefield, eds. 2016. *Museums in Arabia. Transnational Practices and Regional Processes*. London and New York: Routledge.

Fine-Dare, Kathy. 2002. *Grave Injustice: The American Indian Repatriation Movement and NAGPRA*. Lincoln: University of Nebraska Press.

Flynn, G. and D. Hull-Walski. 2001. "Merging Traditional Indigenous Curation Methods with Modern Museum Standards of Care." *Museum Anthropology* 25(1):31–40.

Frese, H. H. 1960. *Anthropology and the Public: The Role of Museums*. Leiden, the Netherlands: E.J. Brill.

Gaskell, Ivan. 2003. "Sacred to Profane and Back Again." In *Arts and Its Publics. Museum Studies at the Millennium* edited by Andrew McClellan, 148–162. Oxford: Blackwell.

Glass, Aaron. 2015. "Indigenous Ontologies, Digital Futures: Plural Provenances and the Kwakwaka'wakw Collection in Berlin and Beyond." In *Museums as Process: Translating Local and Global Knowledges*, edited by Raymond A. Silverman, 19–44. London and New York: Routledge.

Guerzoni, Guido. 2015. "The Museum Building Boom." In *Cities, Museums and Soft Power*, edited by Gail Dexter Lord and Ngaire Blankenberg, 187–198. Washington, DC: American Alliance of Museums.

Gurian, Elaine. 2006. *Civilizing the Museum*. London and New York: Routledge.

Haakanson, Sven. 2015. "Translating Knowledge: Uniting Alutiiq People with Heritage Information." In *Museums as Process: Translating Local and Global Knowledges*, edited by Raymond A. Silverman, 123–129. London and New York: Routledge.

Handler, R. and E. Gable. 1997. *The New History in an Old Museum. Creating the Past at Colonial Williamsburg*. Durham, NC: Duke University Press.

Hannerz, Ulf. 2010. *Anthropology's World. Life in a Twenty-first Century Discipline*. London: Pluto Press.

Harrison, Faye V., ed. 1991. *Decolonizing Anthropology: Moving Further for an Anthropology for Liberation*. Washington, DC: American Anthropological Association.

Harrison, Julia D. 1993. "Ideas of Museums in the 1990s." *Museum Management and Curatorship* 13:160–176.

Harrison, Rodney, Sarah Byrne, and Anne Clarke, ed. 2013. *Reassembling the Collection. Ethnographic Museums and Indigenous Agency.* Santa Fe, NM: School for Advanced Research Press.

Hays-Gilpin, Kelley and Ramson Lomatewama. 2013. "Curating Communities at the Museum of Northern Arizona." In *Reassembling the Collection. Ethnographic Museums and Indigenous Agency*, edited by Rodney Harrison, Sarah Byrne, and Anne Clarke, 259–284. Santa Fe, NM: School for Advanced Research Press.

Hitchcock, Michael, Victor King, and Michael Parnwell. 2010. "Heritage Futures." In *Heritage Tourism in Southeast Asia*, edited by Michael Hitchcock, Victor King, and Michael Parnwell, 264–273. Copenhagen: NIAS Press.

Hooper-Greenhill, E. 2000. *Museums and the Interpretation of Visual Culture.* London and New York: Routledge.

Hoskins, Janet. 1998. *Biographical Objects: How Things Tell the Stories of People's Lives.* London and New York: Routledge.

Hymes, Dell, ed. 1969. *Reinventing Anthropology.* New York: Random House.

Isaac, Gwyneira. 2007. *Mediating Knowledges.* Tucson: University of Arizona Press.

Isaac, Gwyneira. 2009. "Responsibilities toward Knowledge: The Zuni Museum and the Reconciling of Different Knowledge Systems." In *Contesting Knowledge. Museums and Indigenous Perspectives*, edited by Susan Sleeper-Smith, 303–321. Lincoln and London: University of Nebraska Press.

Isaac, Gwyneira. 2015. "Museums and the Practice of Anthropology: Whose Responsibility Is It?" *Practicing Anthropology* 37(3):19.

Jacknis, Ira. 1985. "Franz Boas and Exhibits: On the Limitations of the Museum Method in Anthropology." In *Objects and Others: Essays on Museums and Material Culture*, edited by George Stocking, 75–111. Madison: University of Wisconsin Press.

Jones, Anna Laura. 1993. "Exploding Canons: The Anthropology of Museums." *Annual Review of Anthropology* 22:201–220.

Kaplan, Flora. 1992. "Growing Pains." *Museum News* 71(1):49–51.

Kaplan, Flora. 1994. "Introduction." In *Museums and the Making of "Ourselves." The Role of Objects in National Identity*," edited by Flora E. S. Kaplan, 1–15. London and New York: University of Leicester Press.

Kaplan, Flora. 1996. "Museum Anthropology." In *Encyclopedia of Cultural Anthropology*, edited by David Levinson and Melvin Ember. New York: Henry Holt and Company.

Kaplan, Flora. 2006. "Making and Remaking National Identities." In *A Companion to Museum Studies*, edited by Sharon Macdonald, 152–169. Oxford: Wiley-Blackwell.

Karp, Ivan and Steven Lavine. 1991. "Introduction." In *Exhibiting Cultures: The Poetics and Politics of Museum Display*, edited by Ivan Karp and Steven Lavine. Washington, DC: Smithsonian Institution Press.

Kirshenblatt-Gimblett, Barbara. 1991. "Objects of Ethnography." In *The Poetics and Politics of Museum Display*, edited by Ivan Karp and Steven Lavine, 386–443. Washington, DC: Smithsonian Institution Press.

Kirshenblatt-Gimblett, Barbara. 2006. "World Heritage and Cultural Economics." In *Museum Frictions. Public Cultures/Global Transformations*, edited by Ivan Karp, Corinne A. Kratz, Lynn Szwaja, and Tomas Ybarra-Frausto, 161–202. Durham and London: Duke University Press.

Knell, Simon, ed. 2007. *Museums in the Material World, Leicester Readers in Museum Studies.* London and New York: Routledge.

Kopytoff, Igor. 1986. "The Cultural Biography of Things: Commoditization as Process." In *The Social Life of Things*, edited by Arjun Appadurai, 64–91. Cambridge: Cambridge University Press.

Kramer, Jennifer. 2015. "Mobius Museology: Curating and Critiquing the Multiversity Galleries at the Museum of Anthropology at the University of British Columbia." In *Museum Transformations*, edited by Annie E. Coombes and Ruth B. Phillips, 489–510. Oxford: Wiley Blackwell.

Kramer, Jennifer. 2017. "Betting on the Raven. Ethical Relationality and Nuxalk Cultural Property." In *The Routledge Companion to Cultural Property* edited by Jane Anderson and Haidy Geismar, 152–167. London and New York: Routledge.

Kreps, Christina. 1988. "Decolonizing Anthropology Museums: The Tropenmuseum, Amsterdam." *Museum Studies Journal* 3(2):56–63.

Kreps, Christina. 1994. "The Paradox of Cultural Preservation in Museums." *The Journal of Arts Management, Law, and Society* 23(4):291–306.

Kreps, Christina. 1998. "Museum-Making and Indigenous Curation in Central Kalimantan, Indonesia." *Museum Anthropology* 22(1):5–17.

Kreps, Christina. 2003a. *Liberating Culture: Cross-Cultural Perspectives on Museums, Curation, and Heritage Preservation* London: Routledge.

Kreps, Christina. 2003b. "Curatorship as Social Practice." *Curator: The Museum Journal* 46 (3):311–323.

Kreps, Christina. 2008. "Appropriate Museology in Theory and Practice." *Museum Management and Curatorship* 23(1):23–42.

Kreps, Christina. 2009. "Indigenous Curation, Museums, and Intangible Cultural Heritage." In *Intangible Heritage*, edited by Laurajane Smith and Natsuko Akagawa, 193–208. London and New York: Routledge.

Kreps, Christina. 2011. "Changing the Rules of the Road: Post-Colonialism ad the New Museum Ethics of Museum Anthropology." In *Routledge Companion to Museum Ethics*, edited by Janet Marstine, 70–84. London and New York: Routledge.

Kreps, Christina. 2012. "Intangible Threads: Curating the Living Heritage of Dayak Ikat Weaving." In *Safeguarding Intangible Cultural Heritage*, edited by Michelle Stefano, Peter Davis and Gerard Corsane, 177–192. Woodbridge: Boydell Press.

Kreps, Christina. 2014. "Thai Monastery Museums. Contemporary Expressions of Ancient Traditions." In *Transforming Knowledge Orders: Museums, Collections, and Exhibitions*, edited by Larissa Forster, 230–256. Paderborn, Germany: Wilhelm Fink.

Krmpotich, Cara. 2014. *The Force of Family: Repatriation, Kinship, and Memory on Haida Gwai*. Toronto, Buffalo, London: University of Toronto Press.

Kurin, Richard. 1997. *Reflections of a Culture Broker. A View from the Smithsonian*. Washington, DC: Smithsonian Institution Press.

Levitt, Peggy. 2015. *Artifacts and Allegiances. How Museums Put the Nation and the World on Display*. Berkeley, CA: University of California Press.

Lonetree, Amy. 2012. *Decolonizing Museums. Representing Native America in National and Tribal Museums*. Chapel Hill: University of North Carolina.

Luri, Nancy O. 1981. "Museumland Revisited." *Human Organization* 40(2):180–187.

Macdonald, Sharon. 2002. *Behind the Scenes at the Science Museum*. Oxford: Berg.

Macdonald, Sharon. 2005. "Enchantment and Its Dilemmas: The Museum as Ritual Site." In *Science, Magic, and Religion. The Ritual Processes of Museum Magic*, edited by Mary Bouquet and Nuno Porto, 209–227. New York: Berghahn Books.

Macdonald, Sharon. 2006. "Expanding Museum Studies: An Introduction." In *A Companion to Museum Studies*, edited by Sharon Macdonald, 1–12. Oxford: Wiley-Blackwell.

Macdonald, Sharon and Gordon Fyfe. 1996. "Introduction." In *Theorizing Museums*. Oxford: Blackwell.

Marcus, George 1995. "Ethnography In/Of the World System: The Emergence of Multi-Sited Ethnography." *Annual Review of Anthropology* 24:95–117.

Marcus, George and Michael Fischer 1986. *Anthropology as Cultural Critique: An Experimental Moment in the Human Sciences*. Chicago, IL: University of Chicago Press.

Marstine, Janet. 2006. "Introduction." In *The New Museum Theory*, edited by Janet Marstine, 1–36. Oxford: Blackwell.

Marstine, Janet. 2011. "The Contingent Nature of the New Museum Ethics." In *Routledge Companion to Museum Ethics*, edited by Janet Marstine, 1–12. London and New York: Routledge.

Mason, Rhiannon. 2013. "National Museums, Globalization, and Postnationalism: Imagining a Cosmopolitan Museology." *Museum Worlds* 1:40–64.

Matar, Hayfa. 2015. "Museums as Signifiers in the Gulf." In *Cities, Museums and Soft Power*, edited by Gail Dexter Lord and Ngaire Blankenberg, 87–98. Washington, DC: American Alliance of Museums.

McCarthy, Conal. 2011. *Museums and Maori*. Wellington: Ta Papa Press.

McCarthy, Conal. 2015. "Introduction: Grounding Museum Studies." In *Museum Practice*, edited by Conal McCarthy, xxxiii–lii. Oxford: Wiley Blackwell.

McCarthy, Conal. 2019. "Indigenisation: Reconceptualising Museology." In *The Contemporary Museum. Shaping Museums for the Global Now*, edited by Simon Knell, 37–54. London and New York: Routledge.

Mead, Sidney M. 1983. "Indigenous Models of Museums in Oceania." *Museum International* 35(139):98–101.

Memmi, Albert. 1965. *The Colonizer and the Colonized*. Boston: Beacon Press.

Message, Kylie. 2014. *Museums and Social Activism. Engaged Protest, Museum Meanings*. London and New York: Routledge.

Meyers, Fred, ed. 2001. *Empire of Things. Regimes of Value and Material Culture*. Santa Fe, NM: School of American Research.

Mithlo, Nancy. 2004. "'Red Man's Burden': The Politics of Inclusion in Museum Settings." *American Indian Quarterly* 28(3&4):743–763.

Morphy, Howard. 2015. "Open Access Versus the Culture of Protocols." In *Museums as Process. Translating Local and Global Knowledges*, edited by Raymond A. Silverman, 90–104. London and New York: Routledge.

Nader, Laura. 1969. "Up the Anthropology—Perspectives Gained from Studying Up." In *Reinventing Anthropology*, edited by Dell Hymes, 284–311. New York: Random House.

Nicks, Trudy. 2003. "Museums and Contact Work: Introduction." In *Museums and Sources Communities*, edited by L. Peers and A. Brown, 19–27. London and New York: Routledge.

Onciul, Bryony. 2013. "Community Engagement, Curatorial Practice, and Museum Ethos." In *Museums and Communities. Curators, Collections and Collaboration*, edited by Viv Golding and Wayne Modest, 79–97. London: Bloomsbury.

Onciul, Bryony. 2015. *Museums, Heritage, and Indigenous Voice: Decolonising Engagement*. London: Routledge.

O'Neill, Mark. 2011. "Religion and Cultural Policy: Two Museum Case Studies." *International Journal of Cultural Policy* 17(2):225–243.

Paine, Crispin. 2013. *Religious Objects in Museums: Private Lives and Public Duties*. London: Bloomsbury.

Parezo, Nancy. 2015. "Museums: Sites for Producing Anthropology that Matters." *Practicing Anthropology* 37(3):10–13.

Peers, Laura and Alison Brown, ed. 2003. *Museums and Source Communities*. New York and London: Routledge.

Phillips, Ruth B. 2005. "Re-Placing Objects: Historical Practices for the Second Museum Age." *The Canadian Historical Review* 86(1):83–110.

Phillips, Ruth B. 2011. *Museum Pieces. Toward the Indigenization of Canadian Museums.* Montreal: McGill-Queen's University Press.

Rosoff, Nancy. 1998. "Integrating Native Views into Museum Procedures: Hope and Practice at the National Museum of the American Indian." *Museum Anthropology* 22 (1):33–42.

Rowlands, Michael. 2006. "Presentation and Politics. Introduction." In *Handbook of Material Culture*, edited by Chris Tilley, Webb Keane, Susanne Kuchler, Mike Rowlands, and Patricia Spyer, 443–445. London and Thousand Oaks, California.

Sabloff, Jeremy. 2011. "Where Have You Gone, Margaret Mead? Anthropology and Public Intellectuals." *American Anthropologist* 113(3):408–416.

Sanjek, Roger. 2015. "Introduction. Deep Grooves: Anthropology and Mutuality." In *Mutuality. Anthropology's Changing Terms of Engagement*, edited by Roger Sanjek, 1–7. Philadelphia, PA: University of Philadelphia Press.

Schildkrout, Enid. 1991. "Editorial Statement: On Becoming a Journal." *Museum Anthropology* 15(2):5–6.

Schorch, Philipp, Conal McCarthy, Eveline Dürr. 2019. "Introduction: Conceptualizing Curatopia." In *Curatopia. Museums and the Future of Curatorship*, edited by Philipp Schorch and Conal McCarthy, 1–16. Manchester: Manchester University Press.

Schorch, Philipp, Conal McCarthy, and Arapati Hakiwai. 2016. "Globalizing Maori Museology: Reconceptualizing Engagement, Knowledge, and Vitality through Mana Taonga." *Museum Anthropology* 39(1):48–69.

Schultz, Lainie. 2011. "Collaborative Museology and the Visitor." *Museum Anthropology* 34 (1):1–13.

Shannon, Jennifer. 2009. "The Construction of Native Voice at the National Museum of the American Indian." In *Contesting Knowledge. Museums and Indigenous Perspectives*, edited by Susan Sleeper-Smith, 218–247. Lincoln, NE: University of Nebraska Press.

Shannon, Jennifer. 2014. *Our Lives: Collaboration, Native Voice, and the Making of the National Museum of the American Indian.* Santa Fe School for Advanced Research.

Shannon, Jennifer. 2017. "Collections Care Informed by Native American Perspectives." *Collections: A Journal for Museum and Archives Professionals* 13(3/4):205–224.

Shelton, Anthony. 2001. "Unsettling the Meaning. Critical Museology, Art and Anthropological Discourse." In *Academic Anthropology and the Museum. Back to the Future*, edited by Mary Bouquet, 142–161. New York and Oxford: Berghahn Books.

Shelton, Anthony. 2006a. "Museums and Anthropologies: Practices and Narratives." In *A Companion to Museum Studies*, edited by Sharon Macdonald, 64–80. Oxford: Wiley-Blackwell.

Shelton, Anthony. 2006b. "Museums and Museum Displays." In *Handbook of Material Culture*, edited by Chris Tilley, Webb Keane, Susanne Kuchler, Mike Rowlands, and Patricia Spyer, 480–499. London and Thousand Oaks, California: Sage Publications.

Shelton, Anthony. 2013. "Critical Museology: A Manifesto." *Museum Worlds* 1:7–23.

Silverman, Raymond A., ed. 2015. *Museums as Process: Translating Local and Global Knowledges.* London and New York: Routledge.

Simpson, Moira. 1996. *Making Representations: Museums in the Post-Colonial Era.* London and New York: Routledge.

Simpson, Moira. 2006. "Revealing and Concealing: Museums, Objects, and the Transmission of Knowledge in Aboriginal Australia." In *New Museum Practice and Theory*, edited by Janet Marstine, 153–177. Oxford: Blackwell Publishing.

Sleeper-Smith, Susan. 2009. *Contesting Knowledge: Museums and Indigenous Perspectives.* Lincoln: University of Nebraska Press.

Smith, Laurajane and Natsuko Akagawa, ed. 2009. *Intangible Heritage.* London and New York: Routledge.

Smith, Linda Tuhiwai. 2012. *Decolonizing Methodologies. Research and Indigenous Peoples.* Second ed. London and New York: Zed Books.

Stanley, Nick. 1998. *Being Ourselves for You: The Global Display of Cultures.* London: Middlesex University Press.

Stanley, Nick, ed. 2007. *The Future of Indigenous Museums.* New York and Oxford: Berghahn Books.

Stefano, Michelle and Peter Davis, eds. 2017. *The Routledge Companion to Intangible Cultural Heritage.* London and New York: Routledge.

Stefano, Michelle, Peter Davis, and Gerard Corsane, ed. 2012. *Safeguarding Intangible Cultural Heritage, Heritage Matters.* Woodbridge: The Boydell Press.

Stocking, George. 1985. "Essays on Museums and Material Culture." In *Objects and Others: Essays on Museums and Material Culture,* edited by George Stocking, 3–14. Madison: University of Wisconsin Press.

Sullivan, Bruce. 2015. *Sacred Objects in Secular Spaces. Exhibiting Asian Religions in Museums.* London: Bloomsbury.

Sullivan, Lawrence and Alison Edwards, ed. 2004. *Harvard. Stewards of the Sacred.* Harvard: American Association of Museums and Center for the Study of World Religions.

Sully, Dean, ed. 2008. *Decolonising Conservation: Caring for Maori Meeting Houses Outside New Zealand.* Walnut Creek, CA: Left Coast Press.

Swan, Daniel. 2015. "A Museum Anthropologist in Academic Practice." *Practicing Anthropology* 37(3):65.

Tapsell, Paul. 2015. "Ko Tawa: Where are the Glass Cabinets?" In *Museums as Process: Translating Local and Global Knowledges,* edited by Raymond A. Silverman, 262–278. London and New York: Routledge.

Taylor, Charles. 1992. "The Politics of Recognition." In *Multiculturalism: The Politics of Recognition,* edited by Amy Gutman, 25–74. Princeton, NJ: Princeton University Press.

Thomas, Nicholas. 1991. *Entangled Objects: Exchange, Material Culture, and Colonialism in the Pacific.* Cambridge, MA: Harvard University Press.

Tilley, Chris, Webb Keane, Susanne Kuchler, Mike Rowlands, and Patricia Spyer. 2006. "Introduction." In *Handbook of Material Culture,* edited by Chris Tilley, Webb Keane, Susanne Kuchler, Mike Rowlands, and Patricia Spyer, 1–6. London and Thousand Oaks, California.

Trope, J. and W. Echo-Hawk. 2000. "The Native American Graves Protection and Repatriation Act." In *The Repatriation Reader: Who Owns Native American Remains?,* edited by D. Mihesuah, 123–168. Lincoln and London: University of Nebraska Press.

Varutti, Marzia. 2012. "Towards Social Inclusion in Taiwan: Museums, Equality and Indigenous Groups." In *Museums, Equality, and Social Justice,* edited by Richard Sandell and Eithne Nightingale, 243–253. London and New York: Routledge.

Vergo, Peter. 1989. *The New Museology.* London: Reaktion Books.

Wali, Alaka. 2006. "The Spiral Path: Toward an Integrated Life." *NEPA Bulletin* 26:209–222.

Wali, Alaka. 2015a. "Listening with Passion: A Journey through Engagement and Exchange." In *Mutuality: Anthropology's Changing Terms of Engagement,* edited by Roger Sanjek, 174–190. Philadelphia: University of Pennsylvania Press.

Wali, Alaka. 2015b. "Centering Culture in Museum Work/Centering the Museum in Culture Work." *Practicing Anthropology* 37(3):24–25.

Wali, Alaka and Madline Tudor. 2015. "Crossing the Line: Participatory Action Research in a Museum Setting." In *Public Anthropology in a Borderless World,* edited by Sam Beck and Carl A. Maida, 66–88. New York and Oxford: Berghahn.

Weil, Stephen. 1990. *Rethinking the Museum and Other Meditations.* Washington, DC: Smithsonian Institution Press.

Wintle, Claire. 2016. "Decolonizing the Smithsonian: Museums as Microcosms of Political Encounter." *American Historical Review* 121(5):1492–1520.

Zauzmer, Julie. 2016. "Acts of Faith: The Smithsonian Now Has Its First Religion Curator Since the 1890s." *Washington Post.* Accessed 2 October 2018. www.washingtonpost.com/news/acts-of-faith/wp/2016/.

3

MUSEUM AND APPLIED ANTHROPOLOGY

Shared Histories and Trajectories

Museum and applied anthropology are usually considered two separate subfields in American anthropology each with their own areas of specialization, professional organizations, journals, and conferences. But over their lifetimes they also have shared much in common. Most notable is their practical application and dedication to speaking to audiences and serving constituencies beyond the academy. In short, they have been dedicated to making anthropology useful, and to fulfilling the discipline's fundamental mission to produce and disseminate knowledge "on the nature and lifeways of people worldwide, and to understand the human condition in broader comparative, perspective" (Beck and Maida 2015, 1).

Although museum anthropology now encompasses a far wider range of work than in the past, historically it has involved making, caring for, and managing collections, research, and communicating anthropological knowledge and insights about the world's peoples to the public through exhibitions, programming, publications, and a variety of other media. Applied anthropology, simply put, has been devoted to using anthropological research methods and theories to understand and help solve humanity's problems. Today many museum anthropologists view their work as a form of applied anthropology, and see the two fields as converging around the common cause of engagement (Carattini 2015, Nash, Colwell-Chanthaphonh, and Holen 2011, Wali 2015).

Museum and applied anthropology also overlap in their origins and historical trajectories. The discipline of anthropology started out in the nineteenth century partly as an applied field based in museums. But in time, as anthropology became ensconced in universities and more academically oriented, specialized, and fragmented, museum and applied anthropology evolved into their own subfields. By the mid-twentieth century, both had also receded to the margins of academic, university-based anthropology partly due to their applied and public orientations.

As will be shown in this chapter, the two also have shared a history of criticism and the development of critical practice, or in other words, practice that is both self-reflexive and provides critical perspectives on society (Ames 1992, Beck and Maida 2015, Comaroff 2010, Handler 2005, Marcus and Fischer 1986).

In this chapter, I look at the changing status of museum and applied anthropology within academic anthropology by charting their origins and historical trajectories. One of my aims is to illuminate how the fields and publicly engaged work at various times and places have been "dominant, residual, and emergent" (Williams 1977, 121) within American anthropology. I highlight how the fields not only share a history of criticism, but also how many of the criticisms of museum anthropology have been the same as those directed toward applied anthropology. I suggest that criticism, both external and internal to the fields, has contributed to their on-going transformation and re-emergence as exemplary models of engaged research, scholarship, and practice.

As stated in the introductory chapter, genealogical histories of a field are instructive for illuminating "what from the past defines us now" (Clifford 2013, 34). Genealogical histories are also powerful tools for making the invisible visible, surfacing assumptions, identifying contradictions, and improving possible critical practice (Beck and Maida 2015, 2). Following Hannerz's recommendation, I look into the "nooks and crannies" (Hannerz 2010, 138) of history and shine light on that which has been overlooked, ignored, forgotten, or dismissed. My purpose is not to provide a comprehensive and detailed historical account of museum and applied anthropology. Instead, it is to consider certain movements and tendencies and "outline a general process and speculate about the implications of that process" (Ames 1992, 15). In so doing, I am concerned with processes of continuity *in* change as much as with moments of "crisis and critique" (Comaroff 2010, Hannerz 2010).

Museum Anthropology: A History of Continuity *in* Change

Perhaps more than any other anthropological subfield the past has inordinately shaped and defined museum anthropology. This is largely because the objects in anthropology museums are objects of "Others" (Stocking 1985). They stand as physical reminders of the field's history of "othering," its colonial roots, and the Eurocentric ideologies on which museums were founded. For this reason, Stocking contends in the introduction to *Objects and Others: Essays on Museums and Material Culture*, that "it is hard to locate the historical moment when the situation of anthropology within the institutional 'homeland' of the museum was not intensely problematic" (1985, 8).

Objects and Others is now seen as a seminal text in postcolonial, critical museum anthropology. But some 25 years prior to this publication, H. H. Frese, a Dutch museum anthropologist, emphasized the "ambivalent nature of anthropology museums" in his 1960 book *Anthropology and the Public: The Role of Museums.*

Fundamentally, the anthropology museums are western institutions, employing scientific means of interpretation and explanation developed in western society, and serving a western public. The non-western cultural heritage, which they dutifully store, is made subservient to such use. At the same time, however, the museums, as well as anthropology itself, are bound to store and preserve artefacts and related documents which in themselves, though being in the possession of western institutions, originated in other cultures. For this reason the anthropology museums are the virtual outposts of a non-western world within western culture and society ... In brief, they are a meeting place for different cultural traditions.

(1960, 97)

The incongruities of anthropology museums as "self-appointed keepers" of world cultural heritage with dual obligations to those who count as "the public" and those who count as "other peoples" (Bouquet 2012, 90) have haunted museum anthropology from its beginnings.

Besides this fundamental dilemma, critical debates on the role of anthropology in museums and the purposes and interests it should serve have long been integral to the field and date back to the late 1800s. One example is the classic debate between Franz Boas and Otis T. Mason (published in *Science* in 1887) over the arrangement of collections in exhibits and their interpretation at the American Museum of Natural History (Jacknis 1985, 77–83).

Freed contends that early criticism was mainly self-criticism and was chiefly concerned with how scientific theory would be reflected in exhibits (1991, 60). Symptomatic of growing anxieties around the changing status of museum anthropology within anthropology, a number of papers appeared in the 1950s and 1960s in which authors reflected on the historical development of the field and assessed its present state and possible futures. As Sturtevant emphasized in his often cited paper "Does Anthropology Need Museums?" published in 1969: "During the last 15 years, North American anthropologists have published at least 10 papers deploring the situation of museum anthropology" (1969, 625).

Yet in reading the literature on the history of museum anthropology produced over the last few decades one gets the impression that critical reflection on the field's problematic nature and failings is relatively new, emerging only in the 1980s. What's more, much of the literature depicts museum anthropology as moribund from the time of its "Golden Age" (Sturtevant 1969, 625) at the turn of the twentieth century until it was "rediscovered" by academic anthropologists and other scholars toward the end of the twentieth (Bouquet 2012, Jones 1993, Phillips 2011, Redman 2011). Many have recounted how the museum played a central role in anthropology's early development. But by the mid-twentieth century, anthropology in museums had begun to diminish in importance as anthropology moved into its complementary but eventually dominant institutional setting, the university (Stocking 1985, 8). From this moment forward, museum anthropology is said to have entered a "period of neglect" (Bouquet 2001, 1), and did not re-surface until "museums became the subject of academic scrutiny rather suddenly during the 1990s, as evidenced by the tremendous growth of the small, existing literature on museums" (Phillips 2011, 18).

This burgeoning literature covered academic debates surrounding museum practices, for example on several highly controversial exhibits and closely related topics like the nature of ethnographic authority and the politics of cultural representation; the ethical responsibilities of anthropologists and museums; and the epistemological status of analytical categories such as art, text, and culture (Jones 1993, 201). Alternately labeled "poststructuralist," "deconstructionist," "postmodern," and "postcolonial," these critiques as well as the "crisis in representation" in anthropology in general, are credited with igniting renewed interest in museums. Coupled with activism on the part of Indigenous and other communities, this criticism contributed to an unprecedented theorizing of museums as well as a radical transformation of practice.

These late twentieth-century intellectual and political developments clearly had a profound impact on museum anthropology, giving rise to a "new" museum anthropology (as discussed in Chapters 1 and 2). Nevertheless, the "new" museum anthropology did not replace the "old" or completely reinvent it since traces of the old are always embedded in the new. I argue that an emphasis on this more recent moment in the field's history elides movements and tendencies during its "period of neglect" (Bouquet 2012). Rather than a history marked by stasis and rupture I suggest one characterized by continuity in change and relatively constant criticism both internal and external (cf Marstine 2006, 21–22). This perspective does not render the critiques and developments of the 1980s and 1990s less important or influential. On the contrary, this period was marked by many watershed events that have had deep and lasting effects due to the ways in which they challenged the power and authority of museums and anthropological epistemology. Instead, my aim is to add a layer of complexity and nuance to what have become self-perpetuating narratives by emphasizing how the critiques and developments of the 1980s and 1990s added new energy and momentum to many of those that came before.

A number of anthropologists have scrutinized how the tendency to focus on moments of rupture and radical change in anthropology, such as the crisis of representation of the 1980s, has obscured how these movements are the culmination of long-term trends.[1] They have also pointed out how this tendency can lead to a misrepresentation of the field's history. Following White, I maintain that "In order to understand the legacy of any paradigm shift in scientific discourse we have to explore the play between continuity and rupture … and how the need to break with the past can lead to erasure or distortion" (2012, 72–73).

Accordingly, in the following historical sketch of American museum anthropology I consider how recent paradigmatic shifts in the field are the outcome of a long-standing tendency toward critical reflection and reform. I attempt to show how criticism has not only been fairly constant in museum anthropology over its lifetime, but also how the nature of criticism has shifted over the decades in terms of areas of concern and sources. An additional aim is to illuminate how many contemporary movements such as public engagement and collaboration with source communities have deeper roots than often presumed, underscoring Kratz and Karp's observation that "we tend far too easily to forget that the goals of the past also can serve the needs of the present" (2006, 5).

The Shifting Status of Anthropology in Museums

Museums are often cited as the "institutional homelands" of anthropology (Ames 1992, Lurie 1981), even though anthropology is also said to have grown out of learned societies and universities in the mid-1800s (Bouquet 2012, Shelton 2006, Stocking 1985). Historical accounts of American museum anthropology frequently begin with what Sturtevant called the "Museum Period," the 1840s to 1890s, of anthropology (1969, 622).[2] During this formative period, museums served as a primary center of teaching and research, and heavily influenced the direction of the discipline (Collier and Tschopik 1954, Frese 1960, Sturtevant 1969, 622–623). It was around this time that the great ethnographic, archaeological, and paleontological collections of America were being assembled and housed in newly established museums—the Smithsonian National Museum in 1846; the Peabody Museum of Archaeology and Ethnology at Harvard in 1866; New York's American Museum of Natural History and the Chicago Museum of Natural History in 1893. Collections were amassed in the course of scientific expeditions and fieldwork; as byproducts of world fairs and expositions; through purchases and trading; and donations from private collectors (Cole 1985, Collier and Tschopik 1954, Lonetree 2012, Jenkins 1994, Stocking 1985).

The collection and study of Native American material culture during the late nineteenth century was driven by the impulse of "salvage ethnography," or "a feeling among American anthropologists that the aboriginal cultures of the New World should be studied immediately before the native way of life vanished forever" (Collier and Tschopik 1954, 770). At the time, Native cultures were experiencing rapid change as a consequence of the disintegrative impact of Euro-American expansion, colonialism, and domination. Anthropologists, many working for the United States government's Bureau of American Ethnology (BAE) founded in 1879 and recently established museums, spread out across the continent to document seemingly disappearing ways of life. The work of salvage ethnographers fed museum collections and archives. It was in these institutions rather than in their originating communities where Native American cultural materials could be preserved for the sake of scientific research (Stocking 1985, 114), and for publicly displaying the "vanishing" cultures of Native Americans (Cooper 2008, Lonetree 2012).

The amassing of objects, or examples of material culture, was central to anthropological research at a time when "knowledge itself was thought of as embodied in objects" (Stocking 1985, 114). But in addition to material culture, anthropological research also involved documenting aspects of intangible culture, such as language and oral traditions; religious beliefs, rituals, and ceremonies; and systems of kinship and social organization (Lamphere 1993, 160). It was a time of near feverish "gathering up of culture," and the quest to survey and map the Native peoples of the continent became a defining trait of American anthropology (Darnell 1998). In short: "The history of anthropology in America is largely a history of the encounters of scientists, explorers, and traders among Native American communities" (Mithlo 2004, 748).

Salvage ethnography was grounded in the ideology of inevitability and collecting of this era rested on the belief that "it was necessary to use the time to collect before it was too late" (Cole 1985, 50). Salvage ethnography, or what Clifford has referred to as the "salvage paradigm" (Clifford 1987, 121), epitomized the paradox of cultural preservation. Although it is true that much Native American material culture may have been lost without these preservation efforts, it is also true that they undermined the perpetuation of many aspects of living culture. As Nash, Colwell-Chanthaphonh, and Holen put it:

> With Native Americans threatened from every quarter, early museum anthropologists indeed were able to save many objects that otherwise would have been lost to time … [But] this progress came at a steep price. Often the goal of cultural preservation contradictorily led, in fact, to the destruction of native traditions and the rupture of communities. In the name of science, vast numbers of objects were taken without regard for their spiritual and cultural contexts.
>
> *(2011, 138)*

At the Zuni Pueblo alone between 1879 and 1885 some 12,609 objects were collected for the Smithsonian from a community with fewer than 2000 individuals (Mithlo 2004, 748). Although some Native individuals willingly participated in the trade or sold items under conditions of severe economic distress, there also was resistance to this plundering. Colwell reports how the Zuni, despite their desperate economic circumstances, were especially reluctant to part with sacred and ceremonial objects (2017, 17). Native communities were particularly aggrieved by the desecration of burials and the removal of human remains and "grave goods." Some sought the return of their ancestors' bodies through legal channels. For example, the Cowichan of British Columbia hired a lawyer to press claims against Franz Boas and his accomplices for "grave robbing" (Mithlo 2004, 748, Cole 1985, 191–121). While mostly known for his ethnological work Boas was also interested in physical anthropology early in his career. He amassed a collection of several hundred skeletal remains, mostly from the Northwest Coast, which he eventually sold to various museums and universities (Cole 1985, 119–121).

Stocking writes that anthropology's "object orientation" fit a "discipline organized around the principle of change in time, and devoted primarily to groups that had left no written records" (1985, 114). Working within an evolutionist framework and the paradigm of natural history,[3] anthropological research was driven by a logic that the study of physical remains, archaeological finds, and contemporary material culture was "the most ready means of graphically illustrating the development of mankind" (Stocking 1985, 114). Museum collections furnished evidence for establishing taxonomies of the world's diverse peoples, and how they fit into linear models of cultural evolution—ranging from the "simple" to the "complex" and from the "primitive" to the "civilized." In the expansive phase of Western colonialism, evolutionism in anthropology was both a reflection of and justification for the subjugation of the "savage," "barbarian," and "uncivilized" regions of the world (Stocking 1991, 4). Evolutionism produced taxonomies of racial and culture "types," which later served as the foundation for the development of the "culture area" concept—a central organizing principle for the arrangement of artifacts in museum displays (Bennett et al. 2017, Fenton 1960, Parezo and Hardin 1993, 272).

Boas strongly opposed the evolutionist practice of regarding all cultures as the manifestation of human culture at large in various stages of development. He stressed the need for detailed research through fieldwork on individual cultures, and opposed the typological arrangement and display of objects according to form and function, inspired by the evolutionary framework. Instead, Boas emphasized the need to consider historical and geographical factors for a deeper understanding of a particular culture, as well as cultural processes. He argued that the meaning of an ethnological specimen could not be comprehended "outside of its surroundings, outside of other inventions of the people to whom it belongs, and outside other phenomena affecting that people and its productions" (Boas 1887 quoted in Jacknis 1985, 79). Boas suggested a "tribal arrangement of collections" and what came to be known as the "life group" mode of display, which accentuated the local and contextual meanings and functions of objects (Jacknis 1985, 97).

The formal teaching of anthropology in universities began in the 1880s and 1890s, and it was common for anthropology departments to grow out of or in conjunction with university or large natural history museums (Parezo and Hardin 1993, 272). Museums and universities continued to be complementary institutions into the early decades of the twentieth century, even though according to Sturtevant, "nearly all the jobs were in museums, and most of the teaching was done by anthropologists who also held museum appointments" (1969, 623–624). Financial support for research was likewise mostly channeled through museums, and universities provided little money for anthropological research (Sturtevant 1969, 624). Museum curators formed the core of many university teaching staffs, and most of the "founding fathers" of American anthropology were "museum men" or "former museum men" (Collier and Tschopik 1954, Fenton 1960). Boas, for example, held a joint appointment in the American Museum of Natural History and at Columbia University in New York from 1895 to 1905 (Sturtevant 1969, 624).

By the beginning of the 1930s, anthropology had begun to move its base from museums to universities, which then became the foremost training ground for new generations of anthropologists (Sturtevant 1969, 624, Fenton 1960, 4). Except for archaeologists and physical anthropologists, interest in material culture studies and the use of collections for research started to wane with the shift toward a more behaviorally oriented anthropology. In an article published in 1954, Collier and Tschopik state that by the 1940s and 1950s "most social and cultural anthropologists have become less and less concerned with historical problems and descriptive ethnography, and have generally speaking lost interest in material culture and technology, the traditional and most fruitful stock-in-trade of museums" (1954, 772–773).

Since museum anthropologists were exerting little influence on current trends in anthropological theory they were not attracting many students to museum work. This development, in the words of Collier and Tschopik, "is evidenced by the number of graduate students and recent PhDs who think of museums as intellectually low grade, if they think of them at all ... [and] the opinion of some university anthropologists that museums have nothing to offer their students" (1954, 775).

As anthropology's retreat from museums progressed, it became more and more common for anthropologists to begin their careers in museums and then move to other institutions, such as research centers, universities, and government agencies (Sturtevant 1969). Museums increasingly came to be seen as places of employment for anthropologists who could not "make it" in the university. Universities, not museums, were thought to be where major intellectual breakthroughs were made and new knowledge generated (Parezo and Hardin 1993, 272–273).

Many women anthropologists found employment in museums at a time when positions in universities were still reserved for men. According to Parezo and Hardin, women were welcomed into museums because they were perceived as being naturally suited to caring for and studying objects. "Once inside the museum, women found open to them those aspects of museum work that emphasized their nurturing and handmaidenly role in society" (1993, 277).[4] Women worked primarily with collections because caring for objects (cleaning, cataloging, and preparing them for storage) was akin to "housekeeping." Secretarial work and education were other areas of museum work open to women since these too were seen as traditionally female occupations. Outside of a few exceptions, women were largely relegated to supportive roles while men occupied the more prestigious positions of director and curator that involved research and university-level teaching.[5] This did not mean, however, that women were not making significant scientific contributions to the field during these early years. On the contrary, besides other duties, many conducted field research and published their findings in scholarly journals in addition to producing anthropological literature for the general public (Leckie and Parezo 2008, Parezo and Hardin 1993).

The contributions of women museum anthropologists are not mentioned in most early reviews of the field, which were predominantly authored by men.[6] Native American anthropologists are also largely absent despite the roles they played in shaping American museum anthropology as curators, administrators, and scholars, not just objects of study. One example is the Seneca archaeologist Arthur C. Parker who was born and raised on the Cattaraugus Reservation in New York. According to JoAllyn Archambault (Standing Rock Sioux, Director of the

American Indian Program at the Smithsonian National Museum of Natural History), Parker was one of the first American Indian museum professionals on record in addition to being the first president of the Society for American Archaeology. He began working as a volunteer at the American Museum of Natural History in 1898 and in 1906 was appointed the first state archaeologist of New York, a position based in the New York State Museum. Parker later became Director of the Rochester Museum of Arts and Sciences in 1925. Over his career he published many books and articles on Iroquois archaeology and ethnology, "firmly establishing himself as a major figure in museum anthropology and exhibition" (Archambault 2011, 16).[7]

Parker also was very much a "public anthropologist." He distributed educational materials to local schools; wrote educational scripts for public radio shows; placed temporary exhibits in public buildings; sponsored amateur hobby shows, with one in 1935 pulling in 100,000 people over a period of just six days; and formed the Seneca Arts Projects, which at the height of the depression employed 100 Seneca artists (Nash et al. 2011, 135).

Museum Anthropology and the Public

From the time of their founding, educating the public about the world's peoples and their diverse ways of life was one of the primary functions of anthropology museums and a justification for their existence (Conn 2010, Ewers 1955, Frese 1960, Wissler 1942). Nevertheless, the form and content of public education as well as how much attention it deserved was a topic of ongoing assessment.

Collier and Tschopik maintained that public education in the form of popular lectures, publications, and exhibits were an essential component of a museum anthropologist's work. They stated that exhibits were especially important because they were a museum's "basic and unique form of communication for transmitting anthropological knowledge and concepts to the public" (1954, 777). Nonetheless, they admitted that "the majority of exhibits are out of date in terms of present theoretical positions in anthropology, in terms of educational effectiveness for either students or the public, and in terms of the role that anthropology would like to play in the present world crisis" (1954, 774). The authors made specific recommendations on how to upgrade out-of-date exhibits and improve their effectiveness for teaching anthropological concepts to students and the general public. They asserted that exhibits should be kept up to date not only in reference to anthropological advancements, but also regarding contemporary issues. Moreover, they emphasized that exhibits should be made understandable to the public, echoing the arguments of Boas and other early museum anthropologists (Wissler 1942, Ewers 1955). Moreover, they recommended that systematic studies be made on the public's reaction to exhibits as well as on the anthropological museum as a medium of mass communication (1954, 776).

Actually, at the time of Collier and Tschopik's writing, the evaluation of exhibitions and visitors' responses to them was becoming a common practice in some museums. John C. Ewers, a curator at the United States National Museum (later the Smithsonian National Museum of Natural History), in an article published in *American Anthropologist* in 1955, wrote about a trend in many large, public natural history museums to redesign their exhibits to "render them more instructive and more entertaining to the millions of school children and casual visitors who comprise the very great majority of viewers of their exhibits" (Ewers 1955, 1).

In his article titled "Problems and Procedures in Modernizing Ethnological Exhibits," Ewers described the components of a "Critical Survey of Existing Exhibits" that was conducted by the Department of Anthropology to ascertain what remedial measures needed to be taken to improve their educational effectiveness and entertainment value. Ewers related that after World War II, museum administrators, "aware of their responsibility to the public," encouraged members of their scientific staff to "become more exhibit conscious and to devote time and thought to exhibit planning as well as research" (1955, 2). The survey indicated that many of the existing exhibits had been designed for specialists in the field rather than with the interests and aptitudes of the majority of visitors in mind. Ewers asserted that "clearly, the locus of our interest in planning exhibits should be the museum visitor" (1955, 5), foretelling the contemporary focus on visitor studies and audience research.

The attention given to public education, the visitor, and a concern for contemporary relevance during the 1940s and 1950s, can now be seen as an example of early publicly engaged practice. But it was also a contributing factor to what Collier and Tschopik labeled the "schizophrenic role of the museum anthropologist" (1954, 773) and what Fenton called the "curator's dilemma" (1960, 335).

The curator's dilemma, as discussed in the previous chapter, is an on-going tension and rests on the museum anthropologist's dual obligations to personal research and collections, and to "the museum's recognized obligation to educate the public" (Collier and Tschopik 1954, 772). In contrast to anthropologists working in universities, the authors stated that museum anthropologists usually pursued research in addition to or "in spite of" other museum activities.

> At best this schizophrenic role of the museum anthropologist is a difficult one to maintain, and at worst there is a tendency to slight curatorial duties by those curators who are concerned more with their professional standing as anthropologists than with the effectiveness of their museum work ... There results the paradox that the better a man is as an anthropologist in terms of current value judgements of the profession, the poorer he is likely to be in performing curatorial duties and in contributing to a more vital museum program.
>
> *(1954, 773)*

The curator's dilemma has deep roots in American museum anthropology, dating back to Boas's time. In his classic essay "Some Principles of Museum Administration" (1907), Boas discussed the challenges of successfully balancing what to him were the three main functions of large public museums like the

American Museum of Natural History where he worked. Boas argued that "museums may serve three objects ... healthy entertainment ... instruction and ... the promotion of science" (1907, 921). After debating the merits and limitations of each of these "objects," in the end he wrote that "the question arises, in how far the interests of the public and the interests of science can be harmonized?" (1907, 931). Boas resigned from his post at the museum in 1905 largely owing to these and other conflicts, and particularly those related to approaches to cultural representation (Jacknis 1985, Jenkins 1994).

Boas used the essay to illuminate what he saw as "the limitations of the museum method of anthropology" (Jacknis 1985) in conveying the complexities and the non-material dimensions of a people's culture:

> An assemblage of material such as is found in anthropological collections consists entirely of things made by the various peoples of the world—their tools, household utensils, their ceremonial objects, etc. All of these are used in the daily life of the people, and almost all of them receive their significance only through the thoughts that cluster around them ... It even happens frequently in anthropological collections that a vast field of thought may be expressed by a single object or by no object whatsoever, because that particular aspect of life may consist of ideas only; for instance, if one tribe uses a great many objects in its religious worship, while among another, practically no material objects of worship are used, the religious life of these tribes, which might be equally rigorous, appears quite out of its true proportions in the museum collections.
>
> *(1907, 928)*

Nonetheless, Boas believed that exhibits could make important scientific points and warned against under-valuing popular entertainment as part of the museum's mission to serve the public. The essay is still relevant because in it Boas discusses subjects that continue to be debated to this day, including the proper scope of museums; reactions of visitors to exhibitions; the use and value of collections to research and exhibitions; and the appropriateness of exhibiting non-European cultures alongside animals, plants, and dinosaurs in museums of natural history (Nash et al. 2011, Stocking 1985, Sturtevant 1969).

Regardless of the curator's dilemma and the changing conditions of their field, Collier and Tschopik and others remained optimistic about the role of museums in anthropology. In the concluding section of their article, they suggested measures for strengthening and revitalizing the field. These included supporting both established and new lines of research they believed were important to current and future anthropological theory. For example, they argued that collecting was still necessary to museum anthropology, and that it was especially important to acquire "acculturated objects" for studies on culture change. "Investigations of contemporary or recent acculturation would enrich our knowledge of culture change generally, and would add much to our understanding of changes in the past" (1954, 776). Such activities, they added, might help counter the prevalent view that material culture is of no use to social anthropologists, and that acculturated objects held no interest for museums. They stressed that many aspects of culture change could be studied through material culture, "yet few modern studies of this nature have been made" (Collier and Tschopik 1954, 776).

Mounting Criticism and Anxiety

In the article "Everyone is Breathing on Our Vitrines: Problems and Prospects of Museum Anthropology," published in 1991, Stanley Freed, a curator of anthropology at the American Museum of Natural History, observed that assessments of the state of museum anthropology and its future in the 1950s remained generally optimistic, and were for the most part constructive. However, he states that reviews of the field not only increased in the 1960s, but became more pessimistic, taking decline of the field for granted (1991, 62). More and more critics were viewing collections as irrelevant to research, and material culture studies as outdated, "non-theoretical, non-progressive, intellectually low grade, and generally to be avoided" (1991, 62). Freed describes how papers evaluating the status of museum anthropology during this period move beyond discussion of specifics related to collections, research, and exhibits to more general questions regarding the relationship between anthropology and museums. Articles began to appear with titles along the lines "Are Museums Necessary? (Washburn 1968) and Sturtevant's previously referenced "Does Anthropology Need Museums?" (1969). Freed states that usually the answer to these questions was in the affirmative, provided that major changes were made in the field (1991, 63).

Sturtevant's historical review focused mainly on research, the use of collections, and the scholarly consequences of anthropology's departure from museums. Although he was disturbed by how "other" anthropologists paid little attention to museum work and that museum jobs no longer carried the prestige they once did, he was mostly concerned by the lack of support for research "on huge and irreplaceable collections." Collections, he pointed out, "represent a large investment over many years of time, thought, and money, but seemingly have very little importance for current anthropological research" (1969, 625). Similar to other authors, Sturtevant provided justifications for why research on material culture was imperative to the science of anthropology, and suggested how to "increase the quantity, quality, and prestige of ethnological research on museum collections" (1969, 637). He emphasized how collections are not only of value to museum ethnology, but also to other areas of anthropology such as archaeology and physical anthropology. Sturtevant decried what he saw as the increasing fragmentation of anthropology, stating that after all "anthropology is fundamentally a single field" (1969, 637).

While Sturtevant made no reference to how collections might be of importance to Native Americans and other originating communities, in this article he too returned to the fundamental problem of positioning anthropology in natural history museums. Reiterating the stance of Boas, he argued that anthropology did not belong in a natural history museum. He declared that:

> In fact, the United States is behind the rest of the world in this respect: except in North America, Australia, and New Zealand, nearly all important anthropological collections are either housed in independent museums of anthropology or of man, or they are joined with collection of history, folklore, prehistory, and Classical archaeology, while natural history collections are separately housed.
>
> *(1969, 642)*[8]

In his concluding remarks, Sturtevant turns his attention to exhibits in American anthropology museums, claiming that they lagged behind those of ethnographic museums in other countries regarding advances in display methods and styles. In keeping with other authors, he was critical of how exhibits did not reflect "the principles of modern anthropology" and were based, for example, on outdated concepts such as the "culture area" approach "elaborated for museum exhibits over 60 years ago" (1969, 644). Even worse, exhibits tended to perpetuate stereotypes of non-Western people, cultivating images of "savages" with "primitive" culture, or presenting romanticized views of exotic tribal people in peculiar attire staged in sentimental settings. Exhibits also frequently appealed to a sense of the macabre, showing mummies, skeletons, and shrunken heads (Borhegyi 1969 cited in Sturtevant 1969, 644). Sturtevant argued that exhibits should not only be brought in line with modern anthropology, but they should also demonstrate how anthropological knowledge can be relevant to understanding "the difficulties of the modern world" (1969, 644).[9]

Given this concern, it is curious that Sturtevant did not acknowledge the work being done during the 1950s and 1960s in his own department and museum connected to post-World War II global social, political, and economic developments, and in particular, the decolonization of Africa and Asia. During that time, the Smithsonian's Museum of Natural History was instrumental in educating the American public about the histories, cultures, and contemporary worlds of people living in the newly independent nations of Asia and Africa. Wintle describes how after World War II the National Museum of Natural History embarked on a major redevelopment program, opening 22 new galleries between 1958 and 1959. The Asia and Africa galleries were reconstructed between 1950 and 1970. Two new curators specializing in Asia and Africa were appointed to oversee these projects. Eugene I. Knez was assigned to Asian collections and Gordon D. Gibson was responsible for African materials. Both Knez and Gibson carried out collecting and research expeditions in preparation for the new installations. The "Cultures of the Pacific and Asia" gallery was inaugurated in June 1962, and the "Cultures of Africa and East Asia" gallery opened in August 1967. According to Wintle, "these galleries would necessarily respond to a world in which many of the countries portrayed were undergoing major political shifts and social and economic changes" (2016, 1496).

Wintle notes how Knez was keen to demonstrate the contemporary, urban, and modernizing nature of many nations and communities across Asia, incorporating these dimensions of life into displays (2016, 1504).[10] He also worked closely with Asian colleagues, scholars, and officials, and followed their advice on how to present and interpret objects on display. For Wintle, his displays bore the mark of "genuine collaboration" long before collaboration became paramount in museum anthropology (2016, 1499). What's more, they counter the entrenched view that "museum displays are assumed to have been divorced from the academic and applied anthropology of the period … In Knez's work, applied anthropology and museum work closely aligned" (2016, 1505).

To some, Knez's applied curatorial work at the Smithsonian could be seen as a form of socially engaged research and practice intended to promote cross-cultural exchange and understanding during a period of heightened international tensions. Indeed, this was one of Knez's stated missions. But to others, it can be characterized as propaganda driven by the ideology behind "Cold War" geopolitics. Wintle points out that Knez's curatorial requirements and exhibit narratives matched, to a certain extent, the political intention of the United States government. And despite his "remarkable postcolonial attitude," his practice "provides an intriguing mirror of the 'imperialism of decolonization'" (2016, 1506). It is worth noting here that Knez came to the Smithsonian with a recent PhD in the anthropology of Korea from the Maxwell School of Citizenship and Public Affairs at Syracuse University. Between 1945 and 1946 he directed the Army's Bureau of Culture in Korea. And from 1949 to 1953 he worked for the federal government first in cultural and public affairs at American embassies in Korea and Japan, and then as chief of branch operations for the United States Information Service in Korea (Wintle 2016, 1506).

Social Relevance and the Politics of Cultural Representation

The Smithsonian case raises questions regarding how socially relevant and engaged practice has been viewed in museum anthropology (and anthropology in general) at various points in time and in different places. Indeed, Beck and Maida note that: "Calls to connect anthropology to real world contexts, conditions, and processes have episodically elicited movements in the discipline's history" (2015, 3). Correspondingly, Freed points out that "ideas about social relevance in museums go back over 100 years," but by the mid-twentieth century they were "picking up steam" and becoming more politically and ideologically driven (1991, 66). He cites several authors who argue that greater attention should be given to social issues as a function of the museum's "liberalizing influence"; and traditional museums that are dedicated only to acquisition, care, and display of objects are "outdated and inadequate." He mentions Margaret Mead as an example of a museum anthropologist who saw social relevance as an important role for museums (1991, 66–67). Freed concedes that "museums should not avoid socially relevant issues if they can contribute to the understanding or resolution of issues and problems and act in good faith" (1991, 67). Yet he warns against museums taking sides on emotionally and politically charged issues, and "abandoning objectivity, however imperfect, for politics" (1991, 67).

As a case in point, Freed references controversies (or in his words "headaches") that arose around the exhibit *The Spirit Sings: Artistic Traditions of Canada's First Peoples* mounted by the Glenbow Museum in conjunction with the 1988 Calgary Winter Olympics. Whereas Freed uses *The Spirit Sings* as a cautionary tale, the exhibit and its ripple effects are now seen as having helped usher in a new era of museum/community relations and postcolonial practice.

Much has been written about *The Spirit Sings*, which brought together over 650 pieces of Canadian Aboriginal art from museums around the world (Ames 1992, Jones 1993, Simpson 1996). According to Phillips, most of the work had been collected during the early years of European contact, and few of the pieces had been exhibited or published. Thus, they were largely unknown to Indigenous people, curators, and scholars. Several years before the exhibit opened, however, it became embroiled in controversy that sent "shock waves" around the international anthropological museum community (Phillips 2011, 49).

The cause of the controversy was an international boycott of the exhibit called by the Lubicon Lake Cree of Alberta. The Lubicon sought to draw attention to an unresolved land-claims dispute with the Province of Alberta. The boycott was sparked by the Glenbow Museum's announcement that Shell Oil (Royal Dutch Petroleum) was to be the main corporate sponsor of the exhibit. During the 1970s, the Lubicon had been forced off their ancestral lands when oil companies began drilling despite the lack of a settled land claim. "The announcement that one of the companies exploiting the oil on their traditional lands was to fund an exhibition celebrating the glories of early contact-period Aboriginal cultures struck the Lubicon strategists as the ultimate hypocrisy" (Phillips 2011, 49).

The exhibit presented the Lubicon with the opportunity to draw international attention to their land claim dispute with the provincial government. In addition to seeking support from the public at large, the Lubicon requested that museums that had been approached to loan objects to the Glenbow deny the request. The exhibit went ahead largely as planned, in spite of support for the boycott among activist groups, academics, Aboriginal organizations, and numerous museums. Nonetheless, it came to be seen as a major turning point in museum and originating community relationships, and to many a major stimulus for the reflexive critique of exhibiting practices in Western museums (Phillips 2011, 48).[11] As Karen Coody Cooper (Cherokee) states in her book *Spirited Encounters: American Indians Protest Museum Policies and Practices*:

> The exhibition was a watershed for North American Indian/museum relationships. Had it not been for the Lubicon boycott which drew worldwide attention and created a call for action to which Canada responded in an enlightening fashion while the world watched, positive changes in policy and practice regarding First Nations (and, quite likely, indigenous people throughout the world) would have been, I believe, slower to come ... No

other exhibition led to the creation of a task force ... caused active debate within museums ... attracted support from so many diverse quarters ... and caused museums to address questions on a variety of fronts including financial sponsorship, equally-shared ethnic participation, and acknowledgement of contemporary issues.

(2008, 27)

Today many museum anthropologists look back on *The Spirit Sings* and other controversial exhibits like *Into the Heart of Africa* (shown at the Royal Ontario Museum in Toronto in 1990 and described in the previous chapter) as constructive case studies. But at the time they provoked critical debates not just among museums and stakeholder communities but also among various camps within museum anthropology, underscoring how the field was not homogenous in its views and responses. As Harrison summed it up:

> The controversies revolved around the issue of museum authority and the right of curators to determine and interpret information in exhibitions. These were issues which challenged the entire discipline of anthropology, but the 'poor sister' of anthropology—museum anthropology—because of its public profile, bore the brunt of the criticism from both the community at large and the academic world ... Some museum professionals rose to the challenge and launched into co-operative and productive discussions with minority peoples ... Others preferred to defend the solid foundations of museums and museum anthropology, and while acknowledging that change is necessary, set fairly rigid parameters for the change that they would be willing to accept.
>
> *(1993, 169)*

Freed acknowledges that criticism has long been a part of museum anthropology and was healthy to the field. Nevertheless, he strikes out against mounting criticism coming from academic anthropologists and other scholars, and in particular those he labels "deconstructionists." Whereas earlier criticism was mostly internal to the field and in the form of "self-criticism," he writes that "today's criticism comes from academia as well and is quite different in approach and tone" (1991, 60). Freed states that this criticism ranges from practical suggestions for improving exhibitions to "retrospective moral judgements of little help in creating an exhibit" (1991, 68). In his opinion, this criticism is "harsher," more "heavy-handed," and "rhetorical" in nature. He asserts that "the chief value of deconstructionist analysis is in calling attention to important and remedial failings, such as the absences of historical components in older ethnographic exhibits." But, in his view, "deconstructionists often pose problems without regard to solutions" (1991, 68).

In his defense of museum anthropology, Freed maintains that museum and academic anthropology are "not separate worlds," and indeed, the "alleged failures of museum anthropology are failings of anthropology generally" (1991, 70). He argues that:

If exhibits decontextualize and recontextualize other cultures, so do classroom lectures, books, and journal articles. And while classroom lectures by academic anthropologists reach a limited number of students … permanent exhibit halls in large museums may take 10 or more years to build and are seen by millions of visitors … Exhibits are an easy mark for critics.

(1991, 70)

Freed calls for greater cooperation between universities and museums for "a richer, more holistic anthropology" (1991, 75). He allows that museum anthropology benefits from criticism, and that the field must be ready for change. Freed cites Ames as an example of a museum anthropologist who "looks at museums with unsparing criticism and sees their limitations but does not despair or let them paralyze him" (1991, 75).

Forgotten Narratives: Museum Anthropology Prior to the 1980s

While the controversies and critical debates of the late 1980s and early 1990s and the radical changes they spawned have come to define contemporary museum anthropology, it is important to point out that the field did not remain static prior to this time. During its so-called "period of neglect" by academic anthropologists, museum anthropologists were conducting research and publishing on their findings, teaching in universities and museums, curating exhibitions and developing public programming. Many museum anthropologists were not just prolific scholars and museum professionals, but were also active in professional organizations and were committed advocates for the field. Surveys and studies on the state of anthropology in museums also continued to be conducted that highlighted both the limitations and potential of anthropology in museums (Lurie 1981, Osgood 1979). There were also institutions that recognized the importance of being up to date and socially relevant, and that presented exhibits that addressed pressing issues of the day.

For instance, *The Urban Habitat: The City and Beyond* opened in 1976 at the Milwaukee Public Museum. The 5000-square-foot exhibit traced the origin and course of urbanism from a 20,000-year-old Paleolithic campsite to projections into the year 2000. According to an announcement that appeared in the *Council for Museum Anthropology Newsletter* in 1976, "The city is used as the focus for understanding the increasing and threatening human impact on the natural environment" (Council for Museum Anthropology Newsletter 1976, 12). Themes covered in the exhibit included accelerating population growth, efforts to obtain resources to keep up with population needs, and expanded and improved techniques to harness energy. As stated in the announcement: "The hall shows how past solutions of problems of population, resources, and energy led, in turn, to new problems requiring new solutions, culminating in the problems and alternatives available in the present." Funding for the exhibit came from a grant from the United States National Endowment for the Humanities, and from private donations.

During the 1960s and 1970s, there are also examples of museums that collaborated with Native communities on exhibits about their history and culture, past and present. Archambault describes several exhibits that took place during this time. She states that none of the non-Indian curators involved in mounting these exhibits "thought they were doing something revolutionary, unprecedented or visionary. Instead, they were being responsible anthropologists making sure the presentation was 'accurate' within the notions of the period" (2011, 17). One example is an exhibit on the Bole Maru religion led by Essie Parrish, the religious leader of the Kashaya Pomo of northern California, that opened in 1962 at the Hearst Museum of Anthropology at the University of California, Berkeley. In Archambault's words:

> The Pomo were presented in this exhibit as contemporary Americans, simultaneously living within an enclosed tribal community with its own traditions and history. Their oppositional history, the loss of their original territory, their persecution by white settlers and their survival was part of the storyline.
>
> *(2011, 18)*

Archambault also discusses how the Denver Museum of Natural History (now the Denver Museum of Nature and Science) formed a Native American Advisory Council (NAAC) in 1973 after the Crane American Indian Collection was donated to the museum (Colwell 2017, Herold 1999, Hill 2000). The Council, a multitribal, Denver-area group, was coordinated by Patty Harjo, of Seneca and Seminole ancestry, who was one of the few Native Americans then employed by an American museum (Colwell 2017, 79). The Council was charged with guiding and consulting on all museum activities that involved Native Americans, including exhibit production. It formalized a partnership with the Denver Indian community, "who wanted the exhibits to display the continuity between their ancestors and themselves with dignity and respect" (Archambault 2011, 18). The Council assisted the museum in planning exhibitions in the new Crane American Indian Hall that opened in 1978, providing museum staff with advice on how to curate the collection in a culturally sensitive manner. Particularly important to the Council was that the exhibits should dispel popular stereotypes of Native peoples, portray continuity with their ancestral past, and the fact that Native people had not become extinct.

In this spirit, the museum opened a photography exhibit titled *Moccasins on Pavement: The Urban Indian Experience: A Denver Portrait* in 1979, co-curated by Joyce Herold (Curator of Ethnology) and Michael Taylor (Oglala Sioux). The NAAC established the policies for the project and community members provided the text, which mainly consisted of quotes from interviews (Archambault 2011, 18). Funded through a grant from the National Endowment for the Humanities, the exhibit portrayed Indians living and working as modern Americans at home, in the work place, at school, playing sports, attending pow-wows, and on visits back home on the reservation. The photos documented a modern, urban Indian community engaged in day-to-day activities.

In the "Prologue" to the exhibit catalog, co-curator Joyce Herold wrote that the exhibit:

> portrays people and activities drawn from the estimated seven to ten thousand Indian people who live in metropolitan Denver. They have been chosen for our focus because they are our neighbors and they can give us insights into other present-day Indian people … Images of Denver Indian people, seen by both Indian and non-Indian photographers and interpreters, can contribute much to the sparse documentation of Indians who live off reservations (estimated at over half the present Native American population).
>
> *(1978, 2)*

Co-curator Michael Taylor wrote most of the catalog text interspersed with quotes and statements from the many Indian people contacted to work on the exhibit. As Herold's words, these included "some highly visible leaders of conservative to radical bent and other people of 'average' mold. Not apologists for the plight of Indians past or present, these spokespeople are committed to remembering real Indian history while working toward a proud Indian future" (Herold 1978, 3).

Archambault reports that even though the Denver Indian community's response to the exhibit was "enthusiastic approval," the exhibit was not well-attended by the general public. And although the exhibit traveled throughout Colorado and Europe, no other American museums outside the state were interested in booking it. Archambault suggests that the exhibition did not draw large non-Native audiences because it did not live up to popular, stereotypical images of Native Americans as either romanticized, heroic figures living in tune with nature or as downtrodden and poverty stricken. Instead it showed middle-class Americans leading ordinary lives (2011, 18–19).

Examples of socially relevant exhibits and fruitful collaborative projects such as these have not received much attention in the literature. Nonetheless, they illustrate the directions museum anthropology was taking, and how it was evolving prior to the 1980s. Especially significant is how they represent changes in the nature of relationships between originating communities and museums. Native and other source communities were no longer just the subjects of anthropological investigation and objects on display in museums. Increasingly, they were becoming vocal actors in changing museums from the "inside out" and the "outside in" (Lonetree 2012, 17). Given that Native Americans were pivotal in the shaping of American anthropology from Boas onward, it is not surprising that they would be some of museum anthropology's most ardent critics and influential agents of change (Shannon 2014, 22).

Native American Activism

In her book *Decolonizing Museums*, Amy Lonetree points out that many scholars have emphasized the role postmodern and postcolonial critiques, self-reflection, and the international discourse on human rights have played in leading museums in new directions. But it is equally important, she argues, to keep in mind that American Indian activism has also played a significant role in changing museum practices. Since the 1960s, American Indians, as well as Canadian First Nations and other Indigenous peoples, have been protesting stereotypical displays of American Indian culture and history; challenging the museum's authority to represent Native cultures without including Native perspectives; protesting the collecting, displaying, and holding of American Indian ancestral remains; and making claims for the repatriation of remains, ceremonial, funerary objects, plus objects of cultural patrimony. Moreover, American Indian activists have sought to change the museum from the inside out by having Native people enter the museum profession (2012, 17). In sum, Lonetree contends that even though much has been made of collaboration and Native involvement in the museum world, these developments did not happen merely because of "academic epiphanies by non-Native academics or curators, but as a result of prolonged and committed activism" (2012, 18).

Native activism during the 1960s and 1970s in the United States was not only directed at reforming mainstream museum practices, but also extended to strengthening existing tribal museums and cultural centers and establishing new ones. Such efforts were part of larger, community-based efforts to improve socioeconomic conditions, rebuild community identities, and foster cultural renewal. In addition to tribal governments, the movement to develop tribal museums was supported by national, pan-Indian organizations such as the American Indian Museum Association (AIMA), which was renamed the North American Indian Museums Association (NAIMA). The association was formed in 1978 during a Smithsonian workshop attended by over 20 American Indian museum directors and curators. As Message states:

> It was designed to be a 'call to arms' of the tribal museum community that sought to improve knowledge about and access to resources through building collaborative relationships with other institutions at tribal, regional, state and federal levels ... [T]he establishment of the association was also recognized as an indication of the achievements of American Indian activism, the museological sector, and a range of other spheres.
>
> *(2014, 140)*[12]

The first NAIMA conference was held at the Denver Museum of Natural History (Denver Museum of Nature and Science) from April 30 to May 3, 1979 (and incidentally, during the *Moccasins on Pavement* exhibit run). The museum was nominated to host the conference because of its active involvement with American Indian communities (Message 2014, 143). Eighty-five delegates representing tribal museums and cultural centers throughout the United States and Canada, along with observers and participants from other institutions and foundations, attended the conference (Message 2014, 143). Message states that the NAIMA lasted for about ten years, and was most active during its formative phase when its officers promoted support for tribal museums and political advocacy. The organization lobbied federal agencies and federally funded museums to operate in accordance with the American Indian Religious Freedom Act passed by Congress in 1978, and to establish policies for the repatriation of ancestral remains and religious objects (Message 2014, 144–145).

The passage of the National Museum of the American Indian (NMAI) Act and the Native American Graves Protection and Repatriation Act (NAGPRA) in 1989 and 1990 respectively by the United States Congress were also the culmination of decades-long American Indian activism. In fact, the development of the National Museum of the American Indian was proposed as early as 1973 (Message 2014, 129). Needless to say, these acts have had an immeasurable impact on museum anthropology and continue to shape it to this day.

Richard West, founding director of the NMAI, in an address made to the American Anthropological Association (AAA) not long after the act was passed, outlined the approach to scholarship and research at the NMAI. He emphasized how scholarship on Native peoples must be guided by principles that include the voices of Native peoples. And while West stressed that non-Native scholars and researchers would not be excluded from the NMAI, he also asserted that they must keep in mind that the "rules of the road have changed." West stressed that it was not so much that the anthropological enterprise had been wrong as much as it had been incomplete because it had not included the Native voice to any sizable degree (1993, 5–8).

The on-going development of Native American museums and cultural centers has also been a channel for highlighting Indigenous perspectives and providing alternative narratives and museum models (Cooper 2008, Lonetree 2012, Kreps 2003a). As Sleeper-Smith asserts, "Indigenous people are using museums to emerge from invisibility and to deconstruct the colonization narrative from the viewpoint of the oppressed. At the heart of these projects is a multiplicity of voices, a variety of narratives, and the use of museums as tools of revitalization" (2009, 4). As many scholars have noted, substantive change or paradigmatic shifts in a field are often generated from the periphery and by those who have occupied its borders and margins (Harrison 1993, Hooper-Greenhill 2000, Kreps 2003a).

Referring to developments since the 1980s, Phillips wrote in 2005 that: "The post-colonial and post-structuralist critiques in the academic community, and political pressures for decolonization outside of it ... [have] dramatically raised the profile of museum-based research, radically altered the environment in which it is conducted, and stimulated the development of a range of new institutional practices" (2005, 84). Nevertheless, and as the above section shows, critique, both internal and external, has been integral to museum anthropology since its beginnings. And while developments since the 1980s have been instrumental in reinventing museum anthropology, they were not unprecedented. Rather, they brought the field's problematic aspects into sharper focus, added weight and momentum to on-going movements, and raised new issues for critical analysis.

Museum anthropology has been moving back to the center of academic anthropology and regaining its standing partly due to new theoretical orientations, but also because of how it exemplifies the ways anthropology can be continually responsive to critique, and in turn, transform its practice. Similar statements can be made for anthropology's other "poor sister," applied anthropology.

Applied Anthropology or "Putting Anthropology to Use"

The discipline of anthropology has had since its early days a practical side, dedicated to addressing and solving practical problems. But as the field developed from the late nineteenth century onward, this arena of anthropological work came to be known as applied anthropology. Over the decades, a number of terms have come into usage to describe the various forms of practice and the different ways anthropologists apply their knowledge and skills to activities other than basic research and teaching. These include practicing anthropology, action anthropology, development anthropology, and advocacy anthropology (Van Willigen 2002, ix), and increasingly today, public and engaged anthropology (Beck and Maida 2015). Even though each of the various forms of applied anthropology carries its own specific meanings related to their specific activities and circumstances, what they all share in common is a tradition and commitment to being "useful." Van Willigen uses applied anthropology as a "general label for the entire array of situations and approaches for putting anthropology to use" (2002, ix). Thus, the question of relevance has never been a matter of debate within applied anthropology as it has been in academic and museum anthropology.

Typically, applied anthropologists have worked in the areas of education, public health, international development, environmental conservation, social impact assessment, public policy and analysis, urban planning, social justice and human rights. Many museum anthropologists and archeologists, especially those working in cultural resource and heritage management, also label what they do applied anthropology. Much like museum anthropology, applied anthropology was central to the founding of the discipline. According to Rylko-Bauer et al. in their article "Reclaiming Applied Anthropology" (2006),

> the genesis of applied anthropology cannot be so easily separated from the birth and evolution of the discipline as a whole. The term applied anthropology has been in use for more than a century; it was associated with the creation of early academic departments of anthropology and played an essential role in laying the foundations for the general discipline's infrastructure.
>
> *(2006, 179)*

Applied Anthropology's Colonial Legacy

The idea of applying anthropological methods and knowledge to social problems and public policy dates back to the mid- to late nineteenth century when anthropology was heavily entangled in European colonialism. Ethnology played an important role in the colonial enterprise of many countries whose governments supported the establishment of academic departments to serve colonial interests. For example, the anthropology department at Oxford University was initially set up to be a kind of applied training program in which many faculty members had either worked for or were preparing to work for colonial administrations. As will be discussed in the next chapter, in the Netherlands a number of institutes and university departments were established specifically to train colonial civil servants. For instance, in 1887, a chair in "Geography and Ethnology of the East Indian Archipelago" was established at Leiden University to provide formal instruction in anthropological subjects tied to meeting the needs of colonial policy (Ellen 1976, 312). "Thus within the history of anthropology, application came first" (Rylko-Bauer et al. 2006, 179). Many of what are now considered classic ethnographies were originally written as reports, funded by government agencies to inform administrators (Rylko-Bauer et al. 2006, 180).

In the United States, the new field of anthropology also advanced in tandem with colonial exploits. Simonelli and Skinner describe how the "development of anthropology in the United States was shaped by the country's expansion and nation-building in a land where others had a prior claim, and early anthropologists were caught up in this endeavor" (2013, 554). The BAE employed anthropologists to provide research reports to congressional policy makers. Such reports provided crucial information to guide their decision-making on matters related primarily to Native Americans. John Wesley Powell, an anthropologist and one-time head of the BAE, convinced the United States Congress in 1879 that "anthropology would be useful in getting the Indians peacefully allocated to reservations" (Stocking 1985, 113). And as noted previously, many anthropologists employed by the BAE were also charged with collecting Native American artifacts that formed the museum collections on which early American anthropological research was based.

According to Simonelli and Skinner, anthropologists working for the BAE approached their work in two ways: one was through Boasian "salvage ethnography," or, in their words, "the gathering up of culture in the face of assimilation." The other was through planning and advocacy. "Thus, anthropology in the United States *began* as an applied, engaged, and public enterprise. Practical research, whether funded by the government or by developing university anthropology departments, was aimed at making inevitable change easier" (2013, 554, emphasis in the original).

But there are also examples of applied anthropologists who questioned the policies and approaches of the government agencies that employed them. For instance, Ruth Underhill, a student of Boas, worked for the United States Bureau of Indian Affairs (BIA) in various capacities from 1938 to 1944. One of her jobs was to provide ethnological training to BIA agents as well as to teachers who worked on reservations. During this time, she gave lectures and authored pamphlets for the BIA's *Indian Life and Customs Series* that illustrated various aspects of Native American culture. These pamphlets were intended to reach wide audiences (Halpern 1993, 191).

Underhill's association with the BIA was terminated when she criticized the adoption of a BIA-proposed constitution for the Tohono O'odham Reservation tribal government on the grounds that it did not reflect Tohono O'odham social and political organization. Underhill was well-acquainted with the subject since her PhD dissertation, based on extensive fieldwork, focused on it. After her separation with the BIA, she continued to maintain strong connections to the Tohono O'odham and gained their respect. In 1980, Underhill was honored at a banquet and in a parade on the Tohono O'odham reservation in Arizona. The tribal chairman at the time, Max H. Norris, wrote in a tribal resolution, "It was through your works on the Papago People that many of our young Papagos, in search of themselves, their past, their spirit, have recaptured part of their identities" (Colwell-Chanthaphonh and Nash 2014, 14). Underhill was committed to making anthropology useful to the wider society, the profession, and the people she studied. She was a prolific writer of both scholarly and popular books (Tisdale 1993, 329), and over her long career she also taught at several colleges and universities, including the University of Denver from 1948 to 1952 (Colwell-Chanthaphonh and Nash 2014).

The Public Uses and Abuses of Anthropology

The ideology that culture change and assimilation into the dominant Euro-American culture was inevitable continued to inform the work of many anthropologists well into the twentieth century. For instance, Margaret Mead (based at the American Museum of Natural History in New York) and Ruth Benedict (at Columbia University), both trained by Boas, saw themselves as "cultural brokers" who could help spread mainstream culture through projects that encouraged acculturation and assimilation into dominant Euro-American society (Simonelli and Skinner 2013, 554). During World War II and in the early years of the Cold War, Mead and Benedict also sought to make the cultures of both enemies and allies understandable to the United States government and general public by founding Columbia University's Bureau for Contemporary Culture research project (Beck and Maida 2015, 10).[13]

Outside the United States during the 1950s and 1960s, applied anthropologists were also enlisted to act as culture brokers and agents of change in so-called "developing countries," and to help government agencies facilitate modernization efforts. Even though many saw the transformation to modernity as a foregone conclusion (Simonelli and Skinner 2013, 554–555), there were also those who were critical of top-down, paternalistic approaches to development and modernization.

Sol Tax was an applied anthropologist who thought that anthropologists should work with community members to meet development goals they set for themselves and that would support their self-determination. He was not only concerned with doing basic research, but also helping people deal with the problems they faced in their daily lives. Tax blended theory with practice, maintaining that practical activities were testing grounds for theoretical constructs. For Tax, the value of theory rested on its usefulness. Although his ideas foreshadowed the anthropological critique of development as neo-colonialism and he pioneered methods such as action, collaborative, and participatory anthropology, his ideas and approaches were not well received by academic anthropologists of the day (Simonelli and Skinner 2013, 554, Van Willigen 2002, 32).

Aside from its practical applications, a number of other reasons have been given for applied anthropology's peripheral position within the discipline. During the 1960s and 1970s, Simonelli and Skinner state that "applied anthropologists were seen to be agents of (neo-) colonialism, at a time when the discipline's connection to colonialism was a growing concern" (2013, 555). Van Willigen recounts how from the 1970s forward applied anthropology began to be singled out from the rest of anthropology for its questionable linkages to Cold War machinations;[14] for working within hegemonic power structures rather than critiquing them; and for its complicity with those who create rather than solve social problems such as governments, international development agencies, and corporations. However, as Van Willigen and many other authors have pointed out, "the history of anthropology, both basic and applied, is the history of power relations between anthropologists and the people studied" (2002, 43). And as Rylko-Bauer et al. also suggest, "assigning more blame to one subfield over another glosses over the fact that all of anthropology equally shares these problematic pasts" (2006, 179).

Applied anthropology's marginal status within academic anthropology has also rested on the assertion that it is "a-theoretical." Rylko-Bauer et al. contend that this view derives partly from the perception that applied documents such as project reports and evaluations often focus on hard data, methods, and concise policy recommendations for use by policy makers. Theory, they argue, is often hidden in such research. "Practitioners use theoretical and conceptual frameworks from anthropology and other disciplines to shape their questions, design methodology, and link knowledge with policy, program development, and action. Theory commonly guides applied research to one degree or another" (2006, 184).

Sanjek has pointed out how the work of applied anthropologists has been undervalued because it is often published in the form of "gray literature" rather than in peer-reviewed scholarly journals or books. Gray literature, among other things, consists of policy papers, consultancy reports, evaluations, recommendations, guidelines, editorials, essays, and articles for newsletters. Much gray literature is aimed at influencing policy outcomes and actions. Sanjek emphasizes, however, that "writing gray literature is an important part of what many, perhaps most, anthropologists actually do, occasionally or often, and some reports might be read more widely, and by key readerships, than the anthropologist's 'theoretical' writings" (2015, 300).

The Rise of Engaged and Public Anthropology

In spite of such criticism, applied anthropology has continued to grow, take on new labels, and become increasingly influential within anthropology as a whole. Its growth can be attributed to changes in the understanding and nature of research; in how theory is generated; and the shrinkage of academic, university-based positions for anthropologists. Its growth also reflects the general shift to a more engaged and public anthropology. Rylko-Bauer et al. argue that

> contemporary applied anthropology emerges from a closer look at its history, its role in shaping the discipline, and the current diversity of perspectives and practice. It is more accurately conceived as a complex and broad 'anthropology in use,' united by the goal and practice of applying theories, concepts, and methods from anthropology to confront human problems that often contribute to profound human suffering.
>
> *(2006, 179)*

The continuing growth and significance of applied anthropology can be seen in the subfield's increasing visibility in the AAA. The AAA has changed its goals and direction in the past ten years or so in order to attract the growing number of applied anthropologists, and to keep step with developments in the field. This is reflected in the changing content of AAA's publications and conferences (Simonelli and Skinner 2013, 555–556).

In March 2010, a new section in *American Anthropologist* (the discipline's flagship journal) titled "Public Anthropology Reviews" was inaugurated with the essay "A Sea Change in Anthropology? Public Anthropology Reviews" by editors of the section Melissa Checker, David Vine, and Alaka Wali. In this essay, they write that the new section reflects:

> significant change underway in the discipline, including the expansion of the kind of work that is valued by anthropologists, new ways in which anthropological knowledge is produced and disseminated, and an acknowledgement that anthropologists have a responsibility to dedicate their skills to issues of broad public concern.
>
> *(2010, 5)*

The section was intended to expose readers to new anthropological work being done in a wide array of media and nontraditional academic formats, and that communicated with non-academic audiences on critical issues of social significance. The changes that have been occurring in the discipline, they assert, are a result of demands for the field to break free from its traditional confines, and its insular and exclusionary conversations. Such demands are being made by students and those working inside and outside academic anthropology who are "insisting that anthropologists regain, reinvigorate and institutionalize the political and social engagement that has been part of the discipline almost from its beginnings" (Checker, Vine, and Wali 2010, 5).

Although public anthropology has become one of the many labels used to describe an ever growing concern regarding anthropological relevance, numerous anthropologists from across the disciplinary spectrum had been advocating for a more engaged, publicly faced, and ethically motivated anthropology for decades (Hymes 1969, Peacock 1997, Eriksen 2006, Scheper-Hughes 1995). Low and Merry point out that James Peacock introduced the idea of public anthropology in his presidential lecture to the AAA in 1997 (2010, s207). Nevertheless, the movement is often associated with Robert Borofsky, who has become a strong advocate for public anthropology within the AAA. He also established the Center for a Public Anthropology in 2001. In an essay that appeared in *Anthropology News* (the AAA newsletter) in May 2000, Borofsky presented his views on what constitutes public anthropology.

> It is an anthropology that engages issues and audiences beyond today's self-imposed disciplinary boundaries. The focus is on conversations with broad audiences about broad concerns ... The hope is that by invigorating public conversations with anthropological insights, public anthropology can re-frame and reinvigorate the discipline.
>
> *(2000, 9)*

For Borofsky, one of public anthropology's jobs is to critique the state of anthropology or what it has become, i.e., an overly differentiated, specialized, insulated discipline (2000, 10). Borofsky recognizes that public anthropology is closely aligned with applied anthropology, but the two "dance an ambiguous minuet." Indeed, "it is difficult to differentiate the two because theory and application merge in both." He questions applied anthropology's low status within the discipline, stating that "applied anthropology today tends to be depicted, often unfairly, as focusing primarily on concrete, practical problems that others have conceptually defined for them" (2000, 9). The Center for a Public Anthropology seeks to encourage academics to move beyond the traditional "do no harm" ethos of funded research to one that strives to "do some good."

Even though public anthropology continues to grow in popularity across the discipline, debates continue to surround the use of the term "public," and the directions the movement has pursued. To Beck and Maida, public anthropology is not just about conversations and narrowly confined intellectual exchanges. Rather, it concerns "the co-construction of knowledge, the communication of that knowledge to diverse publics, and as appropriate, various forms of intervention, including political action" (2015, 3).

In the commentary, "Public Anthropology: An Idea Searching for Reality," Trevor Purcell allows that public anthropology holds promise for contributing to "the general public good" but questions its capacity to contribute substantially to social change and equity when many in the field remain averse to activism, socio-political participation, and engagement in the real lives of the people studied. He claims that anthropologists remain too invested in their careers and their institutional values to assume a truly critical participatory stance. What's more, he argues that there still exists a lack of consciousness regarding the compatibility of scientific practice and public praxis on the grounds that the latter compromises neutrality or objectivity. To Purcell, "this collective state of 'objective' detachment has helped to create the need for a public anthropology" (2000, 31). Purcell further emphasizes the need to think critically about who constitutes "the public" of public anthropology. He argues that we need to include the people we study in our conceptualizations of the public as well as ourselves, asserting that "We are *all* part of the historically constituted modern public" (2000, 31, emphasis in original).

Some critics have questioned the need for yet another subfield within the discipline, contending that many applied anthropologists already do the kinds of things that are now being labeled public anthropology. Singer fears that a full establishment and acceptance of public anthropology will lead to the creation of a two-tier system of "anthropological relevance." The upper tier will most likely comprise academic anthropologists or "intellectuals" who will get highlighted in the media as "Anthropological Spokespersons" while applied anthropologists will "become an underclass of laboring grunts who sell their labor on the open market for immediate application" (2000, 6).

Singer's repudiation of public anthropology, in Beck and Maida's view, rearticulates a major disciplinary divide between those who practice applied anthropology and those who do not. This dichotomous stance is misguided, they contend, because it fails "to acknowledge that anthropology departments teach applied anthropology and academically employed anthropologists practice application; further, anthropologists employed outside universities may also teach in academic departments" (2015, 4).

For many, public anthropology is seen as a unifying term and includes forms of practice that are closely aligned with applied, engaged, or practicing anthropology (Lassiter 2008, 73). Over the last decade, numerous articles and books have appeared that address what can now be seen as various manifestations of and approaches to public and engaged anthropology.

In their article "Engaged Anthropology: Diversity and Dilemmas" (2010), Low and Merry discuss the importance of developing an engaged anthropology that addresses public issues. They provide an overview of the scope of engaged anthropology, including its major approaches and historical development. Low and Merry suggest that there is a wide range of practices that fall within engaged anthropology and that these practices can take place in a variety of contexts. Engaged anthropology can take the form of teaching and public education, social critique, collaboration, and advocacy and activism (2010, S204) for example. They declare that their particular interest in engaged anthropology is grounded in their commitment to "an anthropological practice that respects the dignity and rights of all humans and has a beneficent effect on the promotion of social justice" (2010, S204).

In contrast to Simonelli and Skinner cited above, Low and Merry take a less critical stance to what they see as examples of early engaged anthropology in the United States. For instance, they relate how in 1879, the first director of the BAE, John W. Powell, testified before the Congress about the genocide of Native peoples following the building of the railroad and westward expansion. They also discuss how before World War II there were numerous anthropologists, such as Boas, who were exposing economic problems, class divisions, and the effects of racism and inequality in American institutions and society at large (Low and Merry 2010, 205).

The authors also present Margaret Mead's work in a positive light, identifying her as "a pioneer of engaged anthropology." They relate how she was active as a writer for popular publications and as a public speaker on pragmatic problems such as housing, urban development, race, and pollution. Mead also was known for collaborating with a broad range of professionals and academics (Low and Merry 2010, S205). Today, Mead is often extoled as one of anthropology's most notable public intellectuals, and for upholding one of anthropology's central missions "to awaken the Western world to the multiplicity of the human experience" (Nash et al. 2011, 138). But her celebrity status and critiques of American society based on her studies of non-Western cultures were not accepted within the academy, and in recent years, the scientific merit of her work has been heavily scrutinized (Low and Merry 2010, S205).

Low and Merry curiously fail to mention that Mead achieved her notoriety while working within a museum, and was also one of museum anthropology's most renowned figures. Mead became a museum anthropologist in 1926 when she was hired as an assistant curator of ethnology at the American Museum of Natural History (AMNH). She retired from the Museum in 1969 with the title of Curator Emeritus of Ethnology. During her tenure at the AMNH she assembled a sizable ethnographic collection from her fieldwork in the Pacific, and orchestrated the renovation of several exhibition halls. Her *Peoples of the Pacific Hall* was completed in 1971. Although the museum remained her primary professional affiliation, Mead also served as an adjunct professor of anthropology at Columbia University, and was a visiting lecturer at more than a dozen other universities around the world (Thomas 1980, 354–356). Not in the least, Mead was a staunch proponent of the museum's public role. In a 1970 article published in *Museum News* (the magazine of the American Alliance of Museums), Mead called social relevance a major challenge for modern museums. She maintained that the modern museum must be prepared to respond to rapid change, and transform its traditional methods to keep up with social developments and new technologies. Mead urged museums to assume an added social responsibility and educate the public on issues of contemporary concern (Thomas 1980, 360, Mead 1970).

In "Where Have You Gone, Margaret Mead? Anthropology and Public Intellectuals," Sabloff upholds that anthropologists have important, practical knowledge, and in its rich diversity has a great deal to offer the public in general and policy makers in particular. Yet anthropologists must do a better job of informing the public about what they do through greater public outreach and communication. We need public intellectuals like Margaret Mead more than ever, Sabloff attests, who can speak to the myriad crucial issues facing the world today through popular media and channels like museum exhibits (2011).

The Convergence of Applied and Museum Anthropology

Sabloff's comments on the role of museum work in popularizing anthropology support recommendations made by other anthropologists. In "The Convergence of Applied, Practicing and Public Anthropology in the 21st Century" (2004), Lamphere highlights how anthropologists across the discipline's subfields, such as archaeologists, cultural anthropologists, and museum specialists, are joining applied and practicing anthropologists in conducting research on and communicating about critical social issues.

Lamphere reiterates what museum anthropologists have been saying for a long time, and that is that museums are ideal venues for outreach to the public and bringing anthropological knowledge to audiences outside the academy. She suggests that "a museum exhibit is an extraordinary opportunity to present anthropological knowledge on a variety of different levels through the use of objects, graphics, interactive video, and text" (2004, 438). As an example, Lamphere cites the exhibit *RACE: Are We So Different?* produced by the AAA in collaboration with the Science Museum of Minnesota (SMM) with funding from the National Science Foundation and the Ford Foundation. This multimedia, traveling exhibit, which opened at the SMM in 2007, sought to educate the public about the biology of human variation as well as racism as a social construct and structural reality. Accompanied by various forms of educational materials for teachers and museum staff, the exhibit served as a catalyst and forum for dialogues on race and racism in communities across the United States (Lamphere 2004, Moses 2015).

Lamphere is optimistic about the future of applied, practicing, and public anthropology, and sees the convergence of these fields as an opportunity to overcome historical divisions within anthropology. She stresses how "At a time when some of our colleagues are still decrying the disunity of our discipline, there are signs of increased unity and the potential for increased communication across the subfields as we look for better strategies for collaboration, outreach, and advocacy" (2004, 440).[15]

Despite debates over labels, there are many indications that the divisions between basic and applied research, and academic and practicing anthropology, are dissolving. Applied anthropology is resuming its standing in anthropology as a whole, as is museum anthropology. Together, they are providing models for more socially relevant and engaged research, scholarship, and ethical practice in anthropology.

In the next chapter, I look at the historical development of museum anthropology in the Netherlands to provide a comparative perspective on the public role of anthropology in and through museums and its applied dimensions. I consider the forms public engagement has taken in different institutional settings and points in time, particularly, in colonial and postcolonial contexts. In this respect, my aim is to show how processes of decolonization in a former European empire, i.e., the Netherlands, compare to those in a settler-colonial nation like the United States. Thinking historically, or the assembling of genealogical histories, is valuable for discovering what is useful for today and tomorrow, since the past can be the source of new insights and ideas (Lubar 2017, 6–7). So too can be a comparative perspective.

Notes

1 In addition to obfuscating its own historicity, one of the strongest arguments against the crisis of representation movement in anthropology has been that it focused too much on writing and text and not enough on the practice of fieldwork or "doing" ethnography (Shannon 2014, 22, also see Bunzl 2005, 2008). Furthermore, White maintains that the movement is "symptomatic of a much larger problem in the discipline of anthropology's deep-seated anxiety about relevance" (2012, 71). The development of more collaborative strategies, such as the co-production of texts and need for multivocality in cultural representations, has been posited as one of the more significant responses to critiques of the movement (Shannon 2014, 22). Needless to say, critiques of representational strategies have had a particularly significant impact on museum anthropology given its historical task of representing culture through visual technologies such as exhibitions. The work of James Clifford has been especially influential in this regard (see Clifford 1988, 1997).

2 Sturtevant notes that his periodization of museum anthropology's history is developed from that implied by Collier and Tschopik's paper of 1954 (1969, 622). Fenton references a periodization from an even earlier work by Clark Wissler (1942).

3 It should be noted here that in contrast to the situation in Europe where anthropological collections were housed in museums devoted solely to ethnology or "museums of man," natural history museums, for the most part, were home to anthropological collections in the United States. See Frese 1960 for a detailed description, or typology, of the variety of anthropology museums in Europe and North America.

4 See Bennett for a discussion on the gendered aspect of the social space of the museum, and how women became "culture's gentle handmaidens" (1995, 29).

5 Parezo and Hardin note that the first female curator in the department of anthropology at the Smithsonian National Museum of Natural History was not hired until the 1980s (1993, 280). It is now well-known that women outnumber men in the museum profession, and increasing professionalization of the field coincided with its feminization. What Parezo and Hardin noted in 1993 remains true today: "Museum work has become a female-dominated occupation, but this does not mean that women control institutions. Women are instead concentrated at the bottom of the prestige scale (1993, 277).

6 For instance, many of the authors cited in this review were curators of anthropology employed in museums at the time of their writing. William Sturtevant (Smithsonian National Museum of Natural History); Donald Collier (Chicago Natural History Museum [Field Museum]); Harry Tschopik (American Museum of Natural History). William Fenton was Assistant Commissioner of New York State Museum and Science Service.

7 Also see Colwell-Chanthaphonh 2009.

8 Needless to say this is an enduring problem in American museum anthropology, and has not only been troubling to anthropologists but also to many Indigenous people who do not appreciate having their cultures displayed in proximity to fossils, stuffed animals, and other natural history specimens (Cooper 2008).

9 Like Collier and Tschopik, Sturtevant also suggests that anthropological methods can be useful to the development of "visitor studies." "Anthropology, as the only social science well established in museums, seems the ideal field to study the educational effectiveness of various exhibit techniques, to conduct research on visitor reactions" (1969, 644).

10 See Wintle for a discussion on how the Smithsonian's focus on modernization in displays of new nations undergoing decolonization echoes certain developments taking place at the Imperial and Commonwealth Institutes in London at the same time (2013, 187).

11 Freed notes that 22 of the 55 museums contacted by the Lubicon participated in the boycott, five in the United States and the rest in Europe (19, 91, 76). Following the controversy over *The Spirit Sings*, the Canadian Museum Association and the Assembly of First Nations established a joint Task Force to "develop an ethical framework and strategies for Aboriginal nations to represent their history and culture in concert with cultural institutions" (Task Force quoted in Peers and Brown 2003, 12).

12 See Message 2014, chapter 4 "Activism and the Tribal Museum Movement," for a discussion on the role of the Smithsonian's Office of Museum Programs' Native American Training Program, established in 1977, and the American Indian Cultural Resources Training Program created by the National Anthropological Archives in 1973 in the support and development of tribal museums.

13 According to Beck and Maida, when World War II revealed that Americans were relatively ignorant of the cultures of both enemies and allies, the United States government recruited anthropologists to support the war effort. For instance, George Murdock's Cross-Cultural Survey at Yale University's Institute of Human Relations, funded by the Carnegie and Rockefeller Foundations, hired anthropologists to help the military's wartime operations in the Pacific and then to help govern Pacific nations after liberation from the Japanese (Beck and Maida 2015, 13).

14 Much has been written about anthropologists' participation in the American war in Southeast Asia, specifically their role in assisting the US military's counterinsurgency efforts in Thailand and elsewhere (Beck and Maida 2015, 12–13, Price 2016).

15 Another progressive step is the heightening presence of museum anthropology within the Society for Applied Anthropology's (SfAA) annual meetings and publications. The leadership of SfAA has been encouraging, for several years now, the organization of sessions at its annual meetings devoted specifically to museum and heritage topics. The Society's publication, *Practicing Anthropology*, regularly includes articles and special issues on museum work and related topics.

References

Ames, Michael. 1992. *Cannibal Tours and Glass Boxes: The Anthropology of Museums*. Vancouver: University of British Columbia.

Archambault, JoAllyn. 2011. "Native Communities, Museums and Collaboration." *Practicing Anthropology* 33(2):16–20.

Beck, Sam and Carl A. Maida. 2015. "Introduction." In *Public Anthropology in a Borderless World*, edited by Sam Beck and Carl A. Maida, 1–35. New York and Oxford: Berghahn.

Bennett, Tony. 1995. *The Birth of the Museum*. London and New York: Routledge.

Bennett, Tony, Fiona Cameron, Nelia Davis, Ben Dibley, Rodney Harrison, Ira Jacknis, and Conal McCarthy. 2017. *Collecting, Ordering, Governing*. Durham and London: Duke University Press.

Boas, Franz. 1907. "Some Principles of Museum Administration." *Science* 25(649):921–933.

Borhegyi, Stephan. 1969. "The New Role for Anthropology in the Natural History Museum." *Current Anthropology* 10(4):368–370.

Borofsky, Robert. 2000. "Public Anthropology: Where to? What next?" *Anthropology News* (May 2000):9–10.

Bouquet, Mary. 2001. "Introduction: Anthropology and the Museum. Back to the Future." In *Academic Anthropology and the Museum. Back to the Future*, edited by Mary Bouquet. New York and Oxford: Berghahn.

Bouquet, Mary. 2012. *Museums. A Visual Anthropology*. London: Berg.

Bunzl, Matti. 2005. "Anthropology Beyond Crisis: Toward an Intellectual History of the Extended Present." *Anthropology and Humanism* 30(2):187–195.

Bunzl, Matti. 2008. "The Quest for Anthropological Relevance: Borgesian Maps and Epistemological Pitfalls." *American Anthropologist* 110(1):53–60.

Carattini, Amy. 2015. "Contemporary Perspectives: In, Out and Around Museums." *Practicing Anthropology* 37(3):4–6.

Checker, Melissa, David Vine, and Alaka Wali. 2010. "A Sea Change in Anthropology? Public Anthropology Reviews." *American Anthropologist* 112(1):5–6.

Clifford, James. 1987. "Of Other Peoples: Beyond the Salvage Paradigm." In *Discussions in Contemporary Culture*, edited by Hal Foster, 121–150. Seattle, WA: Bay Press.

Clifford, James. 1988. *The Predicament of Culture. Twentieth-Century Ethnography, Literature, and Art*. Cambridge, MA: Harvard University Press.

Clifford, James. 1997. *Routes. Travel and Translation in the Late Twentieth Century*. Cambridge, MA: Harvard University Press.

Clifford, James. 2013. *Returns. Becoming Indigenous in the Twenty-First Century*. Cambridge, MA: Harvard University Press.

Cole, Douglas. 1985. *Captured Heritage. The Scramble for Northwest Coast Artifacts*. Seattle: University of Washington Press.

Collier, Donald and Harry Tschopik. 1954. "The Role of Museums in American Anthropology." *American Anthropologist* 56:768–779.

Colwell-Chanthaphonh, Chip. 2009. *Inheriting the Past: The Making of Arthur C. Parker and Indigenous Archaeology*. Tucson: University of Arizona Press.

Colwell, Chip. 2017. *Plundered Skulls and Stolen Spirits. Inside the Fight to Reclaim Native America's Culture*. Chicago, IL: University of Chicago Press.

Colwell-Chanthaphonh, Chip and Stephen Nash. 2014. *An Anthropologist's Arrival. A Memoir. Ruth M. Underhill*. Tucson: University of Arizona Press.

Comaroff, John. 2010. "The End of Anthropology, Again: On the Future of an In/Discipline." *American Anthropologist* 112(4):524–538.

Conn, Steven. 2010. *Do Museums Still Need Objects?* Philadelphia: University of Pennsylvania Press.

Cooper, Karen C. 2008. *Spirited Encounters. American Indians Protest Museum Policies and Practices*. Lanham, MD: Alta Mira Press.

Council for Museum Anthropology Newsletter. 1976. "Milwaukee Opens 'Urban Habitat'." Edited by Richard I. Ford. University of Michigan, Museum of Anthropology.

Darnell, Regna. 1998. *And Along Came Boas: Continuity and Revolution in the History of Americanist Anthropology*. Amsterdam: John Benjamins.

Edson, G. 1997. *Museum Ethics*. London and New York: Routledge.

Ellen, Roy. 1976. "The Development of Anthropology and Colonial Policy in the Netherlands 1800–1960." *Journal of the History of the Behavioral Sciences* 13:303–324.

Eriksen, Thomas Hylland. 2006. *Engaging Anthropology*. Oxford: Berg.

Ewers, John. 1955. "Problems and Procedures in Modernizing Ethnological Exhibits." *American Anthropologist* 57(1):1–12.

Fenton, Willian N. 1960. "The Museum and Anthropological Research." *Curator: The Museum Journal* 34(4):327–355.

Freed, Stanley. 1991. "Everyone is Breathing on Our Vitrines: Problems and Prospects of Museum Anthropology." *Curator: The Museum Journal* 34(1):58–79.

Frese, H. H. 1960. *Anthropology and the Public: The Role of Museums*. Leiden, the Netherlands: E.J. Brill.

Halpern, Margaret. 1993. "Women in Applied Anthropology in the Southwest: The Early Years." In *Hidden Scholars: Women Anthropologists and the Native American Southwest*, edited by Nancy Parezo, 189–201. Albuquerque: University of New Mexico Press.

Handler, Richard. 2005. *Critics Against Culture. Anthropological Observers of Mass Society*. Madison: University of Wisconsin Press.

Hannerz, Ulf. 2010. *Anthropology's World. Life in a Twenty-first Century Discipline*. London: Pluto Press.

Harrison, Julia D. 1993. "Ideas of Museums in the 1990s." *Museum Management and Curatorship* 13:160–176.

Herold, Joyce. 1978. *Prologue: Moccasins on Pavement. The Urban Indian Experience. A Denver Portrait*, edited by Denver Museum of Nat Hist. Denver, CO: Denver Museum of Nat Hist.

Herold, Joyce. 1999. "Grand Amateur Collecting in the Mid-Twentieth Century." In *Collecting Native America. 1870–1960*, edited by Shepard Krech and Barbara Hail, 259–291. Washington, DC: Smithsonian Institution Press.

Hill, Richard W. 2000. "The Museum Indian: Still Frozen in Time and Mind." *Museum News* 79(3):40–44, 58–66.

Hooper-Greenhill, Eilean. 2000. *Museums and the Interpretation of Visual Culture*. London and New York: Routledge.

Hymes, Dell, ed. 1969. *Reinventing Anthropology*. New York: Random House.

Jacknis, Ira. 1985. "Franz Boas and Exhibits: On the Limitations of the Museum Method in Anthropology." In *Objects and Others: Essays on Museums and Material Culture*, edited by George Stocking, 75–111. Madison: University of Wisconsin Press.

Jenkins, David. 1994. "Object Lessons and Ethnographic Displays: Museum Exhibitions and the Making of American Anthropology." *Comparative Studies in Society and History* 36 (2):242–270.

Jones, Anna Laura. 1993. "Exploding Canons: The Anthropology of Museums." *Annual Review of Anthropology* 22:201–220.

Kratz, Corinne and Ivan Karp. 2006. "Introduction: Museum Frictions: Public Culture/ Global Transformation." In *Museum Frictions. Public Cultures/Global Transformations*, edited by Ivan Karp, Corinne A. Kratz, Lynn Szwaja, and Tomas Ybarra-Frausto, 1–31. Durham and London: Duke University Press.

Kreps, Christina. 2003. *Liberating Culture: Cross-Cultural Perspectives on Museums, Curation, and Heritage Preservation* London: Routledge.

Lamphere, Louise. 1993. "Reichard, Gladys." In *Hidden Scholars. Women Anthropologists and the Native American Southwest*, edited by Nancy Perezo, 157–188. Albuquerque: University of New Mexico Press.

Lamphere, Louise. 2004. "The Convergence of Applied, Practicing, and Public Anthropology in the 21st Century." *Human Organization* 63(4):431–443.

Lassiter, Luke. 2008. "Moving Past Public Anthropology and Doing Collaborative Research." *NAPA Bulletin* 29:70–86.

Lavender, Katherine and Nancy Parezo. 2005. "Ruth Murray Underhill. Ethnohistorian and Ethnographer of Native Peoples." In *Their Own Frontier: Women Intellectuals Re-Visioning the American West*, edited by Shirley Leckie and Nancy Parezo, 355–372. Lincoln and London: University of Nebraska Press.

Leckie, Shirley and Nancy Parezo, ed. 2008. *Their Own Frontier: Women Intellectuals Re-Visioning the American West*. Lincoln and London: University of Nebraska Press.

Lonetree, Amy. 2012. *Decolonizing Museums. Representing Native America in National and Tribal Museums*. Chapel Hill: University of North Carolina.

Low, Setha and Sally Engle Merry. 2010. "Engaged Anthropology: Diversity and Dilemmas." *Current Anthropology* 51(Supplement 2):s203–226.

Lubar, Steven. 2017. *Inside the Lost Museum. Curating, Past and Present*. Cambridge, MA: Harvard University Press.

Lurie, Nancy O. 1981. "Museumland Revisited." *Human Organization* 40(2):180–187.

Marcus, George 1995. "Ethnography In/Of the World System: The Emergence of Multi-Sited Ethnography." *Annual Review of Anthropology* 24:95–117.

Marcus, George and Michael Fischer. 1986. *Anthropology as Cultural Critique*. Chicago, IL: University of Chicago Press.

Marstine, Janet. 2006. "Introduction." In *The New Museum Theory*, edited by Janet Marstine, 1–36. Oxford: Blackwell.

Mead, Margaret. 1970. "Museums in a Media-Saturated World." *Museum News* 49(1):23–25.

Message, Kylie. 2014. *Museums and Social Activism. Engaged Protest, Museum Meanings.* London and New York: Routledge.

Mithlo, Nancy. 2004. "'Red Man's Burden': The Politics of Inclusion in Museum Settings." *American Indian Quarterly* 28(3&4):743–763.

Moses, Yolanda. 2015. "The American Anthropological Association RACE: Are We So Different? Project." In *Mutuality: Anthropology's Changing Terms of Engagement*, edited by Roger Sanjek, 29–44. Philadelphia: University of Pennsylvania Press.

Mullins, Paul. 2011. "Practicing Anthropology and the Politics of Engagement: 2010 Year in Review." *American Anthropologist* 113(2):235–245.

Nash, Stephen, Chip Colwell-Chanthaphonh, and Steven Holen. 2011. "Civic Engagement in Museum Anthropology: A Prolegomenon for the Denver Museum of Nature and Science." *Historical Archaeology* 45(1):135–151.

Osgood, Cornelius. 1979. *Anthropology in Museums of Canada and the United States.* Milwaukee, WI: Milwaukee Public Museum.

Parezo, Nancy and Margaret Hardin. 1993. "In the Realm of the Muses." In *Hidden Scholars: Women Anthropologists and the Native American Southwest*, edited by Nancy Parezo, 270–293. Albuquerque: University of New Mexico Press.

Peacock, James. 1997. "The Future of Anthropology." *American Anthropologist* 99(1):9–29.

Peers, Laura and Alison Brown, ed. 2003. *Museums and Source Communities.* New York and London: Routledge.

Phillips, Ruth B. 2005. "Re-placing Objects: Historical Practices for the Second Museum Age." *Canadian Historical Review* 86(1):83–110.

Phillips, Ruth B. 2011. *Museum Pieces. Toward the Indigenization of Canadian Museums.* Montreal: McGill-Queen's University Press.

Price, David H. 2016. *Cold War Anthropology. The CIA, The Pentagon, and the Growth of Dual Use Anthropology.* Durham and London: Duke University Press.

Purcell, Trevor. 2000. "Public Anthropology: An Idea Searching for Reality." *Transforming Anthropology* 9(2):30–33.

Redman, Samuel. 2011. "The Hearst Museum of Anthropology, the New Deal, and a Reassessment of the 'Dark Ages' of the Museum in the United States." *Museum Anthropology* 34:43–55.

Rylko-Bauer, Barbara, Merrill Singer, and John Van Willigen. 2006. "Reclaiming Applied Anthropology. Its Past, Present, and Future." *American Anthropologist* 108(1):178–190.

Sabloff, Jeremy. 2011. "Where Have You Gone, Margaret Mead? Anthropology and Public Intellectuals." *American Anthropologist* 113(3):408–416.

Sanjek, Roger. 2015. "Introduction. Deep Grooves: Anthropology and Mutuality." In *Mutuality. Anthropology's Changing Terms of Engagement*, edited by Roger Sanjek, 1–7. Philadelphia, PA: University of Philadelphia Press.

Scheper-Hughes, Nancy. 1995. "The Primacy of the Ethical. Propositions for a Militant Anthropology." *Current Anthropology* 36(3):409–418.

Shannon, Jennifer. 2014. *Our Lives: Collaboration, Native Voice, and the Making of the National Museum of the American Indian.* Santa Fe School for Advanced Research.

Shelton, Anthony. 2006. "Museums and Anthropologies: Practices and Narratives." In *A Companion to Museum Studies*, edited by Sharon Macdonald, 64–80. Oxford: Wiley-Blackwell.

Simonelli, Jeanne and Jonathan Skinner. 2013. "Applied and Public Anthropology in the United States and the United Kingdom." In *The Handbook of Sociocultural Anthropology*, edited by James Carrier and Deborah Gewertz, 553–587. London: Bloomsbury.

Simpson, Moira. 1996. *Making Representations: Museums in the Post-Colonial Era*. London and New York: Routledge.

Singer, Merrill. 2000. "Why I Am Not a Public Anthropologist." *Anthropology News* 41 (6):6–7.

Sleeper-Smith, Susan. 2009. *Contesting Knowledge: Museums and Indigenous Perspectives*. Lincoln: University of Nebraska Press.

Stocking, George. 1985. "Essays on Museums and Material Culture." In *Objects and Others: Essays on Museums and Material Culture*, edited by George Stocking, 3–14. Madison: University of Wisconsin Press.

Stocking, George. 1991. "Colonial Situations." In *Colonial Situations: Essays on the Contextualization of Ethnographic Knowledge*, edited by George Stocking, 3–5. Madison: University of Wisconsin Press.

Sturtevant, William. 1969. "Does Anthropology Need Museums?" *Proceedings of the Biological Society of Washington* 82:619–650.

Thomas, David Hurst. 1980. "Margaret Mead as a Museum Anthropologist." *American Anthropologist* 82(2):354–361.

Tisdale, Shelby. 1993. "Women on the Periphery of the Ivory Tower." In *Hidden Scholars: Women Anthropologists and the Native American Southwest*, edited by Nancy Parezo, 311–333. Albuquerque: University of New Mexico Press.

Van Willigen, John. 2002. *Applied Anthropology. An Introduction*. Third ed. Westport, Connecticut: Bergin and Garvey.

Wali, Alaka. 2015. "Listening with Passion: A Journey through Engagement and Exchange." In *Mutuality: Anthropology's Changing Terms of Engagement*, edited by Roger Sanjek, 174–190. Philadelphia: University of Pennsylvania Press.

Washburn, Wilcomb. 1968. "Are Museums Necessary?" *Museum News* 47(2):9–10.

West, Richard. 1993. "Research and Scholarship at the National Museum of the American Indian: The New 'Inclusiveness'." *Museum Anthropology* 17(1):5–8.

White, Bob W. 2012. "From Experimental Moment to Legacy Moment: Collaboration and the Crisis of Representation." *Collaborative Anthropologies* 5:65–97.

Williams, Raymond. 1977. *Marxism and Literature*. Oxford: Oxford University Press.

Wintle, Claire. 2013. "Decolonising the Museum: The Case of the Imperial and Commonwealth Institutes." *Museums and Society* 11(2):185–201.

Wintle, Claire. 2016. "Decolonizing the Smithsonian: Museums as Microcosms of Political Encounter." *American Historical Review* 121(5):1492–1520.

Wissler, Clark. 1942. "The American Indian and the American Philosophical Society." *Proceedings of the American Philosophical Society* 86(1):189–204.

4

MUSEUM ANTHROPOLOGY IN THE NETHERLANDS

Colonial and Postcolonial Narratives

Since the 1980s, "Much printer's ink has been expended in explorations of the colonial baggage of museums and their associated academic disciplines" (Dudley 2015, 2).[1] Yet despite the abundance of literature on the topic, it is surprising how rarely it ranges across national boundaries to provide comparative perspective (Bennett et al. 2017).

The previous chapter examined the history of museum anthropology in the United Sates and changes that have contributed to the development of more publicly engaged, socially relevant, and decolonizing practice. In this chapter, I look at the history and changing landscape of museum anthropology in the Netherlands through case studies of two museums: the National Museum of Ethnology in Leiden and the Tropenmuseum (Tropical Museum) in Amsterdam.[2] I trace the metamorphosis of the museums from the time of their founding during the Dutch colonial era to the present to show how they evolved in correspondence with changes taking place in Dutch society and the wider world. My purpose is to provide a comparative perspective on the relationships between museums and anthropology, and especially, variations in the decolonization of museums (Phillips 2011).

In charting the evolution of the National Museum of Ethnology and the Tropenmuseum, I pay special attention to the public role of museums and anthropology, and the morphology of engagement in colonial and postcolonial settings. What did engagement look like in these different historical contexts and institutions? How were the world's cultures visualized and presented to the public and for what purposes (Bouquet 2012)?

As suggested in the last chapter, an historical perspective allows for a deeper understanding of the complexities of the current moment (Marstine 2006, 21), and reveals narratives that have been overlooked, forgotten, or dismissed. Thinking comparatively about anthropologies and museologies "elsewhere" throws our own canons into relief for closer scrutiny, freeing us from an all too common tendency toward national provincialism (Hannerz 2010, Gingrich and Fox 2002). Thinking comparatively, or what Nader calls "comparative consciousness" (1994), makes visible similarities and differences among phenomena in different times and places, plus patterns and connections, points of intersection and divergence. Combined, an historical and comparative consciousness opens channels for exploring such questions as: What has been shared across national frames and what is unique to a particular context? What has connected us in the past and what connects us now? Under what conditions have change and transformation come about? And what lessons can be learned for the further development of postcolonial, decolonizing museum practice in an interconnected world?

The biographies of the National Museum of Ethnology and the Tropenmuseum encompass decades of change in the history of collecting, exhibiting, and studying the countries and cultures displayed within their exhibition halls. They tell the story of changing relations between those who held the power to display and those put on display. In many respects, what follows is a narrative of the museums' reckoning with the implications of their colonial legacies, and how this reckoning has been entangled in global processes of colonization and decolonization. It also underscores our need to keep in mind the genealogies of museums in diverse environments, and what Erikson refers to as "museum subjectivity." She suggests that "museum subjectivity is the product of interactions between the institution, individuals, and organizations and of broad, social processes. The concept of museum subjectivity, then, refers to the institution's sense of self as related to and shaped by the world around it" (2002, 30). The idea of museum subjectivity reminds us that museums are not independent of their contexts, but rather, are relational and made up of myriad interconnections and relationships (Gosden and Larson 2007, Handler 1993, Kreps 2003a).

The stories of the two museums illustrate how the impact of globalization on museums is not a new phenomenon, but stretches back several centuries. In this regard, museums can be seen as "global theaters" in which international actors have been "part of various global orders for a long time" (Kratz and Karp 2006, 4). I consider how museums, as actors on a global stage, have "managed the pushes and pulls that derived from globalizing processes" (Kratz and Karp 2006, 5).

In the chapter, I revisit research I conducted on Dutch anthropology museums in 1987. I begin with the story of how I became interested in Dutch museums and then describe my fieldwork and research methods as well as initial findings. In the remaining sections of the chapter, I reinterpret my findings in light of more recent research and scholarship on the National Museum of Ethnology and Tropenmuseum, and on the intersection of museums, colonialism, and decolonization more generally. In this sense my account reflects advancements in the critical theory and anthropology of museums since the 1980s, in addition to on-going changes at the museums. Altogether, my aim is to offer an example of how museum ethnography can be enriched by an historical and comparative approach. In Gingrich and Fox's words, "as we make comparisons across space and time we [can] conserve some of the ethnographic richness of context" (2002, 10).

One of my intentions, as in the last chapter, is to draw attention to gaps in the literature on the history of museum anthropology, and specifically, to what Wintle refers to as the "under-examined middle years of the twentieth century" (2013, 185). Wintle writes that much scholarship has been devoted to exposing the links between European museums and imperial agendas before 1945, and on displays of once colonized communities in museums after the 1970s. However, scant attention has been given to the connections between exhibition spaces and the politics of decolonization during the decades in between, which, Wintle argues, offer lessons for the development of postcolonial museum practice today. Especially important, she contends, is how museums concerned with world culture not only reflected political change, but also exercised agency on processes of decolonization.

> Museums helped multiple stakeholders in both metropole and (ex)colony to trial and enact decolonization, neo-colonialism, independence and anti-colonial resistance and acted as microcosms of wider political encounters: the practices of display and acquisition allowed the subjects of a crumbling empire to retain a sense of control over the process of decolonization, but importantly they also provided an arena for emerging powers from the former colonies to assert their own agendas and forced staff at such institutions to take this influence seriously.
>
> *(2013, 185)*

These processes are further illustrated in the next chapter in which I give an account of my research on museum development in Indonesia where the sediment of Dutch colonialism remained legible not only in museums established during the colonial era, but also in the ideology buttressing the postcolonial, national museum system. I address the on-going influence of Dutch museum professionals and other agents in museum and heritage projects. Respectively, this chapter provides historical background for better understanding the narratives presented in later ones. Together they underscore Fanon's assertion that "decolonization is a historical process [that] cannot be understood, cannot become intelligible nor clear to itself except in the exact measure that we can discern the movements which give it historical form and content" (Fanon 1963, 36).

Even though "much printer's ink has been expended" on the subject of museums and colonialism, the subject still demands attention, for as Gosden contends:

> Colonialism is *the* major cultural and historical fact of the last 500 years and to some extent the last 5000 years, although it is said that now we live in a post-colonial world. In some formal sense this is true: colonies are few and empires are absent from the contemporary scene. On the other hand, we are still wrestling with the economic, social, and intellectual consequences of colonialism. When colonialism is viewed comparatively it is disruptive of our views of people, power and objects. By looking at the varying forms of power can take we learn much about the past and unlearn much about the present.
>
> *(2004, 6, emphasis in the original)*

Encountering History

I first became interested in Dutch anthropology museums when I read a set of articles in a 1983 issue of the International Council of Museums (ICOM) journal *Museum* under the theme "New Approaches to Other Cultures in European Museums." Two authors in particular, Guiart and Lightfoot, described trends that had been taking place in a group of European ethnographic museums since the 1970s. The articles can now be read as an early incarnation of the postcolonial critique of museums and critical, reflexive museology. They explain how current practices grew out of a period of "deep self-questioning" regarding museum anthropology's colonial roots and the Eurocentric assumptions and biases on which their institutions rested. Given this history, they asked: What is the contemporary purpose of ethnography and ethnographic museums? And what are the museums' responsibilities not only to their home societies, but also to those that have been the subject of their museums? In the following statement the French anthropologist Jean Guiart contests the museum's "ethnographic authority," and calls for the sharing of that authority.

> By force of circumstance, ethnology has been very much a Western discipline. It must become the property of all, or else it will fall into oblivion. It is not enough to be interested in other people, even if, for a long time, this has been a sign of real progress. There must also be the wish for what they have to say to be of equal weight to what we say ... We are to listen to them first and then to hold a dialogue with them.
>
> *(1983, 138)*

Fred Lightfoot, director of the Commonwealth Institute in London at the time, stressed how museums could not remain stuck in the past, only representing people's traditional and former ways of life. He asserted that it was no longer acceptable to study and present the cultures of "distant peoples," or people who were now living in a "developing Third World," without taking into account their current conditions and realities. The "new type of ethnographical museum," he declared, must "interpret non-Western cultures honestly and sympathetically," be "a meeting place of cultures," and a "platform for the expression of concern for man and his problems" (1983, 140–141).

Among the museums highlighted in the issue was the Tropenmuseum (hereafter TM), which featured exhibitions on development in the "Third World." From what I read, the museum appeared to be radically different from the American anthropology museums with which I was familiar. I was struck by its focus on international development cooperation; nations and constructs such as "the Third World" instead of "culture areas"; and contemporary life, cultural change and survival in place of "vanishing races" and cultures "frozen in time." I was impressed with how the TM openly advocated for the rights and well-being of people living in developing countries, eschewing the scientifically objective and politically neutral stance typical of most anthropology museums. As Lightfoot put it, the museum mounted temporary exhibitions on topics that would be regarded as "no go" subjects in most museums (1983, 143). Additionally, the TM housed a research, documentation, and information center for the public, a theatre that featured international performers, and a children's museum. Altogether, the TM seemed much more dynamic and socially relevant than the typical American anthropology museum (Kreps 1988a).

I traveled to the Netherlands in 1985 to see the TM first hand, and to inquire into the possibility of doing research on the museum. I returned in 1987 to begin what would become an historical study of Dutch ethnographic museums in colonial and postcolonial contexts.[3] This research was not only my first venture into the anthropology of museums and museum ethnography, but also the beginning of an abiding interest in the public role of anthropology museums.

When I began my research there was little literature to draw on for theoretical and methodological guidance since the postcolonial critique and anthropology of museums were just emerging.[4] Consequently, I arrived in the Netherlands without a preconceived theoretical framework and methodological toolkit. The questions driving my research were fairly straightforward, however.

Anthropology museums in both the Netherlands and United States owed their existence to Western expansion and colonialism, and the emergence of anthropology in the nineteenth century. Plus they were part of an international network of museum professionals in which a great deal of information was exchanged regarding museum theory and practice. Given these connections, what accounted for the differences between American and Dutch anthropology museums in their approaches to the representation of non-Western cultures? And what strategies did the museums use to encourage cross-cultural awareness and understanding in the public (Kreps 1988a)?

Not long into my research I realized that in order to answer the first question I needed to look at the larger social and cultural contexts of Dutch museums, and to work backwards, that is, to trace the histories of particular museums to understand how their pasts had informed and shaped their current practices. Thus, what I thought would be an ethnographic account of current museum practices ended up being an historical study of Dutch museums and their transformation.

A few months into my fieldwork, a colleague recommended that I look at H. H. Frese's *Anthropology and the Public: The Role of Museums* (1960). The book proved to be a crucial source of historical information in addition to a conceptual and methodological guide for my research. It can also now be seen as a pioneering work in the anthropology of museums and comparative museology.

Frese was a staff member of the National Museum of Ethnology (NME) in Leiden when he was given the task of setting up a new educational department in the museum to further develop its educational activities. From 1957 to 1958 he took a leave from his post to conduct research on educational work in anthropology museums in Europe (including the United Kingdom), Canada, the United States, Australia, and New Zealand. In his book, Frese states that although his research largely concerned educational theory and pedagogy, his study "remains within the realm of cultural anthropology." By this he meant that the same approach to the study of non-Western cultures that had been the subject of museums was taken to the study of the institutions themselves "with respect to their origins and typological diversity" and their "interaction with the main schools of thought in anthropological theory"; and finally as "an attempt to give an anthropology of the western public" (Frese 1960, 3). Frese further explains that the concept of education was "treated mainly in its anthropological implications ... [I] it is formally defined as referring to the ways in which the museums perform their intermediary role for the public" (Frese 1960, 3).

From the beginning of my research, I had struggled with how to define and classify anthropology museums due to the many kinds of museums that house anthropological collections. Frese's typology of museums was particularly useful in this regard. He proposed that the main criteria for categorizing museums should be the "motivation or orientation of the institution" (1960, 5). In spite of their diversity, Frese suggested that museums with significant anthropological collections could be divided into two main categories: "those with an orientation predominantly if not exclusively in the field of science and those founded for reasons outside the field" (Frese 1960, 15). Within the first category, Frese lists encyclopedic, natural history, archaeology, ethnology, and museums of "man." The second category encompasses geography-economy (colonial museums), missionary museums, and art museums.

Based on Frese's typology, my study primarily focused on the TM, the NME, and the Afrika Centrum (Africa Center) in Cadir en Keer near the Dutch city of Maastricht. I was interested in how the different "motivations and orientations" of these institutions influenced why and how they represented non-Western cultures. The NME was the only museum in my survey that was explicitly oriented to science, or ethnology, whereas the other two, the TM and Africa Center, respectively, were founded as colonial and missionary museums.

Over an eight-month period I combed through museum guides, catalogs, reports, bulletins, brochures, scholarly publications, and any other pertinent material available in English to reconstruct the histories of the individual institutions as well as Dutch anthropology museums in general. I visited seven anthropological museums, one history, and one educational museum where I interviewed curators, museum educators, and directors to gain insight into past and current practices and the philosophical perspectives that informed them. I also created an exhibition evaluation instrument to critically assess various display methods and content.

In brief, I learned that the origin and growth of these, as well as several other Dutch anthropology museums, was inextricably linked to the expansion of the Dutch empire and subsequent colonialism. Beginning in the early 1600s, the Dutch, through the aegis of the United East Indies Company (Verenige Oost-Indische Compagne—VOC), gained control of territories in the East Indies or what is now the Republic of Indonesia.[5] In 1800, the Dutch Crown took possession of the Company's holdings in the East and West Indies, ushering in the era of political colonialism. In the case of Indonesia, this period lasted until 1949 when

Indonesia gained independence from the Dutch (Benda 1965, Chamberlain 1999, Ellen 1976).

How and why non-Western cultures had been represented in museums was, in many regards, based on particular kinds of interests in and relationships with non-Western peoples, i.e., scientific (ethnology), commercial (trade and industry), and religious (missionary). Collections had been assembled as a result of scientific research, military expeditions, commercial trade and economic exploits as well as missionary work in the colonies. After World War II, the Netherlands lost control of their colonial territories and the era of decolonization commenced. As relations between the Dutch and non-Western people began to change, these changes were mirrored in the museums. But museums, throughout this time, were not simply mirroring the changes taking place. They were also helping shape them. Basically, Dutch anthropology museums had been undergoing a process of decolonization since the mid-twentieth century—a process that involved critically reflecting on their pasts and reorienting their purposes (Kreps 1988a, 56).

I also learned that Dutch anthropology had grown up in tandem with colonialism as it had in the United States. During the latter half of the nineteenth century as colonial exploits intensified, the need of the Dutch government to know more about colonial subjects grew steadily. Ethnographers were employed by the colonial government to study Indigenous cultures, especially their social and political structures, customary law, and economic relationship with other groups to inform policy. Ethnographic museums benefited from the work of ethnographers in the colonies since some of the collections they made ended up in the museums of their homelands (Avé 1980, Bouquet 2012, Ellen 1976).

Not surprisingly, I also became aware of the differences between Dutch and American colonialism. Aside from temporal and spatial variations the most profound difference was that unlike the Dutch, who were forced to relinquish political control of and leave their colonies, the United States was (and continues to be) a settler-colonial nation.[6]

Founding Narratives

The National Museum of Ethnology in Leiden was founded on Enlightenment ideals and from its beginning was invested in the scientific pursuit of ethnology, or the newly emerging "science of man." In 1831, Dr. Philip Franz Von Siebold, a physician-scholar and early ethnographer, presented a letter titled "On the Suitability and Usefulness of an Ethnographical Museum in the Netherlands" to King Willem I of the Netherlands, requesting support for the establishment of an ethnology museum. In the letter, Von Siebold expounded upon the scholarly merits and moral virtues of the ethnographic endeavor:

> Man in his manifold developments under foreign climates is the principal subject of an ethnographical museum. An entertaining and instructive and therefore useful occupation is provided by following the inhabitants of foreign

countries and studying their peculiarities. It is even a moral, religious work to occupy oneself in this way with one's fellow man, to learn the good qualities in him and to get nearer to his self by becoming more familiar with an alien exterior which frequently repels us without our knowing why.

(Rijksmuseum voor Volkenkunde 1962, 2)

Von Siebold also offered the following definition of an ethnology museum, which, in Bouquet's view, was "little short of a manifesto."

An ethnographic museum is a scientifically arranged collection of objects from different lands—mainly outside of Europe—which both in their own right and in relation to other objects further acquaint us with the people to whom they belong. Placing before our eyes their religion, manners, and customs, the museum provides us with a clear idea of the state of their arts and sciences, their rural economy, handicrafts, industry and trade.

(Von Siebold quoted in Bouquet 2012, 63)

But ethnographic museums for Von Siebold were not to be the exclusive domain of scholars and elites. He argued, like Boas did at the turn of the twentieth century, that an ethnographic museum should also be a place of amusement and education for the general public (Bouquet 2012, 72). Von Siebold insisted that taking an enlightened and noble interest in one's "fellow man" was the "mark of civilization," and believed that a museum was a place where the public could learn about the customs, religions, and ways of life of foreign peoples. Notwithstanding these enlightened principles, Bouquet injects that an ethnographic museum at home made it possible for those who had never travelled to distant lands to imagine the people whom their fellow countrymen were conquering, administering, converting, and educating. The museum was a place where members of the public could learn about themselves and their own position in a world order divided among colonizers and colonized, civilized and uncivilized (2012, 76–77).

In making his case to the King, Von Siebold recommended that an ethnographic museum would be an appropriate environment for training civil servants, missionaries, administrators, officers, traders, and seamen preparing for tours of duty in colonial territories. "Simply by looking at the objects on display, he explained, one could gain a clear idea of the level of civilization, the arts and sciences there and the people whom they hoped to convert, rule, trade with or otherwise manage, in an engaging and intelligent way" (Bouquet 2012, 74). Von Siebold's arguments were convincing and the Rijks Etnografisch Museum (Royal Ethnographic Museum) was formed in 1837.

The founding collection of the museum contained some 5000 objects that Von Siebold collected when he was stationed in Japan from 1823 to 1830 at the Dutch trading post on the island of Deshima off the coast of Nagasaki. At that time, the Dutch had already enjoyed 200 years of exclusive trading rights with Japan (Van Gulik 1980, 40). The first displays open to the public featured, in addition to

Japanese and Chinese art objects, the raw materials and tools used by artisans and craftspeople and other objects of daily life (Staal and de Rijk 2003, 32). Von Siebold is often acknowledged as one of the forefathers of "scientific" museum ethnography in his attempt to apply systematic scientific principles of classification to collections (Shelton 2006, 66). He believed that objects should be classified and presented according to their geographical place of origin first and secondarily by function. Van Gulik, the director of the NME at the time of my research and a curator of Japanese art and culture, also acknowledged Von Siebold's contributions to the nascent field of museum anthropology.

> From the outset Von Siebold had well-defined plans for the collecting and researching of Japanese material culture and during his stay in Japan indeed managed to bring together a substantial collection of ethnographic material based on a level of systematics, insight and approach which was surprisingly ahead of his time.
>
> *(1980, 40)*

While Von Siebold's motivations have been presented as being primarily scientific and educational, they aligned with the King's own ambitions. In 1820, he formed the Natural Science Committee (Natuurkundige Comissie), which was entrusted with conducting research in the colonies and making collections of natural history specimen and artifacts. As true for other monarchs across Europe at the time, amassing collections and erecting museums was part of the King's plan to bring status and prestige to his emerging nation (ter Keurs 2012, 170–174)[7]

Between 1857 and 1870, the museum developed into a small institute chiefly concerned with China and Japan. Collections from King Willem's Royal Cabinet of Curiosities were added in 1883, which contained objects from Japan, China, Indonesia, and West Africa (Frese 1960, 7). The museum's collections were greatly enlarged when it received a significant share of the Dutch exhibits featured in the International Colonial Exhibition held in Amsterdam in 1883. This collection included a number of model houses from different parts of the Dutch East Indies complete with furnishings and mannequins in traditional dress (Bouquet 2012, 84).

Into the late nineteenth and early twentieth centuries the museum's collections continued to expand with objects obtained from the Pacific, Africa, the Americas, Siberia and the Arctic. But much of the collection came from the East Indies, some of which was a result of several military and scientific expeditions. The most important addition at the time was a collection of Hindu-Buddhist stone sculptures and other classical antiquities from the islands of Java and Sumatra. Thus, the museum's collection comprised an array of objects of art (particularly Buddhist and Hindu religious art), classical antiquities, ceremonial regalia and ritual objects, and ethnographic objects (Frese 1960)[8] By the 1930s, housing and properly caring for the growing collection, which was scattered across a number of buildings in Leiden, became a problem. In 1931, the collection was consolidated and moved to a nineteenth-century building that had served as a university hospital. The museum re-opened to the public in 1937 in this building that remains its home to this day.

The forerunner of the TM was the Colonial Museum (Koloniaal Museum) in Haarlem, organized as a private collection in 1824 by a group of wealthy colonial entrepreneurs that constituted the Dutch Trading Society (Nederlandisch Handel-Maatschappij). With the support of King Willem I, the purpose of the Society was to promote commercial interests in the colonies. In 1871 the Colonial Museum was opened to the public, and began to receive support from the Ministry of Colonies (Van Brakel 2002, 169). The museum displayed colonial products and the raw materials used to manufacture them, such as tropical woods, bamboo, rubber, and palm oil as well as native-made items like handicrafts, weapons, vehicles, and musical instruments. One floor of the museum was set aside for research with study collections. The museum also contained a Pharmaceutical Room and Herbarium where medicines, seeds, herbs, and fruits from all over the world were shown (Bouquet 2012, 84). The museum's aim was to encourage the commercial exploitation of natural resources and agricultural products from the colonies (Van Duuren 2011, 13).

In 1910 the Colonial Museum was transferred to Amsterdam and merged with the Colonial Institute that was to be dedicated primarily to research and training colonial civil servants, traders, missionaries, military personnel, and others conducting business in the colonies. Private banking interests, trading companies, the Ministry of Colonies, and Amsterdam city council donated funds for the construction of a new building to house both the Colonial Institute and Colonial Museum, which was opened to the public in 1926 by Queen Wilhelmina. Described as "massive and flamboyant" (Aldrich 2009, 141–142), the 44,000-square-meter building was decorated with colonial motifs along with allegorical figures depicting the virtues of introducing European science, government, and religion to native populations.

The Colonial Museum's collection contained some 30,000 artifacts (mainly ethnographic and trade objects) transferred from the museum in Haarlem as well as some 12,000 ethnographic objects previously held by the Amsterdam Zoo (Naturis Artis Magistra) (Van Brakel 2002, 169, Bouquet 2012). In addition to these collections, the building also housed a library, research laboratories, photography archives, a conservatory with collections of seeds, wood samples and other tropical products. In general, the Institute served as a center of research for the development of expertise in the fields of colonial trade, tropical medicine, agriculture, and anthropology. Another central purpose of the Colonial Museum was to give the Dutch public a view of life in the colonies and the "great achievements of the Kingdom" (Tropenmuseum 1987).

Whereas the NME in Leiden was oriented toward science and aesthetics, the Colonial Museum was driven mainly by commercial and colonial interests and existed to promote these interests at home and abroad. In a passage describing colonial museums in Europe, including the one in Amsterdam, Frese describes the motivations behind their establishment:

Stemming from an economic and commercial interest or motivated by political reasons, they were the results of a feeling of dissatisfaction with the existing more scientifically oriented museums, and the desire to create a new type of institution for the information of the larger public on all matters pertaining to the colonies.

(1960, 29)[9]

Because the Colonial Museum was intended to give the public a picture of life in colonial territories, that of the colonized and colonizers, special attention was paid to how goods were produced and the people who produced them. Its collections contained examples of commodities that were being extracted from the colonies, in addition to ethnographic materials. Displays of spices, coffee, tobacco, sugar, rubber, and technology used in their processing were shown alongside dioramas and models of plantations and factories. According to Frese, even though examples of the native populations' material culture were displayed in a fashion similar to more scientifically oriented museums like the NME, they were also "intended to show the simple means the indigenous people used in their technology and subsistence economy" (1960, 29). Ritual and religious objects were shown to highlight the strange and exotic customs of "primitive" peoples. And as the museum strived to provide up-to-date information on the colonies and how they were developing, exhibitions often portrayed the changes taking place in Indigenous cultures (Kal 1981, 59). The ideology behind the exhibits was clear: colonialism could be justified on the basis of how it was bringing progress and "civilization" to the colonies.

Tony Bennett, in his essay "The Exhibitionary Complex," describes how this was a common strategy deployed in imperial displays.

In the context of imperial displays, subject peoples were thus represented as occupying the lowest levels of manufacturing civilization. Reduced to displays of 'primitive' handicrafts and the like, they were represented as cultures without momentum except for that benignly bestowed on them from without through the improving mission of the imperialist powers.

(1999, 353–354)

Reflecting the thinking of the time, the Netherlands was presenting itself as an "enlightened colonizer" that was "duty bound to develop colonial society overseas not only for its own benefit, but also for the benefit of its colonial subjects" (Legêne and Van Dijk 2011, 10). The public, in looking at the exhibitions, was effectively looking at the populations of its empire, and government support for public museums was a way in which Dutch citizens were encouraged to participate in the colonial enterprise and its "civilizing" mission (Bouquet 2012, 90).

In addition to presenting visual reports of the successes of colonialism, the Colonial Museum and Institute also served as a training center, as noted above, for civil servants, military personnel, missionaries, and commercial agents traveling to the colonies. Training included instruction in the languages of the territory, and specific information on the culture of the people and region in question (Avé 1980, Nauta 1980, Van Brakel 2002). Anthropology as practiced within the Colonial Museum was a decidedly applied science that largely functioned as an "enabling technology" of the state (Bennett 1995).

The Dutch anthropologist, J. B. Avé, in his "Ethnographical Museums in a Changing World,"[10] generalizes the character of ethnographic museums during the colonial era:

> Collections pertain almost exclusively to the Dutch East Indies ... Collecting is unsystematic ... [and] the description and classification of the object is defective. In most cases, only the form of the objects is described. There is little or no information about their function in society or on their makers ... The presentation corresponds to colonial times: it is the foreign, the differences from Western culture, the exotic aspects which are shown and stressed ... No reference is made to the history of the colonized peoples, and thus no mention is made of changes or innovations which have occurred or are occurring in that culture ... Finally, the organization of areas in an ethnographical museum is a reflection of colonialistic thinking. Individual cultures are grouped into 'cultural regions,' regardless of their ethnic history.
>
> *(1980, 12–13)*

The End of Empire and Beginning of Decolonization

After World War II and with the Dutch imperial era drawing to a close, the two museums began to experience the impact of decolonization. The Colonial Museum and Institute especially had to reorient their mission and purposes to remain relevant and in step with the changing ethos of the times. As such, they began to mirror changing relations between the colonizers and the colonized brought on by the restructuring of the world order, as well as changes occurring in Dutch society. As Buettner suggests, decolonization involved not just relinquishing formal control over colonial territories. It also involved coming to terms with the loss of the colonial order that had benefitted many Europeans and grappling with colonialism's far-reaching implications.

> Decolonization was never merely a chronologically and politically contained 'transfer of power' from rule by Europeans to independence as new Asian, African, and Caribbean nations after 1945. It had a pre-history stretching back through decades of rising contestation and lacked tidy closure when some flags were lowered and others raised at staged independence ceremonies. Just as important, it involved (ex-)colonizers and (ex-)colonized alike at every turn, whether the actors in question were situated in the empire, in Europe, or having undertaken journeys bridging metropolitan and colonial worlds. Not only were former colonies remade as a result of the path to decolonization: so

too was Western Europe, both nationally as well as on local and international levels, which needed to decolonize itself.

(2016, 4–5)

A nationalist movement in the Netherlands East Indies declared independence in 1945 giving birth to the Republic of Indonesia, although the formal transfer of sovereignty to Indonesia did not occur until 1949 (Chamberlain 1999, 85). The Colonial Institute changed its name in 1945 to the Indies Institute (Indisch Instituut) with the hope of maintaining ties with the Netherlands' most economically and politically important colony. But with the impending loss of the East Indies and under threat of being closed it was pressed to adopt a new name and mission. In 1950, the Colonial Institute was renamed the Royal Tropical Institute (Koninklijk Instituut voor de Tropen—KIT) and the Colonial Museum became the Tropenmuseum (Hildering et al. 2015, 312). At this point, the KIT and its museum broadened their geographical scope to include all the tropical regions of the world (not just those of former colonies). They also began to revise their missions to align with a new government mandate to promote international development cooperation. Correspondingly, in 1952, funding for the Institute and museum shifted from the Ministry of Colonial Affairs to the Ministry of Foreign Affairs (Hildering et al. 2015, 315).

During the 1960s, the KIT intensified its research and training in tropical agriculture, health care, trade and economics, in addition to cultural anthropology. Staff members were sent to tropical countries throughout the "Third World" to provide technical assistance as part of development aid and cooperation (Legêne and Van Dijk 2011, 11). As the public face of the KIT, the TM became more and more devoted to "visualizing development" (Hildering et al. 2015, 315), and educating visitors about the connections between the Netherlands and the tropical regions of the world.

After World War II, the Netherlands and other former colonial powers still needed raw materials and agricultural products from their erstwhile colonies to fuel their rapidly industrializing economies. Newly independent, developing nations were also viewed as valuable markets for European products as well as a reservoir of cheap labor. The development of Third World economies and societies was critical to the further development of the free market economies of Europe (Avé 1980, 14). "Cold War" politics and economics also came into play as "First World" nations saw international development cooperation and aid as an instrument for maintaining world peace and checking the spread of communism (Hildering et al. 2015, 312–313).

Dutch anthropology, or ethnology, was also being recalibrated in the face of postcolonial developments. Avé states that during this time ethnologists started to realize that many ethnological theories and approaches like functionalism and material culture studies had become "unusable" (1980, 15). In turn, new fields such as "non-Western sociology" and political anthropology emerged, often informed by Marxist perspectives that critiqued socio-political structures, colonialism, and neo-colonial approaches to development. Moreover, the ethics of the profession were increasingly scrutinized as anthropologists became evermore concerned about their responsibility to the people with whom they lived and worked. Debates arose surrounding the misuse of data in the past, and the need to revise existing methods for more practical application in the present. This criticism was heightened by the fact that the new nations now had their own anthropologists who were highly critical of the neo-colonialism and paternalism behind "development" and "modernization" (Avé 1980, 16).

The ethnic makeup of Dutch society was also changing during this period. Between 1948 and 1962, some 300,000 Indonesian-Dutch and Moluccans (who had sided with the Dutch during the revolutionary period) along with West Indians were resettled in the Netherlands. Large numbers of migrants from southern Europe, North Africa, and the Middle East were also flowing into the country to work in its busy harbors and factories. The Netherlands was becoming an increasingly multicultural country (Buettner 2016, 375).

Visitors to Dutch museums were also changing in character. They were better educated and more aware of the economic, social, and political realities of people living in developing countries as seen on television, in films, and in their travels. Yet in anthropology museums visitors largely saw idyllic and romanticized portrayals of exotic people and ways of life. What's more, former colonial subjects and the people who had historically been the subjects of anthropology museums were now part of the museums' increasingly diverse public (Avé 1980, 16) and members of the museums' staff. Given these social and cultural dynamics both the TM and NME recognized the need to broaden and enhance their educational services (Avé 1980, 16).

An Educational Service was set up in the TM in 1969 to design educational programming for the public. Paul Berghuis, an educator working at the museum during this period and one of my research partners, stressed that the service's goals were to present a more realistic picture of life in developing countries and to create empathy within the public for people and their problems (Berghuis 1979). This "emancipatory" approach was intended to raise public awareness of the disparities between the developed and developing worlds (Avé 1980, 16). Temporary exhibitions reflected the times. For example, *India Now*, presented in 1969, depicted modernization and development in India and the problems they engendered. A subsequent exhibit, *Thailand: Between City and Countryside*, was the product of a joint expedition anthropologists from four Dutch ethnographic museums made to Thailand. It was planned and executed in collaboration with a Thai university and museum.[11] The TM, however, did not just confine its exhibits and programming to people and problems abroad. It also tackled the struggles of "minorities" in Dutch society, such as problems related to immigrants' social integration and welfare (Avé 1980, 23).

Although the Tropenmuseum had been devoting space to exhibits on international development since the 1960s, B. J. Udink, then Minister of Development Cooperation, made the following proposal to the staff in his annual address to the KIT in 1970:

> I would like to examine the possibility of expanding the museum's field of operation to make it a national centre for exhibitions about development cooperation. A dynamic meeting place which would make use of visual techniques with an appeal to the wide public and which would stage ever changing exhibitions in order to present the many facets of development in a clear fashion to a vast number of visitors … a centre every bit as vital as the process of development itself.
>
> *(Udink quoted in Lightfoot 1983, 141)*

The staff saw Udink's challenge as an opportunity to completely renovate and transform the museum. It closed in 1975 and much of the museum's ethnographic and historical objects went into storage since development cooperation, it was believed, could not be represented with objects from the past. This remit required new acquisitions and new exhibition strategies that broke with the past and concentrated on the future (Hildering et al. 2015, 317).

Changes in Exhibiting Strategies at the Tropenmuseum

Her Majesty Queen Juliana of the Netherlands re-opened a renovated and re-imagined TM in 1979. Jan de Koning, the Minister of Development Cooperation, and Amadou-Mahtar M'Bow, Director General of UNESCO, delivered speeches in which they stressed the museum's responsibility in "transferring current, realistic information about the Third World countries to the Dutch public" (Tropenmuseum 1979, quoted in Hildering et al. 2015, 316).

According to Harrie Leyten, a former missionary and curator in the Africa Department as well as another research partner, the staff had three main goals for the "new" TM. First, people would be placed at the center and forefront of all museum programs to show the Dutch public that "there are human beings all over the world who, whatever their superficial differences … share fundamental concerns about daily food, a roof over their heads, health for themselves and children, employment and peace" (Leyten 1987, 5). Secondly, the museum was to show the processes of political, economic, social, and cultural development in which people are engaged. The third aim was to highlight the interdependencies between developed and developing nations. Departments and permanent exhibits on world trade, environmental issues, and technology were created to emphasize these connections. Above all, the museum wanted to avoid perpetuating stereotypical images of "primitive" and "exotic" peoples commonly found in more conventional anthropological museums.

The curators of the TM wanted to tell the story of the everyday life of ordinary people. Although this had long been a theme of the museum, the new exhibitions included mass-produced consumer goods such as plastic buckets, aluminum pots and pans, canned foods, Western-style clothing, and motor bikes. These items were often displayed alongside historical ethnographic objects to highlight culture change. A variety of media, such as photography, film, newspaper clippings as well as music was used to provide further context and for telling people's stories.

Even though the TM was using contemporary, mass-produced objects and materials in its exhibitions, according to Wilhelmina Kal, a curator of Southeast Asia at the museum, the authenticity of objects was still important. In Kal's words, "an authentic object which comes from a world which is foreign to us can by itself tell us something about the people who made and used the object" (1979, 16). With this principle in mind, curators and educators traveled to countries to collect and document objects in their original contexts. An object's value was judged to the extent it could tell a story or communicate a message and an exhibit's storyline (Kal 1979).

Exhibition halls were organized by geographical region and particular themes, such as population pressures in South Asia, the disparity between the rich and the poor in Latin America, and religion and history in the Middle East and North Africa. Using what they called the "evocative" approach, curators and educators designed life-size recreations of social settings such as a housing compound in Burkina Faso, a bazaar in Morocco, and slums in Bombay and Calcutta. The evocative approach was intended to give the visitor the feeling of "being there" and the chance to "enter, temporarily, into a world different from one's own" (Avé 1980, 23, Van Wengen 1980) (see Figure 4.1).[12]

As the staff was planning the new museum they were confronted with how to present development topics within the context of a museum since development, in theory and practice, meant different things to different people. Western theories and models of development used as a framework for exhibitions in the 1960s were questioned since they were based on Western ideas of progress and material growth. Staff furthermore recognized that people in developing nations were conscious of the state in which the colonial powers had left their countries—economically dependent and subjugated to Western political and economic interests. To many critics of the museum development was a form of neo-colonialism and the Dutch government had just stepped into the shoes of the business leaders who formerly sponsored the Colonial Institute and its museum (Kreps 1988a). The fact that several members of the KIT's board of directors were top managers of Dutch multinational corporations with substantial investments in developing countries added weight to this argument (Huizer 1979, 38).

The question of how to present problems in a museum was also under discussion. How could a museum primarily concerned with presenting the realities of the Third World not deal with problems and their political underpinnings? How would the public react to exhibitions that focused on problems, and how far should a museum go in presenting them? In a museum such as the TM objectivity was nearly impossible. As Nico Bogart, director of the museum in 1979, attested: "Of course the problem of subjective perceptions returns to haunt us whatever aspects of the Third World and its relations we chose to present in a museum display. Development is one topic that practically defies objectivity" (1979).

In an interview, Kal claimed that one of the museum's aims was to show as many facets of people's lives as possible. For example, she explained that: "If the people live in a poor country then that is part of their reality. But it is not enough

Step into another world in the Tropenmuseum

The Tropenmuseum is located in one of the finest buildings of Amsterdam. As you will see when you are inside the museum, it consists of an impressive hall with a glass dome at a height of 22 meters. This light-hall is surrounded by galleries arranged in three layers. Here, about ten exhibitions offer a many-sided picture of human life in the tropics and subtropics. You will get an impression of the way in which people are housed there, you can hear them talking, laughing and making music, while at the same time you will be informed about the often immense problems confronting them.

In the **Tropenmuseum** you may walk through an Arab street and hear the sound of buyers and sellers, of donkey-drivers and garage mechanics. In the South Asia department you will have to find your way between small hovels where people live and work. These shelters are made of old crates, cardboard, corrugated iron and plastic bags – the same material that is used in the shanty towns of cities like Bombay and Calcutta.

FIGURE 4.1 Fold of brochure collected in 1987 that shows the museum's exhibition style and discourse at the time. An excerpt from the text reads: "You will be able to find answers to the question what people in the Western world have to do with people in the tropics, and you may wonder what it means that we all inhabit one world"

Source: Scanned image. Brochure produced by the Tropenmuseum in 1986. Photographs by Nico Boink.

to just show the gap between rich and poor, or how the poor live in their poverty and the rich live in their richness. One must also try to depict how the disparity developed." The goal was to give a full picture and as many dimensions of the story as possible.[13]

Some exhibitions and programs inspired public opinion to the point of action. In 1982, the museum installed the exhibit *Mother's Milk, Powder Milk*, which sought to establish a causal link between the production of milk-powder in the Netherlands and high infant mortality in developing countries. Organized in conjunction with the United Nations Children's Fund (UNICEF), the exhibition sparked a vehement debate and boycott in Holland, contributing to the decision on the part of one company to change its controversial trademark (Kreps 1988a, 60).

The TM continued to alter its approaches against a backdrop of on-going criticism and societal change. By 1987, when I first began my research, the museum had already started to revise its approach in response to changing attitudes both inside and outside the museum. I was told that the public had grown weary of seeing mostly problems in the museum, such as poverty, hunger, economic inequality, and environmental degradation. Because visitors wanted to have less confrontational experiences in the museum and to see objects presented more attractively, curators were trying to make the exhibitions more aesthetically appealing by focusing more on art, both contemporary and historical. They realized that constantly portraying people as victims also created a distorted view of reality. As H. J. Gortzak, the Director of the TM at the time of my research, put it in a conference presentation: "You cannot present the people in the Third World as poor devils without culture. The people of the Third World don't buy that anymore" (Gortzak quoted in Leijendekker 1987, 8, translated here). However, as Kal told me, just showing "nice" objects in an anthropological museum is not enough either. "Objects without a story are meaningless." She believed that the museum needed to remain true to its primary objective, and that was to educate the public about the world's peoples and cultures through its main medium—objects.

Reassessing Priorities at the National Museum of Ethnology

The changes that took place in the National Museum of Ethnology following the "end of empire" (Wintle 2013) and decolonization were not as radical as those in the Tropenmuseum owing to its particular history and scientific orientation. From its earliest years, the scope of its collections and study areas extended beyond Dutch colonial territories. Furthermore, as a scientific and research institution connected to the University of Leiden and funded by the Ministry of Education, it did not function, at least overtly, as a mouthpiece for colonial propaganda. Nevertheless, the museum was experiencing its own set of challenges.

Museum anthropology in the Netherlands, as in the United States, was being eclipsed by academic anthropology. By the 1950s and 1960s, Avé states that Dutch anthropology's connections with ethnographical museums were minimal, "even though a number of university professors and readers in anthropology and 'non-Western' sociology started their careers as curators in ethnographical museums" (1980, 15). Traditional anthropology museums like the NME contained collections predominantly from the past that had been accumulated during a time in which ethnologists were mostly interested in the study of "primitive" people, inasmuch as they were not in contact with Western culture. Thus, their research, collections, and displays did not reflect the changes that non-Western people were experiencing as a result of colonialism, modernization, and development. According to Frese, museum anthropologists had been slow or reluctant to deal with culture change and acculturated objects largely because such objects were no longer seen as indicators of cultural difference. Their studies were by and large ahistorical and grounded in the "ethnographic present" (Fabian 1983). On the whole, museum anthropology had not kept abreast of developments in anthropological theory, and in many regards, anthropology museums had become akin to history museums. Consequently, the museum was increasingly being pressured to respond to growing criticisms that it was no longer relevant in a rapidly changing world (Frese 1960, 66–67).

The museum's public stance and educational services were also seen as deficient in comparison to that of other museums, especially the TM. Even though public education had been one of the arguments Von Siebold made for the establishment of the museum back in the 1830s, and the museum had begun to increase its educational services in the late 1940s, it primarily remained a scientific institute and the purview of researchers, scholars, and Asian art connoisseurs.

Ongoing efforts to enhance the educational services of the museum, mostly on the part of the museum's educational staff, gained momentum in the 1950s when the Dutch government began to urge all museums to place greater emphasis on serving the educational interests of their visitors. In 1954, the museum enlarged its educational services by formally creating an educational department, which to Frese, was one of the first ethnographic museums in Europe to do so (1960, 76).

Similar to large, public and research-oriented museums in the United States, debates ignited around the NME's obligations to public education. In fact, Frese's study of museums, described earlier, was primarily devoted to this issue. The underlying problem that informed his research was how anthropology museums could meet their multiple demands.

> Museums are institutions whose responsibility it is to store and preserve collections of artefacts. They are virtual archives of objects taken from all over the world. At the same time, they are centres for scientific research, i.e., anthropological research. Their purpose is to study the objects and the related non-western cultures. Last but not least, the museums are to serve the public. It means they are generally considered to be educational institutions as well.
>
> *(1960, 2)*

Frese recounts how lines were drawn between curators, or research staff, and educators. The former argued that public education should be subordinated to scientific work while the latter maintained that the museum should be first and foremost an educational institution in service to the public (Frese 1960, 3, Van Wengen 1980). Vestiges of these frictions were still discernible in the museum in 1987 (the year of my fieldwork), as well as its conventional approaches to cultural representation.

In contrast to the TM, most of the museum's permanent exhibitions resembled older-style ethnographic museums with objects representing past ways of life and texts in the language of outdated anthropology. But the museum was attempting to mitigate its outmoded image through the presentation of thematic, temporary exhibitions. For example, during my research period, the museum, in celebration of its 150th anniversary, installed the jubilee exhibition *The Seasons of Humankind*. The exhibit's theme was the "the most important phases of human life: birth, initiation, marriage, and death" (Van Gulik 1987, 1). Although the "life cycle" is a fairly conventional subject in anthropology museums and carry traces of classic ethnology, the exhibit differed from earlier displays by showing contemporary objects next to older pieces from its collections. Moreover, the exhibit did not just represent the rites of passage of non-Western peoples, but also those of Europeans to give visitors a cross-cultural, comparative perspective on the subject.

The museum had been using this style of temporary, thematic exhibitions that reversed the anthropological gaze ever since the 1950s. According to Van Wengen, who had been working at the museum in the educational department since the 1950s and was still there in 1987, thematic, temporary exhibitions were created to give displays "a more lively aspect" and to make them more appealing to the public. In the essay "Educational Museumwork in Relation to Scientific Work and Presentation in Museums" published in 1980, he described two exhibits that "attracted attention" in the 1950s. *How Others See Us* (mounted in 1955) was an exhibit on how non-Europeans pictured Europeans, and *Strange Origins of Everyday Things* (1952) traced the origin and circulation of objects the Dutch used in everyday life (1980, 140). Moving into the 1960s, the museum progressively mounted temporary, thematic exhibits to present current social topics.

By the 1970s, some of the museum's curators, such as Gerti Nooter, a curator of Native American and Arctic collections from 1970 to 1990, had started focusing their research on culture change and collecting "acculturated" objects. In an interview, Nooter spoke extensively about how museum-based material culture research complements ethnographic fieldwork, and the value of museum collections for the study of culture change: "I don't say that material culture is the only factor in change. But it's not useful to try to study culture or social change without having analyzed changes in material culture in the same period."[14]

Nooter had been documenting changes in traditional technology as well as the impact of new technologies on the hunting practices of Greenland peoples since the 1960s. His research was featured in an exhibition shown in the museum in 1985 titled *Life and Survival in the Arctic: Changes in Polar Regions*. The exhibit highlighted the contemporary socioeconomic conditions of Arctic peoples and the politics surrounding hunting. Nooter shared that the exhibition had drawn protests from members of Greenpeace and the World Wildlife Fund. Protests, however, did not bother him. In fact he said he invited debate and controversy, and thought it was crucial for the museum to take a position on matters of importance to the people featured in the museum. But at the same time, he stressed that if a museum is going to present exhibitions on controversial topics then that exhibition has to be based on solid scientific research. For Nooter, museums had a responsibility to present truthful information to the public.[15] Interestingly, during our interview, he also shared that the NME had denied the Glenbow Museum's request to borrow objects for *The Spirit Sings* exhibit, discussed in the previous chapter.

In spite of these efforts to keep up with the times and be relevant, in 1987 the NME had the reputation of being less progressive and publicly engaged in comparison to other museums. In an interview, W. R. Van Gulik, director of the museum, acknowledged that the museum had lagged behind other museums in its educational services and public stance. In his mind, this was largely due to the museum's history and scientific orientation. And although he stated that the museum was continually striving to "catch up" with other museums, he emphasized that it was also important for it to maintain its integrity as a scientific institution. In the following passages, Van Gulik muses over the museum's past, its changing priorities, and possible future directions:

> I think the time has passed that museums are considered institutions of research and learning as a goal in itself. We have the duty and also necessity to approach the public and see how the public reacts, which means there is a shift in attention from pure research, conservation, and collecting to the public and its behavior ... Historically we were part of the Ministry of Education and the university [Leiden]. That means the accent on research and the results of research were considered more important. We were generally considered a place where one would study and the public would be considered more or less a nuisance. But I think since the Second World War museums are more aware of themselves as a social institution ... with a specific role for society in terms of education, recreation, and information. It is true that we as a museum have lapsed behind developments and we have to catch up ... But it is never possible, I think, without the necessary basis of scientific research because the exhibitions we present should be based on sound fieldwork and analysis derived from scientific anthropological research.[16]

Van Gulik also talked about the museum's need to adapt to a fluctuating economic climate as it was most likely facing cuts in government funding, and was increasingly being pressured to better market itself. He was quick to point out, however, that the Dutch situation could not be compared to that in the United States where "the culture and approach [to funding] is quite different."

All museums are rather dependent on the income of visitors and so you are forced now to organize exhibitions which attract attention of the greater public. It is becoming increasingly interesting for us to see what they [visitors] think, what they like to see, what they expect from the museum, which means that more than in the past we have to be aware of marketing. So here you see how museums are directed more toward business-like institutions where the principles of profit making become more interesting than the non-measurable results of scientific research ... Where funds are limited people are forced to think about other ways of deriving funds. The United States is already very far in that where the whole culture is different. But I think it's rather dangerous to compare both our countries in the field of sponsoring exhibitions. It is a completely different approach.[17]

Indeed, differences between American and Dutch attitudes toward and sources of funding for museums became an important topic in my research, and I had many discussions with museum staff on public versus private, especially corporate, sponsorship. Whereas Dutch museums had long enjoyed support primarily from public sources, i.e., the government, museums in the United States relied on the American tradition of public/private partnerships and had evolved within a culture of private philanthropy and self-sufficiency (Wyszomirski 1999). Several interviewees told me they looked to the United States for ideas on public relations and marketing since it was a "world leader" in this aspect of museum work. Although generating income by increasing visitor numbers was not something they had to worry much about at the time, they feared that this was a challenge they would be forced to face in the future.

Funding was an important interview topic because I was interested in how this factor might influence the content and message of exhibitions. In an interview with Kal at the TM, I was told that even though the museum was funded by the Dutch Ministry of Development Cooperation the museum did not necessarily reflect its policies and ideology. She said that when staff members accepted Minister Udink's challenge to turn the museum into a Third World information center they insisted that the museum remain independent and not be an instrument of the Ministry. The staff argued that if the museum strictly abided by government policies then every time the government changed, the museum would have to change, and this "would not be in the best interests of the public." Yet, Kal added that the staff understood that it was expected to not act too strongly against government policies.[18]

Overall, my study of Dutch anthropology museums revealed the degree to which the TM and NME were products of their particular histories and social contexts, or their own "subjectivity" (Erikson 2002). The extent to which they had been publicly engaged, and in what ways, appeared to have been largely influenced by their motivation and orientation (Frese 1960). Furthermore, whereas public education was always central to the TM's mission, the NME's commitment to public education waxed and waned and was a matter of on-going debate. And while the NME was dedicated to the "science of man" early on, anthropology at the TM was coupled with other interests and always had practical applications. Only in later years was the TM identified as an anthropology museum. Finally, both museums had been undergoing decolonization, but in their own ways and in response to different pressures at different times.

On the whole, both museums had had a long history of change. They had continued to reflect on their pasts and adapt to changes taking place within and beyond their walls albeit to greater and lesser degrees. In short, each museum had experienced a "history of transformation" (Bouquet 2015).

Creating a Museum Ethics and Culture of Change

Marstine in her discussion of the new museum ethics states that it is now well documented that museums have become increasingly responsive to the shifting needs of society, and have come to accept and even embrace change as a defining element of policy (2011, 5). For Marstine, substantive change in policy and practice requires a "museum ethics of change" (2011, 5). What's more, progressive, socially responsible, and dynamic museums do not ignore or shy away from key ethical issues of the day or from controversy. Instead, they enter debates as participants in civic discourse. Museums that are driven by a museum ethics of change discourse and practice are often grounded in or open to creating a "culture of change" within their institutions that disrupts the status quo and existing interests (Lynch 2011). Embracing an ethics and culture of change allows museums to recalibrate as the needs and interests of its various constituencies and society move in new directions.

Since my initial research in 1987, I have visited the Netherlands on numerous occasions for research and to attend conferences and meetings. Over the years, I have witnessed the changes that have continued to take place at both the NME and the TM in response to internal, institutional dynamics and external energies. In many respects, the museums epitomize what it means to cultivate and enact a "culture of change."

Redesigning and Restructuring the National Museum of Ethnology

Change was at the forefront of thinking about the renovation of the NME that took place from 1996 to 2001. In the introduction to *IN side OUT: ON site IN: Redesigning the National Museum of Ethnology*, a book that describes the processes behind the renovation of the museum, Gert Staal and Martijn de Rijk state that the publication

> deals with a methodology designed to handle the elaborate task of turning the respectable but old-fashioned National Museum of Ethnology into a modern museum that entices 21st century visitors to enjoy and investigate culture from around the world, and link their visual impressions to their understanding of

cultural interdependence. This book is about change and the management of change. Change in the way that museums operate and changes in the methodology of design itself.

(2003, 17)

The primary impetus for renovating the museum came in the form of an announcement from the Minister of Culture in 1988 that all national museums were to be "privatized" and transformed into "private-sector organizations." This decision was based on a report from the National Audit Office that determined that national museums were in "dire straits" in terms of the state of collections and their management (Engelsman 1996). According to Engelsman, director of the NME at the time, "privatization" was a misleading term since it suggested that the public funding of museums would be replaced by private funding. Instead, privatization essentially meant that national museums—as organizations—were no longer state institutions, staffed by civil servants operating under the political responsibility of the Minister of Culture (2006, 39).

The move to privatize, or to reorganize the administrative structure of national museums, was prompted by the finding that their management had become, in Engelsman's words, "utterly deadlocked." All formal authority had been vested in the Ministry of Culture and responsibilities related to running museums had been scattered across various government offices, including the management of museum budgets (1996, 50). "The prime motive for privatization was to clear this situation up, to clarify tasks and responsibilities, and to shift the operational responsibility and authority to museum directors" (Engelsman 1996, 39). Within this new organizational structure, museum directors became chief executive officers who reported to a board of trustees appointed by the Minister. The board's mandate was to supervise and give advice as well as oversee museum finances. Collections and the buildings that housed them remained state property (Engelsman 1996, 50). This restructuring, Engelsman states, allowed national museums to better concentrate on their two main tasks: the professional care of collections and the provision of public services. Making museums independent forced them to be more "accountable" and "transparent" not only to the Ministry of Culture, board of trustees, and other government bodies, but also to the public.

Engelsman reported in 2006 that government spending on the museum actually increased by 30 percent as a result of privatization; and that remarkably, the 1990s proved to be "the single most important decade in two centuries of museum history in the Netherlands" since never before had museums attracted so much government attention (2006, 38). Moreover, Engelsman attested that the privatization of national museums was not a "political issue, and not driven by neo-liberal ideology." Rather, it could be "rightfully regarded as an appropriate means to improve the position and performance of national museums" (2006, 40).

Viewed within a larger context, NME's restructuring fit into a pattern emerging in museums across Europe and Britain that Shelton characterizes as "the rise of managerial dominance," and part of a growing "audit culture."

Shelton has observed how managerial dominance has been responsible for "the implementation of policies designed to introduce greater accountability and supposed transparency into institutions, while making them more responsive to the majority population that funds them" (2006, 76). He points out that while "these structures should theoretically be helpful in narrowing the gap between museum activities and the wider society," in practice they have had a number of repercussions, one being a shift in "power and influence away from a curatorial coterie into the hands of professional managers and administrators" (Shelton 2006, 76).

Interestingly, in light of Shelton's observations, the NME's renovation was executed by an outside design, architectural, and management firm. The firm was entrusted with not only redesigning exhibitions and the building, but also with reconfiguring the museum's organizational structure. When the firm first visited the museum they found that it had become "an impressive culture of departmental islands" in which "eleven curators each ruled their own piece of the globe" (Staal and de Rijk 2003, 24). Consequently, one of their tasks was to create cohesion throughout the museum across departments and exhibitions. To this end and in keeping with the museum's new emphasis on public services, exhibitions were no longer to be "the exclusive domain of scholarly curators," but were to be planned in collaboration with exhibition curators specializing in identifying and reaching out to the museum's "target groups" (Engelsman 1996, 53).

According to Staal and de Rijk, representatives of the firm, the starting point for the new permanent exhibition was the museum's mission:

> The National Museum of Ethnology wants to provide this and future generations with an insight into the history and development of non-Western cultures. An important element thereof is the emphasis on the interaction between cultures and the contacts with our own culture. In so doing the National Museum of Ethnology hopes to stimulate a lasting understanding and respect for other cultures.
>
> *(2003, 43)*

Staal and de Rijk describe how two floors covering more than 3000 square meters of exhibition space were transformed into a new "home" for more than 3000 objects (of some 200,000 total). Separate spaces were to highlight different areas of the world, "each with its own formal characteristics." Yet at the same time, the exhibitions were to visualize connections and interactions among these areas and different cultures (Staal and de Rijk 2003, 17). The aim was to accentuate how worldwide migration and contact among peoples has been a pivotal impulse for cultural innovation. The original regional divisions within the museum were retained with galleries devoted to Asia, Oceania, Africa, the Americas, and Arctic regions. The authors note that the curators selected the artifacts for display, but decisions regarding the number of objects, the themes of displays, and what the displays would look like in addition to the floor plan were all placed in the hands of designers and architects. The communication and education department played a key role in drawing up plans for public programming and visitor experience (Staal and de Rijk 2003, 40).

Although the museum had emphasized aesthetics in its display of classical Asian art and antiquities since its early days, in the newly renovated museum all exhibitions were designed with aesthetics in mind. Staal and de Rijk stress that objects and cultures were positioned "to speak for themselves" (2003, 43), and visitors were to engage with objects on both aesthetic and intellectual levels. Objects were selected for inclusion in exhibitions on the basis of their "beauty, interest, and uniqueness," first and foremost, and then on how they fit into each gallery's storyline (Staal and de Rijk 2003, 121).

Contemporary visual arts were also featured in the refurbished museum in accordance with a Dutch law that stipulates that publicly funded buildings must allocate a percentage of total building costs to visual arts. In 1999, the museum organized a symposium on the relationship between ethnography and art, in which international artists and critics participated. As a result of the symposium, the museum commissioned 12 artists to create work that in some way addressed the interaction between culture and identity (Staal and de Rijk 2003, 141).

The NME's emphasis on aesthetics and art was congruent with a trend in what Shelton calls the "adoption of aestheticized or 'art-type' displays" that began to take hold in anthropology museums in the late twentieth century, especially in Europe (Shelton 2006, 74). The newly built Musée du Quai Branly in Paris (which opened in 2006) is often cited as an example of this aestheticizing penchant with its emphasis on showing "masterpieces" of non-Western art with minimal ethnographic and historical contextualization (Shelton 2006, 75, Debary and Roustan 2017).[19] But while the Quai Branly was criticized for abandoning anthropology in favor of the art paradigm, the NME sought to demonstrate how an aesthetic approach could enhance what was believed to be the mission of a contemporary anthropology museum, and that is to provide insight into "how cultures differ, correspond, and globally interweave … [and] to promote mutual understanding and respect for other cultures and identities among as wide and diverse an audience as possible" (Staal and de Rijk 2003, 46–47).

To fulfill this mission and in line with other Western anthropology museums, the NME has sought to build stronger relationships with originating communities. One example of this effort is the meeting "Sharing Knowledge and Cultural Heritage, First Nations of the Americas," hosted by the museum in 2007. The meeting brought together Indigenous and non-Indigenous curators, scholars, and museum professionals from the Americas and Europe to share their views, experiences, and examples of successful collaborations. According to Buijs and Van Broekhoven, although the museum's curators had a great deal of experience working in international locations such as Mali, Indonesia, Afghanistan, Suriname, and other countries in Latin America they had done less with source communities on-site at the museum. In addition to building alliances, Buijs and Van Broekhoven state that the meeting turned out to be a catalyst for instituting a philosophy and practice of multiple voices into general museum policy in 2008. The policy rests on a commitment to community consultation and collaboration, and a wish to change a former colonial and paternalistic attitude toward originating communities to one of "nothing about them without them." Through such work, curators hope to make the museum a model of "post-colonial museum praxis" (Buijs and Van Broekhoven 2010, 7–15).

"Tropenmuseum for a Change!"

In the article "Decolonizing Anthropology Museums: The Tropenmuseum, Amsterdam" (1988a), I portrayed the TM as a model for decolonizing anthropology museums. I wrote that rather than denying its colonial past,

> in dealing with development and the Third World, the museum in many respects is addressing the consequences of colonialism and its own history. The Tropenmuseum's past is, in many ways, why it is what it is today. The museum has been transformed from being a product and tool of colonialism, upholding values of superiority and dominance over non-Western people, into an institution dedicated to promoting greater understanding and cooperation among peoples. The Tropenmuseum, in many respects, has undergone decolonization.
>
> *(1988a, 61)*

I saw the TM's transformation as exceptionally progressive at the time, especially in comparison to American anthropology museums. While I still maintain that the museum was comparatively progressive then and still is, I have come to see how its decolonization was incomplete, and indeed is, as in all places, an ongoing process. Over the years I have witnessed how the TM, in particular, has continued to transform by putting the postcolonial critique of museums and reflexive museology into practice.

From 1994 to 2008 the TM underwent another round of renovations that more directly addressed the colonial heritage embedded in its building and collections. Legêne and Van Dijk relate that when the TM was renovated in 1979 and was charged with educating the public about international development it largely ignored the most visible reminder of its past—its colonial-era building. In their words, the building had become an "unacknowledged frame for a story about change around the world" (2011, 12). And because most of the colonial-era collections went into storage when the new exhibitions were created, the museum had not overtly connected its past to its present. This renovation was intended to make that erasure visible.

Eastward Bound! Art, Culture, and Colonialism was the first exhibition to open in 2003 that covered one floor of the museum and encompassed four refurbished exhibitions. The title was taken from the travelogue *Oostwaarts* (Eastward Bound) written by the Indonesian-Dutch writer Louis Couperus about his trip to the Netherlands East Indies, China, and Japan in 1923 (Figure 4.2).

FIGURE 4.2 Entrance to *Eastward Bound* exhibition. Tropenmuseum, Amsterdam
Source: Photograph by C. Kreps, 2008.

The exhibitions revolved around the museum's core collections from South Asia, Southeast Asia, and Oceania dating back to the nineteenth century and earlier. One section titled *The Netherlands East Indies at the Tropenmuseum—A Colonial History*, portrayed the many aspects of colonialism as a history, a culture, and legacy (Figure 4.3).

In planning the exhibitions, Legêne and Van Dijk state that the staff wanted to highlight the museum's colonial collections that were classified into three types: 1) objects related to the culture of colonialists overseas; 2) objects that expressed the colonial relationship at home in the Netherlands; and 3) objects that visualized the colony. Through theatrical-style displays the exhibition explored ten collectors and ten collection genres relevant to the TM's history. The main themes of the exhibits were expansion, education, economics, social relations, culture, and science (2011, 13–14).

Legêne and Van Dijk explain that this renovation was motivated by the realization that three decades after the TM reopened in 1979 its exhibitions had not only become outdated, but had "musealized Third World problems." Essentially, this strategy "was an expression of how the Netherlands had dealt (or better, *not* dealt) with its *own* decolonization process" (2011, 13, emphasis in the original). A central message conveyed through the new exhibition was that the collections from and exhibitions about colonized people said more about the collectors and colonizers—traders,

FIGURE 4.3 Model of a seamstress in *The Netherlands East Indies at the Tropenmuseum—A Colonial History* exhibition. Model originally produced in the 1920s for display in exhibit on different ethnic groups in Indonesia. Tropenmuseum, Amsterdam

Source: Photograph by C. Kreps, 2008.

administrators, missionaries, scientists, plantation owners, art dealers—than about the people on display.

Bouquet, in the article "Reactivating the Colonial Collection," critically examines the creative process behind the renovation and some of the intentions behind the project:

> The decision to recover, re-examine, research, and display the colonial collection to the public—both national and international—was partly an attempt at rethinking the collections ... The activation of the collection was accomplished as a project that concentrated the efforts of curatorial staff (of Oceania, Southeast Asia, the film and photographic archive, textiles, and paintings) to try to articulate colonial history through the ethnographic collections.
>
> *(2015, 139)*

Susan Legêne, Head of the Curatorial Department from 1997 to 2008 and scholar of Dutch cultural history, states that a critical element of the refurbishing process was establishing new connections with originating communities abroad and with target groups in the Netherlands. She recounts how the project team wanted to create new connections among the institute, the building, the collections, Dutch society, and communities from where collections came and still come from, but to do so by going "beyond the ethnographic canon" (2009, 16). Thus, it was important to interrogate and display collecting and exhibiting practices of the past by taking the same objects that had been collected and displayed during the colonial period and presenting them to "entirely new visitors" living in an "entirely new social environment." In this way, the project team sought to historicize the museum's own display tradition from multiple perspectives and with diverse voices (Legêne and Van Dijk 2011, 18). What's more, the team wanted to highlight how the TM seeks to make Dutch society an integral part of the stories it tells, and how changes made in the TM happen in interaction with changes taking place in Dutch society (Legêne 2009, 20).

Another section of the exhibition called *The Colonial Theatre* further interrogated, or "reversed," ethnographic modes of display by placing seven life-size mannequins representing archetypal colonial figures in glass boxes shaped like scientific test tubes (Figure 4.4).

These figures included: the highest colonial official, the artist, the soldier in the Royal Netherlands Indies Army, the "*inlandse*" (Indigenous) administrator, the European housewife, the missionary wife, and the tobacco planter (Legêne and Van Dijk 2011, 21). The stories of these characters are told not as the stories of stereotypical "Others." In Legêne's words: "As founders of the museum, they also speak *for* the museum about the past of its collections" (2009, 18). For reviewers Bodenstein and Pagani: "The Colonial Theatre offers an inversion of how the world was visualized in colonial museum culture by adopting the use of the diorama to stage anew the layout introduced into the museum in 1938" (2014, 42).

In December 2008, the TM held the international symposium "Tropenmuseum for a Change!" to mark the completion of the first phase of renovations. Dozens of international heritage and cultural workers, curators, educators, scholars, policy makers, and community members were invited to "analyze the current museum critically and to find common denominators for the next phase of renovation" (Faber and Van Dartel 2009, 7). The symposium was organized around a set of "discourses" on museum policy, interaction between museums and society, contemporary collecting, and the public and presentation. Although the symposium focused on the TM, it was meant to address the many dilemmas and challenges anthropology museums in general continue to face.

During the workshop I participated in, "Social discourse: interaction between museums and society," there were heated debates not only about the TM's history, but also about its role in contemporary society. A number of participants argued that it could never aspire to be anything more than a "closed off museum of colonial history," while others asserted that it should be more engaged in its own neighborhood primarily made up of immigrants and ethnic minorities. They noted that the museum had been concerned with international development for a long time, and with showing the realities of people living in other countries. But why had it not paid more attention to the realities of local community members?

FIGURE 4.4 Mannequin of JHR. Mr. Bonifacious Cornelis De Jong, Governor General
of the Netherlands East Indies from 1931–1936. In the *Colonial Theatre*
exhibit. Tropenmuseum, Amsterdam

Source: Photograph by C. Kreps, 2008.

I was surprised by these assertions since in my view the museum had been on the forefront of socially engaged practice. It had mounted numerous exhibitions on minorities in the Netherlands over the decades, and had actively dealt with immigration issues. As I observed during my research and wrote about in the article referenced above:

> The museum is increasingly working with artists, anthropologists, and educators from around the world as well as with members of local minority groups to incorporate their views into the planning and production of exhibitions and special activities. It is a goal within the museum to give non-Western people and minorities the opportunity to present themselves.
>
> *(Kreps 1988a, 61)*

Along these lines, several participants asked how the museum conceptualizes its community: Who constitutes its community and public? Who is the museum really for and about? Moreover, with collections originating primarily from non-Western peoples, how could the museum and anthropology museums in general overcome their history of "othering"? How could they be relevant to everyone in today's globalized world? As Okwui Enwezor, one of the symposium's keynote speakers, pointed out, "The other is no longer over there, but over here. How other is that Other still today?" (quoted in Van Dartel 2009, 81).

In a published report on the symposium Faber and Van Dartel stress that

> the Tropenmuseum will never be finished. It must continually re-evaluate its existence and identity, especially since the world around us is changing so quickly and fundamentally. At the same time, with every change the museum must always take its own history along as a unique part of its cultural heritage ... for better or worse.
>
> *(2009, 9)*

Faber and Van Dartel relay that the TM persistently struggles with questions of identity, and settling on a name befitting a twenty-first-century anthropology museum. While "ethnographic museum" with its nineteenth-century origins is no longer preferred in practice, "Tropenmuseum now too sounds a bit strange and outdated, just as later concepts as 'the Third World' and 'non-Western people' have become obsolete. So what kind of museum is it then?" (2009, 10).

In a summary statement Van Dartel acknowledges that the symposium raised many questions for the TM to reflect upon, some of which were new while others had been on the table for many years. However, one point had been made clear and that was that the scientific and cultural authority of the TM, and indeed of all ethnographic museums, was waning. In conclusion she writes: "A new era has begun that forces them to become relevant institutions again, supporting the well-being of society at large" (2009, 79).

Tropenmuseum for a Change—Again: The Creation of the National Museum of World Cultures

In October 2011, the TM faced yet another major challenge in its long history when the Dutch Junior Minister of Foreign Affairs announced that the ministry would cut all funding to the museum by the end of 2012. The ministry eventually reversed its decision and promised further funding after months of negotiation and petitioning on the part of the museum, the public, and the international museum community. Nevertheless, with this reversal came the news that the TM would be merged with the NME in Leiden and the Africa Museum in Nijmegen to form the National Museum of World Cultures. Each museum, however, was to remain in its location and retain its own name. The merger was to be completed by April 1, 2014, at which time, the TM's collections, which had been owned by the KIT, were to be nationalized and become state property.

Also significant was how the merger entailed transferring responsibility for the TM from the Ministry of Foreign Affairs to the Ministry of Education, Culture and Science. As Hildering et al. recount, this decision was based on the argument that the Dutch government could no longer justify funding a museum out of its budget for international development (2015, 310). The authors contend that while on the one hand this decision seemed logical, on the other hand, it suggested that the minister did not comprehend the long and complex relationship between the TM and Dutch policies and practices connected to development cooperation. To them, the decision showed that "he held a rather outmoded idea of development as happening 'over there'" missing the role the museum played in making development "visible and relevant" to Dutch audiences at home (Hildering et al. 2015, 310).

The authors further argue that while the decision to move the TM out of the Ministry of Foreign Affairs' development portfolio might have made sense in the short run, it was short sighted because it ignored how the museum had been instrumental in supporting Dutch cultural diplomacy, for example, through assisting museums and heritage institutions abroad, especially in former colonial territories. The museum had also played an important role in cultural diplomacy by serving as a training center for international cultural workers, and as a performance venue for world music, theater, and dance. In their view, this work, carried out under the aegis of development aid and cooperation, had helped make amends for injuries committed in the past. In their view, the decision effectively overlooked the museum's position in shifting colonial and postcolonial relations, and how this history had provided grounding for its international projects (Hildering et al. 2015, 329–330).

Examples of these historical relationships are presented in the next two chapters, in which I describe the history of museum development in Indonesia during colonial and postcolonial eras. I illuminate how both the NME and the TM played central roles in this process, and how, in Appadurai's words: "For the former colony, decolonization is a dialogue with the colonial past, and not a simple dismantling of colonial habits and modes of life" (1996, 89).

An Invitation

At the end of my fieldwork in the Netherlands in August 1987, I presented my findings at a conference organized by the International Committee for Museums of Ethnography (a subcommittee of UNESCO's International Council of Museums), held at the National Museum of Ethnology on the occasion of its 150th anniversary. Museum professionals from throughout Europe, the United States, Canada, Africa, Asia, and the Pacific attended the conference titled "The Presentation of Culture: Problems and Challenges."[20] The conference addressed how Western ethnographic museums needed to continually modify their practices, and adapt to changing views on culture and its representation. Also on the agenda was the role of museums in nation-building and development, and the need to increase international cooperation and exchange.

After my presentation, two Indonesian participants, Bambang Sumadio from the Indonesian Directorate of Museums and Suwati Kartiwa, Curator at the National Museum of Indonesia, approached me. Given their own country's history as a former Dutch colony they found my research intriguing and invited me to come to Indonesia to study their museums. In Indonesia, they suggested, I could see how museums were being deployed for national development and "to serve the people." Four years later I arrived in Indonesia to begin research on this question.

Part of what I learned from my early research on Dutch anthropology museums was that museums articulate with larger historical, political, and cultural movements made up of interconnections among individual actors and agents, international organizations, and governmental bodies that influence (and sometimes control) the direction of museums and cultural work. In the next chapter, I examine some of the "frictions" (Tsing 2005) that are generated by these interconnections, and how they are negotiated on local, national, and global levels. I consider the interests and purposes museums serve during colonial and postcolonial periods, and what engagement, or the public role of museums, looks like within a context of state-controlled museum development.

Notes

1 For example, see Aldrich 2009, Anderson 1991, Barringer and Flynn 1998, Bennett 1995, Boswell and Evans 1999, Clifford 1997, Gosden and Knowles 2001, Kaplan 1994, Prössler 1996, Stocking 1985, Thomas 1991.

2 In this chapter, I use English translations for the names of Dutch institutions and organizations but will refer to the Tropenmuseum in Dutch since this is its internationally recognized name.

3 This research formed the basis of my Master's thesis in International Studies titled *Decolonizing Anthropology Museums: The Dutch Example*, 1988, University of Oregon. Much of the material presented in this chapter is taken from the thesis as well as subsequent publications as cited. During my research period, January to August, 1987, I was a research fellow at the Reinwardt Academy in Leiden, which at that time was classified as a higher vocational training center in museology and applied science in the museum field. Today, it is part of the Amsterdam University of the Arts. It celebrated its fortieth anniversary in 2016.

4 Although Ames's *Museums, Anthropology and the Public* had been published in 1986, for instance, I was not aware of this work until after returning from doing my fieldwork in the Netherlands.

5 The Dutch East Indies Company became active in the Spice Islands (now the Moluccan Islands in Indonesia) at the close of the sixteenth century. The Company controlled the area from the early 1600s until it was dissolved in 1799. The monarchy of King Willem I re-established control of the Indies in 1816 and the Dutch governed the islands until Indonesia achieved independence in 1949 (declared in 1945). Using the term "Indonesia" to refer to what during the colonial era was called "The Netherlands East Indies" is historically incorrect since such a unified polity did not exist prior to the formation of the Republic of Indonesia. As Anderson points out, "Indonesia is a twentieth century invention" (1991, 11 note 4), largely created by the Dutch. The "Netherlands," in turn, was the "Dutch Republic" (1581–1795), the "Batavian Republic" (1795–1806), and the "Kingdom of Holland" (1806–1810). The Kingdom was controlled by the French and British from 1810 until 1816, when it became the "Kingdom of the Netherlands" (Mohr 2014, 18 note 5).

6 Coombes writes that the term "settler" has a "deceptively benign and domesticated ring which masks the violence of colonial encounters that produced and perpetuated consistently discriminatory and genocidal regimes against the indigenous peoples of these regions" (2006, 2).

7 See ter Keurs (2012) for an insightful historical account of the relationships between collecting, nation-building, and international politics in the Netherlands in the late 1700s and early 1800s. The chapter is especially interesting in revealing the roles of local middlemen, leaders, and traders in early collecting.

8 See Bouquet 2012 for a description of early displays in the NME.

9 See Aldrich (2009) for a comparative analysis of colonial museums in London, Paris, Brussels, and Amsterdam.

10 Avé (1980) provides a highly informative overview of the historical development of ethnology and ethnographic museums in Europe with a focus on the Netherlands. Particularly interesting is his list, by year, of exhibit themes during colonial and post-colonial (or pre- and post-World War II) periods.

11 See Hildering et al. (2015) for descriptions of other exhibits installed in the Tropenmuseum during the 1960s and 1970s with similar themes.

12 See Shelton (2006, 73) for examples of similar movements in several European museums in the 1970s and 1980s. Of particular interest here is his mention of an exhibit held in 1979 at the Delft Nusantara Museum (a museum devoted entirely to Indonesia), titled *Toys for the Soul*, which examined cultural disruption brought on by deforestation and forced resettlement in Indonesia.

13 Interview with W. Kal, April 15, 1987.

14 Interview with Gerti Nooter, May 20, 1987.

15 Interview with Gerti Nooter, May 20, 1987.

16 Interview with W. Van Gulik, June 16, 1987.

17 Interview with W. Van Gulik, June 16, 1987.

18 Interview with W. Kal, April 15, 1987.

19 The museum has been heavily criticized for abandoning anthropology in favor of the art paradigm, and for neglecting to acknowledge the colonial legacies of collections. Debary and Roustan point out, however, that despite its scholarly detractors the museum has "enjoyed popular success" (2017, 6).

20 As a point of interest, Michael Ames was one of the conference participants along with Steven Lavine who would go on to organize with Ivan Karp the Smithsonian-sponsored conferences that led to the two seminal volumes *Exhibiting Cultures: The Poetics and Politics of Museum Displays* (1991) and *Museums and Communities: The Politics of Public Culture* (1992).

References

Aldrich, Robert. 2009. "Colonial Museums in Postcolonial Europe." *African and Black Diaspora: An International Journal* 2(2):137–156.

Anderson, Benedict. 1991. *Imagined Communities*. London and New York: Verso.

Appadurai, Arjun. 1996. *Modernity at Large*. Minneapolis and London: University of Minnesota Press.

Avé, J. B. 1980. "Ethnographical Museums in a Changing World." In *From Field-Case to Show-Case. Research, Acquisition and Presentation in the Rijksmuseum voor Volkenkunde (National Museum of Ethnology) Leiden*, edited by H. S. van der Straaten and W. R. Van Gulik, 9–28. Amsterdam: J.C. Gieben, Publisher.

Barringer, Tim and Tom Flynn. 1998. "Introduction." In *Colonialism and the Object. Empire, Material Culture and the Museum*, edited by Tim Barringer and Tom Flynn, 1–8. London: Routledge.

Benda, Harry J. 1965. "Decolonization in Indonesia: The Problem of Continuity and Change." *The American Historical Review* 70(4):1058–1073.

Bennett, Tony. 1995. *The Birth of the Museum*. London and New York: Routledge.

Bennett, Tony. 1999. "The Exhibitionary Complex." In *Representing The Nation: A Reader. Histories, Heritage and Museums*, edited by David Boswell and Jessica Evans, 332–361. London and New York: Routledge.

Bennett, Tony, Fiona Cameron, Nelia Davis, Ben Dibley, Rodney Harrison, Ira Jacknis, and Conal McCarthy. 2017. *Collecting, Ordering, Governing*. Durham and London: Duke University Press.

Berghuis, Peter. 1979. "A New Style of Education." Vision and Visualization, Amsterdam.

Bodenstein, Felicity and Camilla Pagani. 2014. "Decolonising National Museums of Ethnography in Europe: Exposing and Reshaping Colonial Heritage (2000–2012)." In *The Postcolonial Museum. The Arts of Memory and the Pressures of History*, edited by Iain Chambers, Allessandra De Angelis, Celeste Ianniciello, Mariangela Orabona, and Michaela Quadraro, 39–49. London and New York: Routledge.

Bogart, Nico. 1979. "Vision and Visualization". Opening Address at the Symposium Vision and Visualization, Amsterdam.

Boswell, David and Jessica Evans, ed. 1999. *Representing the Nation: A Reader. Histories, Heritage, and Museums*. London and New York: Routledge.

Bouquet, Mary. 2012. *Museums. A Visual Anthropology*. London: Berg.

Bouquet, Mary. 2015. "Reactivating the Colonial Collection: Exhibit-Making as Creative Process at the Tropenmuseum, Amsterdam." In *Museum Transformations*, edited by Annie E. Coombes and Ruth B. Phillips, 133–156. Oxford: Wiley-Blackwell.

Buettner, Elizabeth. 2016. *Europe after Empire. Decolonization, Society, and Culture*. Cambridge: Cambridge University Press.

Buijs, Cunera and Laura Van Broekhoven. 2010. "Introduction." In *Sharing Knowledge and Cultural Heritage: First Nations of the Americas*, edited by Laura Van Broekhoven, Cunera Buijs, and Pieter Hovens, 7–16. Leiden, the Netherlands: Sidestone Press.

Chamberlain, M. E. 1999. *Decolonization*. Oxford: Blackwell Publishers. Original edition, 1985.

Clifford, James. 1997. *Routes. Travel and Translation in the Late Twentieth Century*. Cambridge, MA: Harvard University Press.

Coombes, Annie E. 2006. "Introduction: Memory and History in Settler Colonialism." In *Rethinking Settler Colonialism. History and Memory in Australia, Canada, Aotearoa New Zealand and South Africa*, edited by Annie E. Coombes, 1–12. Manchester: Manchester University Press.

Debary, Octave and Melanie Roustan. 2017. "A Journey to the Musee du Quai Branly: The Anthropology of a Visit." *Museum Anthropology* 40(1):4–17.

Dudley, Sandra. 2015. "Civilizing Museums: Editorial." *Museum Worlds* 3:1–6.

Ellen, Roy. 1976. "The Development of Anthropology and Colonial Policy in the Netherlands 1800–1960." *Journal of the History of the Behavorial Sciences* 13:303–324.

Engelsman, Steven. 1996. "Dutch National Museums Go 'Private'." *Museum International* 48(4):49–53.

Engelsman, Steven. 2006. "Privatization of Museums in the Netherlands: Twelve Years Later." *Museum International* 58(4):37–42.

Erikson, Patricia. 2002. *Voices of a Thousand People. The Makah Cultural and Research Center*. Lincoln and London: University of Nebraska Press.

Faber, Paul and Daan Van Dartel. 2009. "Introduction." In *Tropenmuseum for a Change! Present Between Past and Future. A Symposium Report*, edited by Daan Van Dartel, 7–11. Amsterdam: KIT Publishers.

Fabian, Johannes. 1983. *Time and the Other: How Anthropology Makes Its Object*. New York: Columbia University Press.

Fanon, Frantz. 1963. *The Wretched of the Earth*. New York: Grove Press, Inc.

Frese, H. H. 1960. *Anthropology and the Public: The Role of Museums*. Leiden, the Netherlands: E.J. Brill.

Gingrich, Andre and Richard G. Fox. 2002. "Introduction." In *Anthropology, by Comparison*, edited by Andre Gingrich and Richard G. Fox, 1–24. London and New York: Routledge.

Gosden, Chris. 2004. *Archaeology and Colonialism. Cultural Contact from 5000 BC to the Present*. Cambridge: Cambridge University Press.

Gosden, Chris and Chantal Knowles. 2001. *Collecting Colonialism: Material Culture and Colonial Change*. Oxford: Berg.

Gosden, Chris and Francis Larson. 2007. *Knowing Things: Exploring the Collections at the Pitt Rivers Museum 1884–1945*. Oxford: Oxford University Press.

Guiart, J. 1983. "Ethnological Research: An Infinite Richness." *Museum International* 35 (139):136–138.

Handler, Richard. 1993. "An Anthropological Definition of the Museum and Its Purposes." *Museum Anthropology* 17(1):33–36.

Hannerz, Ulf. 2010. *Anthropology's World. Life in a Twenty-first Century Discipline*. London: Pluto Press.

Hildering, David, Wayne Modest, and Warda Aztouti. 2015. "Visualizing Development: The Tropenmuseum and International Development Aid." In *Museums, Heritage, and International Development*, edited by Paul Basu and Wayne Modest, 310–332. London and New York: Routledge.

Huizer, G. 1979. "Anthropology and Politics: From Naivete Toward Liberation." In *The Politics of Anthropology: From Colonialism and Sexism Toward a View from Below*, edited by G. Huizer and B. Mannheim, 3–41. The Hague: Mouton Press.

Kal, Wilhemina. 1979. "Realization and Presentation." Amsterdam.

Kal, Wilhemina. 1981. "Museum Anthropology." In *Current Issues in Anthropology: The Netherlands*. Rotterdam: The Netherlands Sociological and Anthropological Society.

Kaplan, Flora, ed. 1994. *Museums and the Making of "Ourselves." The Role of Objects in National Identity*. London and New York: University of Leicester Press.

Karp, Ivan and Steven Lavine, eds. 1991. *Exhibiting Cultures: The Poetics and Politics of Museum Display*. Washington, DC: Smithsonian Institution Press.

Karp, Ivan, Christine Mullen-Kreamer, and Steven Lavine, eds. 1992. *Museums and Communities*. Washington, DC: Smithsonian Institution Press.

Kratz, Corinne and Ivan Karp. 2006. "Introduction: Museum Frictions: Public Culture/ Global Transformation." In *Museum Frictions. Public Cultures/Global Transformations*, edited by Ivan Karp, Corinne A. Kratz, Lynn Szwaja, and Tomas Ybarra-Frausto, 1–31. Durham and London: Duke University Press.

Kreps, Christina. 1988a. "Decolonizing Anthropology Museums: The Tropenmuseum, Amsterdam." *Museum Studies Journal* 3(2):56–63.

Kreps, Christina. 1988b. *Decolonizing Anthropology Museums: The Dutch Example*. Master of Arts, International Studies, University of Oregon.

Kreps, Christina. 2003. *Liberating Culture: Cross-Cultural Perspectives on Museums, Curation, and Heritage Preservation*. London: Routledge.

Legêne, Susan. 2009. "Refurbishment: The Tropenmuseum for a Change." In *Tropenmuseum for Change!*, edited by Daan Van Dartel, 12–22. Amsterdam: KIT Publishers.

Legêne, Susan and Janneke Van Dijk. 2011. "Introduction: The Netherlands East Indies, a Colonial History." In *The Netherlands East Indies at the Tropenmuseum*, edited by Susan Legêne and Janneke Van Dijk, 9–25. Amsterdam: KIT Publishers.

Leijendekker, M. 1987. "Wat Bewegt de Volkenkundige Musea? (What Changes the Ethnology Museum?)." *Culturen* 1(1):6–11.

Leyten, Harrie. 1987. "Concepts and Realizations: Four Models of an Ethnographic Exhibition." In *The Presentation of Culture: Problems and Challenges*. Leiden, the Netherlands.

Lightfoot, Fred. 1983. "New Approaches to Other Cultures in European Museums." *Museum International* 139(35):139–144.

Lynch, Bernadette. 2011. "Collaboration, Contestation, and Creative Conflict: On the Efficacy of Museum/Community Partnerships." In *The Routledge Companion to Museum Ethics*, edited by Janet Marstine, 146–163. London and New York: Routledge.

Marstine, Janet. 2006. "Introduction." In *The New Museum Theory*, edited by Janet Marstine, 1–36. Oxford: Blackwell.

Marstine, Janet. 2011. "The Contingent Nature of the New Museum Ethics." In *Routledge Companion to Museum Ethics*, edited by Janet Marstine, 1–12. London and New York: Routledge.

Mohr, Sonja. 2014. *Displaying the Colonial. The Exhibitions of the Museum Nasional Indonesia and the Tropenmuseum*. Berlin: Regiospectra Verlag Berlin.

Nader, Laura. 1994. "Comparative Consciousness." In *Assessing Cultural Anthropology*, edited by Robert Borosky, 84–96. New York: McGraw Hill, Inc.

Nauta, S. 1980. "From Military Academy Museum to Ethnographic Museum. 'Justinus van Nassau' in Breda." In *From Field-Case to Show-case*, edited by J. B. Ave, 97–112. Amsterdam: J. C. Gieben, Publisher.

Phillips, Ruth B. 2011. *Museum Pieces. Toward the Indigenization of Canadian Museums*. Montreal: McGill-Queen's University Press.

Prössler, Martin. 1996. "Museums and Globalization." In *Theorizing Museums*, edited by Sharon Macdonald and Gordon Fyfe, 21–44. Oxford: Blackwell.

Rijksmuseum Voor Volkenkunde. 1962. *Guide to the National Museum of Ethnology, Leiden*. Leiden: Rijksmuseum Voor Volkenkunde.

Shelton, Anthony. 2006. "Museums and Anthropologies: Practices and Narratives." In *A Companion to Museum Studies*, edited by Sharon Macdonald, 64–80. Oxford: Wiley-Blackwell.

Staal, Gert and Martijn de Rijk. 2003. *IN side OUT: ON site IN*. Amsterdam: Bis Publishers.

Stocking, George. 1985. "Essays on Museums and Material Culture." In *Objects and Others: Essays on Museums and Material Culture*, edited by George Stocking, 3–14. Madison: University of Wisconsin Press.

ter Keurs, Pieter. 2012. "Agency, Prestige and Politics: Dutch Collecting Abroad and Local Responses." In *Unpacking the Collection: Networks of Material and Social Agency in the*

Museum, edited by Sarah Byrne, Anne Clarke, Rodney Harrison and Robin Torrence, 165–182. New York: Springer.

Thomas, Nicholas. 1991. *Entangled Objects: Exchange, Material Culture, and Colonialism in the Pacific*. Cambridge, MA: Harvard University Press.

Tropenmuseum. 1987. *Guide to the Tropenmuseum*, edited by Tropenmuseum. Amsterdam: Tropenmuseum.

Tsing, Anna. 2005. *Frictions. An Ethnography of Global Connections*. Princeton and Oxford: Princeton University Press.

Van Brakel, Koos. 2002. "Hunters, Gatherers, and Collectors: Origins and Early History of the Indonesian Collections in the Tropenmuseum, Amsterdam." In *Treasure Hunting? Collectors and Collections of Indonesian Artefacts*, edited by Reimar Schefold and Han F. Vermeulen, 7–16. Leiden: Rijksmuseum Voor Volkenkunde and Research School of Asian, African, and Amerindian Studies.

Van Dartel, Daan. 2009. "Towards the Change: Summary of Thoughts." In *Tropenmuseum for a Change! Present Between Past and Future. A Symposium Report*, edited by Daan Van Dartel, 79–85. Amsterdam: KIT Publishers.

Van Duuren, David. 2011. "Introduction." In *Oceanis at the Tropenmuseum*, edited by David Van Duuren, 13–17. Amsterdam: KIT Publishers.

Van Gulik, W. R. 1980. "'Made in Japan': Aspects of Culture Interpretation in Ethno-Museology." In *From Field-Case to Show-Case*, edited by W. R. Van Gulik, H. S. Van Der Straaten, and G. D. Van Wengen, 35–50. Amsterdam: J. C. Gieben, Publisher.

Van Gulik, W. R. 1987. *Foreword: Seasons of Humankind*, edited by National Museum of Ethnology. Leiden: National Museum of Ethnology.

Van Wengen, G. D. 1980. "Educational Museumwork in Relation to Scientific Work and Presentation in Museums." In *From Field-Case to Showcase*, edited by W. R. Van Gulik, H. S. Van Der Straaten, G. D. Van Wengen, 139–146. Amsterdam: J. C. Gieben, Publishers.

Wintle, Claire. 2013. "Decolonising the Museum: The Case of the Imperial and Commonwealth Institutes." *Museums and Society* 11(2):185–201.

Wyszomirski, Margaret. 1999. "Background on Cultural Policies and Programs in the U.S." In *Comparing Cultural Policy*, edited by Joyce Zemans and Archie Kleingartner, 113–202. London and Walnut Creek: Alamira Press.

5

"MUSEUM FRICTIONS" IN COLONIAL AND POSTCOLONIAL INDONESIA

In their introduction to *Museum Frictions: Public Cultures/Global Transformations*, Corinne Kratz and Ivan Karp chronicle developments that have been taking place in the museum and heritage sector around the world since the 1990s. The authors point out that although international connections and global orientations have become a major trend in museum and heritage practice in recent decades, the particularities and implications of this trend remain relatively unexamined. They go on to say that neither has much attention been given to how museums have managed the often contradictory pushes and pulls, tensions, and "frictions" generated by globalizing processes and "from the history of museums, which is sedimented in their organization, collections, and exhibitions" (2006, 5). Kratz and Karp developed the idea of "museum frictions" to

> shift attention toward the ongoing complex of social processes and transformations that are generated by and based in museums, museological processes that can be multi-sited and ramify far beyond museum settings. 'Museum frictions' incorporates the idea of the museum as a varied and often changing set of practices, processes, and interactions. This sense of the museum as a social technology is a crucial addition to considering the museum as an institution of public culture and the different meanings and histories of the concept of the museum.
>
> *(2006, 2)*

International connections and globalizing processes have always been a prominent factor affecting museums. Yet Kratz and Karp suggest that it has become increasingly important to understand how these connection and processes have influenced and continue to spark new museum frictions and recast old ones. Furthermore, we need to consider conditions under which globalizing processes occur and what they mean for differently situated actors and institutions. It is equally important to examine how local institutions and conditions affect how broader processes are shaped and played out (2006, 2–7).

The previous chapter illustrated how international connections and global orientations influenced the development of museums in the Netherlands in colonial and postcolonial contexts, as well as the kinds of frictions that were generated along the way. I highlighted how museums mirrored and were agents of changing relationships between the Dutch and former (ex)colonial territories. In this chapter, I examine colonial and postcolonial museum development in Indonesia, formerly the Dutch East Indies, and its concomitant frictions. The time period covered is roughly 300 years, i.e., from the late 1700s to the early 2000s. Together, this chapter and the last underscore Kratz and Karp's assertion that the current focus on globalization should not mask the fact that many globalizing processes have deep historical roots, and in some cases, global connections and communications are centuries old (2006, 5).

Western-style museums were first established in Indonesia by Dutch and other Europeans as far back as the eighteenth century. An historical account of this genealogy illuminates how during Dutch occupation museums existed primarily to serve economic, political, scientific, and cultural colonial interests. After Indonesia gained independence in 1949, museums were deployed to aid in processes of decolonization and nation-building that involved a specific agenda for socio-economic development and modernization, and the construction of a national culture and identity. I show how these processes, along with on-going international connections, especially with the Netherlands, shaped museum development in the new Republic. I am also concerned with the relationships between museums and anthropology and their public roles. Particularly important is how anthropology, as an applied science, was put to use by the Dutch colonial government. As will be shown, decolonization rarely, if ever, entails a complete severing of ties with dominant power structures and institutions. Instead, it requires on-going processes of negotiation and the restructuring of power relations, discourses, and ideologies (Aldrich 2009, Anderson 1991, Appadurai 1996, Fanon 1963).

As a case study in the myriad ways in which global and national processes impact those on the regional and local level, the chapter focuses primarily on my ethnographic study of the Provincial Museum of Central Kalimantan, Museum Balanga in the early 1990s. I consider the role Museum Balanga played in national development, and how the museum idea was interpreted in a setting where people purportedly had "no idea of what a museum is" and were "not yet museum-minded." Given this, I was interested in how the museum concept was interpreted in Museum Balanga and how museum work was actually carried out. Contrary to assertions that Indonesians were "not yet museum-minded," I discovered that the people of Central Kalimantan were museum-minded, but in their own ways. In the last sections of the chapter, I describe how local museological practices and approaches to cultural heritage preservation were being mixed with Western-style professional museum practices in Museum Balanga. Also of importance is how the museum approached community engagement, and how community members perceived the museum. Here questions are raised regarding the forms public engagement takes under conditions of state-controlled cultural policy and development, and within a context in which the apparatuses of civil society are relatively weak or emergent. In brief, I consider both the governmentality of museums (Bennett 1995) and resistance to it.

My study of Museum Balanga is presented as an example of multi-sited museum ethnography (Levitt 2015) as I position the museum and my field research within the larger context of the national museum system and international museum profession. I give a detailed description of my research methods, building on the knowledge gained and methodology used in my ethnographic study of Dutch museums that was enriched by an historical and comparative perspective. A multi-sited, comparative, and historical methodology allows for a more complex understanding and contextualization of the many "museum frictions" exposed during the course of my fieldwork. I begin the chapter with an account of one of the first such frictions I encountered.[1]

Conflicting Founding Narratives

When I arrived in Indonesia in December 1989, the first item on my itinerary was to meet with Bambang Sumadio, the Director of the Directorate of Museums, to discuss possible research sites and a museum suitable for a case study. As related at the end of the last chapter, I had met Sumadio two years prior at an International Council of Museums (ICOM) conference in the Netherlands. It was Sumadio who had invited me to come to Indonesia to study museums and their role in national development. I was intrigued by the idea of working in Kalimantan (Indonesian Borneo). My interest had been piqued by conversations I had had with a colleague at the Tropenmuseum who was working on a museum development project in East Kalimantan.[2] Given this, Sumadio recommended the Provincial Museum of Central Kalimantan, Museum Balanga. In his opinion, Museum Balanga was an ideal case study because it was, in his words, a "brand new" museum situated in a remote province where the people "have no idea what a museum is or should be." Presumably, the museum's "new" status would give me the opportunity to document the museum from its earliest stages of development, and to observe how the museum was perceived by local community members. A few days later I was off to Palangka Raya, the provincial capital and a "frontier" (Tsing 2005) town in the heart of Kalimantan, to see the museum for myself.

I returned to Palangka Raya in February 1991 to begin an 18-month ethnographic study of Museum Balanga. Contrary to what I had been told, I discovered that the museum was not new, but was, in fact, founded in 1973 as a regional museum (*museum daerah*). I made this discovery when I happened upon Museum Balanga publications dating back to the 1980s. What's more, a couple of staff members told me that they had been working at the museum for nearly ten years. Needless to say, I was perplexed by these disparate narratives. I was given a fuller account of Museum Balanga's early history later when I interviewed the first director of the museum, Pak[3] Patianom.

According to Pak Patianom, one of the museum's founders, a group of community leaders and representatives of the provincial-level government created the museum out of a concern for the preservation of Central Kalimantan's cultural heritage. He and other community members began collecting materials in the 1970s that represented the culture of Dayak peoples, the predominant ethnic group of the province.[4] They were worried by the rate at which foreign traders were depleting the province of Dayak art and antiquities, and wanted to collect what they could "before it was too late."[5] Pak Patianom and his colleagues also recognized that Dayak culture was changing rapidly and that at some point in the future many objects would no longer be made and used in everyday life or simply available. Especially important were *balanga*—large, ceramic jars of Chinese origin that had historically been valued as heirlooms (*pusaka*) and as symbols of wealth and status. *Balanga* also figured prominently in marriage and mortuary ceremonies and rituals (Harrisson 1986, Kreps 1998, 2003, 2004). The museum was given the name *balanga* in recognition of the jar's cultural importance in Dayak culture.

There were five staff members working at the museum when it was first established, who, in Pak Patianom's words, worked there out of a "sense of pride." He shared that staff members, even though they were civil servants, were often paid in rice and other staples because funding from the regional office of the Department of Education and Culture was minimal. He further related that none of the staff members had had previous experience working in a museum. On this matter, Pak Patianom offered that prior to requesting to be moved to Museum Balanga, he was the head of Palangka Raya's youth sports program.

I learned from museum records that Museum Balanga began to receive financial support from the central government in Jakarta and technical assistance from the Directorate of Museums as early as 1978. By that time, its staff had grown to 26 (Kreps 1994, 170–171). But it was not officially reclassified a provincial museum (*museum negeri*) until 1990. This reclassification integrated Museum Balanga into the national museum system, placing it directly under the administrative purview of the Directorate of Museums of the Ministry of Education and Culture. In an interview with Museum Balanga's director in 1991, he explained that prior to becoming a *museum negeri* it was not a "real" museum. By this he meant that it was not being managed in line with the state bureaucracy and was not following the Directorate's guidelines on standard museum practices (Kreps 1994, 169).

While the director did not consider Museum Balanga to be a "real" museum until 1990, it appeared to be very much a real museum to me when I first visited it in 1989. Actually, I was surprised by the degree to which Museum Balanga resembled a Western-style museum. Located on the outskirts of Palangka Raya on a main road, the museum consisted of nine concrete buildings enclosed in a five-hectare complex. Interestingly, the central building facing the road was graced with a portico complete with columns and the word "Museum" inscribed on the façade (Figure 5.1).

FIGURE 5.1 Provincial Museum of Central Kalimantan, Museum Balanga, Palangka Raya, Central Kalimantan, Indonesia
Photograph by C. Kreps, 1991.

According to Pak Patianom, the original founders of the museum wanted it to be built in the style of a traditional Dayak dwelling known as a *rumah betang* (longhouse), but the governor of the province believed that such a structure was not a fitting symbol for a "modern" and "developing" town like Palangka Raya (Kreps 1994, 172).

I was also surprised by the extent to which Museum Balanga's exhibits resembled those in Western ethnographic museums. As I discovered later, I was not alone in making this association. Several months into my fieldwork I came across an inscription in the museum's guest book written by two Dutch tourists. It read: "A small Royal Tropical Institute Museum in Kalimantan. *Bagus!* [very good]!" Not surprisingly, I found this ironic since it was precisely because of my earlier research at the Royal Tropical Institute (the Tropenmuseum) that I had ended up at Museum Balanga. I had come to Kalimantan thinking I would find a museum unique in form and function only to discover what appeared, at least on the surface, to be a mini-version of one of the Netherlands' most famous ethnographic museums (Kreps 2003a, ix).

Museum Balanga's similarities to Dutch and Western-style museums began to make more sense as I learned more about the history of museum development in Indonesia. The conflicting narratives of Museum Balanga's history would also become clearer as I came to see how it figured in the country's national museum narrative.

Museum Development in Indonesia: Colonial and Postcolonial Connections

In his classic book *Imagined Communities*, Benedict Anderson asserts that Indonesia inherited the museum idea and many of its "museumizing" practices from its Dutch colonizers (1991, 183). In the book, he presents the museum as one of the technologies, or "institutions of power," the Dutch colonial state deployed to imagine its dominions and the "nature of human beings it ruled, the geography of its domain, and the legitimacy of its ancestry" (1991, 163–164).

Indeed, the origins of museums in Indonesia can be traced back to the seventeenth century and to the activities of the Dutch United East Indies Company (Verenigde Oost-Indische Compagne—VOC). By this time, the Dutch had become the dominant economic and naval power in the Indonesian archipelago, and the VOC held exclusive rights to trade throughout the islands and other parts of South and Southeast Asia. The VOC acted as a governing agent by order of a charter extended by the Netherlands States General in 1602. In 1619 the VOC conquered the kingdom of Jacatra and founded the fort of Batavia, which became the commercial and political center of the East Indies and eventually Jakarta, the capital of Indonesia (Anderson 1991, Ellen 1976, Furnivall 1956).

VOC officers recognized that research would be useful to its enterprise and engaged naturalists, geographers, historians, linguists, missionaries, merchants, and military personnel to provide the Company with information on the islands' natural resources and native peoples. In the course of their investigations, agents of the VOC also made collections of artifacts and specimens thought to be of scientific and cultural interest. Ellen states that this early phase of Dutch contact with the Indies produced some of the earliest systematic records of Indigenous cultures (1976, 304). The author references the work of the celebrated naturalist Georg Everard Rumphuis (1627–1702) as an example. Rumphuis made extensive collections of natural history specimens and other "curiosities" while residing in Ambon, now the capital of the province of Molucca. Once known as the Spice Islands, the Moluccan islands played a pivotal role in the spice trade to Europe from the 1500s to 1800s. It later became a center of Dutch missionary activity (Taylor and Aragon 1991, 229). Amir Sutaarga, a leading Indonesian museologist, has suggested that the first "museum" in Indonesia was Rumphuis's Ambonese Curiosity Cabinet (Het Ambonesche Rariteitenkabinet), created in 1648 (Sutaarga 1987, 1).[6]

The museum most commonly recognized as the first in Indonesia began as a collection formed by the Batavia Society of Arts and Sciences (Bataviaasch Genootschap van Kunsten en Wetenshapen) in Batavia. The purpose of the Society, founded in 1778, was to provide expert scientific research and analysis on all aspects of the culture, ancient and contemporary, of the East Indies and to encourage research in a wide range of fields, including biology, physics, and agriculture (McGregor 2004, Sutaarga 2002, Taylor 1994, Hardiati 2006). The Society published its research in the Batavian Society Reports (*Verhandelingen van der Bataviaasch Genootschap van Kunsten en Wetenshapen*), which appeared from 1799 to 1950

(Hardiati 2006, 11). The first issue of the Society's Reports was mostly concerned with ethnographic description (Ellen 1976, 306). Ellen points out that the aim of the Society was not the pursuit of scientific knowledge for its own sake. "Not only did it have the official blessing of the Dutch East Indies Company, but it seemed very much geared to serve the Company's needs" (Ellen 1976, 306). Based on the Society's charter, Ellen notes that preference was given to research that was useful to the Company and its administration.

Although the Society's motto was "For the Common Good," and collections were opened to the public beginning in 1799 (Hardiati 2006, 11–13), in its early years only high-ranking government officials were directors, and members were drawn from the elite of colonial society (Ellen 1976, 306). Membership in the Society was not limited to Batavian residents, but also included experts who lived in other Dutch colonies or in the Netherlands. Membership for Indonesians was introduced in 1860, and was initially reserved for Javanese noblemen. Indonesians accounted for around 10 percent of the total membership by the 1930s (Hardiati 2006, 12).

When the VOC went bankrupt in 1799 and was dissolved in 1800 the Dutch government replaced the company and took political and economic control of the Indies. Thereafter, the Dutch government became increasingly involved in the Society, periodically subsidizing its research. By the time the VOC was dissolved, Ellen states that "a tradition of scholarship had been established within the context of colonial social relations" (1976, 306).

The Batavia Society was typical of the many literary and philosophical learned societies that sprang up in colonial settings around the world and in Europe during the eighteenth century. They were institutions where "polite discussion of antiquities, curiosities, and natural phenomena" could take place as part of an emerging tradition of bourgeois scholarship associated with the Enlightenment (Sheets-Pyenson 1987, 7). One of the most notable achievements of the Batavia Society was the establishment of the Batavia Museum for the study, preservation, and display of collections acquired by its members and other researchers (McGregor 2004, Taylor 1994). Now considered one of the oldest museums in Asia, it stands as an example of how the founding of museums in the metropole was sometimes preceded by the founding of museums in colonial territories (Bouquet 2012, 76).

From 1811 to 1816 the British ruled the Dutch East Indies under the leadership of Sir Stamford Raffles, the British Lieutenant-Governor. Raffles was captivated by the history and cultures of the Indies and traveled widely throughout the islands of Java and Sumatra. He took special interest in archaeological sites, and ordered a systematic survey of the famous Borobudur Hindu-Buddhist temple complex in central Java. His celebrated two-volume *History of Java* was published in 1817. Raffles also supported the research activities of the Batavia Society and acted as the President of the Board while in Java (Anderson 1991, ter Keurs 2009, 153).

After the Dutch regained control of the Indies in 1816, interest in the study of the islands' Hindu-Buddhist past and in the collection of antiquities increased. King Willem I of the Netherlands created the Natural Science Committee (Naturrkundige Comissie) in 1820 (mentioned in the previous chapter) to promote scientific research in the colonies. As early as 1822 an Archaeological Committee was formed to carry out research in the field of Hindu-Buddhist archaeology, and to protect sites from being pillaged. In 1840, the government issued a decree declaring that antiquities could not be owned by individuals, and no antiquities were allowed to leave the islands without the consent of the government (ter Keurs 2009, 154). According to ter Keurs, prior to this time, many important sculptures were sent to the Netherlands, for example to the Museum of Antiquities in Leiden. After the decree, however, it became regular policy to send antiquities to the Batavia Museum. As a result, "the National Museum in Jakarta now has the best Indonesian Hindu-Buddhist collection in the world" (ter Keurs 2009, 154). Efforts to assemble collections were further supported by a policy implemented by the colonial government in 1862 that encouraged colonial officers to make collections on behalf of the government and ship them to the Batavia Museum. Nonetheless, ter Keurs states that collections were often divided between the Batavia Museum and institutions in the "Motherland" based on the predilections of individual researchers and collectors (2009, 154–155).

In time, it became a matter of policy and practice for colonial administrators, civil servants, and military officers to have knowledge of the languages, history, religions, customs, and institutions (especially *adat* or customary law) of the native populations. To this end, several training institutes and colleges were established in the colony as well as in the Netherlands during the 1800s. The early ethnographic and historical studies on which courses were based laid the foundation for the development of *Indologie*, or anthropology of the Indies, as well as Dutch anthropology in general (Ellen 1976, 308, Prager 1999).

In 1877, a chair in the "Geography and Ethnology of the East Indian Archipelago" was established at the University of Leiden with the aim of improving facilities for training colonial civil servants, and providing formal instruction in anthropological subjects closely tied to the needs of colonial policy (Ellen 1976, 312, Avé 1980). Ellen stresses that "the importance of the Indonesian experience in shaping the character of Dutch anthropology cannot be overemphasized, to the extent that it is impossible to understand its creation, development, and institutionalization as a professional discipline except in relation to colonial policy there" (1976, 304). Thus, the foundation of Dutch anthropology was inseparable from the colonial enterprise, and had applied, practical applications (Held 1953). Indeed, Kennedy, in an article on the "practical" uses of anthropology, praised the Dutch for what he perceived as successful and enlightened colonial administration.

> The colonial problem is the native problem. It is a matter of handling human beings with customs and views widely variant from those of the mother country. And that is where the anthropological training of the Dutch civil service staff in the Indies paid rich dividends. Smooth 'native' level dealing with the Indonesian was, I believe, the master key to Dutch success in the administration of Indonesia.
>
> *(1944, 158)*

Prager points out, however, that many Dutch anthropologists working in Indonesia prior to World War II were critical of colonial policies, and felt morally
conflicted about their work.

> Given their status in the colonial hierarchy they were not just detached
> unconcerned observers, but acted as agents of the colonial system, whose tasks
> involved the implementation of administrative decisions which usually con-
> trasted heavily with the cultural relativism inherent in the ethnological per-
> spective. The juxtaposition of the roles of anthropologist and administrator
> was often experienced as an unresolvable moral conflict, and it left an imprint
> on their studies.
>
> *(1999, 337)*

Because of its deep involvement in colonial administration and instrumentalist
nature, some scholars have argued that early Dutch anthropology cannot be considered true ethnology or a pure science (Held 1953). In fact, Koentjaraningrat, an
Indonesian anthropologist, contends that "in the period before the war, anthropology or ethnology in the strictest sense did not exist" (1987, 217). The use of
anthropology to further colonial interests, furthermore, tarnished how the field was
perceived by Indonesians after independence. Sutaarga points out that "the role of
ethnology within the system of colonialism led to such a negative image that it was
replaced by the term *cultuurkunde* (cultural studies) in the 1950s (2002, 281).

A number of commissions, institutes, foundations, and museums were established in the Indies that supported anthropological and archaeological research and
its dissemination in the early 1900s.[7] In 1914, the Encyclopadisch Bureau (similar
to the Bureau of American Ethnology in the United States) was formed to carry
out and publish ethnographic research. The Java Institute, founded in Yogyakarta
in 1919, was devoted to the study of Javanese culture. This institute also owned a
museum that became the Sonobudayo Museum, now considered one of Indonesia's
most prestigious museums. The Assistant Resident of Bali founded a museum in 1915
that was opened to the public in 1935. The Malinckrodt Foundation in Banjarmasin
on the southern coast of Borneo also supported anthropological research, and created a museum based on the collections of J. Malinckrodt, a Dutch anthropologist
who worked among the Dayaks (Ellen 1976, 314, Sutaarga 2002, 284).

During the 1930s, Sutaarga writes that there was a "rush to establish local
museums" on the part of civil servants, merchants, plantation owners, missionaries
and other prominent figures. But, he adds, because these museums were generally
set up and run by "amateurs," largely for the purpose of amassing antiquities, collections were mismanaged and frequently fell into the hands of art dealers. Many
civil servants, Sutaarga notes, "went back home with valuable souvenirs" (2002, 283).
To curtail the trade in antiquities and to protect monuments and historical sites,
the government enacted the Monuments Ordinance (Monumenten Ordonnantie)
in 1931. Staunching the flow of antiquities and the "cultural pauperization" of
the Indies was, according to Sutaarga, one of the government's primary

motivations for establishing and maintaining museums. It was at this time that the Batavia Society's museum was made the official custodian of antiquities (Sutaarga 2002, 283).

It is important to note that while museums during the colonial era were extensions of the state and means of visualizing its power, they were not the exclusive domain of Dutch and other Europeans. Indigenous rulers and noble families were also creating museums. For example, the Sultan's Palace Museum of Ternate was founded in 1916. While labeled a museum, it continued to function as a palace (Taylor 1994, 73).[8] Indonesians could also be found in leadership positions. For example, the Javanese scholar P. A. Hoesein Djajadiningrat became the president of the Batavia Society in 1936 and remained in that position until 1960 (Hardiati 2006, 14). He also presided over the Java Institute, which owned the Sonobudayo Museum (Sutaarga 1976, 22). Djajadiningrat believed that the main goal of having a museum such as the Sonobudayo was not just to preserve and present cultural heritage. Museums should also provide schooling in native handicrafts so that younger generations could "keep in touch with the art and skills of their ancestors and shape new forms and styles inspired by museum collections" (Sutaarga 2002, 285). Several individuals who later became leaders of the Indonesian museum profession, such as Amir Sutaarga, began their careers while the country was still under Dutch rule. Nonetheless, as Sutaarga himself has emphasized, museums during the colonial era were, for the most part, domains of the elite and educated classes and not oriented toward the needs and interests of the general public (2002, 281).

Decolonizing Museums in the New Republic

The Indonesian nationalist movement proclaimed independence on August 17, 1945. However, the Netherlands did not formally relinquish power and grant sovereignty to Indonesia until December 27, 1949, and a unified Republic of Indonesia did not emerge until August 17, 1950 (Ricklefs 2008, 270). Taking lessons from their colonizers the new government, similar to those of other newly independent nations, recognized the usefulness of museums and cultural heritage to nation building and in the construction of a national identity (Anderson 1991, 178, Kaplan 1994, 2006). The Section for Museum Affairs was established in 1949 to restructure and reorient, or in other words, decolonize existing museums in line with the philosophy and policies of the new state.

In postcolonial Indonesia, museums were no longer to be elite institutions for the benefit of a few. Instead, they were to serve the people and their advancement primarily as social and educational institutions. As stated in a government publication, "The role of the museum in the free Republic of Indonesia has a different role from the museum in the Dutch East Indies. The orientation for museums is that they are to function to develop the people" (Departemen Pendidikan dan Kebudayaan 1987, 7). Museums, along with archaeological sites, monuments, and antiquities, were also seen as valuable resources for raising citizens' consciousness about their history and cultures, a consciousness that had been "awakened" during the nationalist movement (Sutaarga 2002, 281). Leaders of the nationalist movement called for a return to and revitalization of Indigenous cultures and values embodied in pre-colonial village life, religion, and the architecture, sculpture, dance, music, and literature of its ancient civilizations (Acciaioli 1985, Foulcher 1990, Bouchier 2007, Errington 1998).

Sukarno, a leader of the nationalist movement and first President of Indonesia, was an ardent anti-colonialist with socialist leanings, and an outspoken critic of Western, and in particular, Dutch cultural imperialism. He resisted Dutch efforts to maintain an economic foothold in the country through cultural diplomacy, cutting off all diplomatic relations with the Netherlands in 1960. According to Scott, Indonesian "officials rejected an official Dutch cultural presence, and demanded only that certain materials be returned from museums [in the Netherlands] as an outstanding matter of the sovereignty transfer" (2017, 654).

Relations between Indonesia and the Netherlands began to warm after Suharto seized power in 1965 and was installed as Indonesia's second president in 1968. Suharto's administration ushered in the 30-year long "New Order" government (1968–1998) that has been characterized as "authoritarian, strongly anti-communist, and largely supported by Western governments" (Scott 2017, 657). Scott states that within months of the regime change, Dutch Foreign Ministry officials rekindled hopes for a "wider Dutch presence in Indonesia" and the renewal of cultural cooperation. By the late 1960s, Dutch Foreign Ministry officials had begun to link cultural relations to development aid as part of its goodwill gestures toward Indonesia's economic and technical development (Scott 2017, 658–659).

Despite the political turmoil of the 1950s and 1960s and priority given to economic and social restructuring, the development of Indonesia's museums and cultural sector continued to advance. A section devoted to administering and developing a national museum system was set up within the Ministry of Education and Culture in 1955. Upon the request of the Ministry, UNESCO commissioned John Irwin of the Victoria & Albert Museum in London to carry out a study of museum development in Indonesia. Sutaarga writes that after six months Irwin submitted his report and recommendations to the government. It included an open-air, national museum based on "the cultural character of *Bhinneka Tunggal Ika* (Unity in Diversity—the national motto of Indonesia)," and a museum training course "since most of the existing museums were in the hands of unskilled museum personnel" (2002, 284). Professional museum training was also high on the list of Dutch-proposed cultural activities, aimed at tackling the problem of poor museum conditions and improving national repositories (Scott 2014, 658).[9]

In 1962, the Dutch government transferred ownership of the museum and library of the Batavia Society, renamed the Cultural Institute of Indonesia, to the Indonesian government, paving the way for the creation of the National Museum and Library in 1975 (Sutaarga 2002, 284, McGregor 2004). Step by step other museums were handed over to the central government. But in Sutaarga's words, a "real and consistent policy as an integrated part of the national cultural policy in the field of museum development had to wait until the 'New Order Government' started the five-year reconstruction programs" (2002, 284).

Provisions were made in the first Indonesian Five Year Development Plan (1969 to 1974) for the support and growth of museums as part of the state's mission to construct a national culture for a country composed of hundreds of ethnic groups with their own languages and cultures (Errington 1998, Kipp 1993, Kipp and Rodgers 1987). As will be discussed later, under Suharto's New Order government provincial museums like Museum Balanga were to represent this diversity while promoting a sense of national unity and helping build a national culture. Provincial museums, in this light, could be seen as a component of what Levitt has called a city or nation's "cultural armature—its social and cultural policies, history, and institutions." A particularly important piece of this armature, she contends, is a city or nation's "diversity management regime," or in other words, "how diversity is regulated, and distributed through a combination of immigration, socioeconomic, and political policies, and the strategies, labels, and power relations underlying how difference gets talked about, measured, and negotiated" (Levitt 2015, 3).

During the 1970s, museum development gained momentum as the government began instituting a nationwide museum system through the Directorate of Museums initially set up in 1966 under the Ministry of Education and Culture. The Directorate became the primary agency responsible for overseeing the development of museums in Indonesia, including provincial museums (Sutaarga 1987, 4). All provincial museums and other state-run museums were required to follow administrative guidelines formulated by the Directorate. Such guidelines included programmatic statements about the functions of museums as well as details on the design of exhibitions and cataloging methods (Taylor 1994, 73). The Directorate also sponsored training programs for museum workers who were mainly civil servants with little or no museum experience. These programs were generally organized in cooperation with museum professionals from the Netherlands, Germany, Japan, Australia, and the United States.

The Directorate also relied heavily on technical and monetary assistance from UNESCO and other international governmental and non-governmental agencies (Kreps 1994, 140). The Directorate joined UNESCO's ICOM in 1970. Membership in ICOM gave Directorate staff and other museum professionals the opportunity to participate in training programs and conferences, and to cultivate international partnerships and exchanges. The Directorate also adopted the ICOM definition of a museum, and attempted to emulate standard, professional museum methods formulated by the international museum community.

The above narrative shows how museum development in Indonesia was, from its beginnings, entangled in larger global political, economic, and cultural processes. Furthermore, it demonstrates how the Western museum idea was present in the country since the eighteenth century. Yet despite this deep history, the museum was still seen as a relatively new concept in Indonesia when I began my research in 1991.

Becoming "Museum-Minded"

In an interview with Bambang Sumadio in 1991, I asked why the museum, a predominantly Eurocentric institution with colonial roots, continued to be used after independence. In response, he said:

> If you have to decide to do something and you see that something is already well established, you tend to take it. Why do Malaysian soldiers march like the British? They have not created their own way of marching because the British army's name and glories are known everywhere. I think that is a good moral. ICOM has developed this international congress [of museum professionals]. In the first phase [of museum development] people in Indonesia try to follow the ICOM standards as a base. Later on they might develop their own.
>
> *(Sumadio quoted in Kreps 2003, 23)*

Sumadio's pragmatic approach, nonetheless, was tempered with the caveat that because the museum was part of the nation's colonial legacy and not an "Indonesian cultural product," it was still a foreign concept to the majority of Indonesians. In fact, in his view as well as that of other members of his staff, Indonesians were "not yet museum-minded." The absence of museum-mindedness, they maintained, accounted for the public's low level of interest in museums, and stood as one of the main obstacles to their further development and integration into Indonesian society. As stated in one of the Directorate's publications, it was one thing to build a museum infrastructure, that is, buildings and other "hardware." But it was quite another to create a mentality or "software" to go along with it (Direktorat Permuseuman 1989, 10). Accordingly, it was the job of museum leaders and workers to cultivate museum-mindedness in the populace, or rather, a particular kind of consciousness about museums and their purposes. In this sense, what Appadurai and Breckenridge said about museums in India also applied to Indonesia, and that is, that "museums need not worry so much about finding their publics as about making them" (1992, 36).

Indonesians' lack of museum-mindedness was also attributed to the country's status as a "developing" nation undergoing a process of modernization. Becoming developed and modernized was an overriding theme of President Suharto's New Order government (Acciaioli 1985, Errington 1998, Foulcher 1990). Museums, in the eyes of government officials, were emblems of modern and developed nations. "Museums are known to play a role in the modern world and museum development is evidence of a developed nation" (Departemen Pendidikan dan Kebudayaan 1987, 7). Thus, museums were seen as both a symbol of modernity as well as a tool of modernization (Kreps 2003, 24).

I found this preoccupation with museum-mindedness compelling since it implied that such a state of mind actually exists. But what did it mean to be museum-minded, and for that matter, how could the government *make* people *become* museum-minded? In time, I realized that in order to answer these questions and more fully comprehend Museum Balanga's place in these processes, I needed to investigate how it articulated with the national museum system and within the wider international museum community.

Multi-Sited Museum Ethnography

My fieldwork was driven by two key research questions. First, how was the museum concept interpreted and applied in Museum Balanga? Second, what role did Museum Balanga play in the state's regional and national development efforts? I was interested in exploring in what ways Museum Balanga was similar to museums in other countries, and thus part of the global museum community, and in what ways it was different, or rather, an artifact of its own historical, national, and cultural contexts. In this respect, the research was essentially a comparison between Western (mainly Dutch and American) and Indonesian museums.

I was concerned with observing and documenting how the staff carried out the basic museum tasks of collecting, documenting, studying, interpreting, preserving, and representing the cultural heritage of Central Kalimantan. Over the course of 18 months, I interviewed nearly all of the museum's 50 staff members, asking questions about their positions and duties, their educational background and training, how they came to work at the museum, their familiarity with museums in other locales, and about their ethnicity, religion, and family life.[10] I observed and participated in staff meetings and activities related to planning and mounting exhibits, developing educational programs and events for visitors, and in workshops on collections management and conservation. I also spent many days in the museum's library and archives going through official documents and manuals (many produced by the Directorate of Museums in Jakarta), annual reports and plans, and museum catalogs and guidebooks.

Outside the museum, I carried out a community survey to ascertain how the museum was perceived by local community members and to gauge the level of interest in the museum.[11] Additionally, on several occasions I accompanied museum staff on their research trips to villages to document rituals and ceremonies, cultural festivals and events, and to inventory tangible and intangible culture in situ.

A particularly useful source of information about regional culture and history were books, manuscripts, pamphlets, photographic albums, and videos produced by community scholars and what museum staff referred to as "cultural experts." In most cases, these "native" or "auto" ethnographers (Pratt 1992) had no formal training in ethnography or historiography. They were simply passionate about their culture and history and wanted to ensure that it was recorded for posterity.[12] Besides these native ethnographers, I encountered many other individuals that had a sophisticated knowledge of what anthropologists do and their penchant for studying aspects of "traditional" culture. In this regard, they found my interest in the museum curious because it did not fit their image of the typical anthropologist. They were far more accustomed to anthropologists coming to Kalimantan to study religion, language, and mortuary rituals, for which the Dayak are well-known (Metcalf 1982, Schiller 1997).

To gain an understanding of the national museum system and how it exerted its power in Museum Balanga I conducted interviews with the Directorate of Museums staff in Jakarta and examined materials published by the department such as policy papers, manuals, and official directives for museums. These materials provided valuable information on the history of museum development in Indonesia (as referenced above), and the structure, organization, mission, and management of the national museum system. I also attended meetings, conferences, and workshops organized by the Directorate. Additionally, I visited museums in Jakarta and in other cities throughout Indonesia to get an impression of the general state of museum development and the cultural sector in Indonesia.

To gauge the influence of the international professional museum community on the national museum system and Museum Balanga, I observed on-site workshops and training programs sponsored by international museum professionals and consultants, especially from the Netherlands. I attended two training workshops sponsored by the Dutch Ministry of International Development Cooperation during my fieldwork led by instructors from the Reinwardt Academy, a Dutch vocational college for museology, with whom I was acquainted.[13] One workshop took place at Museum Balanga and the other five-week course was held at the Provincial Museum of South Kalimantan, Museum Lambung Mangkurat. Workshops, conducted in English and Bahasa Indonesia, focused on collection documentation, cataloging, and registration; conservation, exhibition design, and education. Instructors emphasized the importance of adhering to professionally recognized "best practices" and standards.

In the mode of reflexive anthropology, I was also cognizant of my own impact on the research as a representative of the international museum and anthropological community, and as someone who was expected to offer professional guidance to Museum Balanga staff.[14]

Museum Balanga as a Provincial Museum

As noted above, Museum Balanga is located in the provincial capital of Palangka Raya, which at the time of my research had a population of around 100,000. The town, situated some 130 kilometers from the Java Sea, was founded in 1957 by President Sukarno to be the commercial and government center of the province. The only means of reaching Palangka Raya in the early 1990s was by air or water. At that time, Kalimantan was considered one of Indonesia's most isolated and undeveloped "outer islands," existing on the periphery of the Java-based central government. Palangka Raya's relatively remote location made it to some an unlikely place to find a museum. As one Australian visitor wrote in Museum Balanga's guestbook, "I hardly expected to find a museum in Palangka Raya or in all of Borneo for that matter" (Kreps 2003, 26).

Like other provincial museums throughout Indonesia, Museum Balanga functioned to collect, conserve, and present objects of historical, cultural, and scientific value; and to carry out research and disseminate publications on the collection. Provincial museums were considered general museums with collections pertaining to regional natural history, archaeology, history, and ethnography. They were said to be educational institutions first and foremost, but were also to serve as recreational outlets for the public. Ultimately, provincial museums were expected to play a role in the nation's socioeconomic development and modernization, mostly as educational institutions and by promoting modern ways of thinking based on science and the use of modern technologies (Sumadio 1987, 5).

Even though provincial museums were directed to concentrate on regional culture and history, they were mandated to promote the development of national culture and aid in national integration. Indonesia is an archipelago nation composed of some 400 ethnic groups spread across some 17,000 islands. Creating unity out of this vast diversity was one of the greatest challenges to the nationalist movement and postcolonial governments (Errington 1998, Kipp 1993). Provincial museums were to show how regional culture contributed to national culture, upholding the national motto of "Unity in Diversity." As stated in a Department of Education and Culture publication, "Museums should cultivate national cultural values, which strengthen national pride and a spirit of national unity" (Soebadio 1985, 1).

The 1945 Constitution provided the legislative basis for cultural policy in Indonesia and placed the responsibility of cultural development in the hands of the government. Article 32 stipulated that the government should develop national culture, theoretically founded on the traditions of all the nation's regional cultures. Regional cultural diversity was seen as a "resource" to be mined for the construction of national culture (Sumadio 1987, 1).

The People's Consultative Assembly outlined policies and programs for cultural development as part of its Five Year Development Plans.

> The government draws up plans for cultural development that imply rediscovering, preserving, developing and telling the people about their cultural heritage, enabling them to avoid the negative effects of certain foreign influences while at the same time being ready to absorb what is good from the outside and can further modernization.
>
> *(Soebadio 1985, 10)*

One of the ways provincial museums promoted the state's idea of national culture was through traveling exhibitions known as *wawasan nusantara*. The phrase *wawasan nusantara* translates as the "archipelago worldview," which was synonymous with the government's concept of national culture. The concept is based on the idea that even though Indonesia is culturally diverse, it is one geographical and cultural area. In these exhibits visual comparisons of local cultural forms were made with those from other provinces, emphasizing how certain cultural "traits" and patterns could be identified across the archipelago. Thus, national culture was portrayed as a synthesis of local/regional culture as well as that of the whole archipelago. "The intended message to the province was: 'We are distinctive as a province, but we are one with the rest of the archipelago'" (Taylor 1994, 81).

Sumadio states that *nusantara* exhibits were intended to foster a sense of "cultural relativism" in citizens, accentuating how the cultures of each province are unique products of their own histories, environmental conditions, and local genius. Thus, no culture should be elevated to a higher status than another and each has its own contribution to make to national culture. The culture concept promulgated through *wawasan nusantara* exhibits was calculated to play down and discourage regional tribalism or *sukuisme*. [15] The exhibitions were furthermore designed to extol the principle of tolerance for diversity embodied in the national motto and one of the doctrines of Pancasila, the Indonesian state ideology, which espoused tolerance of cultural and religious diversity. The exhibits were also in keeping with the 1945 Constitution that theoretically guaranteed equal rights to all Indonesian citizens regardless of their ethnic origin or background. All ethnic groups, numerically large or small, purportedly enjoyed the same rights. For instance, although the Javanese numerically constituted a majority (some 60 percent of the nation's total population), they were not to be officially accorded special status in the national cultural mosaic. However, as many scholars have pointed out and as I observed first hand, even though the government was in principle "ethnically blind," in reality, majority groups were often more successful in asserting their identities and interests, and enjoyed higher positions in a national political and cultural hierarchy. Consequently while *nusantara* exhibitions conveyed the notion that all Indonesian cultures should be respected and treated equally, provincial museums generally highlighted the culture of the most dominant ethnic group in a province (Adams 2006, Aragon 1994, Kipp 1993, Taylor 1994).

As noted earlier, Museum Balanga focused on the collection, preservation, study, and display of objects representing the cultural heritage mostly of Dayaks. Central Kalimantan was in fact known as the "Dayak Heartland" (Widen 2017, Avé and King 1986) due to the predominance of Dayak peoples in the province. At the time of my research Dayaks made up the majority of the province's 1.4 million inhabitants (Potter 1996, 18).[16] And even though a number of different Dayak groups lived in Central Kalimantan (for example, the Ma'anyan, Ot Danum, Luangan and Siang), the museum, for the most part, was devoted to Ngaju-Dayak culture, which had historically been the most politically and economically powerful Dayak group in Central Kalimantan (Widen 2017, King 1993, Miles 1976).[17]

But besides the diversity among Dayaks, many other peoples resided in Palangka Raya. Since the province was created in 1957, it had experienced an influx of migrants from other Indonesia islands and elsewhere (Potter 1996, 4). Newcomers consisted of civil servants stationed in the province, spontaneous immigrants seeking work in the rapidly expanding timber and mining industries, as well as participants in a government-sponsored transmigration program. This program involved relocating poor rural families from the more densely populated "inner islands" of Java, Bali, and Madura to the less populated "outer islands" of Kalimantan,

Sumatra, Sulawesi, and West Papua. The program had a considerable impact on the economic, cultural, and ethnic landscape of Kalimantan. Between 1980 and 1985, the provinces of Kalimantan received nearly 400,000 transmigrants (Potter 1996, 31). At the time of my field research Central Kalimantan was one of Indonesia's fastest growing provinces. The implications of these population shifts and related cultural dynamics will be further explored below in a discussion on the dynamics of museum and community relations.

It is important to point out that even though Museum Balanga was not representing the cultural diversity of the province by focusing on Dayak culture, this focus can also be interpreted as a political strategy. Dayaks had historically been discriminated against and seen as "backward" and "primitive" people in comparison to other Indonesians, even at the time of my research. Stereotypical portrayals of Dayaks as "headhunters" and "savages" still appeared in the Indonesian popular media in the early 1990s (Schiller 1997, 3); and Dayaks were fighting to secure rights to their land, economic opportunities, and to practice their traditional religion (Schiller 1997, Widen 2017). In this context, Museum Balanga was one arena in which Dayak culture was recognized and celebrated. It was also a platform for the assertion of Dayak identity.

In 1991, Museum Balanga's collection contained 1261 objects, and of this number 573 were classified as "ethnographic." The museum followed the guidelines for classifying collections provided by the Directorate of Museums and outlined in the document *Collection Classification for Provincial Museums* (Suyati 1990). As stated in this document, ethnographic objects are objects of human production still in use and which may be used for ethnographic research (Suyati 1990, 9). However, in my conversations with staff members I was told that they found the Directorate's classification system confusing and difficult to follow. For example, they often wrestled with how to distinguish an "ethnographic" from an "historical" object. When I asked one staff member how he defined an ethnographic object he replied that an ethnographic object is "anything made by local people." However, he confessed that he found the category of "still being used" hard to apply since many of the ethnographic objects in the museum's collection were either no longer in use, only used on special occasions, or still in use by some people but not by others (Kreps 1994, 190–191).

Besides the Directorate's collection classification system, Museum Balanga followed its standard formats for exhibitions, which, as already mentioned, strongly resembled exhibition styles commonly found in Western ethnographic museums. Objects were grouped thematically and shown in reconstructed cultural contexts. For example, one of Museum Balanga's main exhibits was on the "life cycle," which was a typical thematic exhibit found in provincial museums throughout Indonesia (Taylor 1994, Adams 2006). It portrayed customs related to birth, courting, marriage, and death. The exhibition was originally designed and installed by staff from the Directorate of Museums in Jakarta. Another exhibit featured a life-size diorama of a house on a river complete with a canoe, fishing nets, weirs, and spears, cooking and other household utensils, carrying baskets, and woven rattan mats. Other displays in the museum featured agricultural tools and hunting gear, such as blowpipes and spears. Also on display were ritual and ceremonial objects associated with Kaharingan, the animist religion of the Ngaju and other Dayak groups in Central Kalimantan (Kreps 2003, 29, Schiller 1997).

Many of the objects displayed in exhibitions were still being used by local people and could be found in their homes, villages, or in the market. For this reason, museum staff and community members saw these objects as ordinary and not very interesting or valuable. The perceived ordinariness of certain objects not only affected how museum staff handled these objects; it also was given as a reason for why local people did not visit the museum. They did not see the point of going to a place to look at things they had in their homes and used in their daily lives. In this respect, Museum Balanga's use of Western ethnographic-style exhibitions did not make sense to some local people or fit the social reality outside the museum where elements of traditional and modern ways of life existed side by side (Kreps 2003, 30).

While Museum Balanga's use of Western ethnographic-style exhibitions did not make sense to some local people, this approach was in line with the state's ideology of modernization and development. Within this paradigm certain aspects of people's traditional culture, for example traditional agricultural techniques and animist religious beliefs and practices, or "superstitions," were seen as "obstacles" to development and modernization (Acciaioli 1985, Dove 1988, Foulcher 1990). Objects related to these cultural elements were collected and preserved in the museum under the assumption they would disappear or become obsolete as Dayak communities became developed and modernized or converted to one of the world religions (Christianity, Islam, Hinduism, or Buddhism). Thus, Museum Balanga was engaged in its own version of "salvage ethnography."

As a government-sponsored provincial museum, Museum Balanga clearly manifested certain aspects of the state's ideology of modernization and development plus its concept of national and regional culture, and how it should be represented through standardized exhibition formats. Nonetheless, I observed how in practice staff members had their own ideas of what constituted regional culture, and how it should be treated and represented.

The Indigenization of Museum Balanga and Local Museology

As true for many other provincial museums, staff members in Museum Balanga were civil servants who had had no formal training in museum work before being placed in museums. They acquired their training "on the job" and through training programs sponsored by the Directorate of Museums. Respectively, the Directorate was not only charged with cultivating museum-mindedness in the general public, but also, in museum workers.

Most of the workers in Museum Balanga were Dayaks who maintained close ties to their culture and communities in Palangka Raya and in villages; and even though none of the staff members had had any formal training in anthropology or ethnography, they had implicit knowledge of their own and provincial cultures. Given this profile of museum staff members, I was interested in how their work did or did not conform to conventional, standard museum practice.

As I discovered, while Museum Balanga on the surface appeared similar to Western ethnographic museums in its functions and exhibitions, the manner in which museum workers carried out museum tasks was informed by local knowledge of and protocol surrounding the proper uses and treatment of certain objects, particularly religious and sacred objects. As a case in point, on one occasion I had the opportunity to observe staff go through the process of planning an exhibit on the *tiwah*.

A *tiwah* is an elaborate "secondary-burial" rite in which the bones of deceased relatives are exhumed and re-interred into charnel houses (*sandung*). During the *tiwah*, which can last several days or weeks, the three souls of the dead are brought back together and escorted to the "prosperous village" through the incantations of ritual specialists called *basir*. The *tiwah* is considered one of the hallmarks of traditional Ngaju-Dayak culture and Kaharingan.[18] Schiller estimated that in the 1980s some 30 percent of the Ngaju followed Kaharingan (1997).

The exhibit on the *tiwah* included objects and ritual paraphernalia, such as *hamputang* and *karuhei* (carved wooden figures), created by *basir*. Each *hamputang* and *karuhei* is considered unique, and endowed with meanings and supernatural powers known only to the *basir* who creates it. Knowledge about these objects is grounded in the *basir*'s individual interpretation of Kaharingan, and is considered sacred and secret (Schiller 1997, Sellato 1989, Taylor and Aragon 1991). As Taylor and Aragon note, "without the detailed information from the individual who created them it is impossible to interpret completely the ritual objects … or to understand the use of Dayak paraphernalia" (1991, 49).

Out of respect for the authority and specialized knowledge of *basir*, museum staff enlisted three *basir* to assist them with the exhibit. The *basir* constructed ceremonial structures, selected objects for display, and arranged them in their appropriate positions all in accordance with Kaharingan protocol. After the exhibit was completed, the *basir* performed a cleansing ritual to cast out any lingering bad spirits residing in the objects, and to summon good spirits to bless the museum, the staff, and visitors (Kreps 2003, 33–34).

Collaboration with *basir* was one example of how Museum Balanga was indigenizing the museum concept to make it fit into the local cultural context and ways of knowing, experiencing, and taking care of things people valued in both tangible and intangible forms. It also exemplified how the museum engaged the participation of community members in the co-curation of exhibitions.

On another occasion, I observed how museum staff collaborated with community members in the production of a temporary exhibit on traditional hunting and fishing technology. For the exhibit, the staff constructed a simulated forest environment in the museum complete with live plants and a stream created from sheets of clear plastic. Nets and fish weirs were positioned strategically in the stream that flowed through the forest. Traps were camouflaged in the forest and spears and blowpipes were hung around the periphery of the exhibition hall. Most of the objects on display were from the museum's collection, while other pieces were either made by museum staff and community members or purchased in the local market. In preparation for the exhibit, staff members and an instructor from the University of Palangka Raya conducted interviews with local people to gather information on traditional hunting and fishing practices. They also photographed traps in use in surrounding forests. Material gathered through this field research was included in the exhibition, and in a brochure made available to visitors. During the exhibit, which lasted five days, museum staff and community culture experts provided additional information to visitors on guided tours.

A blowpipe contest was also held in conjunction with the exhibition. Dayaks are renowned for their skill in manufacturing and using the blowpipe (*sumpitan*). The contest took place on the opening day of the exhibit. Several weeks before the exhibit opened, primary and secondary school children, who belonged to local blowpipe clubs, practiced on the museum grounds. During these practice sessions, I had the opportunity to talk to some of the children, their parents, and instructors. One mother told me that her son had just recently become interested in the "sport" and she was encouraging him because "blowing" was part of his Dayak heritage. One of the instructors, a woman around 30 years old, shared that she was a member of a blowpipe club in Palangka Raya and in fact was the champion "blower" of Central Kalimantan.

Another instructor I spoke with said that he believed the club and competitions like the one held at the museum were important because few people still used the blowpipe for hunting. Guns, often homemade, were becoming more and more common. He said he was also currently writing a book about blowpipes because he wanted to make Central Kalimantan famous for its blowpipe tradition. In the "old days," he related, skillfully crafted and accurate *sumpitan* were highly valued family heirlooms (*pusaka*). For the exhibit, the instructor arranged for an elderly man from a nearby village to demonstrate the art of boring a blowpipe to museum visitors (Kreps 1994, 247–255).

Internal Contradictions and Frictions

The exhibit on traditional hunting and fishing technology turned out to be one of the most successful temporary exhibits in the museum's history, drawing 5011 visitors in just five days. This was an extraordinary number given that the museum's annual attendance for 1991, excluding this exhibit, was 2447 (Kreps 1994, 272). These numbers indicated a pattern at the museum wherein visitor numbers went up during temporary exhibits[19] and then remained static for the rest of the year. In general, the majority of the museum's regular visitors were school children brought to the museum on annual excursions. Based on museum records, in 1991 the museum received 1417 student visitors, followed by 670 from the general public, 128 civil servants on official business, and 62 international tourists (Kreps 1994, 273).

According to staff responsible for compiling visitor data, the museum did not start recording visitor numbers until 1990 when it was officially designated a provincial museum. However, I later discovered data on visitors from 1974 to 1989 in a Directorate of Museums publication. Over this 15-year period the museum received 19,756 visitors with an average of 1283 per year. Museum staff noted in reports that visitor numbers were not stable and, in fact, since 1990 museum visitors numbers had actually declined. In 1990 (the year it was officially designated a provincial museum), the museum received 9124 visitors while in 1992 this number was only 3470. When I asked staff members what might have contributed to this dramatic decline, some suggested that the museum did not do enough to promote itself in the community and had not developed a good "public relations" plan. One staff member told me that she believed that community members, for the most part, did not have a "sense of belonging" or feel that the museum was "their museum" (Kreps 1994, 273–274, 290).

When I asked the director of the museum if he was concerned about the drop in visitor numbers his response was the equivalent of "not really" because the museum was "not yet complete." He did not want visitors to come and get a "bad impression" of the museum for fear they would judge him a poor manager. The director blamed the museum's deficiencies and obstacles to its further development on the staff's lack of professional skills, even though he also had no formal training in museum work. But the lack of formal training was not the only factor holding the museum back, in his opinion. It was also due to the workers' poor *sikap mental* (mental attitude) and sense of apathy. Consequently, a need for "discipline" and a "sense of duty" were on the top of the agenda of most staff meetings I attended.

Indeed, a sense of apathy seemed to be prevalent among the staff and was expressed by a high level of absenteeism and inactivity. On outward appearances, the workers' behavior seemed to confirm claims that the staff was apathetic and unmotivated. Yet on further investigation, I learned that their behavior reflected problems endemic to their position as low-level civil servants, and the bureaucratic nature of the museum in general.[20] Civil servants received relatively low wages compared to individuals employed in the private sector. Consequently, most of the staff had other jobs to supplement their income. Plus, some staff members felt obligated to return to their home villages from time to time to help with the rice harvest, gather marketable forest resources such as sandalwood, and to participate in ceremonies (Kreps 1994, 186–187).

But there were also members of the museum staff that were highly motivated and dedicated to their work as demonstrated in the exhibitions described above, which incidentally took place while the director was away. They had many ideas for projects and events and for how the museum could be improved. They told me, however, that they were rarely asked for their opinions or had a voice in how the museum was being managed. Moreover, they were reluctant to make suggestions for fear that this would be interpreted as criticism or insubordination. Such testimonies indicated that the workers' apathy had more to do with the top-down nature of the management of the museum than with a poor mental attitude or lack of discipline.

Community Relations and Engagement

An important objective of my research was to find out how community members perceived Museum Balanga, and to get a sense of overall museum/community relations. One of the methods used to gather data on the subject was a community survey carried out with the help of museum staff. The sample size was relatively small, only 100. But the information obtained through questionnaires and structured interviews gave me an impression of how at least a slice of Palangka Raya viewed the museum and its work.

For those respondents who had never visited the museum, they saw it as a place to go see "old things" and believed it was mainly for visiting government officials and tourists. Twenty respondents said they did not really understand what a museum is even though they had visited Museum Balanga. The majority of respondents believed the museum needed to do more to make itself known to the public. One woman commented that the museum should not expect people to come to it, but instead, the museum should take itself to the people by sponsoring activities in the community. She said that most people are too busy making a living to think about going to the museum. Nonetheless, she appreciated the opportunity to participate in the survey and believed the museum should do more to reach out to and involve community members (Kreps 1994, 287).

A common criticism of the museum was that it did not represent the cultural diversity of the province since it mainly focused on Dayak culture, and especially Ngaju-Dayak culture. The museum was also criticized for displaying only objects associated with Kaharingan, in light of the fact that the majority of Dayaks were Christian or Muslim (Kreps 2003, 158–159). In fact, I was told that visitors often asked staff why there were no displays devoted to Christianity, Islam, or Buddhism in the museum. Another frequent complaint was that the museum did not reflect the linguistic diversity of the province since most of the text in exhibitions was in Ngaju, Bahasa Indonesia, and English. These critiques illustrate not only how visitors and community members contested the museum's interpretation and representation of the province's cultural heritage, but also the challenges the museum faced "engaging heritage" (Onciul, Stefano, and Hawke 2017) in a highly ethnically and religiously diverse region.

Despite these challenges and criticisms, the survey showed that the majority of respondents had visited the museum at least once to see temporary exhibits or to attend special events. And while they did not go to the museum on a regular basis they thought it served an important purpose in preserving and presenting the province's cultural heritage. Many also had thoughtful and creative suggestions for how the museum could be improved.

Altogether my field research at Museum Balanga revealed that many people in Central Kalimantan were museum-minded, but in their own ways. They were conscious of their cultural heritage, and expressed a desire to protect it and keep certain traditions alive. Moreover, they had their own ways of making sense of the museum idea by integrating it into local methods of caring for, interpreting, representing, and transmitting their cultural heritage (Kreps 2003). Plus, I witnessed how certain members of the museum staff, when given the freedom and opportunity, were highly resourceful and creative in engaging community members not just as visitors but as equal partners in the museum's cultural work.

I also learned, however, that some government officials saw local museological practices, such as working with *basir* and other cultural experts, as unprofessional and not in keeping with the idea of the museum as a modern, secular institution based on scientific principles. As a result, these practices were being discouraged in favor of promoting professional museum methods. What became clear was that being museum-minded to them largely meant being modern, and that certain aspects of traditional culture were valued to the extent that they could stand as symbols of national culture or be turned into tourist attractions (Adams 2003, 2006). Along with many other scholars studying Indonesian cultural politics during Suharto's New Order government, I saw how it was the least threatening aspects of traditional culture, such as dance, music, drama, costumes, architecture, and crafts, that tended to receive the most support from the government (Acciaioli 1985, Dove 1988, Errington 1998, Foulcher 1990, Kreps 2003). Yet to me local museological practices were unique cultural expressions that deserved recognition and respect in their own right as examples of cultural diversity. Moreover, they exemplified how Museum Balanga was helping sustain living cultural heritage in both tangible and intangible forms.

The paradoxical nature of Museum Balanga as an instrument of both cultural heritage preservation and modernization was not lost on museum staff. Shortly after a training workshop at the museum run by Dutch museum professionals, one staff member told me that he was worried about what the museum would be like in the future. He recognized the importance of professional museum training for the on-going development of the museum and protection of collections. But he was also concerned about the fate of representing living traditions in an institution dominated by modern ideas and standard, professional methods. In his opinion, the museum should try to keep traditional values alive while acknowledging and promoting new ones (Kreps 1998, 12).

Imagining Alternatives

Toward the end of my fieldwork in Indonesia I met with Bambang Sumadio in Jakarta (again, the Director of the Directorate of Museums) to discuss the preliminary findings of my research. I told him that I had been impressed by many aspects of Museum Balanga's work, especially the staff's collaboration with community members. I also shared that while at times the museum was animated, for example during temporary exhibits and events, on the whole, it was deserted and lifeless. Overall, my impression was that the museum was not integrated into local society even though some community members believed it served important purposes. Moreover, the staff's power to engage with its community on a regular basis and participate in decision-making was seriously constrained.

As an anthropologist and senior civil servant who had served in the Ministry of Education and Culture for decades, Sumadio had been both a participant in and observer of museum development in Indonesia. Thus, he had a long view of the process and a wealth of knowledge and insights to share. He conceded that provincial museums, like Museum Balanga, had not become what he had envisioned them to be, that is, "popular culture centers that reflect the local culture." Instead, they had become "administrative offices" mired in bureaucracy and national and local political interests. Encumbered by this reality, museums were not serving the needs of their communities nor contributing to their development. To Sumadio, museums should be a point of cultural reference "so as the people develop they don't get lost." Museums should provide the "roots to come back to for consultation." He clarified that he was not saying that people should "stick to old ways" simply for the sake of "tradition," but if they "develop into something it has to be something that fits them so they do not become strangers in their own country and own culture" (Sumadio quoted in Kreps 2003, 136).

Sumadio stressed that it was important for museums to "look for what cultural conditions exist in order to keep them alive." For this reason, he believed that ethnography as presented in museums should not only be in the form of objects. But it should also include "other things that go along with it." To illustrate this point he used the example of displaying a boat, which in his view should not only include the boat but also the technology used for making the boat. And not just the tools, but also the technical engineering or know-how involved in boat making. Sumadio added that when local knowledge is presented in a display, it is also necessary to show how local knowledge systems have modern scientific principles behind them. "The people just call it something else." To him, it was imperative for museums to look for and present the positive and inventive aspects of local culture, and emphasize how these too contribute to development. Furthermore, museums could help people market their arts and crafts, which in turn, could help keep artistic traditions alive and bolster local economies. And while government officials tended to see museums primarily in economic terms, mostly as tourist attractions, he believed that "culture and education should come first." Nor should museums be overtly politicized. Museums "should be a place that inspires local people, not a place to consciously indoctrinate them" (Sumadio quoted in Kreps 2003, 137).

Sumadio was disappointed that government bureaucracy had come to dictate museum operations, and hoped that the situation would improve in the future. From his perspective, the problems facing provincial museums were not created by the museums themselves, but were a result of being part of a larger, bureaucratic system. One solution to this problem, he suggested, was the establishment of more private museums in Indonesia. Private museums could serve as a training ground for museum workers and offer models of "good museum management." He also recommended that museums strive to gain the support of non-governmental organizations involved in cultural development. These organizations, in his mind, were more independent and could work outside the restrictions of government.

Sumadio acknowledged that some sectors of society need control, but "culture needs freedom of movement." In the future, he surmised, museums would hopefully depend less on government and develop in such a way that "society will trust them" (Sumadio quoted in Kreps 2003, 137).

Sumadio's assessment of the state of Indonesian provincial museums confirmed my own observations. I too had come to see how government bureaucracy and control was an obstacle to their further development as meaningful institutions of relevance to local communities. What's more, I realized that while Indonesia, as a former colony, had undergone political decolonization, the decolonization of its museums was an on-going process. Museum-making in the country was not only subject to the hegemony of Western museology, but also the hegemony of the state. Yet at the same time, I witnessed resistance to the government's imaginings of culture and museum-mindedness, for example, in the form of local museology.

Coda

I made two trips to Palangka Raya to visit Museum Balanga after my initial fieldwork from 1991 to 1992. On my first trip in 2000, I was disheartened to find that the museum had fallen into disrepair and was practically moribund, with few staff and visitors present. The director who was in charge of the museum during my initial fieldwork had retired, and several other key staff members had left the museum. A few staff members that I knew remained, however, and were able to provide insights on the museum's decline. They told me that the museum had not had a director in two years, and funding from the provincial and central government had decreased dramatically. Unfortunately, the situation had not changed much by the time I returned for a second time in 2002.

Museum Balanga's condition could no doubt be attributed to its own history and particular political and economic circumstances, but it could also be seen as a reflection of the dramatic changes taking place in Indonesia at that time. Following the collapse of the Suharto regime in 1998, Indonesia was transitioning from an authoritarian and centralized form of government to a decentralized democracy. Greater autonomy and power were being given to provincial and local-level governments, and state institutions like museums were being forced to adjust to this restructuring and the redistribution of resources.[21]

Museum Balanga's condition could also be seen as evidence of the failings of a top-down, centralized approach to museum development consistent with state control of cultural activities, or what Jones describes as "authoritarian" cultural policy (2013) characteristic of President Suharto's New Order government. This approach disempowered museum workers and left them ill-prepared to handle challenges in periods of transition. It also largely denied community members the opportunity to participate more directly in the management and control of the museum, and by extension, their own cultural heritage. The poor state of Museum Balanga not only confirmed Sumadio's assessment of provincial museums many years earlier, but also the need for alternative approaches to museum development designed to address the interests of community members and empower cultural workers. A desire to help devise alternative approaches motivated my future applied work with the Dayak Ikat Weaving Project in West Kalimantan and the Museum Pusaka Nias, described in the next chapter.

Notes

1 The fieldwork described in this chapter was the basis of my dissertation *On Becoming "Museum-Minded": A Study of Museum Development and the Politics of Culture in Indonesia*, carried out in partial fulfillment of the requirements for a Doctor of Philosophy in Anthropology from the University of Oregon, Eugene, Oregon, 1994. Some of the material has also appeared in previous publications, mainly *Liberating Culture: Cross-Cultural Perspectives on Museums, Curation, and Heritage Preservation*. London: Routledge, 2003.

2 Wilhelmina Kal, head curator at the Tropenmuseum, was involved in planning a community museum in East Kalimantan during my fieldwork in the Netherlands in 1987. She described the plan for the museum in a paper presented at the International Committee on Museums of Ethnography conference, "The Presentation of Culture," in Leiden, August 31 to September 4, 1987. The title of the paper was "A New Museum for Kalimantan."

3 "Pak" is an abbreviation for "Bapak," a form of address for older men similar to "Sir" or "Mr."

4 The name "Dayak" is a generic term used to refer to the Indigenous people of Borneo. However, a number of different Dayak groups live in Kalimantan and have their own names, languages, and cultural traditions. Dayaks have historically inhabited the interior and upland regions of the island along its many rivers and tributaries, and subsisted on dry-rice farming, hunting, fishing, and gathering forest products for trade. Over time, many migrated to towns, such as Palangka Raya, became civil servants or went to work in Kalimantan's growing timber and mining industries. King suggests that the name "Dayak" is a European-derived term which means "interior or inland person" and was used to distinguish pagan inland peoples from Muslim Malay. At times, the name Dayak has been considered pejorative akin to "backward" or "primitive" (1993, 29). Today the name is widely used throughout Indonesian Borneo by both Dayak and non-Dayak people, although many Dayak people use Dayak along with the name of their particular ethnic group, e.g., Ngaju-Dayak, Ot Danum Dayak, etc.

5 Errington states that the "massive liberation of Indonesian objects onto the market" from interior Kalimantan, Nias, Java, and other islands "came about during the 1970s and 1980s" (1998, 123). For a popular recent account of international collectors operating in Borneo in the 1970s, see Carl Hoffman's *The Last Wild Men of Borneo: A True Story of Death and Treasure* (2018).

6 Although Rumphuis has come to be identified with the Dutch East Indies and known as a Dutch naturalist, he was actually German in national origin. He went to the Indies as a soldier and later transferred to the civil service. On the life and work of Rumphuis see Beekman (1981). Rumphuis's scientific contributions on the flora and fauna of the Moluccan Islands are acknowledged in the Provincial Museum of Maluku, Siwalima Ambon, in the town of Ambon. A re-creation of Rumphuis and his cabinet is featured in the *Eastward Bound! Art, Culture, and Colonialism* exhibit at the Tropenmuseum discussed in the last chapter. Legène and Van Dijk state that Rumphuis's Cabinet of Curiosities was chosen as an icon of the collecting as a strategy for exploring unknown worlds (2011, 22).

7 These developments coincided with the Dutch government's "Ethical Policy" for the Indies, which, among other things, aimed to provide greater access to a Western-style educational system for native peoples (Anderson 1991, 181). The "Ethical Policy," in

general, was intended to promote a more liberal and humanitarian approach to colonial government (ter Keurs 2009).

8 See Adams for a description of how Toraja elites in Sulawesi used the museum idea to display their power and wealth (1995, 150).

9 Scott situates this gesture within the context of decades-long deliberations in the Netherlands concerning the return of cultural property to Indonesia, and as a means of improving relations and re-establishing a foothold in the former colony for economic purposes.

10 Interviews were conducted in Bahasa Indonesia, the national language of Indonesia.

11 The questionnaire for the community survey was written and administered in the Indonesian language with the help of staff members. Although I had had formal training in the Indonesian language and spoke the language well enough to carry out research, I still required assistance in such instances. What's more, many community members chose to converse in their native Dayak language. In these cases, I relied on staff members to translate. One staff member assigned to assist me in my research was fluent in English.

12 See Adams (1995, 2003, 2006) for accounts of a similar devotion to documenting one's own culture and heritage among the Toraja of Sulawesi, Indonesia.

13 As noted in the previous chapter, I was a Research Associate at the Reinwardt Academy in 1987 while conducting fieldwork on Dutch anthropology museums.

14 See Kreps (2003, 26–34) for commentary on problems that can arise when assuming the dual role of researcher/advisor.

15 Personal communication with Bambang Sumadio, Jakarta, 1991. Sumadio's explanation of the meaning and purposes behind *wawasan nusantara* exhibits matched that of publications distributed through the Department of Education and Culture. Government efforts to check *sukuisme* stemmed from the early days of the Republic when appeals to ethnicity were suspected of fostering tribalism, reminiscent of a divide-and-conquer tactic experienced in the colonial past. Several secessionist rebellions challenged national unity in the 1950s (Kipp 1993), including in Central Kalimantan (Miles 1976, Widen 2017). Interestingly, a contemporary form of "tribalism" has emerged since the resignation of President Suharto in 1998, characterized by a movement to return to and revitalize *adat* (generally translated as "custom," "tradition," and "customary law"). Over the last decade, *adat* has come to be associated with activism, Indigenous peoples' movements, and violent conflict (Davidson and Henley 2007).

16 As of 2017, the population of Central Kalimantan was 2.5 million (Widen 2017, 273).

17 The Ngaju's success has been attributed to the fact that they were the object of early Christian missionization. German missionaries arrived in central Borneo in 1835 and eventually established schools in what had become predominantly Christian Ngaju and Ma'anyan Dayak villages. During the Dutch colonial period, Ngaju were also favored for recruitment into the civil service (Schärer 1963, 2). Ironically, it was also the Ngaju that fought most ardently against the Dutch during the revolution (Avé and King 1986, 113). The Ngaju's modern education and political savvy would later help them and other Dayaks win the right to their own province and the maintenance of their traditional religion, Kaharinga (Schiller 1997).

18 Kaharingan is one of the few Indigenous belief systems that are formally recognized as a religion by the Indonesian government. However, this recognition was not won without a struggle and Kaharingan was not allowed to stand alone. Instead it was designated a Hindu sect, and was labeled Hindu-Kaharingan. Hinduism was one of five government-recognized religions along with Islam, Protestantism, Catholicism, and Buddhism (Schiller 1997).

19 Over the course of my 18 months of fieldwork, the museum mounted three temporary exhibitions. The number of temporary exhibits varied from year to year, depending on the museum's work program, budget, and administrative directives. Temporary exhibits were generally short-term, and focused on themes determined by the museum director and staff from the provincial-level Department of Education and Culture. Temporary exhibits were often created to commemorate national holidays, such as Independence

Day, or important moments in Indonesian history. For example, the traditional hunting technology exhibit was given the sub-theme and title: *Commemorating the Cultural Congress and Cultural Values through Traditional Hunting Implements of Central Kalimantan* (Kreps 1994, 248).

20 The behaviors of many museum staff members, such as high absenteeism, apathy, and "foot-dragging" fit James Scott's description of "weapons of the weak," which he interprets as forms of agency and acts of resistance to dominant power structures and figures of authority on the part of subordinated groups (Scott 1985).

21 As a postscript to this narrative I should add that Museum Balanga has survived. While I have not visited the museum since 2002, I have heard from other researchers and a former staff member that the museum has been rejuvenated. Museum Balanga does not appear to have its own website, but a quick Google search will take readers to numerous sites with photographs of exhibitions and descriptions of the museum.

References

Acciaioli, Greg. 1985. "Culture as Art. From Practices to Spectacle in Indonesia." *Canberra Anthropology* 8(1–2):146–172.

Adams, Kathleen. 1995. "Making-Up the Toraja? The Appropriation of Tourism, Anthropology, and Museums for Politics in Upland Sulawesi, Indonesia." *Ethnology* 34(2):143–153.

Adams, Kathleen. 2003. "The Politics of Heritage in Tana Toraja, Indonesia: Interplaying the Local and Global." *Indonesia and the Malay World* 31(89):91–107.

Adams, Kathleen. 2006. *Art as Politics*. Honolulu: University of Hawai'i Press.

Aldrich, Robert. 2009. "Colonial Museums in Postcolonial Europe." *African and Black Diaspora: An International Journal* 2(2):137–156.

Anderson, Benedict. 1991. *Imagined Communities*. London and New York: Verso.

Appadurai, Arjun. 1996. *Modernity at Large*. Minneapolis and London: University of Minnesota Press.

Appadurai, Arjun and Carol Breckenridge. 1992. "Museums Are Good to Think: Heritage on View in India." In *Museums and Communities. The Politics of Public Culture*, edited by Christine M. Kreamer, Ivan Karp, and Steven D. Lavine, 34–55. Washington, DC: Smithsonian Institution Press.

Aragon, Loraine. 1994. "Multiculturalism: Some Lessons from Indonesia." *Cultural Survival Quarterly* 18(2):72–76.

Avé, J.B. 1980. "Ethnographical Museums in a Changing World." In *From Field-Case to Show-Case. Research, Acquisition and Presentation in the Rijksmuseum voor Volkenkunde (National Museum of Ethnology) Leiden*, edited by H.S. van der Straaten and W.R. van Gulik, 9–28. Amsterdam: J.C. Gieben, Publisher.

Avé, J. B. and V. King. 1986. *Borneo: People of the Weeping Forest*. Leiden: National Museum of Ethnology.

Beekman, E. 1981. *The Poison Tree. Selected Writings of Rumphuis on the Natural History of the Indies*. Amherst: University of Massachusetts Press.

Bennett, Tony. 1995. *The Birth of the Museum*. London and New York: Routledge.

Bouchier, David. 2007. "The Romance of Adat in the Indonesian Political Imagination and the Current Revival." In *The Revival of Tradition in Indonesian Politics. The Deployment of Adat from Colonialism to Indigenism*, edited by Jamie Davidson and David Henley, 113–129. London and New York: Routledge.

Bouquet, Mary. 2012. *Museums. A Visual Anthropology*. London: Berg.

Davidson, Jamie and David Henley, ed. 2007. *The Revival of Tradition in Indonesian Politics. The Deployment of Adat from Colonialism to Indigenism*. London and New York: Routledge.

Departemen Pendidikan dan Kebudayaan (Department of Education and Culture). 1986. *Direktori Museum-Museum di Indonesia*. edited by Kebudayaan dan Pendidikan. Jakarta: Proyek Pengembangan Permuseuman.

Departemen Pendidikan dan Kebudayaan (Department of Education and Culture). 1987. *Sejarah Direktorat Permuseuman* (History of the Directorate of Museums). Jakarta: Direktorat Jenderal Kebudayaan (Directorate General of Culture).

Direktorat Permuseuman. 1989. *Pembangunan Permuseuman di Indonesia Sampai Akhir Pelita IV*. Jakarta: Proyek Pembangunan Museum.

Dove, Michael. 1988. "Introduction: Traditional Culture and Development in Contemporary Indonesia." In *The Real and Imagined Role of Culture in Development: Case Studies from Indonesia*, edited by Michael Dover, 1–37. Honolulu: University of Hawai'i Press.

Ellen, Roy. 1976. "The Development of Anthropology and Colonial Policy in the Netherlands 1800–1960." *Journal of the History of the Behavioral Sciences* 13:303–324.

Errington, Shelly. 1998. *The Death of Authentic Primitive Art and Other Tales of Progress*. Berkeley: University of California Press.

Fanon, Frantz. 1963. *The Wretched of the Earth*. New York: Grove Press, Inc.

Foulcher, Keith. 1990. "The Construction of an Indonesian National Culture: Patterns of Hegemony and Resistance." In *State and Civil Society in Indonesia*, edited by Arief Budiman, 301–320. Victoria, Australia: Monash University.

Furnivall, John. 1956. *Colonial Policy and Practice: A Comparative Study of Burma and the Netherlands East Indies*. Cambridge: Cambridge University Press.

Hardiati, Sri Endang 2006. "From Batavian Society to Indonesian National Museum." In *Indonesia. The Discovery of the Past*, edited by Sri Endang and Pieter ter Keurs Hardiati, 11–15. Leiden: National Museum of Ethnology.

Harrisson, Barbara. 1986. *Pusaka: Heirloom Jars of Borneo*. Oxford and New York: Oxford University Press.

Held, Jan. 1953. "Applied Anthropology in Government: The Netherlands." In *Anthropology Today*, edited by Alfred Kroeber, 866–879. Chicago, IL: University of Chicago Press.

Hoffman, Carl. 2018. *The Last Wild Men of Borneo: A True Story of Death and Treasure*. New York: HarperCollins Publishers.

Jones, Tod. 2013. *Culture, Power, and Authoritarianism in the Indonesian State*. Leiden: Brill.

Kaplan, Flora. 1994. *Museums and the Making of "Ourselves" The Role of Objects in National Identity*, edited by Flora Kaplan. London and New York: Leicester University Press.

Kaplan, Flora. 2006. "Making and Remaking National Identities." In *A Companion to Museum Studies*, edited by Sharon Macdonald, 152–169. Oxford: Blackwell.

Kennedy, Raymond. 1944. "Applied Anthropology in the Netherlands East Indies." *Transactions of the New York Academy of Sciences* 6(5):157–162.

King, Victor. 1993. *The Peoples of Borneo*. Oxford: Blackwell.

Kipp, Rita. 1993. *Disassociated Identities: Ethnicity, Religion, and Class in Indonesian Society*. Ann Arbor: University of Michigan Press.

Kipp, Rita and Susan Rodgers, ed. 1987. *Indonesian Religions in Transition*. Tucson: University of Arizona Press.

Koentjaraningrat. 1987. "Anthropology in Indonesia." *Journal of Southeast Asian Studies* 18 (2):217–234.

Kratz, Corinne and Ivan Karp. 2006. "Introduction: Museum Frictions: Public Culture/Global Transformation." In *Museum Frictions. Public Cultures/Global Transformations*, edited by Ivan Karp, Corinne A. Kratz, Lynn Szwaja, and Tomas Ybarra-Frausto, 1–31. Durham and London: Duke University Press.

Kreps, Christina. 1994. *On Becoming "Museum-Minded": A Study of Museum Development and the Politics of Culture in Indonesia*. Doctorate, Anthropology, University of Oregon.

Kreps, Christina. 1998. "Museum-Making and Indigenous Curation in Central Kalimantan, Indonesia." *Museum Anthropology* 22(1):5–17.

Kreps, Christina. 2003. *Liberating Culture: Cross-Cultural Perspectives on Museums, Curation, and Heritage Preservation*. London: Routledge.

Legêne, Susan and Janneke Van Dijk. 2011. "Introduction: The Netherlands East Indies, a Colonial History." In *The Netherlands East Indies at the Tropenmuseum*, edited by Susan Legêne and Janneke Van Dijk, 9–25. Amsterdam: KIT Publishers.

Levitt, Peggy. 2015. *Artifacts and Allegiances. How Museums Put the Nation and the World on Display*. Berkeley, CA: University of California Press.

McGregor, Katherine. 2004. "Museums and the Transformation from Colonial to Post-Colonial Institutions in Indonesia: A Case Study of the Indonesian National Museum." In *Performing Objects. Museums, Material Culture and Performance in Southeast Asia*, edited by Fiona Kerlogue, 15–30. London: The Horniman Museum and Gardens.

Metcalf, Peter. 1982. *A Borneo Journey into Death: Berawan Eschatology from Its Rituals*. Philadelphia: University of Pennsylvania Press.

Miles, Douglas. 1976. *Cutlass and Crescent Moon. A Case Study of Social and Political Change in Outer Indonesia*. Sydney: Center for Southeast Asian Studies.

Onciul, Bryony, Michelle Stefano, and Stephanie Hawke, ed. 2017. *Engaging Heritage, Engaging Communities*. Woodbridge: Boydell and Brewer.

Potter, Lesley. 1996. "Forest Degradation, Deforestation, and Reforestation in Kalimantan: Towards a Sustainable Land Use?" In *Borneo in Transition: People, Forests, Conservation, and Development*, edited by Christine Padoch and Nancy Lee Peluso, 13–40. Oxford: Oxford University Press.

Prager, Michael. 1999. "Crossing Borders, Healing Wounds: Leiden Anthropology and the Colonial Encounter 1917–1949." In *Anthropology and Colonialism in Asia and Oceania*, edited by Jan Van Bremen and Akitoshi Shimizu, 326–361. Surrey: Curzon.

Pratt, Mary Louise. 1992. *Imperial Eyes: Travel Writing and Transculturation*. London and New York: Routledge.

Ricklefs, M. C. 2008. *A History of Modern Indonesia*. Fourth ed. Stanford, CA: Stanford University Press.

Schärer, Hans. 1963. *Ngaju Religion: The Conception of God among a South Borneo People*. Translated by Rodney Needham. The Hague: Nijhof.

Schiller, Anne. 1997. *Small Sacrifices: Religious Change and Cultural Identity among the Ngaju Dayak of Indonesia*. Oxford: Oxford University Press.

Scott, Cynthia. 2014. "Sharing the Divisions of the Colonial Past: An Assessment of the Netherlands-Indonesia Shared Cultural Heritage Project, 2003–2006." *International Journal of Heritage Studies* 20(4):181–195.

Scott, Cynthia. 2017. "Renewing the 'Special Relationship' and Rethinking the Return of Cultural Property: The Netherlands and Indonesia 1949–1979." *Journal of Contemporary History* 52(3):646–668.

Scott, James. 1985. *Weapons of the Weak: Everyday Forms of Peasant Resistance*. New Haven, CT: Yale University Press.

Sellato, Bernard. 1989. *Hornbill and Dragon*. Jakarta: Elf Aquitaine Indonesie.

Sheets-Pyenson, Susan. 1987. "Cathedrals of Science: The Developments of Colonial Natural History Museums During the Nineteenth Century." *History of Science* 25(1):45–49.

Soebadio, H. 1985. *Cultural Policy in Indonesia*. Paris: UNESCO.

Sumadio, Bambang. 1987. "Provincial Museums in Indonesia: Their Role in National Development." The Presentation of Culture, Leiden, the Netherlands.

Sutaarga, Amir. 1976. *Museums in Indonesia, 1968–1976*. Jakarta: Directorate Permuseuman (Directorate of Museums).

Sutaarga, Amir. 1987. *Introduction to Museums in Indonesia: The International Council of Museums Committee in Indonesia.* Jakarta: Direktorat Permuseuman (Directorate of Museums).

Sutaarga, Amir. 2002. "The Role of Museums in Indonesia: Collecting Documents from the Past and the Present for a Better Future." In *Treasure Hunting? Collectors and Collections of Indonesian Artefacts,* edited by Reimar Schefold and Han F. Vermeulen, 281–288. Leiden: University of Leiden and the National Museum of Ethnology.

Suyati. 1990. *Collection Classification for Provincial Museums.* Jakarta, Indonesia: Direktorat Permuseuman.

Taylor, Paul M. 1994a. "Introduction." In *Fragile Traditions: Indonesian Art in Jeopardy,* edited by Paul M. Taylor, 1–12. Honolulu: University of Hawai'i Press.

Taylor, Paul M. 1994b. "The Nusantara Concept of Culture: Local Traditions and National Identity as Expressed in Indonesian Museums." In *Fragil Traditions: Indonesian Art in Jeopardy,* edited by Paul M. Taylor, 71–90. Honolulu: University of Hawai'i Press.

Taylor, Paul M. and Lorraine Aragon. 1991. *Beyond the Java Sea.* Washington, DC and New York: National Museum of Nat Hist and Harry N. Abrams.

ter Keurs, Pieter. 2009. "Collecting in the Colony: Hybridity, Power, and Prestige in the Netherlands East Indies." *Indonesia and the Malay World* 37(108):147–161.

Tsing, Anna. 2005. *Frictions. An Ethnography of Global Connections.* Princeton and Oxford: Princeton University Press.

Widen, Kumpiady. 2017. "The Rise of Dayak Identities in Central Kalimantan." In *Borneo Studies in History, Society, and Culture,* edited by Victor King, Zawawi Ibrahim Noor and Hasharina Hassan, 273–282. Singapore: Springer.

6

INTERNATIONAL COLLABORATION AND THE VALUE OF CULTURE AND HERITAGE

When asked what the term collaboration means to him, Leigh J. Kuwanwisiwma, Director of the Hopi Cultural Preservation Office and member of the Greasewood Clan, responded: "Collaboration to me means a partnership that is equal and also one of reciprocity ... I think collaboration goes both ways, professionally and ethically" (Kuwanwisiwma 2008, 154).

Nowadays, many anthropologists would agree with Kuwanwisiwma—collaboration is fundamentally about partnerships built on principles of reciprocity and equality. Cultivating collaborative partnerships to many is a moral and ethical responsibility, a cornerstone of engaged research and practice, and a decolonizing methodology. Simply put, collaboration means *working together* to achieve mutually agreed upon objectives and goals in research, scholarship, and practice (Lassiter 2008, Smith and Jackson 2008, Smith 2012). Informed by a code of working *with* people rather than *on* them or *about* them, "Collaboration is an act and a practice, but it can also be thought of as an idealized model that different forms of research seek to achieve" (Colwell-Chanthaphonh and Ferguson 2008, 9).

Like engagement, collaboration takes many forms and encompasses a range of strategies that can be executed to varying degrees. For this reason, Colwell-Chanthaphonh and Ferguson, writing about collaboration in archaeology, suggest that "collaboration in practice exists on a continuum, from merely communicating research to descendant communities to a genuine synergy where the contributions of community members and scholars create a positive result that could not be achieved without joining efforts" (2008, 1).

Drawing from the recent literature on collaboration in anthropology and museum studies, this chapter describes my collaborative work in Indonesia with the Dayak Ikat Weaving Project based in Sintang, West Kalimantan and the Museum Pusaka Nias (Nias Heritage Museum) located in the town of Genungsitoli on the island of Nias. I begin the chapter with an account of my initial fieldwork in

Sintang and Nias in 2002 as part of a consultancy for the Ford Foundation. This narrative includes a description of my activities, observations, and findings at each site. I then discuss the University of Denver/Indonesia Exchange Program in Museum Training, which grew out of this initial fieldwork. The program was envisioned as a means of giving participants the opportunity to share knowledge and experience, and as an experiment in "appropriate museology" grounded in the idea that approaches to museum training and development should be developed in collaboration with partners. They should equally fit the needs, socioeconomic conditions, cultural values, and meanings of their specific contexts.

"Situated," "context-specific," and "culturally sensitive" methodologies have, for some time now, been integral to the approaches of researchers working within postcolonial, Indigenous, and feminist paradigms. Such methodologies are seen as a means of decolonizing and countering the "methodological imperialism" of Western social science (Chilisa 2012, Schlehe and Hidayah 2014, Smith 2012), and the "professional culture of method" (Marcus 2008). At issue is not only a concern for reforming the tools of research and knowledge production, but also the conditions under which research is conducted. Consideration of the situated nature and context of research activities is, as Schlehe and Hidayah have argued, fundamental to collaborative exchanges based on principles of reciprocity and equality rather than the extraction of "data" (2014, 254). I suggest that appropriate museology is a context-specific and situated paradigm that counters the hegemonic discourse and practice of Eurocentric museology and heritage management, and is thus a decolonizing methodology (Kreps 2003, Byrne 1991, 2014, Smith 2006).

I argue that a heightened awareness of appropriate museology is needed as international cooperation and collaborative partnerships increasingly characterize much of what goes on in the contemporary museum world (Kratz and Karp 2006, 5). Appropriate museology's emphasis on the particularities of specific contexts does not diminish the importance of global orientations and interactions. Rather, it accentuates the contingencies of local/global interstitial spaces and their negotiation. One of the aims of this chapter is, in fact, to further underscore the importance of international connections and intercultural dialogue. The case studies presented highlight the significance of these relationships for the development and survival of museums in multiple contexts (Buntinx and Karp 2006, 209), and the benefits of multi-pronged strategies that pull together resources and support from multiple sources, i.e., foundations, governmental and non-governmental organizations and institutions, localized and supra-national agencies, and individuals (Daly and Winter 2012). They additionally illustrate how the museum as a "traveling institution" is invoked, utilized, and vernacularized to provide communities with cultural capital, a set of resources and models, and a social field for addressing community needs and interests (Buntinx and Karp 2006, 208).

The work of the Dayak Ikat Weaving Project and Museum Pusaka Nias, moreover, calls attention to the connections among culture, heritage, and international development. Since the 1990s, interest in integrating culture and heritage into development interventions has grown steadily, and today "culture for development" figures prominently in international development theory and practice (Basu and Modest 2015, Rao and Walton 2004). It is also an arena in which museum anthropologists have been actively engaged along with other applied anthropologists. Basu and Modest argue, however, that despite the many claims being made regarding the value of culture and heritage for development, there has been little critical reflection on and long-term evaluation of projects to substantiate such claims (2015, 2).

The Dayak Ikat Weaving Project and Museum Pusaka Nias fit the "culture for development" paradigm not only because they function within the context of a "developing" country, i.e., Indonesia, but also because their work is intended to contribute to the socioeconomic development and general well-being of their communities. My involvement with the organizations over the years as a consultant, collaborative partner, mentor, advisor, and researcher has allowed me to track and thus, to a certain degree, evaluate their activities and progress. I give examples of their activities and initiatives, which in the case of the Weaving Project also included the creation of a community museum, that demonstrate the intrinsic and extrinsic values of culture and heritage. These examples further shed light on what can be achieved through international collaborations, and the importance of international connections and networks.

One of my intentions in this chapter is to exemplify the many forms museum anthropology and cultural work can take on a global stage, which requires engagement on multiple levels and in different registers. I trace the institutional and professional networks in which we work, following flows of people, ideas, cultural technologies, policies and practices. Special attention is given to the personal and professional relationships that are forged through these encounters, which can ultimately play decisive roles in what gets done where and by whom. In this respect, I explore what it means to do museum ethnography and to be a cultural worker in this age of engagement and globalization. Following Mathur, I suggest that global and cosmopolitan perspectives are necessary for "constructing a critical museum studies for the twenty-first century" (2005, 699). As museums are increasingly being seen as sites of global encounters and transnational/cultural spaces (Levitt 2015, 8), it has become imperative for us to formulate "globalizing methods" that account for hybridity, difference, and allow "epistemological suppleness" (Stoller 1997, 91).

Initial Fieldwork in Sintang and Genungsitoli

I was first introduced to the Dayak Ikat Weaving Project (hereafter the Weaving Project) and Museum Pusaka Nias (MPN) in 2002 when I was a consultant to the Ford Foundation office in Jakarta. The Foundation had been helping fund the Weaving Project and MPN for several years, and my brief was to evaluate their progress, identify needs, and make recommendations for their future work. At the time, the Ford program officer with whom I worked was especially interested in supporting the development of community-based museums in Indonesia.[1]

My fieldwork in Sintang and Genungsitoli was relatively short. I spent four days at each site and my total time in Indonesia amounted to three weeks. Much of my time was spent in transit, getting from one island and site to another. Despite the brevity of my fieldwork, I was able to gather enough information at each site to substantiate my recommendation to the Ford Foundation to continue support for the Weaving Project and MPN, and to eventually fund the University of Denver/ Indonesian Exchange Program in Museum Training (the Exchange Program).[2]

In what follows I describe my fieldwork at each site as well as the history and cultural work of each organization. I not only consider the particularities of MPN and the Weaving Project, but also the larger historical, political, and social conditions that shaped them.

Cultural Revitalization and the Dayak Ikat Weaving Project

The Weaving Project was initiated in 1999 by the People, Resources, and Conservation Foundation (PRCF), an international, non-governmental community development organization, in collaboration with the Kobus Centre Foundation (Yayasan Kobus Centre). The Iban Dayaks of West Kalimantan and Sarawak, Malaysia, are famous for their *ikat* textiles, which have been highly prized by collectors for centuries and can be found in museum and private collections throughout the world.[3] The aim of the Weaving Project has been to enhance the artistic and managerial skills of weavers; contribute to women's empowerment through greater financial security and independence; and foster appreciation of Dayak *ikat* weaving through research and education (Huda 2002). Its overarching purpose has been to revive, strengthen, and preserve the Dayak *ikat* weaving tradition through the development of the Jasa Menenun Mandiri (Weavers Go Independent) weaving cooperative.

The decline of weaving among the Iban, as in the case of many traditional arts, was a consequence of the many forces of culture change and the restructuring of Indigenous societies brought on by colonialism, missionization, and state-driven processes of modernization and socioeconomic development. Christianity was introduced into Kalimantan in the 1800s by Dutch, German, and other European missionaries. Conversion to Christianity undermined traditional religious beliefs, customs, and ceremonies that were inextricably tied to weaving. Commercial cloth and clothing were introduced in the 1800s, which decreased the need for hand-woven cloth (Heppell 1994). Furthermore, during the 1960s the Indonesian government was pressuring its citizens, especially those living in remote regions, to embrace its ideology of modernization and development. As a result, many Dayaks began to reject traditional dress, which they believed marked them as "primitive" and "backward." The use of a certain kind of ceremonial cloth known as *pua kumbu* was especially shunned since it was historically associated with headhunting rituals and warfare, and thus linked to a past identity many were trying to shed. As a result of these various pressures, by the 1990s Dayak traditional weaving was considered a disappearing art form (Gittinger 1979, Heppell 1994, Kreps 2012).

In 2002, the weaving cooperative had some 200 members from 13 villages. At the time of my fieldwork, its administrative office and gallery were based at the Kobus Centre that served as a collection and distribution point for the weavers' products. These included *ikat* cloths, bags, jackets, scarves, as well as other local crafts like basketry. The cooperative bought and sold the weavers' products and provided them with loans to purchase thread and dyes. Through their participation in the cooperative, weavers had the opportunity to earn much-needed cash and acquire skills in financial and business management.

The cooperative additionally sponsored training workshops, for example on natural dyeing techniques, taught by older, more experienced weavers. Research on the technical and cultural aspects of weaving was another important part of the Project's work since knowledge of weaving techniques, the meanings of certain designs and motifs, and customs associated with weaving were thought to be disappearing with the passing of older weavers (Kreps 2012, 2017).

The Kobus Centre was also the residence of Father Jacques Maessen, a Dutch Catholic priest who had been working in the region since 1969. He was also a founder of and senior advisor to the Weaving Project (Figure 6.1).

Father Maessen started collecting *ikat* weavings in the 1970s when he noticed that fewer women were weaving, and that heirloom cloths were rapidly being bought up by collectors. By 2002, his textile collection totaled some 500 pieces.

Father Maessen knew a great deal about Dayak weaving as a result of having spent decades in villages and developing close relationships with weavers. Besides

FIGURE 6.1 Father Jacques Maessen, co-founder and Senior Advisor to the Dayak Ikat Weaving Project. In the village of Ensaid, West Kalimantan, Indonesia Photograph by C. Kreps, 2003.

his familiarity with the designs and styles of particular villages and weavers, he was also keenly aware of the importance of the social and cultural contexts of weaving. Father Maessen told me that women weave in their spare time in between looking after children, working in their gardens and rice fields, and doing chores. Weaving was also a collective activity in which women gathered to help one another in various stages of the process. It was during this time that weavers passed on their knowledge and skills to younger weavers. While Father Maessen acknowledged that weaving had become an important economic activity in villages, he and other Project staff did not want to see production become large scale. They feared that increased production might affect the quality of weavings and have a negative impact on the integrity of village social life. In contrast to some government officials who saw weaving as a resource for economic development, the Weaving Project staff was more interested in promoting women's empowerment and the survival of the art than large-scale production (Kreps 2012, 191).

During my visit, Father Maessen, Immanuel Huda (Director of the PRCF), and I discussed the possibility of establishing a community museum or cultural center in Sintang as one of the Weaving Project's long-term goals. Father Maessen hoped to donate his personal collection to such a museum so the collection would remain in the region and be of benefit to the local people.

While in Sintang, I learned that the *bupati* (head of a regency or *kabupaten*)[4] at that time was also interested in establishing a museum/cultural center in the town. The *bupati* was a professionally trained archivist and former head of provincial archives in Pontianak, the provincial capital. The *bupati* and the local Committee on Museums, History and Antiquities had established an archives center in Sintang that housed historical documents and photographs dating back to the 1800s and the Dutch colonial period. While in Sintang, I attended the formal opening of the archives center along with representatives of the Weaving Project. This facility was intended to be temporary since the Committee was in the process of planning the construction of a new building to house the archives and a library. As a Dayak, the *bupati* was very interested in the preservation of Dayak history, art, and culture. However, he believed a museum should represent and serve all the different ethnic groups living in the Sintang district, not just Dayaks.

One museum already existed in Sintang, the Dara Juanti Museum, located on the site of the former palace of Sultan Nata Muhammed Shamsuddin who died there in 1738 (Sellato 2011). The privately owned museum contained heirlooms, state regalia, ceramics, and archaeological artifacts dating back to the Hindu era in Borneo. When we visited the museum we were given a tour by a descendant of the sultan who described himself as an *ahli warisan* (heritage specialist/caretaker). Although the Dara Juanti Museum was a significant historical landmark, my colleagues informed me that because it focused on the history of the sultanate in the region it was mainly associated with the Malay-Muslim community in Sintang (Kreps 2017, 226).

Like the *bupati*, Father Maessen and representatives of the Weaving Project believed that a new museum in Sintang should represent all the different ethnic groups of the region, i.e., Dayak, Malay, and Indonesian-Chinese. They hoped that such a museum could stimulate more social cohesion and dialogue among the different ethnic groups in the district. A brief note on the history of Sintang and inter-ethnic relations is helpful here for understanding these motivations.

The town of Sintang is situated at the confluence of two large rivers, the Kapuas and Melawi, making it a strategically important economic and political center for centuries. Sintang was originally the seat of a Hindu kingdom that later converted to Islam. It was ruled by Sultan Nata Muhammed Shamsuddin (mentioned above) until the arrival of the Dutch colonial government in 1822. Recognizing its strategic importance for trade and military operations, the Dutch government made Sintang its administrative center, and it remained under Dutch control until Indonesia gained independence in 1949 (Fienieg 2007).

Over the centuries, various ethnic groups settled in Sintang, mainly Dayaks, Muslim-Malays, and Chinese who arrived in the mid-1700s to mine gold (Fienieg 2007, 75). In time, each group came to be defined by its own language, ethnic group, and religious affiliation, and occupied its own riverbank and town quarter (Fienieg 2007, 83).

A history of strong social inequalities and political tensions among the various ethnic groups of Kalimantan is well documented. The Dayaks have been historically discriminated against by Malay sultanates, Dutch colonialists, and later by the Indonesian government that labeled them *orang terasing* or "isolated people," a euphemism for "primitive" people (Davidson and Henley 2007, King 1993, Peluso and Harwell 2001, Schiller 1997, Tanasaldy 2007). The Chinese too suffered discrimination. They were not allowed to openly speak their language or practice their religion until after the collapse of Suharto's regime in 1998 (Van Hout, 2015, Van Klinken 2007). Throughout the 1990s, growing tensions between some Dayak and Malay groups led to violent clashes across Kalimantan. This violence has been at least partially linked to the resurgence of ethnic identity movements in the post-Suharto, post-authoritarian period and the decentralization and reform of the government (Schiller and Garang 2002, Van Klinken 2007).

In light of these recent conflicts, which were still fresh in the minds of community members in 2002, I told Father Maessen about several movements within the international museum community, such as the International Coalition of Sites of Conscience[5] (Rassool 2006, Muan 2006), that are using museums and cultural work as a means of promoting intercultural dialogue, reconciliation, and the promotion of human rights. I also recommended exploring the idea of an ecomuseum as a museum model that rests on strengthening a community's sense of place and identity (Davis 2011, Fuller 1992). Because Father Maessen made regular trips to the Netherlands and was planning one later that year, I also suggested that he meet with staff at the Tropenmuseum in Amsterdam to seek advice and possible help in creating a museum.[6] As noted in previous chapters, the Tropenmuseum has a history of working on international museum and cultural development projects in Indonesia and throughout the world.

Altogether, I was impressed with the progress the Weaving Project had made in a relatively short period of time, and with its culturally sensitive and community-grounded approach to its work. I also concluded that Sintang was a suitable site for the establishment of a museum under the leadership of the PRCF and the Kobus Centre. In my report to the Ford Foundation, I recommended that it continue to support the Weaving Project and its future plans to create a museum, which could not only serve the people of the Sintang district but also possibly become a model for other projects throughout Indonesia dedicated to cultural heritage preservation and community development.

The Museum Pusaka Nias: Narratives of Cultural Loss and Recovery

Similar to the Weaving Project, the Museum Pusaka Nias was founded by a Catholic missionary, Father Johannes Hämmerle, who began working in Nias in 1971. Originally from Germany, Father Hämmerle began collecting Nias art, ethnographic objects, and archaeological artifacts in the 1970s in an effort to preserve what remained on the island.

Nias has been celebrated for its rich artistic traditions and monumental architecture for centuries. In the words of the art historian Jerome Feldman, "the islanders produced some of the most spectacular examples of architecture, stone work, wooden sculpture, gold work, and costumes seen anywhere in the [Indonesian] archipelago" (1994, 43). Indeed, years before I made my first trip to the island I had become fascinated by Nias art and culture, which I had seen examples of in Dutch museum collections and exhibition catalogs. Thus, I was thrilled when the Ford Foundation Program officer asked me to visit Nias. What I did not know beforehand, however, was the degree to which the island had been stripped of its material cultural heritage.

Situated in the Indian Ocean some 100 kilometers off the northwest coast of Sumatra, Nias has long been a site of global encounters. Arab, Chinese, and Indian traders had been visiting the island centuries before Europeans arrived in the 1600s. An officer of the Dutch East Indies Company was one of the first Europeans to mention Nias in a report dated 1664. By 1669 the Company had signed trade agreements with Nias chiefs, and established a post near what is now the town of Genungsitoli (Gronert 1990, 12).

In 1864 the island was officially placed under the authority of the Dutch colonial government (Gronert 1990, 13). In keeping with its policy to gather information on the colony's native populations for administrative purposes, the Dutch government commissioned scientific surveys of the island. The first comprehensive study of Nias was published in 1863, followed by many others written by colonial administrators, military personnel, traders, and missionaries. In addition to documenting Nias and its people, they also made collections of art and artifacts. Collections were sent to scientific institutes and museums, for instance, to the Batavia Society museum in Batavia (now Jakarta), and to museums in the Netherlands (Gronert 1990, 15). Over time, Nias art became a prized commodity and ended up in museum and private collections throughout the world.

The collecting of Nias art was so extensive that in 1902 "controversy arose among concerned Westerners over the role of foreigners in the artistic destruction taking place on the island" (Feldman 1994, 43). But the loss of Nias art was not only a result of voracious collecting. The work of Christian missionaries also undermined Nias artistic traditions. Christianity was introduced into Nias in 1865 when French and German Catholic missionaries arrived and began establishing churches on the island. Although progress in converting the islanders was slow in the beginning, Christianity eventually gained a foothold (Gronert 1990, 13)—so much so that today Christianity remains the majority religion on the island. Religious conversion had a great impact on Nias art since the beliefs and practices that inspired it, such as ancestor worship, were discouraged or forbidden (Taylor and Aragon 1991, 69).

Nooy-Palm, in a description of the work of Protestant and Catholic missionaries in Indonesia during the late 1800s, writes that "missionaries' influence on tribal art was often disastrous" (2002, 52). She recounts how many ancestor statues were destroyed by missionaries or by recent converts. During a movement known as the "The Great Repentance" many Nias people cast their religious figures into fires to demonstrate their rejection of paganism. Nooy-Palm states that as a consequence of missionary activities and such movements, "the art of making beautiful and intriguing objects by local artists was gradually lost" (2002, 52). However, Nooy-Palm also points out that not all missionaries were bent on destroying the material expressions of Nias religious traditions. Some saw an alternative use for such objects and collected them to be sent back to the Netherlands and other European countries to museums set up by their missionary societies (Nooy-Palm 2002, 52–54). "Idols" and ritual paraphernalia were displayed in mission museums to represent the pagan ways of native populations. Their presence in the museums demonstrated the success of missionaries in converting people to Christianity and of colonialism's "civilizing" mission.

But while many missionaries were disposed to obliterating native religion others were committed to studying and documenting Indigenous languages, religions, myths, and legends (Nooy-Palm 2002, 52). Many authors have described how missionary descriptions of artifacts have been of great value to museum curators and anthropologists along with their ethnographies and dictionaries. Because they spent extended periods of time, often decades, in one area living among "their people," many missionaries became fluent in native languages and highly knowledgeable of people's culture (Schefold and Vermeulen 2002).

Museum Pusaka Nias was founded against this historical background of competing interests and narratives of cultural destruction and loss, and no less by a missionary. But while Father Hämmerle followed in the footsteps of his predecessors, he did not begin collecting objects to send back to his home country for display as Christian propaganda or for scientific purposes. Instead, he began recovering Nias art and material culture for the benefit of the Nias people. After nearly two decades of collecting, in 1990 Father Hämmerle was granted permission from his order, Friars Minor Capuchin, to establish a museum in Genungsitoli and to

FIGURE 6.2 Staff of the Museum Pusaka Nias. Nata'alui Duha far right and Father Johannes Hämmerle back center. Genungsitoli, Nias, Indonesia
Photograph by C. Kreps, 2002.

devote time to building the museum in addition to his clerical duties. The Museum Pusaka Nias officially opened in 1995 (Figure 6.2).

The museum's development over the years was made possible through the assistance of a broad range of supporters and international connections. It is a private, non-profit organization that operates under the auspices of the Nias Heritage Foundation (Yayasan Pusaka Nias), created in 1991 with the mission to manage and operate a museum and cultural center for the preservation of Nias cultural heritage. It receives funding from private donations, international foundations, non-governmental organizations, in addition to local government agencies. The overall mission of the museum has been to foster awareness and appreciation of the island's natural and cultural history; to serve as a study, research, and recreation center; and to promote the education and social development of local people (Kreps 2015, 260).

The museum is centrally located near the harbor on a major road passing through Genungsitoli. In 2002, it consisted of a large complex of buildings surrounded by a park that included a small zoo and gardens. Various buildings served as storage and display areas for collections and as administrative offices. A dormitory for students from villages throughout the island was also located on the museum's grounds. At that time, the museum was in the process of completing four pavilions to be dedicated to exhibitions. A Swiss architect, who had done extensive research on Nias architecture, designed the pavilions. Another open-air structure designed in the form of an Indonesian *balai*, or meeting place, was also near completion. The *balai* was to serve as a place for special events and activities, such as dance and music performances. A small café overlooking the beach gave visitors a picturesque spot to relax, buy refreshments, and take in the ocean view.

Father Hämmerle told me that he had tried to create a welcoming and relaxing atmosphere in an attempt to popularize the museum and make it attractive to local people. The museum was open to the public seven days a week and charged a small fee to enter. The museum received 20–30 visitors a day, but was especially crowded on Sundays when community members came to the museum to visit the zoo and to picnic. Staff members said that local people also used the museum as a place to practice traditional dance and music, to hold ceremonies, and for celebrations. But the majority of visitors consisted of school children, visiting dignitaries, researchers, and tourists. Although one of the museum's stated purposes was to help the regional government develop tourism on Nias as a means of economic development, Father Hämmerle emphasized that the museum was first and foremost for the local people.

The museum was engaged in a number of activities that served its mission as an educational resource for the community. It offered workshops on traditional arts such as carving, dance, and music, and sponsored training programs for local students in business administration and tourism development as well as English courses. The museum regularly published a bulletin that contained useful information on topics such as health care and hygiene, sustainable agricultural techniques, and environmental conservation. The bulletin was distributed to communities throughout the island and was published both in Indonesian and local languages. The museum furthermore housed a library, which, at the time, was the only one on the island.

Another program involved the study and promotion of the use of traditional medicines. One of the gardens on the grounds was dedicated to the cultivation of traditional medicinal plants.[7] The garden and a herbarium were used as an experimental laboratory and as a "pharmacy" where local people could collect plants for their use at no cost. The museum wanted to offer community members an alternative to expensive, commercially produced drugs while also documenting and preserving Indigenous knowledge about traditional medicine. This program was in keeping with the museum's mission to promote conservation of the island's flora and fauna.

The museum was actively engaged in research, and published books and other materials on Nias art, culture, history, language, archaeology, and architecture. Father Hämmerle had been conducting research and publishing on these topics for many years. I learned that the museum was also supporting archaeological research on the island in cooperation with a German archaeologist from Heidelberg.

The restoration and preservation of traditional Nias architecture was another project in which MPN was engaged in collaboration with villagers across the island. During my visit, I was taken to several villages to see examples of its spectacular and unique architecture (Figure 6.3).

FIGURE 6.3 Chief's house at Bawömataluo built before 1917. South Nias, Indonesia Photograph by C. Kreps, 2003.

Nias is well-known for its extraordinary vernacular architecture and megalithic monuments, which have received much scholarly attention (Feldman 1979, Fox 1993, Grüber and Herbig 2009, Viaro 1990). Waterson, in *The Living House: An Anthropology of Architecture in Southeast Asia*, suggests that "in the whole of South-East Asia it is perhaps in the southern part of Nias that vernacular architecture has found its most monumental expression" (1990, 82). Monumental architecture and megalithic sculptures were also one of island's main tourist attractions.

In 2002, traditional houses clearly remained an important aspect of Nias's tangible and intangible cultural heritage, yet I was told that fewer were being constructed for a number of reasons (Figure 6.4). First was the growing popularity of modern, concrete houses. In the course of my visit, I learned that it was difficult for families to adequately maintain the old houses due to the high cost and unavailability of building materials such as hardwoods, which were becoming scarce due to their harvesting for export. What's more, it was becoming increasingly difficult to find local craftspeople that possessed the specialized knowledge and skills required for their construction (Kreps 2015, 262).

In an effort to preserve traditional houses, the MPN was providing villagers with funds to repair and restore old houses and for training carpenters in vernacular architecture. It was also encouraging people to build new homes in the traditional style with added modern amenities. Alongside these efforts, Father Hämmerle and staff had been conducting studies of Nias vernacular architecture in collaboration

FIGURE 6.4 Traditional-style house in north Nias region
Photograph by C. Kreps, 2002.

with other researchers, for example from the Institute for Comparative Research in Architecture in Vienna, Austria. They were documenting the different styles of houses in different parts of the island, Indigenous knowledge of building techniques, as well as the iconography, customs, and traditions associated with the houses (Grüber and Herbig 2009). The museum displayed several miniature models of traditional Nias houses made by a local craftsman, and a life-size house model stood on the museum's grounds.

In 2002, the museum's collection numbered some 5000 objects, which consisted mostly of ethnographic and archaeological artifacts. At that time, a small percentage of the collection was on display and the staff was in the process of developing exhibitions that were to be installed in the new exhibition halls under construction. Father Hämmerle explained that the new exhibitions were to be modeled after those in Western ethnographic museums, covering various aspects of Nias art, history, and culture. One exhibition hall was dedicated to showing the museum's collection of Nias megaliths and stone sculpture, composed of both original pieces and reproductions. To make itself known to communities outside Genungsitoli, the museum produced traveling exhibits for staff to take to villages.

Even though the museum was serving the people of Nias and fulfilling its mission through an impressive array of programs and activities, Nata'alui Duha, the Assistant Director of the museum, related that generating greater community interest and participation in the museum was one of the museum's greatest challenges. He lamented that although the grounds were crowded on Sundays, visitors rarely took in the exhibitions. The museum had yet to become, in his view, a "center of education and cultural inspiration" for the local people. Consequently, generating deeper community interest and a "sense of ownership" in the museum was one of his main goals.

One community member with whom I spoke claimed that some community members were not inclined to visit the museum because it was owned and run by the Catholic Church. When I asked Father Hämmerle and the staff about this they acknowledged that it was true that the museum was often associated with the Church. However, they stressed that the museum was not confined to serving only Catholics or Christians. In fact, one of the museum's goals was to promote the idea that it exists for everyone as an institution based on democratic principles and respect for human rights and cultural diversity.[8]

The lack of community involvement in the museum was of particular concern to me given that the Ford Foundation was interested in promoting the development of community-based museums in Indonesia, and in using the MPN as a model. During my visit, I suggested various strategies the staff might use to encourage greater community participation, including the co-curation of exhibits and the care and conservation of collections. Up to that point, the museum had relied heavily on museum experts from other Indonesian museums or from abroad for technical assistance in exhibit design and managing and caring for the collections, which despite this help, remained haphazardly stored and in need of attention.

Notwithstanding the poor state of its collection and the challenge of increasing community participation, I left Nias highly impressed by the museum's facilities, educational programs, activities, and its highly dedicated staff. And although it did not fit an idealized version of a community museum—that is, a museum that grows out of and is controlled by a community (Fuller 1992)—I concluded it was serving the people of Nias in a variety of ways and helping sustain and preserve their rich cultural heritage. In my report to the Ford Foundation, I recommended that it continue supporting the museum, and consider sponsoring training for staff at both MPN and the Weaving Project. However, I stressed that such training should be tailored to the specific needs and local conditions of each organization, or in other words, that it should be context-specific and culturally appropriate.

The University of Denver/Indonesia Exchange Program in Museum Training

Funded by the Ford Foundation and Asian Cultural Council in New York City, the University of Denver/Indonesia Exchange Program in Museum Training consisted of two parts. The first part involved on-site training workshops held in July and August 2003 at the Kobus Centre in Sintang (home of the Weaving Project) and in Genungsitoli at the MPN. Two graduate students from the University of Denver (DU) Department of Anthropology Museum and Heritage Studies Program accompanied me and assisted in the workshops. The second part of the Exchange Program entailed bringing Novia Sagita, an Ot-Danum Dayak researcher for the Weaving Project and Nata'alui Duha, Assistant Director of the MPN, to DU to follow courses in museum studies and anthropology. In the following section, I first outline the contours of appropriate museology as a concept, methodology, and context-specific approach to museum training and development. I then describe each part of the Program in terms of activities, goals, and outcomes.

Appropriate Museology: Context-Specific Methodology

While my work in Indonesia in 2002 was the catalyst for the Exchange Program, the idea of appropriate museology was inspired by my earlier research in Central Kalimantan in 1991 and 1992, described in the last chapter. Over the years, I observed that despite the many training programs sponsored by the Directorate of Museums and other parties such as the Ford Foundation, museum workers in Indonesia continued to remain poorly trained, collections poorly cared for (at least from the perspective of museum professionals), and museums poorly attended (Kreps 1998, 2002, 2003, 2008). Appropriate museology was envisioned as an alternative to top-down approaches to museum training largely designed and executed by outside experts and government administrators.

The state of Indonesian museums, according to Directorate staff, was generally attributed to insufficient technical, financial, and human resources as well as to workers' and visitors' lack of "museum-mindedness." This kind of "deficit thinking" (Chilisa 2012, 57–60), however, obscured the drawbacks of approaches to museum training described above, and the inappropriateness of transferring museum models, technologies, and practices from cultural and socioeconomic contexts dramatically different from those in which most Indonesian museums functioned.

For instance, training programs run by national and international museum experts (discussed in the previous chapter) typically focused on various aspects of collections care and management such as registration, documentation, and conservation. But even though these programs were intended to provide museum workers with training that would help them better care for and protect collections, in both content and manner of delivery, this training generally did not match the trainees' level of preparation or the resources available at their museums. Regular access to "museum quality" materials and equipment was also a problem, especially for museums in remote areas. Although well-intended, I observed that trainers paid little attention to how standard, professional museum practices fit particular museum settings. Nor did the structure of these training programs allow room for exploring how local people may have had their own ways of taking care of and safeguarding their cultural heritage in both tangible and intangible forms (Kreps 2008). The training programs with which I was familiar generally matched what McLeod calls "a sort of commando raid in which outsider experts decide what needs to be done, and then do it, then leave." In his estimation this approach "is usually unproductive" (2015, 145).

In addition to on-site training in Indonesia, museum workers were sent abroad to follow training programs. In fact, I recommended several individuals for such training sponsored by the Ford Foundation., and I kept in touch with them as they followed courses at American universities and visited museums in large cities such as Seattle, Los Angeles, Chicago, New York, and Washington, DC. In follow-up conversations with them, I learned that even though they all greatly appreciated the opportunity to travel abroad and gain new knowledge and experience, they also expressed frustration in not being able to apply what they learned back home in their museums. The differences between their museums and those they visited in the United States were too extreme in terms of size, technical resources and facilities, administrative structures, and the degree to which the public was interested in museums. More times than not, they came away from their experiences with a deeper sense of the gaps between museums in "rich nations" like the United States and "poor nations" like Indonesia.

The idea of appropriate museology, as both concept and method, is based on the principle that approaches to training and museum and heritage work should be tailored to specific socioeconomic and cultural contexts. It is ideally a bottom-up, community-based approach that combines local knowledge, resources, and museological practices with those of the professional museum world to better meet the needs and interests of a particular museum and its community. Individual projects should be site-specific, conceptualized "on the ground" in collaboration with stakeholders, rather than being formulated beforehand, "packaged," and "delivered" (Kreps 2008). Appropriate museology offers an alternative to deficit models of museum training and development by recognizing and affirming the cultural and human capital present in communities. Moreover, it is part of the on-going effort to decolonize international museum development and heritage work.

Appropriate museology is also inherently concerned with fostering self-reliance and autonomy. It is now commonly understood within international development circles that too much dependence on foreign or outside assistance can give birth to "white elephants."

> In such cases, a need is identified, a project planned, money is secured from international sources and the work begins. Foreign experts are flown in, local experts are flown out (for oversees training), and there is a deadline. It is often less time consuming to import materials and skills than to identify (let alone develop) them locally. A shining result is delivered within schedule; it continues to shine for two or three years, and then it starts to fall apart. The project has ended so the foreign assistance is not there anymore, even the spare parts for maintenance are often not available.
>
> (Sheriff, Voogt, and Luhila 2006, 43)

Appropriate museology is a methodology that can help avoid the creation of "white elephants" and counter ineffective and unsustainable approaches to museum training and development.[9]

On the whole, context-specific approaches do not simply entail transferring or reproducing established methods, "skill sets," and technologies from one context to another. Instead, they make museum training programs themselves sites of knowledge production since they create spaces for the emergence of new or alternative ideas and hybrid approaches. As I have discovered in the course of my participation in training programs in Indonesia, Vietnam, and Thailand, such programs can be objects of ethnographic inquiry in themselves, and spaces for theorizing and critically reflecting on diverse approaches to cultural and heritage work in diverse environments (Denes et al. 2013)

Appropriate Museology at Museum Pusaka Nias

When my students and I arrived in Nias in July 2003 our first task was to meet with museum staff members and to discuss their needs and set realistic goals for our two-week training workshop. At the time, there were five full-time staff members working under the direction of Father Hämmerle and Nata'alui Duha. Based on our discussions we collectively decided to concentrate on collection storage and care.

A portion of the collection was on display while the rest was stored in various buildings on the museum grounds. None of the storage rooms and display areas was equipped with any means of climate control and pest management. The exhibit halls that had been under construction the previous year had been completed, but were not designed with the protection of collections or local environmental conditions in mind. Given these conditions, we decided to focus on instructing the staff in the basic principles of preventive conservation, and demonstrating how they could be applied to the storage and display of objects.

The museum had a conservation laboratory and a few staff members had some knowledge of conservation techniques based on their training with conservators from Jakarta and abroad. And although the conservation laboratory did contain manuals, materials, and equipment, staff members told me that they did not feel they had been sufficiently trained in how to use the equipment and materials. Thus, they were reluctant to undertake conservation work.

We began the workshop with a presentation on preventive conservation principles and measures. I explained that preventive conservation is intended to prevent the need for remedial conservation, understood as the process of halting the deterioration of an object and stabilizing its condition using specialist conservator techniques (Ambrose and Paine 2006, 190–191). While necessary under certain conditions, remedial conservation requires the skills of professionally trained conservators as well as expensive materials and equipment. In contrast, I emphasized how preventive conservation was largely a matter of becoming familiar with the basic techniques of object handling, reducing various types of stress on objects, and ameliorating damaging environmental conditions (Kreps 2008, 31–32). My primary concern was for staff members to recognize that they did not have to have highly specialized skills and expensive equipment to apply these measures in their museum.

Following the presentation we toured storage units and exhibits with the staff to identify problem areas. Our next step was to go to the local market to purchase supplies for a hands-on demonstration. At the market we purchased nylon fishing line to replace metal wire; mosquito netting to cover shelving units; linoleum for lining shelves; cotton cloth and batting for object mounts; plastic tubing for object rests; Velcro to replace the use of glue and nails; and cotton swabs and soft bristled paint brushes for cleaning objects. We also obtained cardboard tubes (used for rolling linoleum flooring) and Styrofoam packing (in which electronics had been shipped) from shopkeepers at no cost. The total cost of materials purchased was approximately US$30.

At the museum the students and I showed the staff how to carefully clean and handle objects; construct mounts out of Styrofoam and cotton forms; and how to roll textiles on the cardboard tubes to avoid creasing.[10] We then helped the staff cover wooden shelving with linoleum and to arrange objects in secure positions.

The effectiveness of the workshop was made clear when the students and I returned from a three-day tour of the island. While we were away, staff members refurbished an entire shelving unit. They skillfully crafted mounts for all the objects; covered the unit with mosquito netting to protect objects from dust and falling debris; and closed off the window behind the unit to reduce light exposure. We were impressed with how they had quickly applied what they had learned during the workshop, and by what they had accomplished in just a few days. One staff member in charge of collections told me that as a result of the workshop she felt more confident and better qualified to not only carry out her tasks as the museum's assigned conservator, but also to train other staff members (Kreps 2008).

The workshop on preventive conservation demonstrated the value of "appropriate technology" and its museological applications. Community and culture-based approaches to development often promote the use of appropriate technology defined as:

> any object, process, ideas or practice that enhances human fulfillment through satisfaction of human needs. A technology is deemed appropriate when it is compatible with local, cultural and economic conditions ... and utilizes locally available material and energy resources with tools and processes maintained and operationally controlled by the local population ... Technology is considered 'appropriate' to the extent that it is consistent with the cultural, social, economic, and political institutions of the society in which it is used.
>
> *(Hazeltine and Bull 2003, 3–4)*

Appropriate technology may combine people's indigenous skills with modern knowledge to upgrade indigenous skills (Rahman 1993, 20). As a case in point, my students and I heard how staff members used medicinal plants and other natural substances to protect objects. These traditional conservation measures were similar to those used in other parts of Indonesia and elsewhere (Kreps 2003, 138–144).[11]

And as described later in this chapter, Nias vernacular architectural techniques are very much in keeping with the principles and methods of appropriate technology.

During our stay, we also discussed interpretive exhibition strategies and how the staff might improve the educational value of exhibitions while at the same time encourage greater community participation in the museum. Not much had changed in museum/community relations since my visit the previous year. Crowds of people still came to the museum on Sundays, but there was still limited regular visitation on the part of the general public. The staff was not short on ideas for educational programming and outreach activities, but was less conversant in how to actively involve community members on a regular basis and in day-to-day operations. I offered that this was a challenge for museums in the United States and other countries as well, and shared information about visitor studies, focus groups, and other programmatic strategies that have become common. But again, I emphasized that just like everything else we had introduced during the workshop, it was up to them to determine which approaches, if any, would be useful for application in their museum. I also suggested that they seek advice and ideas from community members since the museum was fundamentally for them and about their cultural heritage.

Envisioning a Community Museum for Sintang

Since my visit to Sintang the year before, the Weaving Project had continued pursuing its goal of creating a community museum in the district and a permanent home for Father Maessen's textile collection. Thus, our work became part of this on-going effort. In initial discussions with Project staff, we decided to concentrate on inventorying and documenting Father Maessen's collection with the idea that it would eventually be donated to a museum. Although Father Maessen knew a great deal about the pieces in his collection, most of this knowledge remained, in his words, "in his head." He had never had the time to make an inventory of his collection, which was stored in a number of different rooms in the Kobus Centre.

Over the next couple of weeks, the students instructed staff in how to number, tag, and enter data on inventory worksheets. In lieu of a computerized database system, the students created an inventory worksheet on which information about each piece could be recorded, including an assigned object number, dimensions, materials, provenience, name of weaver if known, and date of collection if known. The worksheet, in English and Indonesian, also included space for descriptive notes and any relevant information in local languages. Novia Sagita, who had been working with the Project for several years as a researcher, provided additional information on the meanings of motifs based on her research with weavers in their home villages (Figure 6.5).

The students also helped rehouse the textiles in a secured, air-conditioned storage room refitted to better protect the textiles from light, dust, humidity, and pests. This activity gave us the opportunity to train staff in basic preventive conservation measures similar to our work at Museum Pusaka Nias.

FIGURE 6.5 Novia Sagita, second from left, researcher for the Dayak Ikat Weaving Project and participant in the University of Denver/Indonesia Exchange Program in Museum Training with Nata'alui Duha pictured in Figure 6.2. Sagita accompanied by Pak Apan, Ibu Apan (weaver), and Juanti Apan in the village of Ensaid, West Kalimantan
Photograph by C. Kreps, 2003.

During our stay, we toured the site where a new, three-story building for the government-funded archives and library was under construction a few kilometers outside of Sintang. Father Maessen and Project staff saw the buildings as a potential home for the Kobus Centre collection. In addition to housing a library and archives, the building was designed to accommodate computer labs, classrooms, storage, and display areas. They further believed there would be a number of advantages to partnering with local government officials, like the *bupati* on their museum initiative. Consequently, Father Maessen asked if I would write a proposal to the *bupati* recommending that space be set aside in the building for a museum. Novia Sagita translated the report into Indonesian and we presented it to the *bupati*. One month after I left Sintang, I heard from Father Maessen that the *bupati* had accepted the proposal.

In the proposal, I suggested that further research be conducted on traditional conservation methods and local curatorial practices, and how these might be integrated into the museum's practice (Kreps 2003, 2009, Clavir 2002). Novia Sagita had documented examples of these practices during her fieldwork in villages. For instance, she recorded how weavers conserve heirloom cloths by carefully storing them in large ceramic storage jars (*balanga*) or in plaited baskets made from the leaves of a medicinal plant that act as an insecticide. She also documented how they classify textiles based on local taxonomies, aesthetic canons, and spiritual criteria (Sagita 2009).

While in Sintang, the students and I proposed mounting an exhibit on Dayak *ikat* weaving at the University of Denver Museum of Anthropology. Father Maessen agreed and loaned several items from the Kobus collection, including a warped loom, a spinning wheel, cotton gin, and several antique and contemporary *ikat* pieces. We drew up loan forms for each item, and the students and I hand-carried the pieces back to Denver. Father Maessen shipped more textiles to us to sell during the exhibition titled *Woven Dreams: Women and Weaving in Indonesian Borneo*, which opened in May 2004. During the opening, we raised over $1500 for the cooperative.

Altogether, our work with the Weaving Project was productive on many accounts. We helped secure a future home for the Kobus collection, and prepared it for eventual donation. The students were able to share their knowledge and skills in collection care and management, and adapt methods to the local context in collaboration with Project staff. They also spent time in the village where many of the textiles were produced that ended up on display in Denver. Thus, they had the chance to meet weavers and gain first-hand knowledge of the textiles' originating, cultural context.[12]

In both Genungsitoli and Sintang, the students had the opportunity to develop sensitivity to the needs and conditions of museums and heritage work in a country and cultures outside their own. In this regard, they did not just learn how to put the concept of appropriate museology into practice, but more significantly, why it is important to do so. The students also left Indonesia with a sense of the environments in which Duha and Sagita worked, which allowed them to better understand how they could assist them during their stays at the University of Denver. Our on-site training in Genungsitoli and Sintang further demonstrated to the Ford Foundation, and to other sponsors, the value of context-specific, appropriate museology.

The Exchange Program as Transnational, Transcultural Reciprocal Collaboration

Nata'alui Duha and Novia Sagita arrived on September 2, 2004 to begin their studies at the University of Denver. Duha was in Denver for one academic quarter (ten weeks) and Sagita was in residence until May 2005, nearly a full academic year.[13] Both were selected to come to Denver because of the positions they held within their organizations, their proficiency in English, and their desire to expand their knowledge and skills in museum and heritage work. Although each had years of experience working in their respective organizations, neither one of them had had the opportunity to undertake formal training in museum studies and anthropology in an academic setting. This was also the first time they were exposed to critical museology. While at DU, they sat in on classes and worked in the DU

Museum of Anthropology (DUMA). Consequently, their time at DU was devoted to training in both the theory and practice of museum anthropology. They also visited several museums in the Denver area, and thus were exposed to a variety of museum types and sizes.

Duha was especially interested in learning about strategies for creating greater community engagement and participation in museums since this was an on-going challenge in Museum Pusaka Nias. In his final report to the Ford Foundation and Asian Cultural Council, he commented on the insights he had gained about the importance of museum/community relations and the museum's role in society. "New museology theories helped me see and define museums by considering the community's need. Museums are for all people and not for a certain group or individual. They have to be democratic and educational institutions to serve social development" (2004).

Because the use of volunteers in museums is relatively uncommon in Indonesia, Duha was particularly impressed by this aspect of American museum culture. As he wrote: "Volunteers are willing to share their time to participate in museum programs ... The Denver Museum of Nature and Science is a good example. It has 1700 volunteers. This community participation indicates a high civic engagement in the museum" (Duha 2004). He recognized how creating a volunteer program at his museum could be a way of involving community members in day-to-day operations, and creating a "sense of ownership" in the museum.

In her report, Sagita also stressed the value of community involvement in museums based on her experience in Denver.

> Museums in Denver very much impressed me; not only the look of buildings but also the large numbers of visitors ... After I visited many different museums in Denver, I realized that a top down style of museum management in my home country is not ideal for our community. The result is that the community does not have a sense of belonging or feeling of being integrated into the museum. The work now is to learn how to have a museum that integrates the community, since it is the community that owns the culture and all of the resources.
>
> *(2005, 3)*

Especially important for Sagita was recognition of the differences between American and Indonesian museums, and the need to adapt museum methods to local contexts to make museums relevant to community members. In her report she stated:

> Looking at my home country of Indonesia it is common knowledge that our museum institution is a symbolic building. Not only do our museums lack human resources, but also our community does not know the role and functions of museums. Learning about and observing objects in a particular building, is not part of our culture. The fact that museums are not part of the

culture [however] does not mean that museums cannot exist in our country. We have cultural materials which need to be preserved and cared for since they are evidence of our history.

(2005, 2)

Sagita wrote that she hoped she would be able to take what she had learned back to Sintang "to contribute to our museum development in a way that reflects local cultural values and identity" (2005, 2).

One of the values of the exchange program was that it allowed participants to make comparisons across their museological work cultures, and in turn, contemplate what did or did not make sense in their respective contexts. As a "de-naturalizing" method, comparison throws into relief differences as well as commonalities, affinities, and points of intersection.

As members of ethnic groups with a history of marginalization in Indonesia, both Sagita and Duha were drawn to the ways museums are addressing the cultural and human rights of historically oppressed peoples in the United States and other countries. They both found the Native American Graves Protection and Repatriation Act (NAGPRA) and consultation work associated with its implementation particularly compelling. They were introduced to NAGPRA in courses and through their work in the DUMA. Duha highlighted the significance of NAGPRA in his report, stating:

> Museum workers must listen to the voice of the community as culture owners. NAGPRA aims to protect the human rights of Native Americans in cultural terms, giving them a right of possession ... NAGPRA can be a good model for other countries to respect cultural heritage as a human right and a gateway to cultural democracy and civil society.
>
> *(2004)*

Duha related that he had also benefited from the opportunity to work with students from diverse national and cultural backgrounds. At the time of Duha and Sagita's residencies, students from Germany and France were pursuing degrees in anthropology and museum studies at DU. He appreciated the chance to freely engage in critical debates with students on issues related to museums and the politics of culture in their respective countries. In sum, he stated that he had been inspired by his participation in the Exchange Program, and would take all that he had learned and apply it back home in Museum Pusaka Nias. In her report, Sagita also affirmed the value of the Program, saying: "As a cultural worker I see this program as a big achievement in collaborative anthropology" (2005, 19).

"Transnational, Transcultural, Reciprocal Collaboration"

Looking back on the Exchange Program, I see how it embodied many elements of what Schlehe and Hidayah call "transnational, transcultural, reciprocal collaboration" (2014). In their article, "Transcultural Ethnography: Reciprocity in Indonesian-German Tandem Research," the authors describe how, since 2004, the Departments of Anthropology at the University of Freiburg, Germany and Gadjah Mada University in Yogyakarta, Indonesia have been developing a joint student-centered project for fieldwork and teaching based on "cross-national, transcultural collaboration." Through the project students learn to practice ethnography in "tandems" both in Indonesia and in Germany, experiencing both "host/guest" and "insider/outsider" positions. The authors state that their program makes "insider" and "outsider" perspectives "complement one another in an attempt to transcend the dichotomy of Euro-centric and Asia-centric views in a synergistic search for diversity and conversation across cultures" (2014, 258). According to Schlehe and Hidayah, a crucial aspect of the model is "to put to use the multiple differences, positions, and relations between cultures" (Schlehe and Hidayah 2014, 254). They view ethnographic fieldwork as a relational, open-ended, and flexible process for the development of context-specific and decolonizing methodologies.

The authors point out that reciprocal collaboration is not simply a matter of doing research or studying in a country other than one's own. Rather, it requires that participants, as "transcultural partners," approach their work sites reflexively, and become aware of the differences between their own work cultures, the micro-dynamics of their own institutional settings, and the macro-structural issues of inequities related to the geo-politics of knowledge production (Schlehe and Hidayah 2014, 257). Furthermore, it requires participants to reflect on their own individual positionality, and how their perceptions, experiences, values, and back-grounds influence their work. "When students from different backgrounds conduct their fieldwork exercises together, similarities and differences are experienced first-handedly. They can learn from each other, discuss their styles, and either strive for compromises and approximation, or they can make conscious use of their different positions" (Schlehe and Hidayah 2014, 266). Through this relational process, the "insider" can often profit from the "outsider's" perspective, and the "outsider" may get valuable context information from the "insider" partner.

Schlele and Hidayah emphasize that one of the many values of transcultural, reciprocal collaborations is that they can create a sense of camaraderie and com-monality among participants from diverse backgrounds. Difference is not some-thing to be overcome, but rather, is the basis for complementarity and for building relationships that can be long-lasting and transformative. The exchange of knowl-edge, experiences, and diverse perspectives through working together can nurture "transcultural relations" and help dissolve "insider/outsider," "us/them," and "East/West" distinctions (Schlehe and Hidayah 2014, 258).

The University of Denver/Indonesia Exchange Program certainly allowed participants to reflect on differences between museum work cultures in Indonesia and the United States as well as the micro-dynamics of their own organizational settings. It also gave participants the opportunity to explore how their diverse backgrounds could be complementary and engender a sense of "commonality." Duha and Sagita established friendships and professional relationships with DU students, faculty, staff, and colleagues in the Denver museum community that remain intact to this day. But while the Exchange Program lived up to the ideals of transnational, transcultural reciprocal collaboration and a decolonizing methodology in many respects, there were also a number of imbalances and inequalities embedded in the Program that were largely unavoidable yet not wholly irredeemable.

For one thing, the Exchange Program was conducted primarily in English. Postcolonial and Indigenous research paradigms critique the dominance of European languages as a "colonizing instrument" that perpetuates inequalities in knowledge production and distribution (Chilisa 2012, 58). Given this critique, ideally my students should have had language training before going to Indonesia. However, this would have been impractical due to the short period of time they would be spending in the country. Moreover, Indonesia is known for being linguistically and culturally diverse. It is common for most Indonesians to speak one or more local languages in addition to Bahasa Indonesia, the national language. The question thus becomes whose language to learn? Plus, I did not foresee language as a significant barrier since I speak Bahasa Indonesia and several members of the Museum Pusaka Nias and Weaving Project staff spoke English. While one could say that the predominant use of English in the Exchange Program placed the Indonesian participants at a disadvantage, it also gave them the opportunity to enhance their English language skills, which, for better or worse, is social capital in a globalized world in which English has become the dominant lingua franca.

Another obvious imbalance in the Exchange Program was the time participants spent in each "field site." Again my students and I spent approximately one month in Indonesia while Sagita and Duha were in Denver for nine and four months respectively. This disparity too was unavoidable since our work in Indonesia had to be carried out over the summer break and accommodate professional and personal schedules on all sides.

Above all, the Exchange Program embodied imbalances in power. Such imbalances are inherent to most North/South collaborations since they are predicated on differential access to resources, such as funding, institutional support and infrastructure, and other forms of social capital (Crewe and Axelby 2013). Furthermore, in North/South collaborations greater authority is generally consigned to project coordinators and leaders by virtue of their positions. This is something I became acutely aware of in my earlier work on a cultural and environmental conservation project in Kalimantan (Kreps 2002, 2003), as well as during the workshops at Museum Pusaka Nias and the Weaving Project. For instance, even though I envisioned all participants in the training workshops as "differently positioned equals" (Schlehe and Hidayah 2014, 254), I was invariably cast as the "international museum expert" there to bestow knowledge and expertise upon the staff. This "expert/beneficiary" relationship invoked certain expectations and power dynamics despite my efforts to circumvent the "cult of the expert" (Kreps 2003, 8–9, Rassool 2006).

Yet this did not mean that staff members were simply "beneficiaries" or powerless recipients of our "services" or "charity" (Lynch 2011, 2017). On the contrary, in several instances staff members quite consciously used me to gain access to resources like funding, to shore up their own authority, and assert their own agendas in the eyes of local authorities and power brokers. As a case in point, Father Maessen of the Weaving Project convinced the *bupati* of Sintang to make space for a museum in the new archives building on the basis of the proposal he asked me to write. Father Maessen believed, as previously noted, that the proposal would carry more weight coming from an "international museum expert." This example throws light on the agency of differently positioned actors in collaborative partnerships, and how power and authority can be shared and distributed. It further highlights how those involved in creating collaborative partnerships would do well in remembering how their own positions are invariably entangled in and can become subservient to local discourses and politics (Adams 1995, 150).

Indeed, Schlehe and Hidayah's model of transnational, transcultural reciprocal collaboration is intended to make such power dynamics transparent. Differences in power and their implications are "on the table" and a factor to be reflexively acknowledged and interrogated. Accordingly, they regard their model "as a contribution to the restructuring of the global project of anthropology as a debate among equals in a connected world with all of its richness of differences and problems of inequalities" (Schlehe and Hidayah 2014, 254).

Collaborations like the University of Denver/Indonesia Exchange Program can contribute to the restructuring of the global project of museum and heritage work by cultivating global perspectives. Through the Exchange Program participants gained greater awareness not only of their differences, but also of their common-alities as members of a worldwide museum community that despite its diversity is also united by shared values and sense of purpose. They became even more cog-nizant of the importance of international connections and professional networks as resources to draw on when needed. Indeed, developing "human resources" and "capacity building," in the jargon of international development practice (Isar 2015, 33), was initially identified as one of the primary needs of both organizations.

The Value of Museum and Heritage Work

My work with the Museum Pusaka Nias and the Dayak Ikat Weaving Project is but one example of the many kinds of international collaborations and partnerships in which museum anthropologists have been engaged (Adams 2005, Basu and Modest 2015, Basu and Zetterstrom-Sharp 2015, Silverman 2015). Beyond the belief in the inherent value of culture and heritage work, many museum anthro-pologists are committed to collaboration as a potentially decolonizing methodology and ethical responsibility to those with whom they work.

Jennifer Shannon, in "Projectishare.com: Sharing Our Past, Collecting for the Future" describes a collaborative project at the University of Colorado Museum of Natural History and the National Museum of Taiwan carried out with the Paiwan, the Indigenous people of Taiwan, and the Navajo Nation in the United States. The project, titled *iShare: Connecting Museums and Communities East and West*, pro-vides a model "to think about collaborative practice in museum anthropology, as well as issues of translation between different continental traditions of museum anthropology, and between indigenous communities a world apart" (2015, 68). According to Shannon, the principles of decolonizing the museum guided the structure of the collaborative process and were embedded and exemplified in the project's outcomes—mainly a secure web application (*iShare*) and a dynamically linked public website[14] that allows online visitors to access collections, educational and audiovisual materials, and to explore and share stories, oral histories, and knowledge. For Shannon, collaboration, as a decolonizing methodology, entails sharing authority and access to resources, and being reflexive and aware of unequal power relations (2015, 79–83).

Speaking from her standpoint as an American museum curator and professor of anthropology, Shannon maintains that those working with originating communities and that are interested in decolonization want to enhance originating communities' rights and public visibility. They engage in collaboration because:

> Ethically, we want to empower Native peoples to have control over how they are represented to the public, redress past injustices, and include originating communities that have been represented and yet often silenced in the museum. We also want the museum to serve the communities whose objects they house. Finally, epistemologically we value other ways of knowing the world around us and do not want to continue to privilege only Western ways of knowing the world, Native objects, or Native life experiences.
>
> *(2015, 68–69)*

Ultimately, Shannon states that "iShare embraces the idea that anthropology can do some good" (2015, 82). Over the years I too have witnessed examples of this "good" in the ways Museum Pusaka Nias and the Weaving Project have contributed to the safeguarding of their communities' tangible and intangible cultural heritage and well-being. These examples, described below, demonstrate the intrinsic and extrinsic value of culture and heritage.

"A Blessing in Disguise"

Just two weeks after Duha returned to Nias in December 2004, the catastrophic "Boxing Day" tsunami devastated the northwest coast of Sumatra and other coastal regions in the Indian Ocean. Because Nias is situated near the epicenter of the earthquake that spawned the tsunami the island did not suffer as many casualties and as much damage as did other coastal areas. But three months later, on March 28, 2005, an earthquake measuring 8.7 on the Richter scale struck the island. The earthquake and its aftershocks killed nearly 1000 people, and injured close to 12,000. It destroyed much of the island's infrastructure, especially in Genungsitoli, the largest town on the island and home to Museum Pusaka Nias (Kreps 2008, 2015).

In an email message I received from Duha on May 2, 2005 he described the conditions in Nias and damage at the museum. Several buildings used for storing collections and housing students plus a wall surrounding the museum complex had collapsed, and more than 100 pieces in the collection were severely damaged or destroyed. In response to a call for help sent out across the Internet, the museum began to receive aid from a number of international organizations within months after the disaster. Among these was the Cultural Emergency Response (CER) Programme based in the Netherlands, which initially donated €17,000 for the construction of a new storage building (Kreps 2015).

The CER Programme, part of the Prince Claus Fund for Culture and Development based in the Netherlands, offers "first aid" for culture in the form of funding to restore damaged heritage or to protect that which is threatened by natural or human-created disasters. The CER operates on the premise that rescuing cultural resources can help restore a sense of continuity and normalcy to disaster-affected communities. It works directly with individuals and organizations that are the owners of damaged cultural property, and are thus in a position to safeguard it most closely (Chronis and Box 2006, 6–8). CER recognizes the "all pervasiveness of culture," in people's lives, "its intrinsic value as a basic human need, and its relevance as a factor of human resilience" (Frerks, Goldewijk, and van der Plas 2011, 11).[15]

I returned to Nias in August 2008, three years after the earthquake. Although I had been in regular communication with Duha since the disaster and was aware of the museum's reconstruction efforts, I was astounded by the remarkable recovery it had made in just a few years. While touring the newly constructed storage building, I was pleased to see how the museum staff had incorporated many of the preventive conservation techniques we had introduced in our workshop five years earlier. Staff had created storage units and mounts using locally sourced materials to protect fragile objects, such as ceramics and sculptures, from the constant threat of tremors (see Figure 6.6).

FIGURE 6.6 Before and after photographs of collections storage at Museum Pusaka Nias. On the left is an example of storage facilities in 2003 and on the right in 2008. In the photograph Nata'alui Duha is pointing out how the staff has applied preventive conservation techniques in the rehousing of collections in the newly constructed depot. Duha is accompanied by staff member Oktoberlina Telaumbanua
Photograph by C. Kreps, 2008.

Three life-size models of Nias traditional-style houses had also been constructed on museum grounds, which, at that time, were being used to house international aid workers. Contrary to what I expected to see, the museum appeared to be thriving and was in better condition than it had been before the earthquake. In Father Hämmerle's words, the disaster, ironically, had been a "blessing in disguise" because it generated much-needed financial assistance for the museum, and increased awareness of the value of Nias vernacular architecture and efforts to preserve it (Kreps 2008, 2015).

Although the museum had long been working with villagers to restore and preserve traditional houses this work took on added significance after the earth-quake, which destroyed some 16,000 homes and damaged another 62,000, leaving some 70,000 people homeless (Lang 2010, 143). Remarkably, while 80 percent of modern-style, concrete houses and other buildings collapsed, traditional-style houses were left standing (Viaro and Ziegler 2009, 14), some of which were over 100 years old. This is because Nias architecture is highly adapted to the island's geographical location and geological conditions. Nias is situated in one of the most seismically active areas of the world, and due to regularly occurring earthquakes, construction techniques have been developed over the centuries to withstand seis-mic shocks. This feature of Nias architecture had been attracting the attention of researchers since the 1800s (Waterson 1990, 80). However, interest in Nias earth-quake-proof architecture rose dramatically after the disaster (Grüber and Herbig 2009), and was factored into reconstruction and rehabilitation efforts facilitated through the museum (Kreps 2015).

Questioning the "Culture for Development" Paradigm

MPN's story provides a compelling case study in the vital role cultural heritage work can play in humanitarian disaster relief, and for assessing the values of culture and heritage to socioeconomic development more generally. The extent to which scarce resources should be spent on culture in so-called developing countries has been a topic of on-going debate within international development circles for dec-ades, and more recently, within the museum and heritage sector (Basu and Modest 2015, Evans and Rowlands 2015, Kreps 2003, Rao and Walton 2004, Schech and Haggis 2000, Silverman and Ruggles 2007, Warren, Slikkerveer, and Brokensha 1995, UNESCO 1995). At the center of debates have been competing perceptions of the intrinsic and extrinsic values of culture and heritage. Up until recently extrinsic and instrumental values have been prioritized over and above other values, leading Basu and Modest to argue that there is a need to "think outside the instrumentalist logic that dominates much development" (2015, 12). This logic, in their view, reduces the values of culture and heritage simply to "assets," "resources," and "means to an end."

The instrumentalist logic of conventional development strategies has rested on the all too common view of culture as a luxury, existing outside Maslow's "hierarchy of basic human needs," i.e., food, water, shelter, health, and security

(Basu and Modest 2015, 10). Development work has, by and large, generally concentrated on securing basic needs through economic and materialist measures. Basu and Modest, however, contend that rendering culture and heritage subservient to supposedly more fundamental needs denies the cultural subjectivities of the people development seeks to aid, and overlooks the importance of heritage in shaping those subjectivities. To them, culture and heritage have intrinsic value as a "capacity" in terms of how they give structure and meaning to people's lives, inform their aspirations for the future, and contribute to their overall well-being. In short, they assert that greater consideration needs to be given to the multiple regimes of value in which culture and heritage can be conceptualized (2015, 11–12). Indeed, today, heritage is increasingly being seen not so much as a "thing," but as "an act of making meaning" and as a "cultural and social process, which engages with acts of remembering that work to create ways to understand and engage with the present" (Smith 2006, 2). Ultimately, at issue are questions regarding "who defines cultural heritage and who should control stewardship and the benefits of cultural heritage" (Silverman and Ruggles 2007, 3).

The work of Museum Pusaka Nias and the Dayak Ikat Weaving Project has certainly been driven by instrumentalist logic. To greater and lesser degrees, the two have framed culture and heritage as "resources" and "assets" to be mined for development purposes. The Weaving Project's cooperative, after all, was established not only to revive and preserve the *ikat* weaving tradition, but also to empower women through financial independence and, in turn, promote community development. On these grounds, it could be accused of embracing the now highly critiqued "culture for development" approach (Basu and Modest 2015, McLeod 2015, Rao and Walton 2004). Yet the Weaving Project's approach departs from a purely instrumentalist strategy on several fronts, which, in many respects, has contributed to its long-term success (Kreps 2012, 191, Sagita 2009).

One sign of success is the cooperative's growth in membership, which increased from 200 weavers in 2002 to 1500 in 2014.[16] Sagita attributes the cooperative's remarkable success as both an economic development and cultural heritage preservation initiative to multiple factors. First of all, since the Project's founding in 1999, it has received financial backing and endorsement from numerous sources, including the Ford Foundation, local government departments, other non-government and community development organizations, and private, domestic, and international donors. It has also benefited from good marketing. But especially important is how the cooperative has been diligent in building the weavers' capacity to manage the production and distribution of their products, giving them control and power over the direction of the cooperative. Moreover, the Project has sought to respect local knowledge and age-old customs associated with weaving, such as rituals performed during various stages of the weaving process and beliefs regarding the sacred nature of certain types of cloth. Finally, the Project has been tailored to fit into the lives of the weavers and their home communities rather than disrupt them for the sake of development (Kreps 2012, 191). Overall, Sagita credits the cooperative's success and survival to the Project's commitment to creating a collaborative process amenable to all stakeholders. At its roots have been an awareness of and sensitivity to the weavers' cultural subjectivities, and how culture and heritage can be a capacity for empowerment.

A New Museum for Sintang: The Museum Kapuas Raya

After returning from her studies in Denver in 2005 Sagita became the coordinator of the Weaving Project's museum development initiative, and began conducting fieldwork in villages throughout the district to gauge interest in the idea. She even led a group of weavers on a trip to visit the Museum Pusaka Nias, and get advice from staff (Sagita 2009). The Weaving Project's museum initiative was deferred, however, when the Kobus Centre and the government of Sintang partnered with the Tropenmuseum in Amsterdam to create the Museum Kapuas Raya. At this point, Sagita was assigned to the project team dedicated to planning and setting up this museum. The Museum Kapuas Raya opened in October 2008 in the same building under construction when I visited in 2003 (Kreps 2015, 170–171).

I returned to Sintang in August 2008, just a few months before the museum was scheduled to open. As I toured the building, it was rewarding to see what had become of Father Maessen and the *bupati*'s vision for a museum in Sintang. I was especially moved when I entered the gallery dedicated to the display and study of Dayak *ikat* weaving. Father Maessen had found a permanent home for his collection. But even more so, I was struck by how much grander the community museum initiative had become than originally imagined.

The opening of Museum Kapuas Raya was the outcome of at least five years of negotiations, planning, and bidirectional exchanges between representatives from Sintang and the Tropenmuseum. As a collaborative partnership among a district-level government, a local non-governmental organization (the Kobus Centre and Foundation), and a foreign museum, Museum Kapuas Raya represented a new model of museum development in Indonesia. It also departed from the "standardized concept of the provincial museum in Indonesia" (Van Hout 2015, 184) in its approach to the representation of culture. Unlike provincial museums that attempt to represent the history and cultures of an entire province, or just one dominant ethnic group within a province (Kreps 2003, Taylor 1994), the Museum Kapuas Raya was to focus on the specific history and cultural heritage of particular communities within a district of a province.

Itie Van Hout, a senior curator at the Tropenmuseum and leader of the project team, describes, in detail, the process of planning the museum and its exhibits in the book chapter "Museum Kapuas Raya: The In-Between Museum" (2015). According to Van Hout, among the many concerns project team leaders had to take into consideration was how to equally represent the three main ethnic groups of Sintang—Dayak, Malay, and Indonesian-Chinese. This matter was of critical importance in light of the tensions that had historically existed among these groups (as discussed earlier in this chapter), and the *bupati* and Father Maessen's desire to create a museum that would foster intercultural dialogue and social cohesion. And given that the project was to be collaborative and community-based it was imperative that representatives from these communities were involved in all phases of the project, especially in the interpretation and representations of their own cultures. But in Van Hout's assessment, these goals were only partially met.

Van Hout recounts that while community representatives determined the content of their individual exhibits, donated objects, and helped install them, the different groups' level of commitment to the project was uneven. What's more, she states that the groups did not really interact and communicate with one another until the final installation of their exhibits. She discloses that actually certain groups were reticent to participate in the project from the start, and although much work was done to build relationships, a "feeling of separateness" lingered between project leaders and community groups (2015, 183). Van Hout attributes this situation to the project's design, which in her view, did not provide community participants with sufficient opportunities to engage in dialogue with one another and with project staff. Their fluctuating commitment and feelings of skepticism, she surmises, were likely due to the fact that the project was the vision of the *bupati* and Father Maessen and not that of the community (2015, 183–185).

It is also possible that community members were reluctant to engage more fully with the project due to a lagging mistrust of any government-related undertaking, and suspicions regarding its approach to participation. As I experienced during my work on a cultural and environmental conservation project in East Kalimantan in the late 1990s, community members were hesitant to participate because they were far more accustomed to being told what to do rather than being asked to make their own decisions (Kreps 2003, 129–137). Although Indonesia had officially become a democratic state by the mid-2000s, it was still emerging from decades of authoritarian rule (Aspinall and Fealy 2003, Jones 2013). In this light, the Museum Kapuas Raya project raises questions concerning the museum as an institution of civil society within the context of an "emerging democracy," and about how it might be perceived by citizens still leery of the coercive powers of the state. Indeed, considering that the museum was financed by the district government with the aim of shaping a socially cohesive community, Van Hout concedes that the project could be seen as an instrument of governmentality (Bennett 1998), "fashioning how Sintang's various communities should behave as citizens of the Indonesian state" (2015, 185).

Despite these and many other vexing issues, Van Hout believes the Museum Kapuas Raya project was a success because:

> The government museum staff and community of Sintang are creating their own museological form and practice. They are striving to shape a museum that suits the local political, economic, and cultural conditions while accepting that these are dynamic processes. The museum management has recognized that it is only by engaging with the issues of local relevance that the museum can build relationships with the community and in this way flourish as an institution of civil society. In addition to its exhibitions about

Sintang's culture and histories, the museum provides a meeting place to discuss cultural and environmental issues, and has thus begun to play an important role in the complex field of community development.

(2015, 184)

Throughout her chapter, Van Hout reflects on the challenges of international cultural cooperation, particularly between partners that share a colonial history. She speculates on how this history and its concomitant power relationships might have influenced the dynamics of the project. In this light, it is of interest to point out that the partnership between the Tropenmuseum and the Sintang government coincided with the Netherlands–Indonesia Shared Cultural Heritage Project (SCH) that took place from 2003 to 2006 (Scott 2014).

The SCH project, sponsored by the Dutch Ministry of Foreign Affairs, was initiated when the Indonesian government in the early 2000s asked to exhibit Dutch collections, which it argued, the Indonesian public had never seen because they were "stored in a foreign country" (Hardiati and ter Keurs 2006, 7). Beginning in late 2003, the SCH project focused on exchanging information on the collections of the National Museum of Ethnology in Leiden and the National Museum in Jakarta. Curatorial and conservation teams from both museums conducted research to reconstruct the history of collecting and division of collections made between the museums during the Dutch colonial period (Scott 2014, 182). One of the outcomes of the project was a joint exhibition that was displayed at the National Museum in Jakarta in 2005 and in The New Church (Nieuwe Kerk) in Amsterdam in 2006. The project also produced an exhibition catalogue, *Indonesia: The Discovery of the Past*, as well as the edited volume *Colonial Collections Revisited* (ter Keurs 2007). Scott writes that the publications brought "clarity to the varying contexts of colonial museum collection formation," and the SCH project overall "highlighted a convergence between scholarly interest in and official willingness to account for the forgotten colonial history of Dutch museums and their collection" (2014, 181).

Scott argues that the SCH project was a means of forestalling the question of returning objects in Dutch museums to Indonesia (2014, 181). And indeed, the project can be seen as an extension of the Dutch government's longstanding propensity to use culture as a political tool in forging and repairing international relations (Scott 2017). But on the other hand, the project can be viewed as yet another example of how the Dutch have been attempting to confront their colonial legacy through international cooperation and exchange. The Museum Kapuas Raya project is a case in point. In addition to helping establish a museum in Sintang, the project also involved the production of a documentary film on the textile tradition of the region plus research on the history of Sintang. The aim of the latter was to collate primary and secondary archival sources housed in Dutch institutions and to make them available to the people of Sintang. The publication, *Sejarah Sintang—The History of Sintang. A Collection of Books, Manuscripts, Archives and Articles* (Fienieg 2007), was one product of this research.[17] Moreover, Van Hout notes that at the end of the project the Tropenmuseum agreed to transfer ownership of objects to the Museum Kapuas Raya, which it had initially only agreed to loan (2015, 186).

Reflections on the Values of International Collaboration

The stories of the University of Denver/Indonesia Exchange Program in Museum Development, the Museum Pusaka Nias, the Dayak Ikat Weaving Project, and the Museum Kapuas Raya demonstrate what can be achieved through international connections and collaboration. Together, they represent a global community of cultural workers and organizations dedicated to shared interests and concerns. As such, they invite a more expansive and cosmopolitan notion of "community" when doing community-engaged work.

I have not been back to Sintang since 2008 and thus have not seen the Museum Kapuas Raya since it opened. However, I have remained in contact with Father Maessen and Novia Sagita who tell me the museum is doing well, and has become an active educational and cultural hub in Sintang. Father Maessen is no longer directly involved with the Museum Kapuas Raya and the Dayak Ikat Weaving Project, although he continues to support its work through efforts such as the publication in 2014 of *Tenun Ikat Dayak Desa: Cerita dan Motif Kain* [*Ikat Weaving of the Desa Dayak: Stories of Motifs on Cloth*], produced in cooperation with the Indonesian National Crafts Council, the Kobus Foundation, and the Dayak Ikat Weaving Cooperative. He has also moved on to other causes, most notably, the protection of Kalimantan's highly endangered orangutans. Novia Sagita also continues to work with the weavers through the non-governmental organization PlanetIndonesia, which is an environmental and cultural conservation organization she founded with an American environmental activist. I have also not visited Nias since 2008, but have maintained contact with Father Hämmerle and Nata'alui Duha, who is now director of the museum. The museum boasts an impressive website on which one can find a wealth of information on the museum, the history and culture of Nias, research reports, and updates on projects, including its continued work on restoring traditional houses.[18]

Aside from the values of museum and heritage work, one of the many lessons I have learned through my participation in international collaborations is that we can often find ourselves forming alliances and working with what at first may seem like unlikely partners. In Indonesia on three different islands (i.e., West Papua, Kalimantan, and Nias), I discovered how I shared common interests and concerns with missionaries—a community with whom many anthropologists have long been at odds due to the perception that we work at cross-purposes. The commonly held view is that while anthropologists have been intent on documenting and protecting people's cultures (and by extension cultural diversity), missionaries have been devoted to changing them. But in all three cases, the missionaries I have encountered have not been bent on the undoing of Indigenous cultures. Instead, they have been involved in creating museums in their communities and safeguarding their cultural heritage. They all also have been dedicated to protecting people's human rights often in the face of political reprisal.[19] In Thailand, as a "resource person" for the Intangible Cultural Heritage and Museums Field School organized by the Princess Maha Chakri Sirindhorn Anthropology Centre, I was introduced to Buddhist monks and abbots who oversaw community museums housed within their monasteries (Denes et al. 2013, Kreps 2014). During museum training programs in Hanoi, Vietnam sponsored by the Smithsonian Institution and the Ford Foundation, I worked alongside museum directors, curators, and staff that had fought decades earlier in the "American War."

Through these experiences, I have learned that collaboration is a "zone of engagement" (Onciul 2013), and the degree to which partnerships can be "reciprocal" and "equal" (Kuwanwisiwma 2008) is not only contingent on context and the actors involved, but also the willingness of actors to acknowledge their respective power and embrace difference as a "capacity" (Basu and Modest 2015) for engagement. In essence, I have learned that collaboration is largely about "making kin" (Haraway 2016), and finding kinship in what we do.

Notes

1 I began working with the Ford Foundation in Jakarta while conducting research on Museum Balanga in Central Kalimantan. In 1991, Alan Feinstein, a Ford program officer, asked me to visit the Provincial Museum Siwalima in Ambon in the Moluccan Islands and the Museum for Culture and Progress in Agats, West Papua (formerly Irian Jaya). Ford had been funding projects at the museums, and Feinstein needed someone to visit the museums to see what was happening "on the ground" in order to decide whether or not to continue support. Like Museum Balanga, the Museum Siwalima was a government-sponsored, provincial museum (*museum negeri*) that operated within the national museum system. The Museum for Culture and Progress was a private, independent museum established by Catholic missionaries from the American Crosier Order. Both museums were located in remote provinces and islands of eastern Indonesia that required many days' travel from Jakarta to reach. In addition to this work, the Ford Foundation was a sponsor of a World Wildlife Fund environmental and cultural conservation project I worked on in East Kalimantan in 1996 and 1997 (Kreps 2002, 2003).

2 A comment on time and fieldwork is worth making here since many anthropologists have been critical of consultancy work, or applied work in general, on the basis of how it frequently involves relatively short periods of time spent in the field. While extensive knowledge of a particular locale gained through long-term research is one of the values anthropologists can bring to consultancies, in many cases, applied work is carried out under a number of constraints not the least of which is time. Indeed, long-term fieldwork in many instances can be seen as a luxury or even impractical given the limitations of budgets and project cycles, and the demands on stakeholders' time and schedules. Moreover, time constraints need not compromise the quality of work produced. What matters is the quality of data collected, the methods used in its collection (or the research process), and the ultimate outcomes and use of the research (Gardner and Lewis 2015, Nahm 2016, Strathern and Steward 2001).

3 The Iban Dayak are one of the many Dayak ethnic groups inhabiting Borneo. As noted previously, the name "Dayak" is a generic term used to describe the Indigenous peoples of Borneo even though there are dozens of different Dayak ethnic groups with their own names, languages, and cultural particularities (King 1993). *Ikat* is a term used to refer to textiles produced through the *ikat* or tie-dye process. Designs on cloth are

produced through a process of tying or covering sections of the warp yarn to resist dye. The Iban weave on back-strap looms also known as tension looms (Gittinger 1979, 233).

4 A *bupati* holds a position equivalent to that of a mayor.

5 Formed in 1999, the Coalition is a global network of historic houses, museums, and memorials dedicated to educating publics about the contemporary implications of past tragedies, and in many cases, how to work toward reconciliation and rebuilding social cohesion (see www.sitesofconscience.org).

6 On his visit to the Netherlands in 2003 Father Maessen met with staff at the Tropenmuseum to discuss the idea of developing a museum in Sintang (Van Hout 2015, 170). This meeting would turn out to be pivotal, as will be shown later in the chapter.

7 I found this to be a feature of many museums throughout Indonesia.

8 The community member's remark alludes to the pervasive role of religion in Indonesian citizens' lives, as well as how questions of religion have been historically entangled in the politics of culture, ethnicity, and identity in the country. Religious affiliation can determine whom one marries, what kind of school one attends, and one's ability to secure employment in the civil service (see Adams 2006, Kipp 1993, Schiller 1997).

9 See Varutti for a description of inappropriate and unsustainable museum development in Taiwan. The author discusses how the Taiwanese government began establishing museums in Indigenous areas in the early 2000s to showcase the history, culture, and traditions of various Taiwanese Indigenous groups. However, not long after the museums were set up they came to be known as "mosquito museums" since mosquitoes were their main visitors (Varutti 2012, 59).

10 Ideally, these materials should have been tested for their potential deleterious, long-term effects on objects. But in the absence of archival-quality materials they were handy, inexpensive substitutes. Nata'alui Duha told me a year later they had substituted the cardboard tubes with bamboo, which is a material in abundance on the island.

11 For example, see Agrawal's *Appropriate Technologies in the Conservation of Cultural Property* (1981) for a fascinating description of the use of traditional conservation technologies and materials in India.

12 Inspired by her work with the Dayak Ikat Weaving Project one of the students, Catherine Fitzgerald, wrote her Master's thesis on women's weaving cooperatives: *Re-Weaving the Past: Reviving Textile Traditions in Women's Cooperatives*. University of Denver, 2005.

13 Duha's stay in Denver was comparatively short to that of Novia Sagita due to his work and family obligations.

14 http://enprojectshare.com/.

15 In September 2006, Nata'alui Duha participated in the conference "Culture is a Basic Need: Responding to Cultural Emergencies," held in the Netherlands and sponsored by the CER. The conference was convened to celebrate the Fund's tenth anniversary, and brought together representatives of organizations that had received aid from the CER in addition to anthropologists, architects, art historians, photographers, and development policy makers and planners. One of the purposes of the conference was to draw attention to the importance of culture in humanitarian relief, address the impact of disasters on culture and identity, and encourage dialogue on why culture should be regarded as a basic human need and part of humanitarian assistance (Mendez 2006).

16 Personal communication with Jacques Maessen, October 24, 2014.

17 Novia Sagita translated this book into Bahasa Indonesia.

18 I also worked with Sagita and Duha when they were participants in the Intangible Cultural Heritage and Museums Field School in Thailand in 2012 for which I served as an instructor (Denes et al. 2013, Kreps 2014).

19 This was especially true for the Museum for Culture and Progress in Agats, West Papua (formerly Irian Jaya) mentioned in note 1. On the museum's human rights work and its political implications see Schneebaum (1982) and Stanley (2002).

References

Adams, Kathleen. 1995. "Making-Up the Toraja? The Appropriation of Tourism, Anthropology, and Museums for Politics in Upland Sulawesi, Indonesia." *Ethnology* 34(2):143–153.

Adams, Kathleen. 2005. "Public Interest Anthropology in Heritage Sites: Writing Culture and Righting Wrongs." *International Journal of Heritage Studies* 11(5):433–439.

Adams, Kathleen. 2006. *Art as Politics.* Honolulu: University of Hawai'i Press.

Agrawal, O. 1981. *Appropriate Technologies in the Conservation of Cultural Property.* Paris: UNESCO.

Ambrose, T. and C. Paine. 2006. *Museum Basics.* London and New York: Routledge.

Aspinall, Edward and Greg Fealy, ed. 2003. *Local Power and Politics in Indonesia. Decentralisation and Democratisation.* Singapore: Institute of Southeast Asian Studies.

Basu, Paul and Wayne Modest. 2015. "Museums, Heritage and International Development: A Critical Conversation." In *Museums, Heritage, and International Development*, edited by Paul Basu and Wayne Modest, 1–32. London and New York: Routledge.

Basu, Paul and Johanna Zetterstrom-Sharp. 2015. "Complicating Culture for Development: Negotiating 'Dysfunctional Heritage' in Sierra Leone." In *Museums, Heritage, and International Development*, edited by Paul Basu and Wayne Modest, 56–82. London and New York: Routledge.

Bennett, Tony. 1998. *Culture: A Reformer's Science.* London: Sage.

Buntinx, Gustavo and Ivan Karp. 2006. "Tactical Museologies." In *Museum Frictions. Public Cultures/Global Transformations*, edited by Ivan Karp, Corrine Kratz, Lynn Szwaja, and Tomas Ybarra-Frausto, 207–218. Durham and London: Duke University Press.

Byrne, Denis. 1991. "Western Hegemony in Archaeological Heritage Management." *History and Archaeology* 5:269–276.

Byrne, Denis. 2014. *Counterheritage: Critical Perspectives on Heritage Conservation in Asia.* London and New York: Routledge.

Chilisa, Bagele. 2012. *Indigenous Research Methodologies.* Los Angeles and London: Sage.

Chronis, Iwana and Louk Box. 2006. "CER at the Crossroads of Heritage and Humanism." In *Culture is a Basic Need*, edited by Els van der Plas and Caro Mendez, 6–15. The Hague, Netherlands: Prince Claus Fund.

Clavir, Miriam. 2002. *Preserving What is Valued: Museums, Conservation, and First Nations* Vancouver: University of British Columbia Press.

Colwell-Chanthaphonh, Chip and T.J. Ferguson. 2008. "Introduction: The Collaborative Continuum." In *Collaboration in Archaeological Practice. Engaging Descendant Communities*, edited by Chip Colwell-Chanthaphonh and T.J. Ferguson, 1–32. Lanham, MD: AltaMira Press.

Crewe, Emma and Richard Axelby. 2013. *Anthropology and Development. Culture, Morality and Politics in a Globalised World.* Cambridge: Cambridge University Press.

Daly, Patrick and Tim Winter, ed. 2012. *Routledge Handbook of Heritage in Asia.* London and New York: Routledge.

Davidson, Jamie and David Henley, ed. 2007. *The Revival of Tradition in Indonesian Politics. The Deployment of Adat from Colonialism to Indigenism.* London and New York: Routledge.

Davis, Peter. 2011. *Ecomuseums: A Sense of Place.* London: Bloomsbury.

Denes, Alexandra, Paritta Chalermpow Koanantakool, Peter Davis, Christina Kreps, Kate Hennessy, Marilena Alivizatou, and Michelle Stefano. 2013. "Critical Reflections on Safeguarding Culture: The Intangible Cultural Heritage and Museums Field School in Lamphun, Thailand." *Heritage and Society* 6(1):4–23.

Duha, Nata'alui. 2004. *Report to the Asian Cultural Council on Museum Management Training Program at the Department of Anthropology University of Denver-Colorado.*

Evans, Harriet and Michael Rowlands. 2015. "Reconceptualizing Heritage in China. Museums, Development and the Shifting Dynamics of Power." In *Museums, Heritage and International Development*, edited by Paul Basu and Wayne Modest, 272–294. London and New York: Routledge.

Feldman, Jerome. 1979. "The House as World in Bawomataluo, South Nias." In *Art, Ritual, and Society in Indonesia*, edited by Edward Bruner and J. Becker, 127–189. Athens, Ohio: Ohio University Center for Southeast Asian Studies.

Feldman, Jerome. 1994. "The Adaptation of Indigenous Forms to Western Taste: The Case of Nias." In *Fragile Traditions: Indonesian Art in Jeopardy*, edited by Paul Michael Taylor, 43–57. Honolulu: University of Hawai'i Press.

Fienieg, Anouk. 2007. *Sejarah Sintang—The History of Sintang*. Translated by Novia Sagita. Amsterdam: Tropenmuseum KIT Publishers.

Fox, J. J. 1993. *Inside Austronesian Houses: Perspectives on Domestic Designs for Living*. Canberra: Australian National University.

Frerks, G., B. K. Goldewijk, and E. van der Plas. 2011. "Introduction." In *Cultural Emergency in Conflict and Disaster*, edited by G. Frerks, B. K. Goldewijk, and E. van der Plas, 8–19.

Fuller, Nancy. 1992. "The Museum as a Vehicle for Community Empowerment: The Ak-chin Indian Community Ecomuseum Project." In *Museums and Communities*, edited by Ivan Karp, Christine Mullen-Kreamer, and Steven Lavine, 327–365. Washington, DC: Smithsonian Institution Press.

Gardner, Katy and David Lewis. 2015. *Anthropology and Development. Challenges for the Twenty-first Century*. London: Pluto Press.

Gittinger, M. 1979. *Splendid Symbols: Textile Traditions in Indonesia*. Washington, DC: The Textile Museum.

Gronert, Walter. 1990. "Introduction." In *Nias Treasures. Cosmis Reflections in Stone, Wood, and Gold*, edited by Delft Volkenkundig Museum Nusantara, 11–20. Delft: Volkenkundig Museum Nusantara, Delft.

Grüber, Petra and Ulrike Herbig. 2009. *Traditional Architecture and Art on Nias, Indonesia*. Vienna, Austria: Institute for Comparative Research in Architecture.

Haraway, Donna. 2016. *Staying with the Trouble. Making Kin in the Chthulucene*. Durham and London: Duke University Press.

Hardiati, Endang and Pieter ter Keurs. 2006. *Indonesia: The Discovery of the Past*. Leiden: National Museum of Ethnology.

Hazeltine, B. and C. Bull. 2003. *Field Guide to Appropriate Technology*. London: Academic Press.

Heppell, Michael. 1994. "Whither Dayak Art?" In *Fragile Traditions: Indonesian Art in Jeopardy*, edited by Paul Michael Taylor, 123–138. Honolulu: University of Hawai'i Press.

Huda, Immanuel. 2002. *Membangan Program Restorasi Tenun Ikat Dayak di Sintang*. Pontanak, West Kalimantan: PRCF.

Isar, Yudhishthir Raj. 2015. "UNESCO, Museums, and 'Development'." In *Museums, Heritage, and International Development*, edited by Paul Basu and Wayne Modest, 33–55. London and New York: Routledge.

Jones, Tod. 2013. *Culture, Power, and Authoritarianism in the Indonesian State*. Leiden: Brill.

King, Victor. 1993. *The Peoples of Borneo*. Oxford: Blackwell.

Kipp, Rita 1993. *Disassociated Identities: Ethnicity, Religion, and Class in Indonesian Society*. Ann Arbor: University of Michigan Press.

Kratz, Corinne and Ivan Karp. 2006. "Introduction: Museum Frictions: Public Culture/ Global Transformation." In *Museum Frictions. Public Cultures/Global Transformations*, edited by Ivan Karp, Corinne A. Kratz, Lynn Szwaja, and Tomas Ybarra-Frausto, 1–31. Durham and London: Duke University Press.

Kreps, Christina. 1998. "Museum-Making and Indigenous Curation in Central Kalimantan, Indonesia." *Museum Anthropology* 22(1):5–17.

Kreps, Christina. 2002. "Environmental Conservation and Cultural Action." *Practicing Anthropology* 24(2):28–32.

Kreps, Christina. 2003. *Liberating Culture: Cross-Cultural Perspectives on Museums, Curation, and Heritage Preservation* London: Routledge.

Kreps, Christina. 2008. "Appropriate Museology in Theory and Practice." *Museum Management and Curatorship* 23(1):23–42.

Kreps, Christina. 2009. "Indigenous Curation, Museums, and Intangible Cultural Heritage." In *Intangible Heritage*, edited by Laurajane Smith and Natsuko Akagawa, 193–208. London and New York: Routledge.

Kreps, Christina. 2012. "Intangible Threads: Curating the Living Heritage of Dayak Ikat Weaving." In *Safeguarding Intangible Cultural Heritage*, edited by Peter Davis, Gerard Corsane and Michelle Stefano, 177–192. Woodbridge: Boydell Press.

Kreps, Christina. 2014. "Thai Monastery Museums. Contemporary Expressions of Ancient Traditions." In *Transforming Knowledge Orders: Museums, Collections, and Exhibitions*, edited by Larissa Forster, 230–256. Paderborn, Germany: Wilhelm Fink.

Kreps, Christina. 2015. "Cultural Heritage, Humanitarianism, and Development: Critical Links." In *Museums, Heritage and International Development*, edited by Paul Basu and Wayne Modest, 250–271. London and New York: Routledge.

Kreps, Christina. 2017. "The Real and the Ideal: Towards Culturally Appropriate and Collaborative Heritage Practice in Kalimantan." In *Borneo Studies in History, Society and Culture*, edited by Victor King, Zawai Ibrahim, and Noor Hasharina Hassan, 211–234. Singapore: Springer.

Kuwanwisiwma, Leigh J. 2008. "Collaboration Means Equality, Respect, Reciprocity: A Conversation about Archaeology and the Hopi Tribe." In *Collaboration in Archaeological Practice. Engaging Descendant Communities*, edited by Chip Colwell-Chanthaphonh and T.J. Ferguson, 151–169. Lanham, MD: AltaMira Press.

Lang, H. 2010. "Rehabilitation and Reconstruction in South Nias Heritage Villages." In *Rebuilding Lives in Aceh and Nias, Indonesia*, edited by F. Steinberg and P. Smidt, 143–182. Manila: Asian Development Bank.

Lassiter, Luke. 2008. "Moving Past Public Anthropology and Doing Collaborative Research." *NAPA Bulletin* 29:70–86.

Levitt, Peggy. 2015. *Artifacts and Allegiances. How Museums Put the Nation and the World on Display*. Berkeley: University of California Press.

Lynch, Bernadette. 2011. "Collaboration, Contestation, and Creative Conflict: On the Efficacy of Museum/Community Partnerships." In *The Routledge Companion to Museum Ethics*, edited by Janet Marstine, 146–163. London and New York: Routledge.

Lynch, Bernadette. 2017. "The Gate in the Wall: Beyond Happiness Making in Museums." In *Engaging Heritage, Engaging Communities*, edited by Bryony Onciul, Michelle Stefano, and Stephanie Hawke, 11–29. Woodbridge: Boydell Press.

Marcus, George. 2008. "The End(s) of Ethnography: Social/Cultural Anthropology's Signature Form of Producing Knowledge in Transition." *Cultural Anthropology* 23(1):1–14.

Mathur, Saloni. 2005. "Social Thought and Commentary: Museums and Globalization." *Anthropological Quarterly* 78(3):697–708.

McLeod, Malcolm. 2015. "Has It Been Worth It? Personal Reflections on Museum Development in Ghana." In *Museums, Heritage, and International Development*, edited by Paul Basu and Wayne Modest, 143–149. London and New York: Routledge.

Mendez, Caro. 2006. "Foreword: Culture Is a Basic Need." In *Culture Is a Basic Need*, edited by Els van der Plas and Caro Mendez, 4–5. The Hague: Prince Claus Fund.

Muan, Ingrid. 2006. "Musings on Museums from Phnom Penh." In *Museum Frictions. Public Cultures/Global Transformations*, edited by Ivan Karp, Corinne A. Kratz, Lynn Szwaja, and Tomas Ybarra-Frausto, 257–285. Durham: Duke University Press.

Nahm, Sheena. 2016. "Time and the Method of the Unexpected." In *Applied Anthropology. Unexpected Spaces, Topics, and Methods*, edited by Sheena Nahm and Cortney Hughes Rinker, 122–135. London and New York: Routledge.

Nooy-Palm, Hetty. 2002. "Treasure Hunters in the Field: Collecting Ethnographic Artefacts in the Netherlands East Indies (1750–1940)." In *Treasure Hunting? Collectors and Collections of Indonesian Artefacts*, edited by Reimar Schefold and Han F. Vermeulen, 47–80. Leiden: Research School CNWS, University of Leiden.

Onciul, Bryony. 2013. "Community Engagement, Curatorial Practice, and Museum Ethos." In *Museums and Communities. Curators, Collections and Collaboration*, edited by Viv Golding and Wayne Modest, 79–97. London: Bloomsbury.

Peluso, Nancy L. and Emily Harwell. 2001. "Territory, Custom, and the Cultural Politics of Ethnic War in West Kalimantan, Indonesia." In *Violent Environments*, edited by Nancy L. Peluso, 83–116. Ithaca, NY: Cornell University Press.

Rahman, A. 1993. *People's Self-Development: Perspectives on Participatory Action Research*. London: Zed Books.

Rao, Vijaayendra and Michael Walton. 2004. "Culture and Public Action: Rationality, Equality of Agency, and Development." In *Culture and Public Action*, edited by Vijayendro Rao and Michael Walton, 3–36. Washington, DC: The World Bank.

Rassool, Ciraj. 2006. "Community Museums, Memory Politics, and Social Transformation in South Africa: Histories, Possibilities, and Limits." In *Museum Frictions. Public Cultures/ Global Transformations*, edited by Ivan Karp, Corinne A. Kratz, Lynn Szwaja, and Tomas Ybarra-Frausto, 286–321. Durham, NC: Duke University Press.

Sagita, Novia. 2005. *Professional Training in Museum Studies and Anthropology*. University of Denver.

Sagita, Novia. 2009. "Community-Based Museum: Traditional Curation in Women's Weaving Culture." In *Can We Make a Difference: Museums, Society, and Development in North and South*, edited by Paul Vogt, 119–128. Amsterdam: KIT Tropenmuseum.

Schech, S. and J. Haggis. 2000. *Culture and Development: A Critical Introduction*. Oxford: Blackwell Publishers.

Schefold, Reimar and Han F. Vermeulen. 2002. "Introduction: Collectors and the Collecting of Indonesian Artefacts." In *Treasure Hunting? Collectors and Collections of Indonesian Artefacts*, edited by Reimar Schefold and Han F. Vermeulen, 1–22. Leiden: Research School CNSW, University of Leiden.

Schiller, Anne. 1997. *Small Sacrifices: Religious Change and Cultural Identity among the Ngaju Dayak of Indonesia*. Oxford: Oxford University Press.

Schiller, Anne and B. Garang. 2002. "Religion and Inter-Ethnic Violence in Indonesia." *Journal of Contemporary Asia* 32(2):244–254.

Schlehe, Judith and Sita Hidayah. 2014. "Transcultural Ethnography: Reciprocity in Indonesian-German Tandem Research." In *Methodology and Research Practice in Southeast Asian Studies*, edited by Mikko Huotari, Jürgen Ruland, and Judith Schlehe, 253–272. New York: Palgrave Macmillan.

Schneebaum, Tobias. 1982. "The Asmat Museum for Culture and Progress." *Cultural Survival Quarterly* 6(2):36–37.

Scott, Cynthia. 2014. "Sharing the Divisions of the Colonial Past: An Assessment of the Netherlands-Indonesia Shared Cultural Heritage Project, 2003–2006." *International Journal of Heritage Studies* 20(4):181–195.

Scott, Cynthia. 2017. "Renewing the 'Special Relationship' and Rethinking the Return of Cultural Property: The Netherlands and Indonesia, 1949–1979." *Journal of Contemporary History* 52(3):646–668.

Sellato, Bernard. 1989. *Hornbill and Dragon.* Jakarta: Elf Aquitaine, Indonesie.

Sellato, Bernard. 2011. *Sultans, Palaces and Patrimonization in Indonesian Borneo 1950–2010: Nation-State, Political Decentralization, Identity (Re)Localization.* Unpublished paper.

Shannon, Jennifer. 2015. "Projectishare.com: Sharing Our Past, Collecting for the Future." In *Museums as Process: Translating Local and Global Knowledges*, edited by Raymond A. Silverman, 67–89. London and New York: Routledge.

Sheriff, Abdul, Paul Voogt, and Mubiana Luhila. 2006. *The Zanzibar House of Wonders Museums. A Case Study in Culture and Development.* Amsterdam: KIT Publishers.

Silverman, H. and D. F. Ruggles, eds. 2009. *Cultural Heritage and Human Rights.* Dordrecht: Springer.

Silverman, Raymond A., ed. 2015. *Museums as Process: Translating Local and Global Knowledges.* London and New York: Routledge.

Smith, Claire and Gary Jackson. 2008. "The Ethics of Collaboration: Whose Culture? Whose Intellectual Property? Who Benefits." In *Collaboration in Archaeological Practice. Engaging Descendant Communities*, edited by Chip Colwell-Chanthaphonh and T.J. Ferguson, 171–199. Lanham, MD: AltaMira Press.

Smith, Laurajane. 2006. *Uses of Heritage.* London and New York: Routledge.

Smith, Linda Tuhiwai. 2012. *Decolonizing Methodologies. Research and Indigenous Peoples.* Second ed. London and New York: Zed Books.

Stanley, Nick. 2002. "Museums and Indigenous Identity: Asmat Carving in a Global Context." In *Pacific Art. Persistence, Change, and Meaning*, edited by Anita Herle, Nick Stanley, Karen Stevenson, and Robert Welsch, 147–165. Honolulu: University of Hawai'i Press.

Stoller, Paul. 1997. "Globalizing Method: The Problems of Doing Ethnography in Transnational Spaces." *Anthropology and Humanism* 22(1):81–94.

Strathern, Andrew and Pamela Stewart. 2001. "Introduction: Anthropology and Consultancy: Ethnographic Dilemmas and Opportunities." *Social Analysis* 45(2):3–22.

Tanasaldy, T. 2007. "Ethnic Identity Politics in West Kalimantan." In *Renegotiating Boundaries: Local Politics in Post-Suharto Indonesia*, edited by H. Schulte Nordholt and G. Van Klinken, 349–372. Leiden: KITLV Press.

Taylor, Paul M. 1994. "The Nusantara Concept of Culture: Local Traditions and National Identity in Indonesia." In *Fragile Traditions: Indonesian Art in Jeopardy*, edited by Paul M. Taylor. Honolulu: University of Hawaii Press.

Taylor, Paul M. and Lorraine Aragon. 1991. *Beyond the Java Sea.* Washington DC and New York: National Museum of Nat Hist and Harry N. Abrams.

ter Keurs, Pieter. 2007. *Colonial Collections Revisited.* Leiden: CNWS, University of Leiden.

UNESCO. 1995. *The Cultural Dimensions of Development: Toward a Practical Approach.* Paris: UNESCO.

Van Hout, Itie. 2015. "The Museum Kapuas Raya: The In-Between Museum." In *Museums, Heritage and International Development*, edited by Paul Basu and Wayne Modest, 170–187. London and New York: Routledge.

Van Klinken, G. 2007. *Communal Violence and Democratization in Indonesia. Small Town Wars.* London and New York: Routledge.

Varutti, Marzia. 2012. "Towards Social Inclusion in Taiwan Museums: Museums, Equality and Indigenous Groups." In *Museums, Equality, and Social Justice*, edited by Richard Sandell and Eithne Nightingale, 243–253. London and New York: Routledge.

Viaro, A. 1990. "The Traditional Architecture of Nias." In *Nias: Tribal Treasures: Cosmic Reflections in Stone, Wood and Gold*, edited by Delft Volkenkundig Museum Nusantara, 45–78. Delft: Volkenkundig Museum Nusantara.

Viaro, A. and A. Ziegler. 2009. "Nias Reconstruction in the Respect of the Tradition." In *Traditional Architecture and Art on Nias, Indonesia*, edited by P. Gurber and U. Herbig, 140–149. Vienna: Institute of Comparative Research in Architecture.

Warren, L., J. Slikkerveer, and D. Brokensha, ed. 1995. *The Cultural Dimensions of Development: Indigenous Knowledge Systems*. London: Intermediate Technology Publications.

Waterson, Roxana. 1990. *The Living House. An Anthropology of Architecture in Southeast Asia*. Oxford: Oxford University Press.

7

DOING MUSEUM ANTHROPOLOGY "AT HOME"

In the previous three chapters, I provided examples of doing museum anthropology "away" on a global stage. In this final and concluding chapter, I consider doing museum anthropology "at home," mainly within the context of university museums. I elaborate on "tendencies and movements," issues, and challenges in museum anthropology touched on in Chapters 1 and 2, and explore implications of anthropology's "return to the museum." More broadly, I explore the ways in which museum anthropology, as a multifaceted and wide-ranging field, matters both within and beyond the academy.

As stated in the introductory chapter, one of my intentions in this book has been to provide an historical account of the shifting status of museum anthropology within academic anthropology. Relegated to the margins of academic anthropology for decades, I have argued that museum anthropology has regained its standing in the discipline partly because it offers models for engaged research, scholarship, and practice at a time in which engagement permeates the discipline. In Chapter 2, I discussed other movements that have contributed to a revitalized museum anthropology, including the postcolonial critique and theorizing of museums; the rise of the anthropology of museums and critical, reflexive museology; a renewed interest in material culture studies, art, objects, and collections; the ascent of museum and heritage studies as both an academic discipline and career path for anthropology graduates; and not in the least, Indigenous scholarly critique and activism. Combined with the prominence of applied anthropology, I have suggested that museum anthropology has become a site for generating widely applicable theoretical and methodological advancements, and models for ethically grounded and socially responsible practice.

Although much attention in the book has been given to the current accent on engaged research, scholarship, and practice, also understood as the public role of anthropology and museums, I have tried to provide an historical and comparative perspective on the different forms engagement has taken at different moments in time and in various national settings. In doing so, my goal has been to disrupt the notion of engaged work as inherently beneficent, and to highlight how it can also be deployed, for example, as an instrument of governmentality. Remaining mindful of its often contradictory and problematic aspects, I have maintained, nevertheless, that the recent turn toward greater engagement is a progressive move for museums and anthropology. This is because many still view anthropology and its museums as "either a continuing agency of colonial relations and thinking and/or as irrelevant to contemporary social and political life" (Macdonald, Lidchi, and von Oswald 2017, 95–96). Clearly, while much progress has been made in critically addressing museum anthropology's colonial heritage, much decolonizing work remains to be done, as does making museums and anthropology matter to broader and more diverse audiences.

In this chapter, I consider museum anthropology's on-going reconnection to academic anthropology within the setting of university museums. While these museums have historically served as sites for research, teaching, and communicating anthropological knowledge and insights to their audiences, I am especially concerned with how today they are uniquely positioned to make anthropology relevant and useful through publicly engaged research and practice. One of my aims is to show how the perceived divides between theoretically oriented anthropology and applied, publicly engaged work are closing as it becomes ever more clear how theory informs practice and practice informs theory (McCarthy 2015, Thomas 2010). University anthropology museums are at once sites for the representation of anthropological knowledge and for its generation (Thomas 2016a).

Over the past couple of decades, university museums have been experiencing a renaissance as they have sought to better fulfill their parent institution's core mission—education and research. Today, the mission of many universities and colleges also includes serving the public good through increased community engagement (Conn 2016, Jandl and Gold 2014, Merriman 2012). This trend has brought added funding and administrative support for engaged work of all kinds, but especially collaboration with underserved, historically marginalized communities (Kreps 2015b).

The revitalization of university museums has also given rise to a renewed interest in using collections for object-based research, teaching, and experiential, multisensory learning. As academia necessarily becomes ever more reliant on information technology, object-based learning provides students with the opportunity to engage with "real things," minimizing mediation between source and experience and maximizing possibilities for discovery since "objects tend to do more question-raising than answer providing" (Stromberg 2014, 15).

As will be shown in this chapter through a number of examples, university museums are multifunctional sites for inventive teaching, learning, research, professional training, and community collaboration. They contribute to the intellectual and social life of university communities and beyond as places of encounter and exchange among people, things, and ideas. University anthropology museums, in particular, can be leaders in fostering intercultural dialogue and modeling ways of engaging (and sometimes reconciling) difference and "difficult heritage" (Macdonald 2009). In this sense, they can play a key role in cultivating cosmopolitan worldviews and "convivial culture" that "can offer an alternative to the anxiety and fear of otherness, and of the troubled relationships across alterity" (Macdonald, Lidchi, and von Oswald 2017, 95). This is one of the many ways anthropology and museums can make themselves matter and be of relevance in our times.

The Re-Emergence of the University Museum

Steve Conn, the noted historian of American museums and intellectual history, in his article "Do Universities Need Museums/Do Museums Need Universities?" writes: "It does not exaggerate to say that modern higher education and our modern conception of the museum grew up at exactly the same moment and often right next door to one another. It seemed axiomatic: colleges needed museums like they needed libraries and laboratories—to carry out their work" (2016, 310–311). Throughout the second half of the nineteenth century, he points out that colleges and universities saw museums as central to their institutional designs and built accordingly. But by the mid-twentieth century, many college and university museums had begun to languish, especially museums of natural history and ethnography.

> While art museums enjoyed a pride of place across the twentieth century, and universities decided they needed art museums, administrators were ambivalent about their ethnographic and natural historical collections. Higher education no longer needed museums and their collections to get on with their business … [In time], people forgot that these museums had ever been an important part of the work of colleges and universities.
>
> *(Conn 2016, 312)*

Across the Atlantic in the United Kingdom, a similar pattern developed. As Merriman recounts:

> From the 19th century, teaching in many of the new subjects such as geology, archaeology, and natural history was more often than not done in the university museum itself, and the idea of the object lesson or teaching through close contact with actual objects and specimens, was firmly embedded in the higher education experience.
>
> *(2012, 37)*

Yet by the mid-twentieth century, changes in teaching methods, such as a shift towards lab-based work and lectures, and later to the widespread application of information technologies coupled with funding cuts, "led in many instances to university collections being seen as burdens rather than assets by their parent universities" (Merriman 2012, 37).

By the 1980s, university museums in both the United States and the United Kingdom were in crisis not just in terms of funding but also in terms of purpose. As Conn astutely observes: "Museums of all sorts may start with collections of objects, but what turns a mere collection of objects into a museum is the way those collections are given coherence and meaning. Museums need an intellectual architecture as much as they need a physical space in which to exhibit their stuff" (2016, 321).

Nick Merriman of the Manchester Museum at the University of Manchester contends that over the past couple of decades there has been something of a "revolution" in the ways in which university museums have been rethinking their missions. This rethinking has been driven by changes in higher education, by developments in museology, and by the availability of funding streams (2012, 37–38).[1] Concurrently, considerable attention has been given to identifying the distinctive role of university museums within the museum sector. In addition to contributing to research and teaching, Merriman suggests that part of what distinguishes university museums from others is how they embrace (or should) a "university ethos, which is focused on experimentation, innovation, debate, and reflection" (Merriman 2012, 38).

According to Merriman, another impetus behind the reinvigoration of the Manchester Museum, in particular, has been a realignment of the museum's mission and its goals to highlight "research, higher learning, and social responsibility." The latter is focused on "making the university a force for good locally, nationally, and internationally, and includes playing a significant role in the community. Everything the museum does is now aligned to these three goals" (2012, 40–41). The Manchester Museum's realignment of goals and mission has followed a general movement in university museums across the United Kingdom to more purposely focus on social responsibility and community engagement (Nelson and Macdonald 2012, Van Broekhoven 2018).

In Chapter 1, I noted how scholars have linked the push toward greater public engagement in universities and the museum sector to neoliberal economics and the concomitant need for "accountability" in the face of looming budget cuts (Beck and Maida 2013, Crooke 2006, Lynch 2011, 2013, Shelton 2006). I also mentioned that while on the one hand we need to be aware of how larger economic, political, and social forces impact universities and museums, on the other hand, we should not let them overshadow the progressive elements of their "ripple effects." Among these is the revitalization of university museums, and a renewed interest in the value of collections for teaching, learning, and research. It may not be coincidental that the reinvigoration of university museums has overlapped with a burgeoning scholarly, theoretical interest in museums and collections in addition to the rise of museum studies (Conn 2016).[2]

Cycles and Returns

Teaching with objects, a practice that was common or even required a century ago, as noted above, is increasingly being integrated into campus curricula as the value of complementing theoretical work with time-honored, hands-on approaches is being recognized. In the process, the now worn-out dichotomies of "objects versus ideas," "objects versus people," and "theory versus practice" are being eroded. As Kathleen Adams, in a special issue of *Museum Anthropology*[3] devoted to innovative strategies for teaching with objects, succinctly puts it:

> Although a century ago anthropology, museums, and objects were intimately entwined, trends in many museology and anthropology courses have drifted toward focusing on ideas and people rather than on objects. The contributors to this special issue have cultivated new pedagogical approaches that complement or realign literature-focused classroom canons that can distance students from the very objects under study … The articles underscore how object-based teaching can yield new theoretical and practical insights, enhance the social relevance of classroom activities, and facilitate meaningful benefits for local communities.
>
> *(2015, 88)*

Adams, in her introductory article, shares her experience as a graduate student in the 1980s that speaks to the changes that have occurred in the field over the past several decades.

> For some of us who have come of age as museum-oriented anthropologists in the past two to three decades, our graduate school training frequently consisted of bifurcated classroom training experiences. My own experience … entailed taking heavily object-centered museology graduate classes in the campus museum and theoretically oriented anthropology of (ethnic) art classes in the anthropology building. Never once did an artifact cross the threshold of my theory-oriented anthropology or art classes, and only occasionally did we view images of material culture in the classroom (generally slide shows of the professors' fieldwork with material culture). While we gained extensive knowledge of the history of anthropological theories pertaining to objects, the actual material world was palpably absent from the classroom.
>
> *(2015, 89–90)*

My experience was not that different from that of Adams. I began working in a museum as an undergraduate student in anthropology in the late 1970s because, like many museum anthropologists, I was fascinated by the things in museums. The museum in which I worked was not a university museum, but was located across the street from my college campus. Although the museum housed significant Southwestern Native American art collections, not once during my course on the topic did we step foot in the museum. As I wrote in my contribution to Adams's edited issue of *Museum Anthropology*, "by the time I reached graduate school my interests had shifted from doing anthropology *in* museums to doing the anthropology *of* museums. In looking back, I see how this reorientation reflected the diminished status of the museum object at that time and the move toward the more theoretical aspects of museum anthropology" (Kreps 2015b, 96).

I should add, however, that my retreat from museums was not motivated just by a reorientation in academic interests. It was also driven by a "crisis of conscience" brought on by my experience working directly with Native Americans in the early 1980s.[4] I recall several "uncomfortable" moments and especially one encounter in which I was labeled an "anthro-apologist." While the remark was meant as a joke, its sting came from sensing that it harbored an underlying truth. Indeed, my decision to initially pursue graduate work in international studies rather than anthropology hinged on this lurking realization. It was not until after I completed my study of Dutch museums (a cathartic experience in many respects) in 1987, that I felt I could return to anthropology. This decision was undoubtedly influenced by the mounting postcolonial critique of museums and the concurrent crisis of representation in anthropology (Ames 1986, Cole 1985, Comaroff 2010, Stocking 1985, Clifford and Marcus 1986).

Although museums and art remained areas of primary interest over the ensuing decades, I only relatively recently began to consistently integrate objects and collections into my research and teaching. This is despite the fact that I have been director of a museum of anthropology and program in museum studies plus teaching a course in art and anthropology for 20 years. Later in the chapter I provide some examples of this work, but first describe other efforts to reconnect anthropology, museums, and collections.

Smithsonian Summer Institute in Museum Anthropology

Among the many workshops, seminars, and institutes that have been organized over the past decade or so devoted to reviving interest in collections and object-based research, learning, and teaching has been the Smithsonian Summer Institute in Museum Anthropology (SIMA), launched in 2009 at the Smithsonian's National Museum of Natural History Department of Anthropology. Funded through the Cultural Anthropology Program of the National Science Foundation, the idea behind SIMA was to develop a research and training course to "revitalize museums as sites of knowledge production," and "resolve the gap between theory and application" (Greene and Kisin 2010, 25). Designed for Master's degree and doctoral students in anthropology and related fields, the Institute provides a supplement to university training. It seeks to promote a broader and more effective use of museum collections in anthropological research, giving students the tools to utilize collections for investigating research questions. In an article that appeared in *Anthropology News* in January 2010, Candace Greene, the founding director of SIMA, states: "At the start of the program we present the museum as an unfamiliar field site with a distinct language, history and set of customs ... Working with records, students learn ways to approach the complicated histories that moved objects from source communities to collectors to museums" (Greene and Kisin 2010, 25).

Over a period of four weeks between 12 to 14 students were introduced to the scope of collections and accompanying available materials; given training in appropriate methods for collecting and analyzing museum data; and made aware of a range of theoretical and ethical issues pertinent to collections. Greene explains that time was also given, almost daily, to "improving skills in object observation, employing all the senses" (Greene and Kisin 2010, 25). Students came with their own research projects and continually refined them as they encountered new data and new analytical tools using Smithsonian collections. The Institute also offered fellowships to faculty interested in developing anthropology courses on collections-based research methods. By 2018, a total of 146 people had participated in the program, including 104 graduate students, eight faculty fellows, 33 interns, and one fellow of the Research Experience for Graduate Students program (Nichols and Lowman 2018, 5).[5]

In an interview published in *Museum Anthropology*, Greene reflects on the impetus behind the creation of SIMA, saying:

> It was deeply personal. I love the things in museums, and wanted others to love them too and for all the right reasons! They document cultural behavior in unique and revealing ways … Anthropology fell out of love with things a long time ago, but it seems a promising time at present to attempt reconciliation.
>
> *(Nichols and Lowman 2018, 5)*

Greene adds that even though "museum anthropology has become a flourishing field" and "materiality has developed a wealth of new theory around objects," there is still not much engagement with objects and especially those in museums. At a time when members of originating communities are using museum collections in record numbers she asks: "Surely anthropologists could learn a thing or two from them about the power of objects?" When conceptualizing and planning SIMA, Greene recalls how it grew from "the idea of putting theory and things together in ways that would resonate within the current field of anthropology." But she and others involved in SIMA's creation wanted to target those who might have the most long-term impact. "After careful consideration, we decided that the most effective way to re-engage the profession was through training graduate students, reaching people early in their careers when they are most ready to bring new ideas and new questions to old collections" (Nichols and Lowman 2018, 5).[6]

The movement toward more object-based teaching and learning in universities and initiatives such as SIMA represent a reunification of museum anthropology with its ancestral roots, albeit with a new critical and reflexive eye. But it is worth noting here that the field's re-engagement with collections has emerged at a moment in which some have been asking if museums "still need objects" (Conn 2010) with the advent of digital technologies and the growing popularity of interactive and two-dimensional media (Adams 2015, 89, Thomas 2016a).

As will be discussed in the following sections, university anthropology museums are ideal arenas for keeping abreast of current technological and social developments, and exploring how to better use their collections for teaching, research, and training the next generation of museum anthropologists.

University Anthropology Museums

It goes without saying that along with museum anthropology in general, "Over the past several decades, university anthropology museums have faced a profound crisis" (Lubar and Stokes-Rees 2012, 89). But just as crisis and critique has contributed to the transformation of museum anthropology more broadly, it has also been a catalyst for reinvigorating many university-based anthropology museums (Ames 1992, Van Broekhoven 2018, Kramer 2015, Gosden and Larson 2007, Shelton 2015). In this section, I look at initiatives and specific projects in three university anthropology museums: the Haffenreffer Museum of Anthropology, Brown University; the Museum of Anthropology, University of British Columbia; and the University of Denver Museum of Anthropology, my home institution. In the first, I describe how the staff is making the museum's collections and resources more accessible and useful to students, faculty, and researchers, while in the latter two, I focus on exhibitions as sites for community collaboration, public engagement, and the promotion of intercultural dialogue. Together they provide examples of the kind of work being carried out in museum anthropology today that reflects changes that have been taking place in the field over the past decades, and the face of the new museum anthropology.

The Haffenreffer Museum of Anthropology, Brown University

In "From Collections to Curriculum: New Approaches to Teaching and Learning," Steven Lubar and Emily Stokes-Rees describe changes they implemented in the Haffenreffer Museum of Anthropology at Brown University from 2010 to 2012.

> In that period, the museum has increased its presence across the university as a resource for teaching and learning. There is more interaction between staff and faculty and students, exhibits are easier to do, cover a wider range of topics, and a new space, CultureLab, makes the collections more easily available to students and researchers. We have reached out beyond anthropology to departments from history to performance studies and reached beyond our museum space to display elsewhere on campus. We have thought carefully about what museum policies—even what traditional museum standards have been holding us back ... Most importantly, we put student learning from objects first on our list of priorities.
>
> *(2012, 92–93)*

Their first step in this process was to see what other museums were doing. To this end, during the 2010–2011 academic year the Haffenreffer partnered with the Rhode Island School of Design and Brown's John Nicholas Brown Center for Public Humanities and Cultural Heritage to hold a series of workshops on effective ways to enable museums and academic departments to collaborate more fruitfully. *Rethinking the University Museum* brought together academics, museum professionals, and students to discuss how to strengthen the educational role of the museum and put its collections to work in the teaching and training of undergraduate and graduate students. In the process, they learned that they were not alone in seeking ways to reunite the museum with teaching and learning, and in fact, many university art museums had been re-engaging with art history departments since the 1990s thanks to support from the Andrew W. Mellon Foundation (Jandl 2012).

Lubar and Stokes-Rees emphasize that it is essential for university museums to support the core mission of the university, i.e., reaching, teaching, and learning. If it does not, "it will inevitably fear for its life in times of budget cutbacks. More than that, it is missing an opportunity to put its collections to their fullest use" (2012, 96–97). The authors stress that it is imperative for museums to rethink rules about use, and how to make objects accessible to faculty, students, and other users. This may mean compromising on "best practices," and taking time to train users in how to appropriately handle and use objects (Lubar and Stokes-Rees 2012, 102). But first, staff needs to let users know what is available and how it might fit into courses, research, and other activities.

Seeking to go beyond the "behind the scenes" tour of collections, in 2011 staff took part of their exhibit space and converted it into the CultureLab, which "offers an on-campus environment for students and other visitors to learn about, investigate, and interact with museum artifacts" (Lubar and Stokes-Rees 2012, 104). The CultureLab, they explain, is a flexible space for multiple uses. Altogether, it functions as visible museum storage, seminar room, and laboratory space within the museum's gallery.

Lubar and Stokes-Rees recount how they worked to break down the traditional boundaries between disciplines, and draw attention to the historical roots of categories that have separated anthropology museums from other museums and resources on campus, such as libraries and archives. In doing so, they have forged new alliances and created new kinds of exhibitions, and rethought how collections can be interpreted and used. "When you reorient the museum toward teaching and learning, you see the assets of museums in new ways. Small and agile museums like the Haffenreffer have the potential to redefine museum work" (Lubar and Stokes-Rees 2012, 110). They admit that the changes they have made did not always come easily, and came at some cost to on-going museum work. Nevertheless, they hope the Haffenreffer will come to be seen as a center for the educational endeavor at Brown University, and that the "adventuresome work of university museums might serve as a model for museums more generally" (2012, 116).

Janet Marstine has argued that university museums are set apart from other types of museums by their pedagogical mission and identity attached to their particular institutions. As such, they are uniquely positioned to allow risk taking, museological experimentation, and what she calls "messiness." By this she means, "the power to mix things up, to challenge museological rituals, express diverse viewpoints, and experiment with alternative design strategies, even if they run counter to the museum's standard practice" (2007, 305). Below Marstine highlights some of the distinctive qualities of university museums and their potential.

Protected by intellectual freedom, the third space of the university museum can support student-produced, open-ended exhibitions that complicate and sometimes even contradict institutional narratives. As university museums increasingly conceptualize themselves from storehouses to spaces of encounters that foster learning communities, it follows that visitors should experience a multiplicity of voices in university exhibitions.

(2007, 305)

Museum of Anthropology, University of British Columbia

The Museum of Anthropology of the University of British Columbia (UBCMOA) has long been a leader in "mixing things up," destabilizing museological and anthropological orthodoxies, and representing a multiplicity of voices through its pioneering, collaborative exhibitionary practices (Ames 2003). Among its many innovations over the years, has been the transformation of its renowned visible storage research gallery (Lubar 2017, 229–230) and exhibition into one of its new "Multiversity Galleries." The renewal of the exhibition was part of a larger "Partnership of Peoples: A New Infrastructure for Collaborative Research" renovation project, which was to provide the museum with a research infrastructure that enabled it to better meet the requirements of First Nations and other community stakeholders. The Multiversity Galleries, altogether, are intended to make the museum's research philosophy visible to the public (Shelton and Houtman 2009, 12).

According to Jennifer Kramer, faculty in the Department of Anthropology and curator at the museum, in 2003 MOA staff began to redesign the visible storage into an expanded research facility that would be more welcoming and respectful to communities of origin. She states that when the exhibition was created in 1976 it was meant to make portions of the museum's collections more accessible to various stakeholders, especially to First Nation artists, by alleviating the need for them to make appointments with staff to view collections in closed storage. However, as soon as visible storage opened it began to be criticized for, among other things, allowing only partial views of objects and conforming to standard anthropological systems of classification by grouping objects according to culture, area, and type (Kramer 2015, 490). Through consultation with elders, artists, and community members over the years staff learned that this system and style of display did not respect the importance and meaning of objects to originating communities (Shelton and Houtman 2009, 12).

The renovation of the exhibition involved extensive consultation and collaboration with First Nations community members, resulting in the reorganization of collections by classification categories that privileged Indigenous language, cosmology, and local knowledge. MOA opened its renewed visible storage in January 2010. As Kramer notes:

> Renamed the Multiversity Galleries to evoke the guiding principle of multiple ways of knowing, categorizing, and organizing tangible and intangible culture, the space is intended to decolonize older systems of museum classification and radically change the curatorial process that had been used in the first iteration of visible storage.
>
> *(2015, 490)*

Anthony Shelton, director of the museum, further explains that the concept of "multiversity" was originally developed by two postcolonial theorists, Paulo Wangoola and Claude Alvares, to acknowledge that "different cultural communities possess their own epistemologies, values, and classifications, which during the colonial period were repressed, ignored, and subverted by the imposition of positivist scientific models and knowledge" (Shelton and Houtman 2009, 12). By basing the galleries on the idea of multiversity, the museum seeks to recognize these differences, and wherever possible, "give the presentation and voice of interpretation back to originating communities to foster their own use of the spaces and stimulate new dialogues between cultures" (Shelton and Houtman 2009, 12).

The Multiversity Galleries are considered works in progress and are intended to never be completed as the museum continues to edit and add to them in response to on-going critiques and dialogue. For this reason, Kramer states that what is on display in the Multiversity Galleries are the relationships among curators, community members, and critics, plus a collaborative curation methodology (2015, 506). Kramer points out that the processes behind creating the new Multiversity Galleries did not entail making compromises as much as they required translating Indigenous concepts, language, and protocol in a manner that would be understandable to the public.

The Multiversity Galleries illustrate how exhibitions can be based on theoretical concepts, complex histories, and critical museology and be accessible and meaningful to wide audiences. The MOA's deep commitment to collaborative processes, moreover, demonstrates how university museums can be spaces for intercultural dialogue and the practice of intercultural curation. Grounded in the concept of hybridity, intercultural curation is fundamentally a dialogical and relational methodology that suggests a coming together, mixing, and exchange of approaches informed by principles of reciprocity and respect (Gosden and Larson 2007, Kreps 2018, Phillips 2003).

While hybridity remains a contested concept to some, it has become prominent in museological discourse as a way to describe what goes on in the "contact"

(Clifford 1997) and "engagement" zones (Onciul 2013) of museums. According to Marstine, hybridity is a useful methodological approach for subverting hegemonic power structures. She asserts that "Museum interventions that engage hybridity have the capacity to spark the kind of critical, self-reflective thinking, essential to organizational change toward equity and social justice" (2013, 157). Intercultural curation can be seen as a museological intervention in that it consciously disrupts conventional paradigms of practice. It can also create "third" and "in between" spaces" that problematize and transgress boundaries, allowing for multiple subject positions and agency. Marstine points out that the idea of hybridity has been, in fact, central to facilitating reconciliation in conflict resolution situations because it challenges individuals and groups to grapple with complex interrelationships and conflicting interests. Underpinning the museological concept of hybridity as a counterhegemonic method is the notion that museums have the right and responsibility to redress inequalities and advance social justice through a commitment to change (Marstine 2013).

MOA's Multiversity Galleries, in effect, turn the museum "inside out" by making visible to its publics processes behind intercultural curation. In this way, MOA illustrates how university museums can model for their publics ways of engaging with difference. They can show that institutional and social change is possible by creating policies, procedures, and ethical protocol aimed at righting wrongs of the past and acknowledging the claims of historically oppressed groups.

The work of the Museum of Anthropology of the University of British Columbia has been shaped by its particular institutional history (Shelton 2007, 2009), the extraordinary vision and philosophy of its directors,[7] and by, in no small measure, its physical location. The museum sits on the ancestral and unceded territory of the Coast Salish Musqueam people with whom the museum has a special relationship (Kramer 2017, 157). In fact, MOA has built and works closely with First Nations communities throughout the province of British Columbia (Shelton and Houtman 2009, 2). Reciprocal relationships with these communities form the core around which much of its practice revolves. Attuned to the importance of place, it has created a "sense of place" for the museum and its local communities, which is integral to its identity and purpose (Shelton 2007). But as a museum of world arts and cultures, MOA exists in and is connected to an expansive circle of communities.

MOA's research philosophy and collaborative curatorial methodology calls attention to how doing museum anthropology "at home" in a settler nation takes on meanings and responsibilities different from those in museums far removed from originating communities. Thomas draws attention to these differences in a discussion of how consultation with communities and "a commitment to engage" emerged earlier in anthropology museums located in "former settler colonies where museums were located among, or in close proximity to, aboriginal groups" (2016a, 32). Whereas community engagement and consultation with originating and other communities in curatorial practice has now become widespread, he writes:

Until the 1990s there was something of a gulf between the expectations and approaches to work in Auckland, Denver, Sydney, and Vancouver, on the one hand, and on the other those in European museums, far away from native peoples and less subject to immediate pressure from them.

(Thomas 2016a, 32)

In the following section, I describe how a "commitment to engage" with Native American and other communities has been shaping curatorial practice in the University of Denver Museum of Anthropology. Of particular concern is how this commitment reflects institutional philosophies and vision, and the museum's history and geographical locality.

The University of Denver Museum of Anthropology

The University of Denver Museum of Anthropology (DUMA) is a teaching and research museum housed within the Department of Anthropology. It consists of a collections storage room, collections lab, and gallery open to the general public. Its collection of some 160,000 pieces is mostly made up of archaeological artifacts taken from sites in Colorado, the Great Basin, and the American Southwest, and ethnographic objects originating from communities around the world.

The museum was founded in the early 1920s by Dr. Etienne B. Renaud, a Frenchman who was hired by the university in 1916 originally to teach Romance languages and literature. Fascinated by the history and cultures of the region's Indigenous peoples, Renaud turned his attention to archaeology and anthropology.[8] In addition to teaching and chairing the department for 22 years, he excavated archaeological sites throughout Colorado and neighboring states and amassed collections for his research. Over the years, other faculty and researchers associated with the department added collections to the museum.

The University of Denver's (DU) Department of Anthropology and museum has a long history of close ties with the Denver Art Museum (founded in 1893) and the Denver Museum of Natural History (formally opened to the public in 1908 and now known as the Denver Museum of Nature and Science). Many of the museums' curators lectured at DU or held appointments at both institutions. Frederic H. Douglas, appointed curator of Native Arts at the Denver Art Museum in 1930 (Harris 1996, 26), taught courses at DU on the subject beginning in the 1930s. A number of noted women scholars and curators specializing in the arts and cultures of the American Southwest worked at both institutions from time to time, including Ruth Underhill (see Chapter 3), Marie Wormington, Kate Peck Kent, and Clara Lee Tanner (Colwell-Chanthaphonh and Nash 2014, Parezo 1993). Kate Peck Kent, curator of Native arts at the Denver Art Museum from 1942 to 1944, in particular, made sizable contributions to the DUMA's collection through her research on Southwestern Native American and West African textiles. Kent taught at DU from the late 1960s until 1978, when she retired (Spilka 2007, 20).

Given this history, museum studies and museum anthropology have been an integral component of DU's Department of Anthropology since its early years. The department began to offer a credited course in museum studies in 1949 taught by a curator at the Denver Museum of Nature and Science. In 1989, the department revised its Master's program in museum studies under the directorship of Dr. Terry Reynolds with assistance from Helen Pustmueller who served as the museum's curator for some 20 years (Pustmueller 1996).[9] Today, museum anthropology is considered one of the main disciplinary subfields within the department in addition to archaeology and cultural anthropology. Graduate students concentrating on the museum and heritage studies "track" gain hands-on experience in nearly all areas of museum practice, or in Shelton's words, "operational museology," complementing courses in the history and theory of museum anthropology and critical museology.

As director of the museum and the museum and heritage studies track since 1998, I have positioned museum anthropology as a form of applied and public anthropology. My aim has been to train students to be theoretically grounded, practicing anthropologists in museums or related cultural institutions and organizations. This orientation has been in alignment with the direction the department had been taking for a couple of decades. In 2017, faculty created a vision statement to more overtly declare its focus on applied, public anthropology and "commitment to engage," which is: "To be a center of creative research and teaching, and a leading voice for the practice of public, collaborative, and community-engaged anthropology." This vision is in step with the university's motto, "To be a great private university dedicated to the public good." In the same year, the department was awarded "Community Engaged Department of the Year" from the DU Center for Community Engagement and Service Learning (CCESL) "for developing a concentration of faculty members who engage in high quality community-based partnerships; carry out rigorous public good scholarship; and/or teach innovative service learning courses that improve students' academic knowledge." CCESL has funded numerous faculty-led projects over the past decade, including exhibitions created in collaboration with community partners. Below I describe a couple of these projects as examples of community-engaged research, teaching, and practice, and how university museums can be laboratories for experientially exploring subjects of contemporary anthropological and museological concern.

A series of exhibitions titled *Connecting the Pieces: Dialogues on the Amache Archaeological Collections* has been a central feature of Professor Bonnie Clark's advanced seminar course, "American Material Culture," designed to teach students how to conduct research on and interpret material culture and tangible history. The exhibitions have been based on Clark's research at the site of the Amache Japanese confinement camp located in southeastern Colorado near the town of Granada. Constructed in 1942 and occupied until 1945, Amache was one of ten camps built for the express purpose of confining thousands of Americans of Japanese ancestry during World War II. Since 2008, Clark has been conducting a field school in historical archaeology and museum studies biennially at the site to uncover and reconstruct elements of this dark passage in American history (Clark and Amati 2018, Kreps 2015b).

Key to the "Amache Project," has been collaboration with a wide range of participants in the fieldwork as well as in the production of the exhibitions displayed in the DUMA gallery. DU students have served as the core field crew along with Granada high school students, volunteers who identify as former Amache internees, individuals who had family members in Amache or other camps, and individuals with interest in the subject (Clark and Amati 2018, Kreps 2015b, 104).

According to Clark and Amati, the *Connecting the Pieces* exhibitions have given the artifacts excavated at the site "a second life," and created a platform for engaging different stakeholders in the history of Amache and Japanese-American internment more generally (Clark and Amati 2018, 2). The main goal of the exhibition projects has been to use artifacts and a collaborative curating process as a means to connect students with those who had a personal connection to internment history (Kreps 2015b, 104). During the first iteration of the exhibition installed in 2012, students in the class partnered with community members who had personal knowledge about Amache and internment history. Over the course of the ten-week class, students and their partners selected artifacts and composed labels for them drawn from their research and conversations. Each team produced two labels, one written by the student and one by the community partner. Both labels were displayed in the exhibitions to show, according to Clark and Amati, how there are multiple ways of viewing archaeological artifacts and multiple stories that can be prompted by them (2018, 4). Visitors to the exhibit were invited to join the dialogue through interactive exhibit elements, for example, spaces where they could write their responses to the artifacts and the question: "What do these objects say to you?" (Clark and Amati 2018, 6). Two graduate students conducting research on community collaboration in museums designed the exhibition with the input of students in the class and community partners.

Clark and Amati report that the first iteration of *Connecting the Pieces* either met or exceeded expectations on many fronts. For example, they write that "Data from reflective student journals suggested that many of the civic education goals of the project did come to fruition. One student wrote that her work on the exhibit humanized internment history. 'It wasn't just dates and words anymore, but actual objects that families used'" (Clark and Amati 2018, 6–7). Due to the success of the first, a second exhibit was created as a product of Clark's 2014 field season and 2015 "American Material Culture" class. This time the class collaborated with the poet and former Amache internee, Lawson Inada. Inada led students and community members in a haiku-writing workshop that was inspired by poetry written in internment camps. During the workshop, which he called the "Amache Haiku Society," participants composed haiku that were then hung on a "haiku tree" erected in the gallery. Throughout the exhibition's duration, visitors added their own haiku to the tree inspired by objects on display and the larger themes addressed in the exhibition. In Clark and Amati's words: "It was a very popular interaction, encouraging active and creative reflection on the history and experience of internment, as well as the power of objects on display" (2018, 8).

Museums as Places for Intercultural Dialogue

The concept behind *Connecting the Pieces* was inspired by Museums as Places for Intercultural Dialogue (MAPforID), a European Union-sponsored initiative coordinated by the Institute for the Arts and Cultural Good of the Emilia-Romagna Region (Instituto per i Beni Artistici Culturale e Naturali della Regione Emilia-Romagna, or IBC for short) in Bologna, Italy. Carried out between 2007 and 2009, MAPforID's main goals were to develop the potential of museums to be places for intercultural dialogue, and to foster more active engagement between museums and communities, especially immigrant communities (Bodo 2009, 6, Iervolino 2013, 117). The project supported 30 pilot projects in six partner countries (Italy, the Netherlands, Hungary, Spain, Ireland, and the United Kingdom). Museums and cultural organizations located in each country were invited to submit proposals based on guidelines generated by the project's core research group. All of the projects sought to promote intercultural learning opportunities and cross-cultural understanding between migrants and members of the majority population (Iervolino 2013, 188).[10]

Two MAPforID projects, in particular, informed the *Connecting the Pieces* exhibits at DU—*Choose the Piece* and *Tongue to Tongue: A Collaborative Exhibition* (Clark and Amati 2018, 3). The former took place at the Civic Archaeological and Ethnographic Museum in Modena, Italy. The museum was established in 1871 and holds collections representing the historical development of the city and the region from the Paleolithic period to the nineteenth century. The project involved inviting newly arrived immigrants to symbolically adopt an object in the museum's collection, conduct research on it, and then teach other members of their community about it. The museum staff worked with local immigrant aid organizations to identify 60 participants from 18 countries to take part in the project. Most were students enrolled in language training courses at the Centre for Adult Education and Training (CAET).

In collaboration with the museum staff and CAET teachers, the participants (called cultural mediators) each selected an object from the museum's collections. Their choices were said to be guided by personal tastes, interests, memories, and affinities with the objects. Participants were also asked to write down the reasons for why they chose particular pieces along with a short biography. This activity in turn stimulated dialogue around the objects and personal stories. At the end of the program participants received a certificate that documented their symbolic adoption of the piece and their commitment to informing themselves and others about its history and significance. Photographs of the participants with their adopted objects, interpretive text, and the participants' biographies were then made into a "multicultural" calendar for 2010 that was distributed among the participants and made available to the public (Salvi 2009, 58–59).

Choose the Piece was based on the idea that museums should not just be concerned with developing new audiences by reaching out to immigrant communities and trying to get them to come to the museum. Rather, the goal was to involve them in ways that gave them a sense of shared cultural heritage and belonging. One of the outcomes of the project was that participants began to bring their families and friends to the museum outside the framework of the project, which indicated to the staff that they felt comfortable in a place they previously thought was not for them (Salvi 2009, 59).

The other project, *Tongue to Tongue: A Collaborative Exhibition*, was jointly orchestrated by the Museum of Anthropology and Ethnography at the University of Turin, Italy, and Centre for African Studies. The Centre was established in 1983 to foster cultural relations between the Piedmont region of northern Italy and African nations, and to educate the public about African history, arts, languages, and cultures. In 1996, it launched a project to enhance African artistic and ethnographic heritage preserved in regional museums (Bodo 2012, 36). At the heart of *Tongue to Tongue* was a training course for "Cultural Mediators of Intercultural Heritage," in which participants from Chad, Italy, Morocco, Congo, Romania, and Senegal were trained to be interpreters of the museum's heritage and collections. The objective was to bring the "tongue" of the museum, or its language and culture (characterized as institutional, scientific, and didactic), into dialogue with the "tongue" or voice (glossed as autobiographical, evocative, and emotional) of community "cultural mediators" (Bodo 2012, 184–185). Both the course and the exhibition were based on a participatory planning process as a form of cultural empowerment, "providing first and second generation migrants and cultural mediators with genuine opportunities for self-representation and cultural re-appropriation of tangible and intangible heritage" (Pecci cited in Bodo 2012, 184).

The multi-vocal exhibition was executed through collaboration among the mediators, museum staff, an architect, and an exhibition designer. Each mediator was free to choose a piece from the ethnographic collection with which he/she identified emotionally and culturally, but the object was not necessarily directly related to the mediator's own cultural background. Then, together with museum staff, the mediators created a "dialogical narrative route" generated from the interaction and exchange of knowledge, perspectives, and experiences among the participants. The chosen objects were then displayed in the museum alongside the "subjective heritage" (souvenirs, photographs, books, and clothes) of the cultural mediators, creating a range of autobiographical installations (Simone 2009, 36).

According to the project coordinator, Anna Maria Pecci, a museum anthropologist at the University of Turin, the project demonstrated how museum objects can reveal "their capacity to evade the classifications and narratives into which they had been institutionally inscribed and to be re-presented into a new, more connective display" (Pecci and Mangiapane quoted in Bodo 2012, 15). The strengths of the project were its participatory/autobiographical approach; the use of storytelling as a mediation tool; and the recontextualization of collections that stressed their emotional power, which in turn disengaged them from the prevailing rationale of cultural representation (Bodo 2012, 189).

Simona Bodo, a senior researcher for MAPforID, states that the exploratory and experimental nature of the project showed a willingness on the part of museum professionals to go beyond policies targeting individuals and groups according to their national origin and ethnicity. Such initiatives, Bodo asserts, are often based on an over-simplistic assumption that a community will be interested exclusively in objects and issues that are specifically related to its cultural background (2012, 189).

I was introduced to MAPforID in 2008 when I was teaching a course at the University of Bologna and met staff members from the IBC working with the project. The project intrigued me for several reasons. As a museum anthropologist, I had long been concerned with the role museums, especially those with ethnographic collections, could play in promoting cross-cultural understanding and respect for cultural diversity. Plus, I was always looking for ways that anthropological collections could be used for contemporary and socially relevant cultural work. The project was also compelling because it contradicted my impression of Italian museums as rather conservative places that largely adhered to the tenets of "old museology." As the Italian museologist Serena Iervolino has noted, until the early 2000s Italian museums had tended to lag behind their northern European counterparts and had continued focusing on traditional museum practices when others were becoming more community-oriented (Iervolino 2013, 115).

I returned to Italy in 2009 to attend the second MAPforID conference in Rimini, and later visited project sites at museums in Turin, Modena, Parma, Reggio Emelia, and Bologna. I wanted to learn more about the process behind specific projects, such as *Choose the Piece* and *Tongue to Tongue*, and how they were interpreting the concept of intercultural dialogue and applying it in practice. What's more, I was curious to know how they were making meaningful connections to immigrant communities, and in turn, how their approaches might be applied back home in Denver (Kreps 2009).

As stated in one of the project's publications, *Museums as Places for Intercultural Dialogue: Selected Practices from Europe*, intercultural dialogue is:

> a process that comprises an open and respectful exchange or interaction between individuals, groups, and organizations with different cultural backgrounds and world views. Among its aims are to develop deeper understandings of diverse perspectives and practices; to increase participation and the freedom and ability to make choices; to foster equality; and to enhance creative processes.
>
> *(Bodo, Gibbs, and Sani 2009, 6)*

MAPforID's interpretation of intercultural dialogue drew on the ideas of many cultural theorists, but especially Nestor Garcia Canclini's concepts of interculturality. According to Garcia Canclini, "the concept of interculturality reminds us of interaction and encounter, i.e., what happens when a relationship of exchange is established between groups. Whereas multiculturality entails the acceptance of difference, interculturality implies that negotiation, conflict, and mutual exchange exist between groups" (Garcia Canclini quoted in Delgado 2009, 8). Indeed, the project's emphasis on interculturality and intercultural dialogue was conceived as an alternative to models of multiculturalism that had become common throughout Europe. To MAPforID project leaders, these models tended to essentialize and exoticize people and their cultures by focusing on where they came from and their pasts instead of where they live in the present. What's more, multicultural policies were thought to encourage segregation and reinforce discrimination by casting ethnic groups as bounded communities with distinct identities (Delgado 2009, 8). Indeed, the project sought to counter static notions of culture by conceptualizing it as fluid, constantly in flux, and generative. And in keeping with the idea of interculturality, it stressed the reality of cultural mixing, sharing, and integration, and the ideal that societies should strive to go beyond being multicultural, wherein diverse but separate cultures simply co-exist, to being intercultural (Bodo, Gibbs, and Sani 2009, 6–7).

A common thread running throughout all MAPforID projects was the desire to rethink the role of the museum in contemporary society. Project partners were encouraged to see the museum "as an institution which is capable of not only speaking to audiences, but also of listening to its audiences" (Bodo, Gibbs, and Sani 2009, 7). The aim was to re-imagine the museum in the image of Homi Bhabha's idea of "the third space," or an "inter" in between space of translation and negotiation (Delgado 2009, 8).

This theoretical and philosophical approach was behind another European Union-sponsored and IBC-organized project, The Learning Museum, which I participated in as a "third country partner." Carried out between 2010 and 2013, the project was guided by the idea that museums should not only be places of learning, but as learning organizations themselves they should also be learning from their publics.[11]

My exposure to the tremendous variety of innovative projects sponsored by MAPforID and The Learning Museum motivated me to be more experimental and creative in my own curatorial work. Just one example of projects that have been inspired by my experience in Europe is *Making Home: Civic Dialogues on Where We Live and How We Live Together*, installed in 2011 (Kreps 2015b).

The exhibition was initially conceived as a collaborative project between the DUMA and the African Community Center, a refugee resettlement agency in Denver, and a means of creating awareness of the challenges immigrants face in making a home and new life in a new place. As the project evolved, however, it was modified to address how people in general create a sense of home and what home means to them. Ultimately, the project entailed collaboration among members of the local Bhutanese refugee community and students and faculty from the Department of Anthropology as well as from other departments and programs across campus.

In conceptualizing the exhibition, we wanted to create an exhibition that would be experiential, participatory, open-ended, multisensory and inviting in contrast to the more conventional objects in glass cases with "book on the wall" text. To this end, my student co-curator and I designed a month-long series of workshops consisting of activities and performances focused on specific themes related to making home. Our aim was to set the stage for the creation of an interactive, iterative exhibition that took form over time with the addition of new artifacts, traces, and documents produced by workshop participants. We hoped that these newly created forms of material culture and art would stimulate intercultural dialogue among participants around the idea of home (Kreps 2015b, 107).

University museums are still often perceived as "dusty, quiet, and mostly inanimate places where objects are preserved for posterity" (Turin 2015, 122). And anthropology museums have long been criticized for not keeping up with and presenting current developments in the field. *Making Home* was designed to counter these perceptions by animating the gallery and addressing a topic, i.e., migration and immigration, of current concern in anthropology, the museum community, as well as to the wider public. How museums can speak to these issues and promote social cohesion has been on the forefront of the international museum community's agenda for some time now (Crooke 2007, Gourievidis 2014, Iervolino 2013, Levitt 2015).

The above projects are but two examples of the kind of community-engaged work being carried out by various faculty members in and through the DUMA. Moreover, they gave students the chance to explore how museums and exhibitions can be sites for investigating contemporary anthropological topics, arenas for cultural production, and spaces for community and socially engaged practice. Such projects are no longer considered "experimental," even if each project is unique and experimental in its own ways. They have become one of the ways the department makes the philosophy inscribed in its vision statement visible to its audiences. It is important to point out, however, that decades before community engagement became normative practice in the department, or in anthropology in general, faculty and museum staff had been working with Native American communities in various capacities. Similar to other American anthropology departments and museums, practices in the DUMA have been shaped over the years by its special relationship to Native American communities, by the shifting nature of this relationship, and its locality in the heart of "Indian Country."

Historical Reckonings

Changes in the relationships between museums and Native communities are the result of many interventions over the past several decades, among which, the 1990 Native American Graves Protection and Repatriation Act (NAGPRA) has been paramount. NAGPRA has reconfigured the terms of engagement between museums and Native communities. Because the law mandates that museums conduct inventories of their collections and essentially do provenance research, it has also forced museums to uncover and reconstruct their own, particular histories of extractive anthropology and collection formation. In this regard, NAGPRA has been a channel for the critique of museum anthropology and how it has been practiced in specific institutions (Colwell 2017).

Since 1990, the DUMA has been proactively implementing NAGPRA. Recognizing the magnitude of the law as a legal obligation and moral responsibility, the university administration has provided funding for NAGPRA-related work and a designated NAGPRA Coordinator position on the museum staff. This support has allowed the museum to not merely comply with the law, but also to work within the "spirit of the law" and take initiatives aimed at building stronger relationships with Native communities. In addition to presenting exhibitions and programming on Native American arts and culture, often in collaboration with Native artists and organizations, the museum has become a platform for promoting awareness of Indigenous issues on campus. The Department of Anthropology's extensive experience in working with Native communities and on sensitive matters such as NAGPRA made it a key player in actions taken to address the dark history associated with the university's founder in advance of its 150th anniversary.

The University of Denver was founded in 1864 by John Evans, a physician by training, philanthropist, politician, advocate of public education and higher learning, and a central figure in establishing two private universities: Northwestern University in Evanston, Illinois and the Colorado Seminary that became the University of Denver. In 1862, Evans was sworn in as the second Governor of Colorado Territory and Ex Officio Superintendent of Indian Affairs. Just two weeks after the Colorado Seminary opened its doors a heavily armed militia of the First and Third Colorado Volunteers led by United States Army Colonel John Chivington carried out the infamous Sand Creek Massacre.

By 1861 displaced and captive Cheyenne and Arapaho had been forced onto and incarcerated in a military reservation called Sand Creek in southeastern Colorado. According to the Native American historian Roxanne Dunbar-Ortiz:

> They were camped under a white flag of truce and had federal permission to hunt buffalo to feed themselves. But in early 1864, the territorial governor [John Evans] informed them they could no longer leave the reservation to hunt. Despite their compliance with the order, on November 29th, 1864, Chivington took seven hundred Colorado Volunteers to the reservation. Without provocation or warning they attacked, leaving dead 105 women and children and 28 men.
>
> *(Dunbar-Ortiz 2014, 137)*

In its 1865 investigation, the US Congress Joint Committee on the Conduct of War recorded testimonies and published a report that documented the actions of the volunteers and the brutality of their killings. As Dunbar-Ortiz writes, "After the smoke cleared, they had returned and finished off the few survivors while scalping and mutilating corpses—men and women, young and old, children and babies" (2014, 137). Witnesses report that the men decorated their weapons, saddles, and caps with their trophies, which were later paraded through the streets of

Denver. Despite the detailed report of the Massacre, neither Chivington nor any of his men were formally reprimanded or prosecuted.

In 2013, one year prior to the anniversaries of both the University of Denver and the Sand Creek Massacre, a group of concerned DU faculty, including two faculty members of the Department of Anthropology, formed an ad hoc committee to produce a scholarly report on the massacre and the extent of John Evans's involvement. The committee included members of the DU Native Student Alliance, alumni, and representatives of the Cheyenne and Arapaho communities from Wyoming, Montana, Colorado and Oklahoma. In the previous year, Northwestern University, under pressure from Native students and members of the Chicago Native community, appointed a committee to address and compile its own report on Evans's role in the Massacre. Its report was released in May 2014 (Clemmer-Smith et al. 2014, iii–iv).

While the Northwestern report condemned Evans for a "deep moral failure," the committee ultimately exonerated Evans of responsibility for the Massacre. On the other hand, the Report of the John Evans Study Committee of the University of Denver, submitted in November 2014, concluded that Evans shared responsibility for the Massacre because he "created the conditions in which the massacre was highly likely … by fanning the flames of war when he could have dampened them" (Clemmer-Smith et al. 2014, iii). In response to the Report and the committee's recommendations, the University created the Task Force on Native American Inclusivity, on which I served. The Task Force was responsible for making further suggestions to the administration on how it could implement recommendations, and take steps to acknowledge DU's institutional legacy. As stated by the Report's authors:

> This committee's hope is that by understanding our founder's role in this catastrophic event we can unite as a community and begin to forge a new relationship to the past for the benefit of the public good. We offer this report as an initial step to promote empathy and healing, not only for those of us who have inherited this complex legacy, but also for the Arapaho and Cheyenne people, who have displayed an active sense of presence in the face of victimization and, lest we forget, on whose ancestral lands our campus sits.
>
> *(Clemmer-Smith et al. 2014, iii–iv)*

Up to and following the release of the Evans Report, a number of symposia, workshops, and events took place across campus to publicly acknowledge DU's connection to the Sand Creek Massacre and to repair relations with descendant communities. The DUMA participated in this process by hosting several art exhibits that took the Massacre as their main theme and presented it from Native perspectives.

The first of them was an exhibit created in partnership with the DU Native Student Alliance titled *Moving Forward* that featured the work of Native American artists Thomas Greyeyes and Ryan Singer. During the exhibit's run in March 2014, the museum hosted a multi-tribal NAGPRA consultation that took place down the hall from the DUMA gallery. When representatives from the Cheyenne and Arapaho Tribes of Oklahoma visited the gallery one representative made it known that he was disappointed to see that the artists were not Cheyenne or Arapaho. Later he introduced museum staff to George Curtis Levi, a Southern Cheyenne artist, who in turn, organized a group show with four additional Cheyenne and Arapaho artists—Brent Learned, Merlin Little Thunder, B. J. Stepp, and Nathan Hart—who all had family connections to the Sand Creek Massacre. The exhibit, *One November Morning*, was shown in the gallery from January to March 2015 and was accompanied by a panel discussion on the impact of the Sand Creek Massacre on Cheyenne and Arapaho art (Amati 2018) (see Figure 7.1).

Levi curated another exhibit, *Tsitsistas: Our Cheyenne Family*, which focused on the artwork of his family and was shown in the gallery in conjunction with the International Indigenous Film and Arts Festival in October 2016. For nearly a decade, the DUMA has partnered with the International Institute for Indigenous Resource Management's annual Indigenous Film and Arts Festival that features film and art by and about Indigenous peoples from around the world.

The DUMA has been able to contribute to the university's efforts to address its past by drawing on its experience of reckoning with its own checkered history, and as a member of a community of practice that has undergone decades of intensive self-criticism and reform. The museum has recognized and acted on its special relationship, obligations, and responsibilities to Native communities, and especially to those on whose ancestral territories the museum sits. Working with Native

FIGURE 7.1 *Chivington's Victims*. George Curtis Levi, Southern Cheyenne. 2014 Image used with permission from artist.

artists has proven to be a particularly potent means of attending to these "difficult heritages" (Macdonald 2009) because, in Leavy's words, "visual art … can be used to challenge, dislodge, and transform outdated beliefs and stereotypes … Visual images can be used as a powerful form of social and political resistance" (2015, 225). Through this work, the DUMA has attempted to help make the university a more welcoming environment not only for Native communities, but for everyone.

Working with Artists

In recent years university anthropology museums have been increasingly working with artists of all kinds to (re)interpret collections in creative ways to generate alternative histories and narratives, and to forge new kinds of relationships within and across communities. Artist interventions in museums have served as another catalyst for institutional critique by "mining the museum" and turning its inner workings inside out, and in the process, exposing the unspoken value systems of museums and universities (King and Marstine 2006, 266). Artists can do the work of "defamiliarization," pushing viewers to look at something in new and different ways (Leavy 2015, 228). In general, anthropology museums have been enlisting artists to help them breathe new life into collections, exhibitionary strategies, and programing in their attempts to make their institutions more socially relevant, contemporary, and appealing to wider audiences (Lubar 2017, Marstine 2013, 2017, Thomas 2016).

Working with artists also has been part of a trend in anthropology to pay more attention to the "border zones" between contemporary art and anthropological practice. Schneider and Wright in the introduction to the book *Between Art and Anthropology* discuss how "artistic practices can extend anthropological practices and vice versa," and "encourage the kind of experimentation that would result in new and dynamic directions for both contemporary art practices that revolve around various kinds of documentation and to enlarge the range of work being produced within anthropology" (2010, 3). The authors suggest that collaborations between artists and anthropologists can be "starting points for new practices" (2010, 4). As a case in point, my teaching, research, and curatorial practice have taken new directions in recent years as a result of working with the Italian artist Daniele Pario Perra. Our collaboration has dramatically influenced not only what I teach but also how I teach socially, community-engaged museum anthropology (Kreps 2015b, 97).

I first met Perra at an art educator's conference in 2009 at the Museum of Contemporary Art in Bologna, Italy while conducting research on the MAPforID projects described earlier. In his presentation, Perra described graffiti removal and preservation workshops he had been carrying out in cities throughout Europe with marginalized communities, such as Roma youth. Perra explained how he saw graffiti as "spontaneous communication," or a way of communicating outside the filters of mainstream culture and authoritative structures. To Perra, graffiti, or "writings" in his words, can be seen as the "cultural DNA of a city or place" that encodes and represents its *zeitgeist*. It is a medium through which the voiceless and socially invisible can make their opinions, ideas, hopes, and frustrations known in the public sphere.

During the workshops, Perra canvasses neighborhoods with participants and together they identify and map writings that they find particularly meaningful. Then they are removed by transferring the pigments to canvas through a technique used for centuries in Italy to remove and conserve frescoes. The resulting "artifacts" are then archived or installed in a community gallery. For Perra, a critical component of the workshops, and his overall art practice, is the civic dialogue that takes place around these mapping and preservation interventions. The workshops give participants the chance to discuss the meanings and stories behind the writings, and how they connect to local issues and places. They are a means of bringing people together to interrogate nodes of communication within and across communities.

Following his presentation, I talked to Perra about how much his work resembled ethnographic fieldwork and asked if he was familiar with anthropological methods. In response, he said that although he was not a trained anthropologist or sociologist his work was indeed sociological and he considered himself more of a "researcher" than artist. Indeed, he called his work "fieldwork" rather than art. And because his work intersected the fields of design, architecture, urban planning, and community activism he had a hard time classifying it. But if pressed to place his work in a particular art genre then he would label it "relational" art. Being a relational artist to Perra meant bringing people together to engage in dialogue and perform actions around issues of common concern (Kreps 2015b, 97).

Relational art, or rather "relational aesthetics," is a mode of art making codified by the cultural theorist and curator Nicolas Bourriaud in his landmark text *Relational Aesthetics*. According to Bourriaud, relational art encompasses "a set of artistic practices which take as their theoretical and practical point of departure the whole of human relations and their social context, rather than an independent and private space" (2002, 113). Relational art creates interactive, communicative human exchanges and experiences in a particular time and space. The anthropologist Matti Bunzl writes that since the 1990s, relational aesthetics has been a dominant paradigm in avant-garde circles.

> Encompassing a varied range of practices, it is characterized primarily by an attempt to break the ossified relations between art, artist, and viewer. Rather than present spectators with finished products, the products are supposed to become activated as part of the artwork itself. The result is a blurring of various boundaries in a practice that sees itself as radically democratic and open-ended.
>
> *(2016, 143)*

Relational art is akin to or is sometimes seen as interchangeable with "social practice" art in that the latter also extends to and is embedded in social relations and public spaces, "stepping outside the gallery space" social practice artists have "proposed explicitly social and political forms of work. The aim of their projects is not just to enact social relations, but to intervene in actually existing contexts—to have a social and political effect" (Sansi 2015, 13).

Relational and social practice artists, like Perra, are not just interested in the art product itself, but more so, the things one can do with art. Social practice art tends to be highly experimental, participatory, performance-based, open-ended, dialogical, and transformative in its approach. It typically takes place in public spaces in articulation with a specific site, and frequently involves research or fieldwork that addresses issues of immediate political and social relevance to particular social groups (Sansi 2015, 2).

As I listened to Perra's conference presentation I was reminded of the work of the Platteforum, a community arts organization that works with underserved youth in Denver. I thought Perra would be a good fit for their artist-in-residence program and suggested that he apply. Over the next two years, I walked Perra through the application process and met with staff of the Platteforum, the Denver Museum of Contemporary Art (MCA), and a representative of the Denver Office of Cultural Affairs to plan his residency. At the same time, I discussed with Platteforum and MCA staff how I could integrate Perra's residency into my "Art and Anthropology" class. Consequently, Perra's residency became a collaborative project involving the Platteforum, the MCA, the University of Denver, and ultimately, citizens of Bologna, Perra's home town.

Perra arrived in Denver in March 2011 to begin a residency at the Platteforum as part of the Confluence Project, a shared artist-in-residence program between the MCA and Platteforum that brought teens together from the MCA's Teen Council and Platteforum's ArtLab to work with visiting artists. Over a six-week period, Perra conducted research on graffiti in Denver and facilitated workshops with Platteforum and MCA teens as well as students enrolled in my "Art and Anthropology" class (Figure 7.2).

As participant observers, students documented workshop activities through field notes, photography, and videos for the production of an ethnography of the project, focusing on the ways graffiti are variously perceived, as art, communication, or vandalism.

In class, students were assigned to teams charged with investigating the history of graffiti as a means of political and social expression and as urban, street, and unsanctioned public art; civic responses to graffiti in the form of ordinances and initiatives such as the Denver Graffiti Removal Task Force and the criminalization of graffiti; the use and control of public space; and the structure and history of community arts and cultural organizations like the Platteforum. The aim of the students' research was to contextualize the project within larger political, social, and cultural contexts and art movements. In class, we also discussed the "ethnographic turn" in contemporary art practices, and where anthropological and contemporary art practices converge and diverge, raising questions such as: What is meant by "art as ethnography" and "ethnography as art"? Are artists held to the same ethical standards as anthropologists? And to what degree is "artistic license" allowed in ethnography? Over the term, we discovered that Stephen Feld is not overstating

FIGURE 7.2 Daniele Pario Perra, on right, removing graffiti/tagging from abandoned building in Denver. Finished piece featured in exhibit *ANARCH-ETIQUETTE* shown in the Denver University Museum of Anthropology gallery Photograph by C. Kreps, 2011.

the case when he asks: "is it safer and easier to migrate or appropriate anthropology to art than art to anthropology?" (2010, 125).

Aside from these academic questions, the project posed a number of logistical challenges. This was Perra's first project in the United States, and he quickly learned that he had to make dramatic adjustments to his practice to accommodate social circumstances and settings quite different from those in the European cities where he had worked. Early on, he found out that he could not take teens on excursions in search of writings, particularly into what appeared to him to be abandoned buildings and decaying industrial sites. Not only were these sites considered too dangerous and risky for teens, but most were also private property. As he learned, a "NO TRESPASSING" sign in the United States really means no trespassing!

But above all, the greatest challenge was finding writings that met Perra's criteria, i.e., not tagging, not mural art, but writing that conveyed some social or political message. The City of Denver's Graffiti Removal and Abatement Task Force, we found out, is highly efficient. Within days of their appearance, crews are on the scene to paint over markings. As true in many cities, graffiti, or what is more commonly "tagging," is seen as a sign of gang activity and thus its removal is part of anti-gang initiatives (Beck 2015). Added to this, Perra discovered that most wall paint in the United States is latex-based, or essentially rubber, and therefore does not allow saturation of pigments. In most cases, Perra was *peeling* writings from surfaces rather than *transferring* them. Despites these obstacles and contingencies, Perra and workshop participants produced 20 pieces that were exhibited in the MCA alongside pieces Perra had produced in workshops in Europe. The exhibition was titled *ANARCH-ETIQUETTE: The Etiquette of Anarchy and Preserving Writing on the Wall*, and was on display from May through June, 2011 at the MCA.

For me and my students, the exhibition at the MCA and the collaborative, creative process behind it served as a field site for investigating the border zones between art and anthropology, and the different exhibitionary strategies in art and anthropology museums. At the MCA, the unframed canvas pieces hung on white walls with brief labels that gave the title of the piece and place of origin. A short video showed Perra working with participants in the removal and preservation of the writings. An introductory text briefly explained the Confluence Project to visitors and thanked sponsors. Perra and workshop participants were credited with creating the "art," not anonymous graffiti writers.

The process of removing writings, or graffiti, from their original context, transferring them to canvas, and then displaying them in a contemporary art museum clearly demonstrated to students Svasek's concept of "object transit and transition" we had been reading about in class.

> When exploring why objects are considered art in a particular period in a particular social setting it is crucial to analyse two processes … transit and transition. Transit records the location and movement of objects over time and across social or geographical boundaries, while transition analyses how the meaning, value, and status of objects as well as how people experience them, is changed in that process.
>
> *(2007, 4)*

Indeed, throughout the project students asked if graffiti were still graffiti when transferred from the street and on to the walls of a gallery. How did this action change their meaning and value? Furthermore, did Perra and the participants have the right to remove the writings? What about the intentions of the original writers? While we were uncomfortable with some aspects of Perra's practice and the MCA exhibition, we also understood that relational and social practice art is meant to raise questions and be unsettling.

A smaller version of *ANARCH-ETIQUETTE* was installed in the DUMA in July 2011. In this setting, the focus was on graffiti as communication, and more specifically, as a signifier of social and cultural boundaries and a means of marking territory (Beck 2015). The objective was to present graffiti as a cultural phenomenon from an anthropological perspective by placing it in wider social and political contexts.

Perra installed another iteration of the exhibition in the Biblioteca Salaborsa, the municipal library and civic center in Bologna in December 2011. It included pieces created in Denver as well as others produced in workshops held throughout Europe. Here the exhibition served as a platform for a civic dialogue around graffiti. Perra organized an *incontro publico* (public forum) titled "Urban Communication," in which speakers from Bologna's Office of Cultural Affairs, noted "thought leaders" and "trend watchers" (such as Francesco Morace of Futureconceptlab, Renzo di Renzo of Heads Collective of United Colors of Benetton), local citizens, as well as myself and another faculty member from the University of Denver, Roberta Waldbaum, participated. Discussion revolved around the use of public space and freedom of expression in democratic societies, and especially in a place like Bologna where the "right to write" can conflict with a long tradition of protecting the aesthetics of historic buildings and monuments.[12]

The project, overall, threw into relief the degree to which context and locality matter in terms of how its various components were executed and the varied capacities and expectations of those involved. Perra was quick to realize that his practice needed to be adjusted to what was and was not possible in Denver, and to let the project take its own direction. In this regard, the project lived up to the philosophy and principles of relational and social practice art as experimental, open-ended, and above all, context-specific. For the teen and student participants, the project gave them a wider, more cosmopolitan lens through which to view graffiti as a form of expression, in addition to how museums can be "civic laboratories" (Bennett 2005). And for me the experience was liberating. It allowed me to break free from tired pedagogical methods, such as an over-reliance on text, and to become more experimental and creative in my in- and out-of-classroom pedagogy and curatorial work.

The case studies and specific projects described above demonstrate how university anthropology museums are multifaceted sites that represent many aspects of the new museum anthropology. They are reinvigorating their collections by finding novel ways of putting them to use, moving curatorial work in new directions beyond the care and display of collections (Schorch, McCarthy, and Dürr 2019). Nowadays, curatorship in university museums is commonly a matter of co-curatorship and co-creation in the service of diversity and social inclusion. They have become spaces of intercultural curation and dialogue and of encounter not only with objects, but also with people of diverse backgrounds and with stories to tell. What's more, they exemplify how museums can be attuned to the needs and interests of local communities while at the same time promoting global, cosmopolitan perspectives.

Cosmopolitan Museum Anthropology

As museums of world cultures anthropology museums are uniquely positioned to practice "cosmopolitan museology" or a museology that encourages not only visitors but also museum professionals "to step outside of their location and see the world through the eyes of 'others'" and recognize a "plurality of worldviews" (Mason 2013, 59). Cosmopolitan museum anthropology can help foster global perspectives and ways of being in the world that acknowledge connections and obligations to others beyond self, family, and nation (Appiah 2006). It can furthermore expand the notion of community beyond the local, regional, and national to include global/planetary communities.

Museums and anthropology have long struggled with the dilemma of how to engender greater understandings of what unites us as human beings without eliding our differences. Certainly, mapping humanity's similarities and differences, or universals and particularities, has been a classic component of the anthropological enterprise (Hannerz 2010). But in anthropology's contemporary world, similarities and differences are not seen in the oppositional and totalizing terms of yesteryear. Golding and Modest, for instance, suggest a framework that promotes "thinking and working through difference" and seeing "similarity across and within difference" (2019).

In her book *Staying with the Trouble: Making Kin in the Chthulucene*, Donna Haraway urges us to engage in "tentacular thinking," a mode of thinking that involves tracking threads and connections, finding their tangles and patterns, what does and does not connect us, and what is the same and not the same at all. In Haraway's calculation, we have to "relearn how to conjugate worlds with partial connections and not universals and particulars" (2016, 13). Rather than focus on universals and particulars, our task is to "make kin," to find kinship with "oddkin" (human and nonhuman), and become capable of "response-ability" to that kin. To Haraway, "staying with the trouble" means learning to live and make-with diversity, to get on together, and to build more livable futures on a shared, multispecies planet. She says: "Our task is to make trouble, to stir up potent response to devastating events, as well as to settle troubled waters and rebuild quiet places" (Haraway 2016, 1). These too can be tasks for museums and anthropology in our current age of engagement.

Museums and anthropology have undergone radical transformations over the past several decades. They have "stayed with the trouble" of reconciling their colonial pasts with contemporary presents, and their inherent contradictions and dilemmas (Macdonald, Lidchi, and von Oswald 2017). And as I have tried to show in this book, on-going criticism, or making trouble and stirring things up, has been a major force behind this transformation. But change has not come about through criticism alone. It also has required action, and an increasing capacity for response-ability.

Today, most observers of museums would agree that "Public engagement and responsiveness to community are now, in diverse respects, vital to the orientation and work of museums of all kinds" (Thomas 2016a, 11). For anthropology museums, this means engagement with and responsiveness to communities near and far. And many would also agree with Thomas's assertion that the world still needs anthropology museums, "whatever you think of their history" (2016b). For Thomas we need them because they are places that are filled with wondrous things that represent human creativity and ingenuity, tell the stories of adaptation and survival, and of entangled histories of encounter and exchange. Museums are places for making unexpected discoveries and for stimulating and sustaining curiosity through their collections. "Collections do not merely enrich our senses of where we have come from, of the constitution of the cultures we inhabit; they are also resources for the future, creative technologies that people can use to create new things" (Thomas 2016a, 17). To Thomas, this is what museums are good for in the twenty-first century.

While the degree to which anthropology has been publicly engaged has waxed and waned over time, the commitment to safeguard world cultural heritage on the part of its museums has not wavered. What is different today, however, is that Western anthropologists, curators, museologists, and scholars are no longer the self-appointed guardians of that heritage and knowledge about it. Nowadays, this guardianship is shared with, or ceded to, its original keepers. Shared guardianship has become a critical component of the new museum ethics (Marstine 2011), and expanded our knowledge and understandings of the diverse ways people relate to, value, and have cared for their belongings inside and outside of museums. In turn, we now know that there is not one universal museology, but a world full of diverse museologies.

Indeed, much has changed in the landscape of museums and anthropology over the past several decades. Reflecting on this change I am reminded of my 1988 article on decolonizing anthropology museums, which opened with Kenneth Hudson's assertion that the day of the ethnographic museum had gone. Hudson made this claim based on the assumption that such museums were no longer of "influence" mostly owing to their outdated collections (Hudson 1987). Countering this claim, I argued that anthropology museums still played useful roles in society by encouraging cross-cultural awareness and understanding (Kreps 1988, 56). Obviously, much has been done since to revitalize anthropology museums, as this book has shown. Above all, it is now clear that their influence, and indeed future, rests on making both what is in museums and what museums do continually matter.

Notes

1 Thomas writes that over the past 20 years virtually every major institution, and many smaller ones, in Britain have had major extensions or improvements because of the allocation of a share of National Lottery proceeds through the Heritage Lottery Fund (2010, 6).

2 While there has been a remarkable resurgence of interest in and support for university museums over the past 20 years or so, I would be remiss if I did not acknowledge that there is also cause for anxiety in some quarters as discussed in Chapter 2 and in Conn (2016).

3 The special issue titled "Emergent Visions for Object-Based Teaching In and Beyond the Classroom" was the outcome of a 2013 American Anthropological Association Invited Roundtable Session sponsored by the Council for Museum Anthropology and Society for Visual Anthropology. I was one of four panelists that participated in the session and contributed to the issue. Kathleen Adams, Professor of Anthropology at Loyola University in Chicago, organized the session.

4 From 1982 to 1985 I was an employee of Alaska Native Arts and Crafts Cooperative (ANAC), a non-profit marketing association and gallery located in Anchorage. ANAC was initially set up in 1938 as a New Deal economic development initiative for Alaska's Indigenous populations (see McLerran 2004, Moore 2008).

5 In November 2017, the conference titled "Putting Theory & Things Together: Research with Museum Collections" was held at the National Museum of Natural History in recognition of SIMA's tenth anniversary. Over two days, student alumni presented papers on their research and Howard Morphy and Ruth Phillips delivered keynote addresses. The spring 2018 issue of *Museum Anthropology* features six articles by student alumni based on their presentations and on research begun during their time at SIMA.

6 SIMA received additional funding in 2017 from the National Science Foundation to continue the program.

7 Dr. Michael Ames became the director of MOA in 1974 and served in the position until 1997 when Dr. Ruth Phillips took over the directorship until 2002. Dr. Anthony Shelton was appointed director in 2004 (Shelton 2009). Needless to say, all have made their marks as leading figures in museum anthropology, art history, and museology.

8 Renaud earned a Bachelor's degree in 1905 from the University of Paris followed by graduate work in physics, chemistry, and mathematics at Catholic University in Washington, DC from 1907 to 1908. After teaching Greek, algebra, and Roman history at Charles College in Maryland he moved to Colorado and received a Master of Arts from the University of Colorado. In 1920, the University of Denver awarded Renaud a PhD (Spilka 2007, 4).

9 Helen Pustmueller made many significant professional and financial contributions to the Department of Anthropology and DUMA from the 1970s to late 1990s. She received a Master of Arts in anthropology in 1977, and went on to become a research associate in the museum from 1978–1980 and curator until 1996. Before her death in 2013, Pustmueller donated funds to the department for the creation of the Helen M. Pustmueller Endowed Fellowship. www.du.edu/ahss/anthropology/admission/scholarships.html (accessed August 12, 2018).

10 Among the project's many outcomes is the publication *Museums as Places for Intercultural Dialogue: Selected Practices from Europe* (2009) for which I wrote a foreword. The publication is available online at: www.ne-mo.org/fileadmin/Dateien/public/service/Handbook_MAPforID_EN.pdf.

11 The Learning Museum Project produced a number of publications, including two to which I contributed the essays "The Power of Words and Vocabularies" (Kreps 2013a) and "Participation, Museums, and Civic Engagement." (Kreps 2013b).

12 This iteration of the exhibition was supported by a grant from the Fondazione Cassa di Risparmio di Bologna (CARISBO).

References

Adams, Kathleen. 2015. "Back to the Future? : Emergent Visions for Object-Based Teaching in and Beyond the Classroom." *Museum Anthropology* 2:88–95.

Amati, Anne. 2018. "A Roadmap to Repatriation: The Native American Graves Protection and Repatriation Act (NAGPRA)." *Informal Learning Review* (no. 152, September/November):3–8.

Ames, Michael. 1986. *Museums, the Public, and Anthropology. A Study of the Anthropology of Anthropology*. Vancouver and New Delhi: UBC Press Concept Publishing.

Ames, Michael. 1992. *Cannibal Tours and Glass Boxes: The Anthropology of Museums*. Vancouver: University of British Columbia.

Ames, Michael. 2003. "How to Decorate a House. The Renegotiation of Cultural Representations in the University of British Columbia Museum of Anthropology." In *Museums and Source Communities*, edited by L. Peers and A. Brown, 171–180. London and New York: Routledge.

Appiah, Kwame. 2006. *Cosmopolitanism: Ethics in a World of Strangers*. New York: W. W. Norton and Company, Inc.

Beck, Sam. 2015. "Urban Transitions: Graffiti Transformations." In *Public Anthropology in a Borderless World*, edited by Sam Beck and Carl A. Maida, 314–350. New York and Oxford: Berghahn.

Beck, Sam and Carl A. Maida. 2013. *Toward Engaged Anthropology*. New York: Berghahn Books.

Bennett, Tony. 2005. "Civic Laboratories: Museums, Cultural Objecthood and the Governance of the Social." *Cultural Studies* 19(5):521–547.

Bodo, Simona. 2012. "Museums as Intercultural Spaces." In *Museums, Equality, and Social Justice*, edited by Richard Sandell and Eithne Nightingale, 181–191. London and New York: Routledge.

Bodo, Simona, Kirsten Gibbs, and Margherita Sani. 2009. *Museums as Places for Intercultural Dialogue: Selected Practices from Europe*. MAPforID Group.

Bourriaud, Nicolas. 2002. *Relational Aesthetics*. Dijon: Presses du Reel.

Bunzl, Matti. 2016. "But Is It Art? Not Really." In *Curatorial Dreams*, edited by Shelley Butler and Erica Lehrer, 141–152. Montreal & Kingston, London, Chicago, IL: McGill-Queens University Press.

Clark, Bonnie and Anne Amati. 2018. "Powerful Objects, Difficult Dialogues: Mobilizing Archaeological Exhibits for Civic Engagement." *International Journal of Heritage Studies* 1–14.

Clemmer-Smith, Richard, Alan Gilbert, David F. Halas, Billy J. Stratton, George E. Tinker, Nancy D. Wadsworth, and Steven Fisher. 2014. *Report of the John Evans Study Committee University of Denver*. Denver, CO: University of Denver.

Clifford, James. 1997. *Routes. Travel and Translation in the Late Twentieth Century*. Cambridge, MA: Harvard University Press.

Clifford, James and George Marcus, ed. 1986. *Writing Culture: The Poetics and Politics of Ethnography*. Berkeley: University of California Press.

Cole, Douglas. 1985. *Captured Heritage. The Scramble for Northwest Coast Artifacts*. Seattle: University of Washington Press.

Colwell, Chip. 2017. *Plundered Skulls and Stolen Spirits: Inside the Fight to Reclaim Native America's Culture*. Chicago, IL: University of Chicago Press.

Colwell-Chanthaphonh, Chip and Stephen Nash. 2014. *An Anthropologist's Arrival. A Memoir. Ruth M. Underhill*. Tucson: University of Arizona Press.

Comaroff, John. 2010. "The End of Anthropology, Again: On the Future of an In/Discipline." *American Anthropologist* 112(4):524–538.

Conn, Steven. 2010. *Do Museums Still Need Objects?* Philadelphia: University of Pennsylvania Press.

Conn, Steven. 2016. "Do Universities Need Museums/Do Museums Need Universities?" *The Antioch Review* 74(2):309–323.

Crooke, Elizabeth. 2006. "Museums and Community." In *Companion to Museum Studies*, edited by Sharon Macdonald, 170–185. Oxford: Blackwell.

Crooke, Elizabeth. 2007. *Museums and Community: Ideas, Issues, and Challenges*. London and New York: Routledge.

Delgado, Elena. 2009. *MAP for ID and the Museo de America*.

Dunbar-Ortiz, Roxanne. 2014. *An Indigenous Peoples' History of the United States*. Boston: Beacon Press.

Feld, Steven. 2010. "Collaborative Migrations: Contemporary Art in/as Anthropology." In *Between Art and Anthropology*, edited by Arnd Schneider and Christopher Wright, 109–126. Oxford and New York: Berg.

Golding, Viv and Wayne Modest. 2019. "Thinking and Working through Difference: Remaking the Ethnographic Museum in the Global Contemporary." In *Curatopia:*

Museums and the Future of Curatorship, edited by Philipp Schorch and Conal McCarthy, 90–106. Manchester: University of Manchester Press.

Gosden, Chris and Francis Larson. 2007. *Knowing Things: Exploring the Collections at the Pitt Rivers Museum 1884–1945*. Oxford: Oxford University Press.

Gourievidis, Laurence. 2014. *Museums and Migration: History, Memory and Politics*. London and New York: Routledge.

Greene, Candace and Eugenia Kisin. 2010. "A New Museum-Based Research Curriculum: Smithsonian Summer Institute in Museum Anthropology." *Anthropology News* (January):25.

Hannerz, Ulf. 2010. *Anthropology's World. Life in a Twenty-first Century Discipline*. London: Pluto Press.

Haraway, Donna. 2016. *Staying with the Trouble: Making Kin in the Chthulucene*. Durham and London: Duke University Press.

Harris, Neil. 1996. "Searching for Form: The Denver Art Museum in Context." In *The Denver Art Museum: The First Hundred Years*, edited by Marlene Chambers, 21–53. Denver, CO: Denver Art Museum.

Hudson, Kenneth. 1987. *Museums of Influence*. Cambridge: Cambridge University Press.

Iervolino, Serena. 2013. "Museums, Migrants Communities, and Intercultural Dialogue in Italy." In *Museums and Communities. Curators, Collections, and Collaboration*, edited by Viv Golding and Wayne Modest, 113–129. London: Bloomsbury.

Jandl, Stefanie. 2012. "The Andrew W. Mellon Foundation: Transforming College and University Art Museums " In *A Handbook for Academic Museums. Beyond Exhibitions and Education*, edited by Stefanie S. Jandl and Mark S. Gold, 120–147. Edinburgh and Boston: MuseumsEtc.

Jandl, Stefanie and Mark Gold. 2014. *Advancing Engagement. A Handbook for Academic Museums*. Vol. 3. Edinburgh and Boston: MuseumsEtc.

King, Lyndel and Janet Marstine. 2006. "The University Museum and Gallery: A Site for Institutional Critique and a Focus of the Curriculum." In *New Museum Theory and Practice: An Introduction*, edited by Janet Marstine, 266–291. Oxford: Blackwell.

Kramer, Jennifer. 2015. "Mobius Museology: Curating and Critiquing the Multiversity Galleries at the Museum of Anthropology at the University of British Columbia." In *Museum Transformations*, edited by Annie E. Coombes and Ruth B. Phillips, 489–510. Oxford: Wiley Blackwell.

Kramer, Jennifer. 2017. "Betting on the Raven. Ethical Relationality and Nuxalk Cultural Property." In *The Routledge Companion to Cultural Property* edited by Jane Anderson and Haidy Geismar, 152–167. London and New York: Routledge.

Kreps, Christina. 1988. "Decolonizing Anthropology Museums: The Tropenmuseum, Amsterdam." *Museum Studies Journal* 3(2):56–63.

Kreps, Christina. 2009. "Foreword." In *Museums as Places for Intercultural Dialogue: Selected Practices from Europe*, edited by Simona Bodo, Kirsten Gibbs, and Margherita Sani, 4–5. MAPforID Group.

Kreps, Christina. 2011. "Take It to the Wall: Relational Art and Community Engagement." American Anthropological Association Annual Meeting, Montreal.

Kreps, Christina. 2013a. "The Power of Words and Vocabularies." In *Museums and Intercultural Dialogue*, edited by Ineta Zelca Simansone. The Learning Museum Network Project No. 4.

Kreps, Christina. 2013b. "Participation, Museums, and Civic Engagement." In *The Learning Museum. Report 7 New Trends in Museums of the 21st Century*, edited by Anne Nicholls, Manuela Pereira and Margharita Sani. Regione Emilia-Romagna.

Kreps, Christina. 2015a. "Contextualizing Matters: A Biography of a Relational Art and Anthropology Project." American Anthropological Association Annual Meeting, Denver, Colorado.

Kreps, Christina. 2015b. "University Museums as Laboratories for Experiential Learning and Engaged Practice." *Museum Anthropology* 38(2):96–111.

Kreps, Christina. 2018. "Intercultural Curation as a Model for Engaging Difference." SWICH: Multiple Voices of a Colonized World, Vienna, Austria, September 6–7.

Leavy, Patricia. 2015. *Method Meets Art. Art-Based Research Practice*. Second ed. New York: Guilford Press.

Levitt, Peggy. 2015. *Artifacts and Allegiances. How Museums Put the Nation and the World on Display*. Berkeley: University of California Press.

Lubar, Steven. 2017. *Inside the Lost Museum. Curating, Past and Present*. Cambridge, MA: Harvard University Press.

Lubar, Steven and Emily Stokes-Rees. 2012. "From Collections to Curriculum: New Approaches to Teaching and Learning." In *A Handbook for Academic Museums. Beyond Exhibitions and Education*, edited by Stefanie S. Jandl and Mark S. Gold. Edinburgh and Boston: MuseumsEtc.

Lynch, Bernadette. 2011. "Collaboration, Contestation, and Creative Conflict: On the Efficacy of Museum/Community Partnerships." In *The Routledge Companion to Museum Ethics*, edited by Janet Marstine, 146–163. London and New York: Routledge.

Lynch, Bernadette. 2013. "Custom-Made Reflexive Practice: Can Museums Realise Their Capacities in Helping Others Realise Theirs?" *Museum Management and Curatorship* 26 (5):441–458.

Macdonald, Sharon. 2009. *Difficult Heritage: Negotiating the Nazi Past in Nuremberg and Beyond*. London and New York: Routledge.

Macdonald, Sharon, Henrietta Lidchi, and Margareta von Oswald. 2017. "Engaging Anthropological Legacies toward Cosmo-optimistic Futures?" *Museum Worlds: Advances in Research* 5:95–107.

Marstine, Janet. 2007. "What a Mess? Claiming a Space for Undergraduate Student Experimentation in the University Museum." *Museum Management and Curatorship* 22 (3):303–317.

Marstine, Janet. 2011. "The Contingent Nature of the New Museum Ethics." In *Routledge Companion to Museum Ethics*, edited by Janet Marstine, 1–12. London and New York: Routledge.

Marstine, Janet. 2013. "Cultural Collisions in Socially Engaged Artistic Practice." *Museum Worlds: Advances in Research* 1:153–178.

Marstine, Janet. 2017. *Critical Practice: Artists, Museums, Ethics*. London and New York: Routledge.

Mason, Rhiannon. 2013. "National Museums, Globalization, and Postnationalism: Imagining a Cosmopolitan Museology." *Museum Worlds* 1:40–64.

McCarthy, Conal. 2015. "Introduction: Grounding Museum Studies." In *Museum Practice*, edited by Conal McCarthy, xxxiii–lii. Oxford: Wiley Blackwell.

McLerran, Jennifer. 2004. *A New Deal for Native Art: Indian Arts and Federal Policy*. Tucson: University of Arizona Press.

Merriman, Nick. 2012. "Transforming the University Museum: The Manchester Experience." In *A Handbook for Academic Museums. Beyond Exhibitions and Education*, edited by Stefanie Jandl and Mark Gold, 36–59. Edinburgh and Boston: MuseumsEtc.

Moore, Emily. 2008. "The Silver Hand: Authenticating Alaskan Native Art, Craft, and Body." *Journal of Modern Craft* 1(2):197–219.

Nelson, Tonya and Sally Macdonald. 2012. "A Space for Innovation and Experimentation: University as Test Beds for New Digital Technologies." In *A Handbook for Academic Museums: Beyond Exhibitions and Education*, edited by Stefanie Jandl and Mark Gold, 418–441. Edinburgh and Boston: MuseumsEtc.

Nichols, Catherine and Christopher B. Lowman. 2018. "A Common Thread: Recognizing the Contributions of the Summer Institute in Museum Anthropology to Graduate Training with Anthropological Museum Collections." *Museum Anthropology* 41(1):5–12.

Onciul, Bryony. 2013. "Community Engagement, Curatorial Practice, and Museum Ethos." In *Museums and Communities. Curators, Collections, and Collaboration*, edited by Viv Golding and Wayne Modest, 79–97. London: Bloomsbury.

Parezo, Nancy and Margaret Hardin. 1993. "In the Realm of the Muses." In *Hidden Scholars: Women Anthropologists and the Native American Southwest*, edited by Nancy Parezo, 270–293. Albuquerque: University of New Mexico Press.

Phillips, Ruth B. 2003. "Introduction. Community Collaborations in Exhibitions. Toward a Dialogic Paradigm." In *Museums and Source Communities*, edited by L. Peers and A. Brown, 155–170. London and New York: Routledge.

Pustmueller, Helen M. 1996. *A Brief History of the University of Denver Museum of Anthropology*. Unpublished paper.

Salvi, Antonella. 2009. *Introduction to Pilot Projects in Emilia-Romagna*.

Sansi, Roger. 2015. *Art, Anthropology and the Gift*. London and New York: Bloomsbury.

Schneider, Arnd and Christopher Wright. 2006. *Contemporary Art and Anthropology*. Oxford and New York: Berg.

Schneider, Arnd and Christopher Wright. 2010. "Between Art and Anthropology." In *Between Art and Anthropology: Contemporary Ethnographic Practice* edited by Arnd Schneider and Christopher Wright, 1–21. Oxford and New York: Berg.

Schorch, Philipp, Conal McCarthy, and Eveline Dürr. 2019. "Introduction: Conceptualising Curatopia." In *Curatopia. Museums and the Future of Curatorship*, edited by Philipp Schorch and Conal McCarthy, 1–16. Manchester: Manchester University Press.

Shelton, Anthony. 2006. "Museums and Anthropologies: Practices and Narratives." In *A Companion to Museum Studies*, edited by Sharon Macdonald, 64–80. Oxford: Wiley-Blackwell.

Shelton, Anthony. 2007. "Questioning Locality: The UBC Museum of Anthropology and Its Hinterlands." *Etnografica* 11(2):387–406.

Shelton, Anthony. 2009. "A Brief History of the Museum." In *The Museum of Anthropology at the University of British Columbia*, edited by Carol Mayer and Anthony Shelton, 9–13. Seattle: University of Washington Press.

Shelton, Anthony. 2015. "Museum Practice and Mediation: An Afterword." In *Museum Practice*, edited by Conal McCarthy, 613–634. Oxford: Wiley Blackwell.

Shelton, Anthony and Gustaaf Houtman. 2009. "Negotiating New Visions: An Interview with Anthony Shelton by Gustaaf Houtman." *Anthropology Today* 25(6):7–13.

Simone, Vincenzo. 2009. *Turin's Museums as Places for Intercultural Dialogue*.

Spilka, Bernard. 2007. *The Department of Anthropology. University of Denver*. Unpublished paper.

Stocking, George. 1985. "Essays on Museums and Material Culture." In *Objects and Others: Essays on Museums and Material Culture*, edited by George Stocking, 3–14. Madison: University of Wisconsin Press.

Story, Lewis Wingfield. 1996. "Building a Collection." In *The Denver Art Museum: The First Hundred Years*, edited by Marlene Chambers, 75–135. Seattle, WA: Marquand Books, Inc.

Stromberg, John. 2014. "Foreword: Imagining the College Museum in 2050." In *Advancing Engagement. A Handbook for Academic Museums*, edited by Stefanie Jandl and Mark Gold, 8–15. Edinburgh and Boston: MuseumsEtc.

Svasek, Maruska. 2007. *Anthropology, Art, and Cultural Production*. London: Pluto Press.

Thomas, Nicholas. 2010. "The Museum as Method." *Museum Anthropology* 33(1):6–10.

Thomas, Nicholas. 2016a. *The Return of Curiosity. What Museums are Good For in the 21st Century*. London: Reaktion Books.

Thomas, Nicholas. 2016b. "We Need Ethnographic Museums Today Whatever You Think of Their History." *Apollo*, March 29:1–19.

Turin, Mark. 2015. "Devil in the Digital: Ambivalent Results in an Object-Based Teaching Course." *Museum Anthropology* 38(2):123–132.

Van Broekhoven, Laura. 2018. "Calibrating Relevance at the Pitt Rivers Museum." In *Dethroning Historical Reputations: Universities, Museums, and the Commemoration of Benefactors*, edited by J. Pellew and L. Goldman, 65–79. School of Advanced Study, University of London, Institute of Historical Research.

INDEX

Milton Keynes UK
Ingram Content Group UK Ltd.
UKHW022214151223
434481UK00019B/183